The Communicator's Commentary

Judges, Ruth

The Communicator's Commentary Series
Old Testament

I *Genesis* by D. Stuart Briscoe

II *Exodus* by Maxie D. Dunnam

III *Leviticus* by Gary W. Demarest

IV *Numbers* by James Philip

V *Deuteronomy* by John C. Maxwell

VI *Joshua* by John A. Huffman, Jr.

VII *Judges, Ruth* by David Jackman

VIII *1, 2 Samuel* by Kenneth L. Chafin

IX *1, 2 Kings* by Russell H. Dilday

X *1, 2 Chronicles* by Leslie C. Allen

XI *Ezra, Nehemiah, Esther* by Mark Roberts

XII *Job* by David L. McKenna

XIII *Psalms 1–72* by Donald M. Williams

XIV *Psalms 73–150* by Donald M. Williams

XVa *Proverbs* by David A. Hubbard

XVb *Ecclesiastes, Song of Solomon* by David A. Hubbard

XVI *Isaiah* by David L. McKenna

XVII *Jeremiah, Lamentations* by John Guest

XVIII *Ezekiel* by Douglas Stuart

XIX *Daniel* by Sinclair B. Ferguson

XX *Hosea, Joel, Amos, Obadiah, Jonah,* by Lloyd J. Ogilvie

XXI *Micah, Nahum, Habakkuk, Zephaniah, Haggai, Zechariah, Malachi* by Walter C. Kaiser, Jr.

Lloyd J. Ogilvie
General Editor

The Communicator's Commentary

Judges, Ruth

David Jackman

WORD BOOKS, PUBLISHER • DALLAS, TEXAS

Library of Congress Cataloging-in-Publication Data
Main entry under title:

The Communicator's Commentary.
Bibliography: p.
Contents: OT7. Judges, Ruth / by David Jackman
1. Bible. O.T.—Commentaries. I. Ogilvie, Lloyd
John. II. Jackman, David
BS1151.2.C66 1986 221.7'7 86-11138
ISBN 0-8499-0412-9 (V. OT7)

Printed in the United States of America

4 5 6 7 8 9 9 AGF 9 8 7 6 5 4

To my mother
in gratitude for her godly example

Contents

Editor's Preface 9
Author's Preface 15

SECTION ONE THE BOOK OF JUDGES

Introduction to the Book of Judges *19*
An Outline of Judges *31*
1. The Incomplete Conquest (1:1–2:5) *35*
2. Uncovering the Meaning of the Book (2:6–3:6) *51*
3. Patterns of Unpredictability (3:7–31) *64*
4. A Famous Victory (4:1–5:31) *78*
5. Gideon: In God's Base Camp (6:1–32) *100*
6. Proving God (6:33–7:8) *114*
7. Divine Strategy (7:9–25) *125*
8. The Test of Success (8:1–35) *138*
9. The Power That Corrupts (9:1–57) *151*
10. Sin's Dead End (10:1–18) *169*
11. Learning from God's Providence (11:1–28) *181*
12. The Enemy Within (11:29–12:15) *194*
13. Samson: God Intervenes (13:1–25) *207*
14. Samson: God Overrules (14:1–20) *219*
15. Samson: God Empowers (15:1–20) *231*
16. Samson: God Judges (16:1–31) *243*
17. Beware of False Gods (17:1–18:31) *259*
18. The Infection of Godlessness (19:1–20:11) *277*
19. The Purging of Evil (20:12–21:25) *291*

SECTION TWO THE BOOK OF RUTH

Introduction to the Book of Ruth *311*
An Outline of Ruth *313*
1. "When You're at the End of Your Tether ..." (1:1–22) *315*
2. The Mechanics of Grace (2:1–23) *328*
3. Acts of Faith and Love (3:1–18) *339*
4. "There Is a Redeemer" (4:1–22) *351*

Bibliography *365*

Editor's Preface

God has called all of his people to be communicators. Everyone who is in Christ is called into ministry. As ministers of the manifold grace of God, all of us—clergy and laity—are commissioned with the challenge to communicate our faith to individuals and groups, classes and congregations.

The Bible, God's Word, is the objective basis of the truth of his love and power that we seek to communicate. In response to the urgent, expressed needs of pastors, teachers, Bible study leaders, church school teachers, small group enablers, and individual Christians, the Communicator's Commentary is offered as a penetrating search of the Scriptures of the Old and New Testament to enable vital personal and practical communication of the abundant life.

Many current commentaries and Bible study guides provide only some aspects of a communicator's needs. Some offer in-depth scholarship but no application to daily life. Others are so popular in approach that biblical roots are left unexplained. Few offer impelling illustrations that open windows for the reader to see the exciting application for today's struggles. And most of all, seldom have the expositors given the valuable outlines of passages so needed to help the preacher or teacher in his or her busy life to prepare for communicating the Word to congregations or classes.

This Communicator's Commentary series brings all of these elements together. The authors are scholar-preachers and teachers outstanding in their ability to make the Scriptures come alive for individuals and groups. They are noted for bringing together excellence in biblical scholarship, knowledge of the original Hebrew and Greek, sensitivity to people's needs, vivid illustrative material from biblical, classical, and contemporary sources, and lucid communication by the use of clear outlines of thought. Each has been selected to contribute to this series because of his Spirit-empowered ability to help people live in the skins of biblical characters and provide a "you-are-there" intensity to the drama of events of the Bible which have so much to say about our relationships and responsibilities today.

The design for the Communicator's Commentary gives the reader an overall outline of each book of the Bible. Following the introduction, which reveals the author's approach and salient background on the book, each chapter of the commentary provides the Scripture to be exposited. The New King James Bible has been chosen for the Communicator's Commentary because it combines with integrity the beauty of language, underlying Hebrew and Greek textual basis, and thought-flow of the 1611 King James Version, while replacing obsolete verb forms and other archaisms with their everyday contemporary counterparts for greater readability. Reverence for God is preserved in the capitalization of all pronouns referring to the Father, Son, or Holy Spirit. Readers who are more comfortable with another translation can readily find the parallel passage by means of the chapter and verse reference at the end of each passage being exposited. The paragraphs of exposition combine fresh insights to the Scripture, application, rich illustrative material, and innovative ways of utilizing the vibrant truth for his or her own life and for the challenge of communicating it with vigor and vitality.

It has been gratifying to me as editor of this series to receive enthusiastic progress reports from each contributor. As they worked, all were gripped with new truths from the Scripture—God-given insights into passages, previously not written in the literature of biblical explanation. A prime objective of this series is for each user to find the same awareness: that God speaks with newness through the Scriptures when we approach them with a ready mind and a willingness to communicate what he has given; that God delights to give communicators of his Word "I-never-saw-that-in-that-verse-before" intellectual insights so that our listeners and readers can have "I-never-realized-all-that-was-in-that-verse" spiritual experiences.

The thrust of the commentary series unequivocally affirms that God speaks through the Scriptures today to engender faith, enable adventuresome living of the abundant life, and establish the basis of obedient discipleship. The Bible, the unique Word of God, is unlimited as a resource for Christians in communicating our hope to others. It is our weapon in the battle for truth, the guide for ministry, and the irresistible force for introducing others to God.

A biblically rooted communication of the gospel holds in unity and oneness what divergent movements have wrought asunder. This commentary series courageously presents personal faith, caring for individuals, and social responsibility as essential, inseparable dimensions of biblical Christianity. It seeks to present the quadrilateral gospel in its fullness which calls us to unreserved commitment to Christ, unrestricted self-esteem in his grace, unqualified love for others in personal evangelism, and undying efforts to work for justice and righteousness in a sick and suffering world.

A growing renaissance in the church today is being led by clergy and laity who are biblically rooted, Christ-centered, and Holy Spirit-empowered. They have dared to listen to people's most urgent questions and deepest needs and then to God as he speaks through the Bible. Biblical preaching is the secret of growing churches. Bible study classes and small groups are equipping the laity for ministry in the world. Dynamic Christians are finding that daily study of God's Word allows the Spirit to do in them what he wishes to communicate through them to others. These days are the most exciting time since Pentecost. The Communicator's Commentary is offered to be a primary resource of new life for this renaissance.

It has been very encouraging to receive the enthusiastic responses of pastors and teachers to the twelve New Testament volumes of the Communicator's Commentary series. The letters from communicators on the firing line in pulpits, classes, study groups, and Bible fellowship clusters across the nation, as well as the reviews of scholars and publication analysts, have indicated that we have been on target in meeting a need for a distinctly different kind of commentary on the Scriptures, a commentary that is primarily aimed at helping interpreters of the Bible to equip the laity for ministry.

This positive response has led the publisher to press on with an additional twenty-one volumes covering the books of the Old Testament. These new volumes rest upon the same goals and guidelines that undergird the New Testament volumes. Scholar-preachers with facility in Hebrew as well as vivid contemporary exposition have been selected as authors. The purpose throughout is to aid the preacher and teacher in the challenge and adventure of Old Testament exposition in communication. In each volume you will meet

Yahweh, the "I AM" Lord who is Creator, Sustainer, and Redeemer in the unfolding drama of his call and care of Israel. He is the Lord who acts, intervenes, judges, and presses his people into the immense challenges and privileges of being a chosen people, a holy nation. And in the descriptive exposition of each passage, the implications of the ultimate revelation of Yahweh in Jesus Christ, his Son, our Lord, are carefully spelled out to maintain unity and oneness in the preaching and teaching of the gospel.

I am pleased to introduce the author of this commentary on Judges and Ruth, the Reverend David Jackman. After graduating from Cambridge University and attending theological school in Bristol, England, he served as a staff member for Inter-Varsity in Britain. Thereafter, he pastored the Above Bar Church in Southhampton, where his outstanding preaching and leadership made a pronounced impact upon this fine church and the surrounding community. After fifteen years in the pastoral ministry, Rev. Jackman has become the director of the Cornhill Training Course. Located in the heart of the business community of London, this school trains pastors in biblical exposition and ministry skills.

David Jackman is well known throughout Britain—and increasingly throughout the world—as an outstanding teacher of the Bible. He is in demand as a conference speaker, and has been the principal speaker of the Keswick Conference as well as the Religious Emphasis Week at Cambridge. He has also spoken on British television. Rev. Jackman has preached at the church of which I am pastor in Hollywood, where God used him to inspire our congregation, and to challenge us to a Spirit-led life of obedience to Christ.

This commentary exemplifies Rev. Jackman's excellence in biblical exposition. You will appreciate his attention to detail, grasp of theological issues, and ability to allow even the often-ignored books of Judges and Ruth to speak with contemporary power. "My prayer," he writes, "is that the hidden treasures of these books from Israel's history . . . will come alive to us in the contemporary church, with new relevance, as they are studied and taught, learned and obeyed." Undergirding Rev. Jackman's able interpretation of the Scriptures is his conviction that God calls us, in grace, to obey his Word. This conviction gives each chapter a consistent sense of urgency and applicability.

This commentary reflects David Jackman's excellent scholarship and his sensitive pastoral heart. Having preached through Judges and Ruth with his own congregation, he enables the communicator of Scripture to understand the original text and to convey its modern vitality. I thank David for this superb addition to the Communicators Commentary series, and commend it to you with confidence.

LLOYD OGILVIE

Author's Preface

When the idea of writing this volume was first put to me by Dr. Lloyd Ogilvie, longer ago than I care to admit, I knew that I had encountered a challenging task. Apart from odd character studies (often in more senses than one) on the great heroes such as Gideon and Samson, I had rarely heard a sermon from Judges, let alone a series of consecutive expositions. Yet I am a great believer in the fact that the Bible is one book and that without attention to the Old Testament our understanding of the New will always be, at best, fragile. I decided to embark on the adventure of trying to understand the difficult Book of Judges, so that I might learn its lessons and seek to convey them relevantly to the contemporary situation in the congregation I serve.

From September 1987 to March 1988, our Sunday morning expositions at Above Bar Church, Southampton, studied Judges consecutively, with the Book of Ruth included halfway through, as a lead-up to Christmas and because of its context in the Judges period. We learned so much together. The downward spiral of sin and chastening spoke deeply to us all, and we understood more of our own depravity and of God's limitless grace as we came face-to-face with ourselves and saw the depths of our own stubborn, rebellious hearts in the lives of people who lived so many centuries ago.

I am grateful for the response and involvement of this, my own congregation at Above Bar Church, in the preparation of these studies. To preach to a congregation hungry for God's Word is always a great privilege. To their prayer and encouragement I am indebted for some of my life's most fulfilling moments, as I have tried to communicate God's truth to mind, heart, and will.

I want to express my sincere personal thanks to my two preaching colleagues, Peter Baker and Trevor Waldock, who stimulated me in the initial study, and whose own expositions provided valuable insights, some of which have been incorporated into this book. The congregation at Above Bar, an eclectic, city-center community, has always drawn me to seek to give my best in study and preaching over the fifteen years I have been privileged to serve on staff. I would also like to thank the conference guests and staff of Lee Abbey, Devon, with whom I was able to share the revised version of the work on Ruth, in 1990. Finally, I wish to express my sincere gratitude to my secretary Linda Burt, for her typing and retyping of the manuscript for publication, and for her unfailing patience and enthusiasm throughout the project.

My prayer is that the hidden treasures of these books from Israel's history, which have so much to teach us about God's dealings with his people, will come alive to us in the contemporary church, with new relevance, as they are studied and taught, learned and obeyed.

DAVID JACKMAN
Southampton, England
March 1991

SECTION ONE

The Book of Judges

Judges 1:1–21:25

Introduction to the Book of Judges

Every book of the Bible has its own unique contribution to make to the intricate tapestry of God's self-revelation to man. The communicator's task must first be to listen, patiently, questioningly, and above all obediently, to what God is saying if ever he is to have the conviction and clarity to become the channel of that message to his generation at their own unique point in history. All too often we assume that we know what the Bible is saying, because we are more or less familiar with the characters who move through its pages and their historical circumstances. This is particularly the case with an Old Testament history such as Judges. For many of us, the names *Gideon* and *Samson* have been part of our inheritance from early childhood.

But as I have worked on this material, much of it as unfamiliar to most contemporary Christians as its major heroes are well-known, I have tried to ask some fundamental questions. Why is this book here in the Bible at all? What are its essential meaning and message? What would we *not* know about God if we did not have the Book of Judges? Above all, I have been concerned to try to listen to the text and to seek to be guided by its own structures and patterns in my understanding and communication of its timeless truth.

Just as all good preaching is dialogical, involving the hearers in the preacher's presentation, anticipating their questions and stimulating their responses, so all good preparation and study enters into that same process with the text before us. It is my fervent hope that by sharing some of my own dialogue with Judges with other communicators, that you will find stimulus to begin your own conversation, which will broaden out into many lives as you involve your congregation in this much-neglected, but highly rewarding, biblical material.

Judges is not a book to which we instantly turn when we are considering the next expository preaching series. To many it is a story of gloom and doom, a depressing catalogue of unfaithfulness to God on the part of Israel, violence and intrigue, false religion and immorality. We can get enough of that on the nightly newscast without needing to import it into the pulpit on a Sunday morning. But that statement alone gives us an immediate clue as to its pressing relevance. At one level we are dealing with a book not far short of three thousand years old, covering a well-defined but relatively remote and obscure period of Israelite history. A detailed chronology is necessarily difficult to establish, but the parameters of the period are well known. The book deals with the history of Israel from the death of Joshua to the beginning of the monarchy with the accession of Saul. Some scholars would date these two fixed points as c.1200 and c.1020 B.C., giving a total span for the book's events of approximately 180 years.[1] However, if all the figures of the different oppressions and periods of the judges' rule are added up, the total is well over twice that figure.

Many attempts have been made by the commentators, both Jewish and Christian, to solve this problem. The most obvious solution, and this is clearly supported by the text, is that some of the times of oppression and periods of different judges' authority overlapped, as they were happening in different parts of the country. Other scholars, while recognizing this to be so, argue that a much longer period is still required, thus pointing to an earlier date for the conquest of Canaan (c.1380) and, therefore, for the Exodus (c.1450).[2] While these discussions may be important for our confidence in the veracity of the Bible, they do not materially affect our communication of the message. We can be sure that we are dealing with historical reality.

But we are also dealing with a book of *Bible* history, which means that it has a double purpose, just as it has a dual authorship. On the one hand, it is historically accurate as the source of a reliable record of real people and real events. But its selection of material is governed by a theological purpose, to reveal in the arena of human activity the otherwise hidden plans and purposes of the eternal God. The point is underlined by the fact that while we classify Judges among the historical books in the English Bible, the Hebrew classification places it among the Former Prophets, where it is the second book following Joshua.

Contemporary hermeneutical insights warn us against importing a twentieth-century Western concept of history into an interpretation of the biblical manuscripts, and this is a case in point. Israelite historians were not obsessed with facts and statistics in our contemporary way. Undoubtedly they were committed to truth in their compilation of accurate and therefore reliable, authoritative records of their national past. But their governing purpose was always didactic rather than merely descriptive or analytical. Paul catches this point exactly in the New Testament when he writes to the Romans that "For whatever things were written before were written for our learning, that we through the patience and comfort of the Scriptures might have hope" (Rom. 15:4). It is the nature of biblical inspiration not only to record accurately the significant historical events, but with the account to provide also the authoritative divine interpretation.

Again, the New Testament helps us to understand this, in the apostolic ministry. So Peter, concerned at the closing of the apostolic age to keep the purity of the revealed truth of the gospel always central in the church (2 Pet. 1:15ff.), reminds his readers "that no prophecy of Scripture is of any private interpretation, for prophecy never came by the will of man, but holy men of God spoke as they were moved by the Holy Spirit." The parallel to his own experience is exact. The apostles were not the dupes of "cunningly devised fables" but eyewitnesses of the majesty of our Lord Jesus Christ. They saw the events of his miraculous ministry and listened to his gracious words. But they also heard the "voice from the excellent glory" explaining the meaning of this Christ event when they were with him on the holy mountain. "This is my beloved Son, in whom I am well pleased." It is this pattern which runs throughout biblical history which gives it also its unique prophetic focus. The events of God's intervention are recorded together with the divine interpretation of those events, and these together make up the infallible revelation, inspired by the Holy Spirit who "carried along" (literally) holy men of God to speak and write God's unchanging Word (2 Pet. 1:21).

As we approach the Book of Judges, therefore, we come not with an antiquarian interest in a world of long ago and far away. The history, geography, and archaeology of the book will all provide us with valuable insights, but never as an end in themselves. It is possible to teach the Old Testament in that way, but very limiting. We come rather as the people of the living God eager to know more of his character and nature, his mysterious ways in his dealings with men. Our concern is to learn how his unchanging faithfulness matches the unchanging needs of every generation of human experience. For those who lived through the period it was a time of change and transition, in which it must often have seemed that the only certainty was that nothing was certain. Their outward life-style and environment may make that Israelite culture seem a million miles away from us today, but men's heart needs in a time of constant flux and unforeseen developments were surely little different from those of the sophisticated urbanized world of contemporary Western man. We are not traveling to another planet when we look at the Book of Judges; simply looking in a mirror.

There are, however, certain important differences—and one above all which is crucial for the matter of our interpretation and application. Israel was a theocracy. This is not just a statement of fact, but one of the underlying issues of the whole book. Perhaps the most famous statement of the Book of Judges is its closing sentence (21:25), "In those days there was no king in Israel; everyone did what was right in his own eyes."

Joshua's great achievement had been to lead the twelve tribes into the Land of Promise and to begin to settle in the country God had given them. But when he died, the process was far from complete and he left no successor. At the end of our period, Israel was sure that she needed a king "like all the other nations" and Saul was soon anointed. But Israel already had a king—Yahweh (always translated "LORD" in capitals in our English version) was their Sovereign. The issues of the book are concerned with the interrelationship of king and people within the covenant of grace, inaugurated by the blood of the Passover lambs, ratified in the giving of the Law at Sinai, and to be lived out in the daily obedience of loyal and loving service to the Covenant Lord.

This essential context warns us against making oversimplistic applications from the theocracy of Israel to the democracies of our day. It would be very easy for us in seeking to communicate the vital message of Judges to draw direct parallels to the problems of urban violence and social disintegration being faced by the once-Christian democracies of the western world. Undoubtedly those comparisons are in order, but not by a straight equation of Israel to a secular state today.

The equation is of Israel with the church, in that both are what they are solely by the grace of God in saving covenant initiative. As we look at the sad demise of the nation of Israel in this book, we shall be biblically justified in communicating that these evidences are always the marks of a nation that turns its back on God. The parallels to our own current experience in such areas as the sanctity of human life, syncretism in religion, and the dehumanizing exploitation of the weak and defenseless are exact. But these are infringements of the *moral* law of God, given for the good of all human beings, Jew and Gentile. This constitutes the Maker's Instructions, without which we cannot expect the intricate machinery of humanity to function at all effectively. When they are torn up and deliberately rejected, breakdown is the inevitable consequence. To that extent, we are justified in applying the consequences of law rejection to our contemporary nation states who have never existed in a covenant relationship to God, as Israel did. Other passages of the Old Testament, such as Amos 1 and 2, also provide ample support for this position.

But the danger is that in pointing the finger at the easily recognized sins of secularized people we fail to see that the primary application must always be to the people who *are* bound by covenant bonds in a personal relationship with the Covenant Lord. Is there not a danger in Christian circles today that our reforming zeal for society blinds us to our own glaring deficiencies? The beam in our own eye (Matt. 7:3–5) is still likely to be the problem for most of us Christians. In my application of the text I have therefore tried to observe this as the priority, believing this to reflect biblical hermeneutical practice, while neither rejecting nor neglecting a wider relevance where possible.

The Book of Judges is so called from the title given to describe the activities of its leading figures. They are *Sophtim* (Hebrew), or in the Greek Septuagint, *Kritai*. For us the word *judges* immediately conjures up images of courts of law and arbitration between individuals in dispute. This was a part of what the judges did, but not their major role. The twelve characters around which the book centers were "saviors" or "deliverers," raised up by God to rescue the nation, both from itself in its persistent slide into godlessness and then, as a consequence, from its increasingly oppressive enemies. Often it was initial success in this latter area which led to a period of relative peace in which the "judge" ruled over an area as an authority figure dispensing justice and stabilizing the community.

Although a first reading of the book would leave one with a bewildering list of names and places, many unrelated to the others because there are so many separate episodes, closer study discovers a careful structure to the whole composition. Far from being a loose collection of dramatic stories belonging to Israel's folklore, the book bears the mark of carefully selected historical material built on a strong theological foundation. The unmistakable "message" that the book purveys throughout is in itself compelling evidence of its unity. This does not mean, of course, that its author did not utilize older sources and weave them into his overall pattern. This helps to explain also the discrepancy in the length of treatment given to the different judges, ranging from four chapters (Samson) to one verse (Shamgar). Clearly, some records were much more detailed than others. Any book covering a time span as big as that of Judges would almost certainly have to work on that presupposition. It would be a similar process to that which Luke describes as his literary method at the start of his Gospel (Luke 1:1–4).

Clearly, the author was aware of the Book of Joshua and seems to have lived within the early period of the monarchy in Israel. This means that his composition was historically very close to the end of the Judges' period. Internal evidence supporting this is to be found in 1:21 where the Jebusites are described as occupying Jerusalem with the Benjamites "to this day." We know from 2 Samuel 5 that Jerusalem was finally conquered by King David at the beginning of his reign (c.1000 B.C.) so that our author is in the days of Samuel and Saul. It is felt by many commentators that the several repetitions of there being no king in Israel indicate a time of writing when the early success of the monarchy enabled the author to look back on the kingless period in a particularly negative light. This may well be true, but the theocratic rule of Yahweh is his uppermost concern, rather than providing an apologia for any earthly monarch, however apparently beneficial or successful.

The identity of the author is unknown, though there has been considerable and, I must confess, attractive speculation that it may well have been Samuel. The absence of his own story from the record seems unexpected since he was both the greatest of the judges and the first of the prophets, in Jewish tradition. The whole case is fully detailed in Goslinga's commentary where he recognizes it "must remain an unproven hypothesis." But he rightly discerns the spirit of

Samuel in the book's systematic attack on idolatry. His dates and the access he would undoubtedly have had to all the relevant information, through his childhood and youth at Shiloh, reinforce the argument. Moreover, since the task of committing God's revelation to writing was so vital, would it not be likely that the man of God "par excellence" of his time would be God's chosen channel?[3] I find it persuasive reasoning.

However, the contents of the book are thankfully much more certain than the possible identity of its author. It divides clearly into three unequal sections. Perhaps the best way of describing this is to identify firstly the central section (3:7–16:31) which is by far the longest of the three and is clearly the heart of the book. Here we are introduced in succession to the twelve judges, raised up at different times and places but with two common purposes—to defeat Israel's enemies by God's power and to return the people to a living faith in God, a devotion to his purposes and obedience to his commands. They are usually subdivided into six major judges (Othniel, Ehud, Deborah, Gideon, Jephthah and Samson) and six minor judges (Shamgar, Tola, Jair, Ibzan, Elon and Abdon) though this is more on the basis of the amount of information recorded than on their personal success or significance. The two may not, of course, be unrelated.

On either side of this central core there is more general reflective material, in the form of an important theological introduction (1:1–3:6) and a representative summary conclusion (17:1–21:25). The introduction itself falls into two clear halves, the first of which (1:1–2:5) reveals the basic pattern of Israel's behavior toward God, in terms of incomplete obedience. In this record of the military endeavors of the tribes following Joshua's death the point made about all others is that they did not evict the pagan tribes from the land completely, as God had commanded. It is possible to suggest different motivations behind this inactivity—mistaken generosity, fear, or just downright laziness—but the text shows us that God's assessment of it was disobedience, which drew forth the severe rebuke of the angel of the Lord described in 2:1–5. The second part of the introductory material (2:6–3:6) surveys the forthcoming contents of the book from the divine perspective, explaining the patterns we see operating time and time again throughout the story. The commentary on the text (chapter 2) explores this theme in detail.

Chapters 17–21 contain two extensive and detailed narratives which appear to be designed to recapitulate the main lessons of the book and to act as summary statements of all that was going on. Chronologically, the events described seem to have occurred fairly early on in the period of the judges, when there was still a considerable measure of unity and a residue of faithfulness among the people. Yet they stand as a somber reminder of what happens when God allows the cause of rebellion to work out its own destructive effects. As in the chilling catalogue of consequences listed by Paul in Romans 1, when God "gives men over" to the full repercussions of their sins, so these chapters indicate the appalling situations which develop when God allows his people to experience the outworking of their own persistent wrong choices, when the absolute authority of the Lord is exchanged for the relativism of doing what man sees fit. The slide is from disillusionment through despair to anarchy and ultimately to disintegration.

Joshua's death was a watershed in the nation's experience. For the first time since the Exodus they had no universally recognized human leader. They had entered and possessed a large part of the land God had promised to give them, but the greater part of that challenge still lay before them. They had now to live as God's faithful covenant people in the land. For this task God had already provided certain very necessary resources. They had the Law of God, given through Moses, preserved in the Ark of the Covenant at Shiloh, and taught through their tribes, clans, and families.

They also had the land itself, part in fact and part in promise, equally a gift from God; but like all God's gifts of grace it needed to be claimed by obedient faith and worked at. Though there was no visible, earthly king, they had plenty of evidence through many graphic reminders from their past of how committed the unseen leadership of the Lord was to their well-being and prosperity. They only had to remember the Passover, the crossing of the Red Sea, the provision of the manna in the desert and the water from the rock, right through to the fall of Jericho and their other great victories, which had been accomplished by God's strength alone.

But, as we know from our own Christian experience, the second stage can often prove harder than the first. Pioneering is one thing; faithful growth and development another. We are fortunate to have an excellent summary of the period of Judges on the lips of Samuel, recorded in 1 Samuel 12:6–11.

> Then Samuel said to the people, "It is the Lord who raised up Moses and Aaron, and who brought your fathers up from the land of Egypt. Now therefore, stand still, that I may reason with you before the Lord concerning all the righteous acts of the Lord which He did to you and your fathers: When Jacob had gone into Egypt, and your fathers cried out to the Lord, then the Lord sent Moses and Aaron, who brought your fathers out of Egypt and made them dwell in this place. And when they forgot the Lord their God, He sold them into the hand of Sisera, commander of the army of Hazor, into the hand of the Philistines, and into the hand of the king of Moab; and they fought against them. Then they cried out to the Lord, and said, 'We have sinned, because we have forsaken the Lord and served the Baals and Ashtoreths; but now deliver us from the hand of our enemies, and we will serve You.' And the Lord sent Jerubbaal, Bedan, Jephthah, and Samuel, and delivered you out of the hand of your enemies on every side, and you dwelt in safety."

As Samuel surveys the period from the Exodus to his day, his great concern is to remind the people that everything has depended on God's initiative alone (v. 7). It is always a profound stimulus to gratitude and praise, as well as a challenge to further obedience and forward movement, to remember the slavery from which we, the people of God, have been delivered. When we start to get a little lax in our commitment, to drift loose of our spiritual moorings, we need to think back to where we were when he found and rescued us (v. 8). The danger is forgetting (v. 9a) because the immediate crisis has passed and we are lulled into a false sense of security as though the battle is over. But it never is, in this world. Forgetting like that is not a mental process due to old age or being overbusy. It is one of the classic Old Testament ways of expressing unfaithfulness to our covenant obligations and responsibilities. It is the practical unbelief that sooner or later leads to idolatry.

Israel's downfall was so often caused by an overdose of self-confidence which presumed upon the covenant blessings, as though somehow they could be enjoyed independently of the covenant requirements of faith and obedience. That self-confidence led them to squeeze God into the margin of their lives, not denying him *a* place but making sure it was not the *central* place, because deep down they imagined they could get along without him for a while. But Samuel points out that there was a consequence—"He sold them" (v. 9b). That was not vindictive or spiteful; it was the other side of covenant love, designed to be remedial and restorative (v. 10). The indication of its effectiveness is seen in the response of repentance—turning from sin, but also turning back to God in renewed commitment to loyal, devoted service. Then, in his grace, God was pleased to raise up judges to deliver his humbled people (v. 11). But the sad reality is that this pattern became a regular cycle, or really a downward spiral, for not only did it recur again and again, but each time it lengthened and deepened, and each time it became harder to climb out of the vortex.

Why did it have to be that way? Why was it that the Israelites failed to occupy the land of Canaan, which they knew God had promised to them? The Book of Judges is not without answers to that question. Some of them are very down-to-earth, practical explanations of the problems they faced. Judah encountered fierce resistance from the Philistine inhabitants of the plains "because they had chariots of iron" (1:19). When Sisera comes on the scene in 4:3, he is able to subject Israel to his oppressive rule for twenty years because he has nine hundred iron chariots. Israel could not match these superior armaments, but then that was not how she had escaped from Egypt or conquered Jericho either. A whole new generation needed to be trained in war, and God allowed some of the pagan tribes to remain so that they might be able to learn the lessons of practical faith and experience their own mighty victories as they depended on the Lord's direction and followed out his plans (3:1–3). But these thoughts, while explaining to us the outward circumstances which provided such a challenge to Israel, do not reveal why they failed so lamentably.

The seeds of their decline began with spiritual compromise. They were commanded to throw down the pagan altars and not to enter into any alliances with the Canaanites. Presumably, as always in Scripture, these specific instructions were given because God knew that these were the precise dangers which would prove to be their undoing. But instead of Israel ruthlessly destroying these false gods, the pagan tribes were at first tolerated, allowed to live alongside Israel, and then they gradually penetrated the nation's life. Corruption followed. Heathen religious practices began to infiltrate the worship of Yahweh. Their gods were accepted with their families since by now intermarriage was becoming increasingly common. After all, it would be argued, they were pleasant enough people and if one was going to have a Canaanite wife or husband you could not expect her or him to leave the household gods behind. We all know in Israel that Yahweh is stronger, but there's no harm in accepting the other deities alongside him.

Once this happened, the likelihood of Israel waging any sort of continuing conflict against paganism disappeared over the far horizon. Once the Canaanites became Israel's friends they were a far greater danger than they had ever been when they were enemies. The parallels to the contemporary church's wooing of our secularized society clamor to be identified in our application. Our wholehearted acceptance of Mammon, as perfectly able to be worshiped, in practice, alongside the Lord, in spite of Christ's express prohibition (Matt. 6:24), is a clear case in point. Perhaps we should also consider the other "household gods" which occupy their shrines in our contemporary Christian environment—fame, prestige, success, power, attractiveness, popularity, sport, work, even family life itself. Any one of these can prove to be a challenger to the Sovereign rule of Christ in our lives and lead to the sort of syncretism and compromise which brought Israel down.

Once the Lord was displaced, the nation began to fall apart, as will the church which dethrones Christ. Personal interests predominated and so jealousies grew. Bitter hostilities between warring tribes developed and the very concept of the nation as a unity was threatened. But Israel survived. Her spiritual weakness is stressed many times, but not more than the power and grace of the living God, exactly matching the whole color spectrum of our human need. For through it all, there shines the faithful covenant-love of a God who remembers his people even when they choose to forget him, who loves them too much to let them get away with their sin and so pursues them with his grace.

The Book of Judges reveals something of the cosmic dimension to the struggles in which Israel found herself enmeshed. Behind the local battles lies a remorseless enemy who is implacably opposed to the purposes of God. The devil would stop at nothing to destroy the seed of Abraham because he knew that from that seed would come the Deliverer, who would create the new Israel and write his own eternal doom. So there is unrelenting hostility, but often disguised with incredible subtlety.

We need not expect the battle to be any less fierce in our generation since he knows his time is short (Rev. 12:12, 2 Tim. 3:1ff.). But Judges also reminds us that when God's people do not deserve the least of his mercies, he delivers them as an act of pure grace. He is a God of unremitting faithfulness and infinite patience who gladly answers our self-centered cries and freely forgives all who turn to him, in true repentance. Or where would any of us be? What a marvelous thing it is to learn that however adverse the circumstances of life may be, and however much we may be to blame for our own making of them, we still worship the God who never gives up, never lets us down, and never lets us go. His love has the victory for ever!

NOTES

1. See Arthur E. Cundall and Leon Morris, "Judges—An Introduction and Commentary," in *Judges and Ruth, Tyndale Old Testament Commentaries* (London: Inter-Varsity Press, 1968), 30 (see Bibliography).
2. See C. J. Goslinga, *Joshua, Judges and Ruth,* trans. Ray Togtman, *The Bible Students' Commentary* (Grand Rapids: Zondervan, 1968), 223–35.
3. Goslinga, *Judges,* 217–23.

An Outline of Judges

I. The Incomplete Conquest: 1:1–2:5
   A. Poised for Advance: 1:1
   B. Samples of Success: 1:2–18, 22–26
   C. Roots of Failure: 1:19–21, 27–36
   D. The Verdict of the Lord: 2:1–5
II. Uncovering the Meaning of the Book: 2:6–3:6
   A. The Peril of the Second Generation: 2:6–10
   B. The Downward Spiral: 2:11–19
   C. The Mercy of Judgment: 2:20–3:6
III. Patterns of Unpredictability: 3:7–31
   A. Othniel: The Man for the Job: 3:7–11
   B. Ehud: One of God's "Irregulars": 3:12–30
   C. Shamgar: A Rank Outsider: 3:31
IV. A Famous Victory: 4:1–5:31
   A. A Desperate Situation: 4:1–3, 5:6–12
   B. Deborah: A Remarkable Woman 4:4–7, 5:7
   C. Barak: A Hesitant Man: 4:8–9, 22
   D. A Divided Nation: 4:10, 5:13–18
   E. A Miraculous Intervention: 4:11–16, 5:19–23
   F. An Unexpected End: 4:17–24
   G. A Challenging Contrast: 5:1–5, 31
V. Gideon: In God's Base Camp: 6:1–32
   A. God Chastises: 6:1–6
   B. God Convicts: 6:7–10
   C. God Conscripts: 6:11–16
   D. God Confirms: 6:17–24
   E. God Challenges: 6:25–32

VI. Gideon: Proving God: 6:33–7:8
  A. The Transforming Factor: 6:33–35
  B. The Confirming Factor: 6:36–40
  C. The Reduction Factor: 7:1–8
VII. Gideon: Divine Strategy: 7:9–25
  A. From Fear to Faith: 7:9–14
  B. From Faith to Fulfillment: 7:15–25
VIII. Gideon: The Tests of Success: 8:1–35
  A. The Test of Criticism: 8:1–3
  B. The Test of Noncooperation: 8:4–21
  C. The Test of Personal Popularity: 8:22–27
  D. The Test of Retirement: 8:28–35
IX. The Power That Corrupts: 9:1–57
  A. Powerful Arrogance: 9:1–6
  B. Prophetic Insight: 9:7–21
  C. Rampant Evil: 9:22–49
  D. Covenant Discipline: 9:50–57
X. Sin's Dead End: 10:1–18
  A. Sin Restrained: 10:1–5
  B. Sin Resurgent: 10:6–9
  C. Sin Rebuked: 10:10–14
  D. Sin Rejected: 10:15–18
XI. Learning From God's Providence: 11:1–28
  A. In the Early Circumstances of Jephthah's Life: 11:1–3
  B. In the Wise Negotiation of Gilead's Elders: 11:4–11
  C. In the Sovereign Control of Israel's History: 11:12–28
XII. The Enemy Within: 11:29–12:15
  A. Overactive Doubt Brings Tragedy: 11:29–40
  B. Inactive Criticism Brings Tragedy: 12:1–7
  C. Divinely Active Faithfulness Brings Stability: 12:8–15
XIII. Samson: God Intervenes: 13:1–25
  A. On God's Terms: 13:1–7
  B. In God's Time: 13:8–16
  C. Through God's Truth: 13:17–25
XIV. Samson: God Overrules: 14:1–20
  A. Through Apparently Bizarre Behavior: 14:1–4
  B. By Empowering with His Spirit: 14:5–9
  C. In Transcending Human Weakness: 14:10–20
XV. Samson: God Empowers: 15:1–20

- A. Revenge on God's Enemies: 15:1–8
- B. Rejection by God's People: 15:9–17
- C. Recognition Through God's Provision: 15:18–20

XVI. Samson: God Judges: 16:1–31
- A. Strength and Moral Weakness: 16:1–3
- B. Strength and Personal Vulnerability: 16:4–17
- C. Strength and Fatal Presumption: 16:18–21
- D. Strength and Divine Retribution: 16:22–31

XVII. Beware of False Gods: 17:1–18:31
- A. The Marks of False Religion: 17:1–13
- B. The Motivation to False Religion: 18:1–31

XVIII. The Infection of Godlessness: 19:1–20:11
- A. Sexual Immorality
- B. Personal Violence
- C. Moral Paralysis

XIX. The Purging of Evil: 20:12–21:25
- A. No Recognition of Guilt: 20:12–17
- B. No Restriction on Revenge: 20:18–48
- C. No Respect for Human Life: 21:1–24
- D. No Reverence for God: 21:25

CHAPTER ONE

The Incomplete Conquest

Judges 1:1–2:5

One of my early memories is of being a rather nervous new boy. At the age of eleven, I had just arrived with about twenty-five others in a new class at a large, traditional, British grammar school. Bewildered by its size and as yet unfamiliar traditions, we sat petrified while a towering and forbidding master, clothed in a black academic gown, informed us in blood-curdling tones, "If any of you boys should get on the wrong side of me, it will be torture for that boy . . . purgatory!" I can still hear his Rs rolling and our hearts thudding. We quickly learned that first impressions matter and that they can sometimes shape the future course of history. Fortunately, most of us managed to stay on the right side of our pedagogue and I still have no reason to believe in purgatory! However, a new beginning is always a time of challenge, with enormous potential for good or ill. As the Book of Judges opens, the nation of Israel is into something new.

Poised for Advance

> 1 Now after the death of Joshua it came to pass that the children of Israel asked the Lord, saying, "Who shall be first to go up for us against the Canaanites to fight against them?"
>
> *Judg. 1:1*

Joshua had left Israel united with a real vision for the future possibilities that God was wanting to open up to his people. Gathering the leaders of the people together just before his death, he set before them two possible future histories of the nation which their actions would dictate. On the one hand, he outlined the complete occupation of the whole promised land, the settlement of all the tribes in the land they had been allotted and the eviction of all the pagan nations. "The Lord your God himself will drive them out of your way. He will push them out before you, and you will take possession of their land, as the Lord your God promised you" (Josh. 23:5 NIV). All this was promised through the omnipotent strength and help of the Lord, but was dependent upon careful obedience (v. 6), forswearing idolatry (v. 7), and a deep love for Yahweh (v. 11). The alternative scenario was one of apostasy, making alliances with the pagan tribes, worshiping their gods, and intermarrying with their people (vv. 12–13). Such an attitude would forfeit God's blessing and lead to Israel's eventual destruction.

The writer of Judges obviously means us to relate the opening of his book to that solemn event with its promises and warnings, which issued in the renewal of the covenant at Shechem, the protestation of all the people "we will serve the Lord," and Joshua's last recorded act of setting up a stone of witness there, under an oak tree (Joshua 24). The united nation, after mourning the death of their great military leader, came together, spiritually alert and keen to fulfill their promises, as they determined to pursue and extend the conquest. They knew that a huge task lay before them if they were going to enter God's promised inheritance, a task which would require faith and hard work. The two always belong together.

Each tribe would have its own role to play, but it would all be "for us." There was a unity of purpose and devotion which might be expressed as "all for one and one for all." So, they came humbly before God to inquire about his will, presumably through the Urim and Thummin of the high priest (see Numbers 27:21). Which tribe does the Lord want to strike the first symbolic blow to open up the new phase of the struggle? It's a marvelous start to the book, with its picture of harmonious cooperation with God's revealed purposes.

Today's danger is that we expect God to do it all for us. Of course, this was going to be the problem a little later on for Israel, when the continuing battle became very demanding and exhaustion overcame perseverance. A good start is of the utmost importance, but the tragedy was that Israel lacked staying power. In our more passive and relaxed social context where we are used to so much being done for us, when how to use our leisure time responsibly is likely to be a major issue for Christians in the next few decades, it is very tempting for us to distort the living God into an omnipotent spiritual slot machine, whose main purpose is to do for me what I cannot manage on my own. The foam bubble-bath concept of Christianity, where I just have to relax back into the love of God and feel comfortable, has a subtle allurement for us believers. We find it more conducive to sing, "Make my flesh life melt away" than to "put to death the deeds of the flesh" (Col. 3:5). This thinking is in all of our hearts. But the Bible does tell us that while the power belongs to God alone, the responsibility to ask for and exercise that power belongs with us.

Paul knew what it was to labor and struggle in the battle to present everyone mature in Christ while recognizing that all the energy which was so powerfully working in him belonged to God (Col. 1:29). He could counsel the Philippians to continue to work out their salvation because God was working in them (Phil. 2:12–13). Similarly, Peter can exhort his readers to make every effort to add to their faith and to be all the more eager to make their calling and election sure (2 Pet. 1:5, 10). We need to get the balance of dependence on God's resources with the activity of faith clearly settled in our own thinking if ever we are to be able to persevere, for if we do not start right we shall have little hope of winning through when the going gets tough.

Samples of Success

2 And the Lord said, "Judah shall go up. Indeed I have delivered the land into his hand."

3 So Judah said to Simeon his brother, "Come up with me to my allotted territory, that we may fight against the Canaanites; and I will likewise go with you to your allotted territory." And Simeon went with him.

4 Then Judah went up, and the Lord delivered the Canaanites and the Perizzites into their hand; and they killed ten thousand men at Bezek.

5 And they found Adoni-Bezek in Bezek, and fought against him; and they defeated the Canaanites and the Perizzites.

6 Then Adoni-Bezek fled, and they pursued him and caught him and cut off his thumbs and big toes.

7 And Adoni-Bezek said, "Seventy kings with their thumbs and big toes cut off used to gather scraps under my table; as I have done, so God has repaid me." Then they brought him to Jerusalem, and there he died.

8 Now the children of Judah fought against Jerusalem and took it; they struck it with the edge of the sword and set the city on fire.

9 And afterwards the children of Judah went down to fight against the Canaanites who dwelt in the mountains, in the South, and in the lowland.

10 Then Judah went against the Canaanites who dwelt in Hebron. (Now the name of Hebron was formerly Kirjath Arba.) And they killed Sheshai, Ahiman, and Talmai.

11 From there they went against the inhabitants of Debir. (The name of Debir was formerly Kirjath Sepher.)

12 Then Caleb said, "Whoever attacks Kirjath Sepher and takes it, to him I will give my daughter Achsah as wife."

13 And Othniel the son of Kenaz, Caleb's younger brother, took it; so he gave him his daughter Achsah as wife.

14 Now it happened, when she came to him, that she urged him to ask her father for a field. And she dismounted from her donkey, and Caleb said to her, "What do you wish?"

15 So she said to him, "Give me a blessing; since you have given me land in the South, give me also springs of water." And Caleb gave her the upper springs and the lower springs.

16 Now the children of the Kenite, Moses' father-in-law, went up from the City of Palms with the children of Judah into the Wilderness of Judah, which lies in the South near Arad; and they went and dwelt among the people.

17 And Judah went with his brother Simeon, and they attacked the Canaanites who inhabited Zephath, and utterly destroyed it. So the name of the city was called Hormah.

> 18 Also Judah took Gaza with its territory, Ashkelon with its territory, and Ekron with its territory.
>
> *Judg. 1:2–18*

Just as Israel begins in the right way by seeking God's will, so God responds, as always faithful to the covenant promises, by clear guidance coupled with a renewed promise (v. 2). All the land belongs to God and he will give it into the hands of a faithful and obedient people. So Judah is selected to begin the new campaign and Simeon joins with them. This was a natural arrangement as Judah and Simeon had been blood brothers, sons of Leah, and the inheritance of Simeon was within the borders of Judah (Josh. 19:1). Their initial purpose was to drive out the Canaanites who still occupied the territory which had been allotted to them.

Judah's campaign is described as having two major movements. First, the combined tribes went up into the Judean highlands, to win a notable victory at Bezek (vv. 4–8). Later they went down to the coastal plain (vv. 9–17) to win other great victories. For several paragraphs, it seems that the success story of the days of Joshua is going to be repeated. Verses 4–7 present a representative and highly typical account of a military victory, in Old Testament style. The enemy is identified, the battle is joined, and the outcome recorded (v. 4). The casualties are listed—ten thousand men at Bezek—and the fate of the enemy leader is described (vv. 6–7). This outcome is even justified from the victim's own mouth as deserved retribution for the inhuman and shameful way he had treated those whom he had previously conquered. The style of writing is quick, uncomplicated, factual. That much is history, but the theological perspective is also there, tucked into the start of verse 4. The Lord did it.

Now we are swept along on the tide of Judah's success. There is a devastating blow against Jerusalem (v. 8), the city of the Jebusites. Although its king had been killed by Joshua, the city had remained unattacked. This would be a constant threat to the tribes, so it became the obvious target of their next operation. Once subdued, Jerusalem could be left behind as they fanned out south and west. First Hebron fell (v. 10), twenty miles away; then another ten miles further on Debir was taken (v. 11). Modern archaeology has revealed a city of approximately seven and one-half acres, well-fortified but destroyed by fire c.1220 B.C.

Then, suddenly, in the following verses there is an unexpected change of pace and style. Inserted into the Debir narrative, within the flow of the national drama, is a personal perspective; the same story on the microscale. There is Caleb, the sole survivor of the Joshua generation, that great old warrior who at eighty-five was still intent on driving the Anakites from the hill country and taking Hebron as his own, as Joshua had promised him (Josh. 14:13). It was he who drove out Sheshai, Ahiman, and Talmai (see Joshua 15:14), as verse 20 will make clear.

It is worth reflecting on the influence this doughty crusader had on the next generation before he too died. Clearly he was a major stimulus to the tribe of Judah to "possess its possessions" and these verses show him offering a handsome incentive bonus to any of the younger generation who is prepared to follow his Hebron example at Debir. Promised Caleb's daughter Achsah in marriage if he can take the city, Othniel, his nephew, seems to have accepted the challenge with alacrity and received his reward, the hand of his cousin (v. 13). The young lady is equally shown not to be backward in coming forward, urging her husband to ask Caleb not only for a field but for water to irrigate it. It may have been a wedding present, but it was certainly an extremely valuable and generous gift. The text seems to indicate, however, that it would not have been hers had she not taken the initiative to ask Caleb for it (vv. 14–15). What Othniel did, if anything, to further her request is not stated. Perhaps he was still trying to make his mind up about how to approach Caleb! But not for the last time in this book, feminine intuition seizes the moment. Alighting from her donkey would be a special sign of respect toward her father, and what old man could resist a dutiful daughter's request for *"a blessing"*? The result was the generous provision of springs on both higher and lower ground, which would enable the cultivation of the land and ensure the family's future prosperity.

The point of the short episode seems to be that the land is there for the taking. If the men of Israel are like Othniel, responding to the challenge under God's direction, the land will indeed be theirs. If the women are like Achsah, taking their opportunities, there are abundant "blessings" to be obtained. The spiritual equivalent is surely the open promises of Matthew 7:7–11 which offer limitless resources to those whose faith and obedience are sufficient to seize the opportunities—to ask, seek, and knock. The implication for Judges, which we shall sadly spell out with increasing clarity as the book progresses, is that failure to enter into all that God has promised is not due to any deficiency on the part of the gracious provider. He is not niggardly in his provision or arbitrarily restrictive in his blessings. They are for all who will trust and obey. Verse 15 is a picture of a living faith that we need to emulate in our own generation. We should never hesitate to ask for God's best.

Verses 16–18 confirm the expansion south of Jericho. The Kenites of verse 16 are the descendants of Jethro or Reuel, Moses' father-in-law, whose son Hobab accompanied the Israelites on the journey to the promised land (Num. 10:29–33). They had been a nomadic people and when Israel began to settle in the land they seem to have remained in the Jordan area near Jericho, without being involved in Joshua's conquest. Now, with Hebron and Debir in Israelite hands, it made sense for them to join forces as Judah and Simeon moved south toward the Negev. They are to come to Israel's aid late in the unfolding story (4:11, 5:24). In verse 17, Zephath falls and is totally destroyed. It lay in the territory allotted to Simeon on the southern border of Canaan, so the men of Judah now reciprocate the help they had already received. Turning from the desert to the coastal plain, Judah now subdued the three principal Philistine cities of Gaza, Ashkelon and Ekron with the surrounding countryside (v. 18). The order indicates a move from the south, as the armies wheeled west and then proceeded north. What a fantastic success story it seems to be! There was certainly no stopping Israel now! No wonder verse 19a makes the point that all this was evidence of the presence and power of the Lord with the men of Judah. But it was not only Judah.

> 22 And the house of Joseph also went up against Bethel, and the Lord was with them.
>
> 23 So the house of Joseph sent men to spy out Bethel. (The name of the city was formerly Luz.)
>
> 24 And when the spies saw a man coming out of the city, they said to him, "Please show us the entrance to the city, and we will show you mercy."
>
> 25 So he showed them the entrance to the city, and they struck the city with the edge of the sword; but they let the man and all his family go.
>
> 26 And the man went to the land of the Hittites, built a city, and called its name Luz, which is its name to this day.
>
> *Judg. 1:22–26*

These verses record the parallel and probably contemporaneous developments of *"the house of Joseph,"* which Joshua 16:1, 4 identify as Ephraim and the half-tribe of Manasseh. Their land lay in the center of Canaan and so, with the Lord's evident approval, they begin by attacking the key citadel of Bethel (Luz). This city is actually on the border of Ephraim, but belonging to Benjamin (Josh. 18:22). Joshua had attacked and taken it (Josh. 12:16), but, as so often happens, the Canaanites seem to have reoccupied the city. The first task in hand is to reassert Israelite rule. But here we hit a negative note. Even in the midst of this early success there are the seeds of compromise. At Bezek (vv. 4–7) there was in every sense a copybook victory. Adoni-Bezek (the lord of Bezek) suffered exactly the fate which God had commanded upon the pagan nations and their rulers. The men of Judah fought him, pursued him, captured him, punished and eventually executed him. But the story at Bethel is one of opportunism, compromise, treachery and ultimately release.

It has been argued that there is biblical precedent for this in the way Joshua took Jericho, when Rahab (the equivalent to the man of verse 24) hid the spies and saved herself and her family (Josh. 2:1–24; 6:25). But the differences are more marked than the similarities. There, it was Rahab who took the initiative. It was clearly under God's direction that the city was conquered and she was incorporated into Israel (see Matt. 1:5). By contrast, here there is no record of God being consulted. The aim is to find the easiest way through the problem, and the collaborator is allowed to escape scot-free, to found another pagan city. Bethel already belonged to Yahweh. It was there that the Lord had appeared to the patriarch Jacob in a dream, who had set up an altar there to the Lord (Gen. 28:10–19). The place belonged to God as its changed name (Beth-El, the house of God) indicated. Now although the city is taken and its population destroyed (v. 25) instead of that pagan culture being obliterated, it is allowed to move to a new Luz.

The victory, such as it was, achieved by trickery rather than won through God's strength, depended on a traitor rather than the Lord of hosts. The lesson is that when you win that way the pagan culture survives to be replanted and will return to plague you on future occasions. I only have to leave one or two roots of bindweed in my garden for the whole soil eventually to be ruined and taken over by it. One rotten apple in a box is enough to infect all the rest. So often in our

Christian lives we may make good progress in dealing with sin and growing in godliness, until one day we come up against a particularly deeply ingrained habit, a darling sin, which stands like an occupied Bethel in the path of future progress and growth to maturity. The flesh pleads to be spared. Surely we do not need to be ruthless in dealing with something so minor. There must be some compromise possible to prevent its extermination. But as the African missionary story tells us, "Little leopards become big leopards, and big leopards kill." The harmless little cub, so cuddly and cute, ultimately can threaten your very life. Israel failed to take that lesson seriously and suffered the consequences. We need to be extremely careful when our spiritual self-indulgence encourages us to be soft on our favorite sins. We may be signing our spiritual death warrant.

This theme has introduced us to the second and, sadly, very different half of the chapter. In order to appreciate just how different it is, we need to go back a few verses as we begin to uncover the negative side of the story.

Roots of Failure

> 19 So the Lord was with Judah. And they drove out the mountaineers, but they could not drive out the inhabitants of the lowland, because they had chariots of iron.
>
> 20 And they gave Hebron to Caleb, as Moses had said. Then he expelled from there the three sons of Anak.
>
> 21 But the children of Benjamin did not drive out the Jebusites who inhabited Jerusalem; so the Jebusites dwell with the children of Benjamin in Jerusalem to this day.
>
> *Judg. 1:19–21*

Remember that avalanche of successes which dominated the first eighteen verses? When we do, we realize that verse 19 is meant to hit us like a body blow. *"They could not drive the inhabitants of the lowland, . . ."* Again, even worse, is verse 21, they *"did not drive out the Jebusites. . . ."* What has gone wrong? The whole passage suddenly runs into a brick wall. "They could not . . . they did not." Its movement forces us to stop and ask, "but why?" If "*the Lord was with*" them (v. 19a) why this sudden failure?

The whole chapter turns on this curiously unsettling verse with its two paradoxical realities. Why should iron chariots be so effective against Judah if Yahweh was with them? Clearly, they were no problem to God. He was not going to be paralyzed or pulverized by the latest in armament technology of the late Bronze Age. These same troops had received the promise of verse 2 endorsing and reiterating the words of Joshua, "though the Canaanites have iron chariots and though they are strong, you can drive them out" (Josh. 17:18 NIV). The story of Deborah in chapter 4 will show that chariots of iron were by no means invincible and were certainly no match for God's power. So, why the collapse?

The problem lay not in any inadequacy on God's side (of that we can always be sure) but in the Israelites' perception of the chariots. They were persuaded that these awesome weapons, which they were totally unable to match, were too powerful. The task was too difficult, the odds were all stacked against them, and so it would be folly to take them on. When that is the real reason behind "they could not," it is as inevitable as night following day that the next stage will become "they did not." The damaging result was that although they took the cities of the plains, they did not establish Israelite settlements there. Instead, they opted for a break in hostilities, slackened their effort, rested on their laurels, and soon the Philistines drifted back and reoccupied the territory.

Similarly, at Jerusalem, their great victory (v. 8) was not followed up by any serious or persistent attempt to root out the Jebusites. So the pagans soon rebuilt and fortified their city, which remained a thorn in Israel's side as a foreign stronghold deep in the heart of the country until the time of King David (2 Sam. 5:6ff.). Instead of trusting the Lord for even greater things, they began to succumb to negative thinking, which led them out of victory into failure. Ultimately, they brought about their own defeat by convincing themselves that they could not succeed.

Perhaps the most vivid biblical parallel is the incident in the Gospels of Peter walking on the water (Matt. 14:24–31). In response to the Lord's clear call Peter was able to do the impossible, until he began to think too hard and too humanly about it. As he took his eyes off the Lord who called and looked instead at the stormy sea, he began to sink.

It was doubt that was Peter's problem, as it is ours. The immediacy of the very real challenges, their tangibility and power, begin to paralyze faith and prompt the response, "I can't." The remedy is in seeing the Lord more clearly and determining to rely upon his Word of promise, irrespective of the circumstances. It's a lesson we all have to learn and relearn.

Take a sports team that has lost confidence in its ability to win. It's on a losing streak that seems unending. Then a new coach or manager takes over. He renews morale, develops new skills and techniques, reinvigorates the training program. Above all, he commands a personal loyalty, bred from confidence in his ability, from each member of that defeated team. They begin to work together, instead of criticizing and attacking each other. They no longer look at the opposition imagining what can't be done. Because they are not playing for themselves, or even their supporters, much less to the gallery, they are liberated to believe in victory. The difference is that they are playing for one person only, to whom they all relate and whose word is law, and what they are really bothered about is his assessment and his verdict. In a world of fallible human beings it does not often work out that way, but when it does the combination is unstoppable! When Judah lost sight of the manager, she lost. Her past victories became memories, but her present experience became paralysis.

> 27 However, Manasseh did not drive out the inhabitants of Beth Shean and its villages, or Taanach and its villages, or the inhabitants of Dor and its villages, or the inhabitants of Ibleam and its villages, or the inhabitants of Megiddo and its villages; for the Canaanites were determined to dwell in that land.
>
> 28 And it came to pass, when Israel was strong, that they put the Canaanites under tribute, but did not completely drive them out.
>
> 29 Nor did Ephraim drive out the Canaanites who dwelt in Gezer; so the Canaanites dwelt in Gezer among them.
>
> 30 Nor did Zebulun drive out the inhabitants of Kitron or the inhabitants of Nahalol; so the Canaanites dwelt among them, and were put under tribute.
>
> 31 Nor did Asher drive out the inhabitants of Acco or the inhabitants of Sidon, or of Ahlab, Achzib, Helbah, Aphik, or Rehob.

32 So the Asherites dwelt among the Canaanites, the inhabitants of the land; for they did not drive them out.
33 Nor did Naphtali drive out the inhabitants of Beth Shemesh or the inhabitants of Beth Anath; but they dwelt among the Canaanites, the inhabitants of the land. Nevertheless the inhabitants of Beth Shemesh and Beth Anath were put under tribute to them.
34 And the Amorites forced the children of Dan into the mountains, for they would not allow them to come down to the valley;
35 and the Amorites were determined to dwell in Mount Heres, in Aijalon, and in Shaalbim; yet when the strength of the house of Joseph became greater, they were put under tribute.
36 Now the boundary of the Amorites was from the Ascent of Akrabbim, from Sela, and upward.

Judg. 1:27–36

Since the other tribes had achieved nothing comparable to Judah's victories, it is hardly surprising that the latter's willingness to submit to compromise was even hastier. But from verse 27 onward the record of these northern tribes is uniformly depressing. Because they did not drive out the Canaanites, they were constantly in conflict. There were periods when they used the pagan tribes as forced labor, but never drove them out completely. The idea of leniency on the part of Manasseh (vv. 27–28) was in direct contradiction of the policy God had commanded them to follow (Deut. 20:16–17).

The root of the problem was that, not unnaturally, they encountered determined resistance from the Canaanite settlements. These enemies were entrenched in their strongholds, with weapons and fortifications to support them, so the Israelites decided to opt for the easy life and learn how to develop a working relationship of relatively peaceful coexistence. Thus the catalogue of failure runs on through the tribes—after Manasseh, Ephraim (v. 29), Zebulun (v. 30), Asher (v. 31), Naphtali (v. 33) and worst of all, Dan (v. 34) where the Israelites were actually driven back into the hills by the Amorites, although the inheritance they had been given under Joshua was mainly on the plain.

So the chapter that begins with elation ends in collapse. The best that Israel can hope for seems to be periods of relative superiority, when the tribes with whom they have decided to coexist become forced laborers for them. This is a far remove from the vision of the whole promised land which had animated the earlier settlers. The observant reader is driven by the text to ask again and again why this should be so, but we have to wait for chapter 2 for the ultimate and definitive answer.

The Verdict of the Lord

> 1 Then the Angel of the Lord came up from Gilgal to Bochim, and said, "I led you up from Egypt and brought you to the land of which I swore to your fathers; and I said, 'I will never break my covenant with you.
>
> 2 "'And you shall make no covenant with the inhabitants of this land; you shall tear down their altars.' But you have not obeyed My voice. Why have you done this?
>
> 3 "Therefore I also said, 'I will not drive them out before you; but they shall be thorns in your side, and their gods shall be a snare to you.'"
>
> 4 So it was, when the Angel of the Lord spoke these words to all the children of Israel, that the people lifted up their voices and wept.
>
> 5 Then they called the name of that place Bochim; and they sacrificed there to the Lord.
>
> *Judg. 2:1–5*

How does God view it all? Whatever the issue or debate, that is always the ultimate and most significant question. There were doubtless those then, as there are many today, who would want to argue that Israel was entirely right to avoid bloodshed. How could a God of love destroy "innocent" people? It is, of course, our reasoning that is on trial in a question like that, not God's morality. When we remember that "there is none righteous, no, not one" (Rom. 3:10) and that "the wages of sin is death" (Rom. 6:23), the concept of innocence disappears. Instead of querying God's justice we stand amazed at his patient, long-suffering mercy. "Because of the Lord's great love we are not consumed" (Lam. 3:22 NIV). And when we bow in worship before that grace expressed in the cross of Calvary, where the sinless Savior carried our sin and atoned for our transgressions, we realize that peace at any price is never God's way.

In 1:4, Judah *"went up"* and won great victories over the Canaanites and Perizzites. In 1:22, Joseph *"went up"* and attacked Bethel. The same verb is used in both cases and is translated "attacked" in the New International Version. Here, in 2:1, it is used again, but this time the subject is the "Angel of the Lord." God is speaking to the people in divine wisdom and with divine authority.

Once again, all Israel is assembled, presumably at a festival gathering, at a location in the hill country later named Bochim ("weeping") because of the response generated by the divine visitation. He comes to review the present state of the nation and its affairs. This is God on the attack.

Characteristically, the divine message begins by looking back to remind the Israelites of the great deliverance he had secured for them in the Exodus, which had made them what they now are. In view of the charge that he is about to lay, the messenger refers this to the Lord's unswerving faithfulness to his covenant promises (v. 1b). This opens the way for the charge in verse 2 which concerns Israel's disobedience to her covenant obligations to Yahweh, as Lord. This is demonstrated in the nation's readiness to make covenants with the Canaanites and corresponding unwillingness to break down the pagan altars.

It is important to note that the charge is not one of failing to expel the Canaanites from the land, for that was always Yahweh's responsibility, as verse 3 clearly implies (*"I will not drive them out . . ."*). The charge against Israel is her rebellion against her covenant Lord by coming to peace terms with his enemies. Later, in 2:21–3:4, God explains the reasons for what might have been interpreted as his delay in this matter, but at this point there is simply the chilling statement that the people have forfeited his blessing. All that he had promised would have been fulfilled, in God's own time and way, had they been prepared to obey his commands. Now, all that he had threatened as the consequences of disobedience must inevitably follow. They will not be able to rid themselves of the pagan tribes. They will be the source of constant harassment to them physically (*"thorns in your sides"*) and a continuing snare, spiritually. It is an awesome prospect, but it is clearly not unjust. There is an ironic appropriateness about the sentence on a people who were only too ready to embrace God's enemies that they are condemned to live with the consequences. God often allows us to be ensnared in our own foolishness, to learn how bitter sin is by its long-term consequences.

Perhaps that was the thinking of the father in Jesus' parable of the prodigal son (Luke 15:11–32). Why else should a loving father have sold part of his property to give his son the inheritance before his death? Did he not realize that the son's heart was already in the far country and that the only way to win him back was to let him go and experience all that it had to offer, including, and especially, the pig-trough? That was when the boy's heart turned back to home, and then his body was not far behind! Isn't Jesus telling us something about how our loving heavenly Father habitually deals with his recalcitrant, ungrateful, sinning children? So it is here. If Israel refuses to recognize that her inheritance belongs to the Lord, that it is *his* land, divine property, then she must learn it the hard way. If she will not purge her Lord's land of cultic idolatry and pagan altars, planted by his arch-enemy the devil, then her sins of disobedience will come back to mock and haunt her. We are all, however blessed, only stewards of God's good gifts. "For who makes you different from anyone else? What do you have that you did not receive?" (1 Cor. 4:7a NIV) Well, then, says Paul, "it is required that those who have been given a trust must prove faithful" (1 Cor. 4:2 NIV).

So, what is the answer? Verses 4–5 spell it out. The people heard and received the Word of God, as it was delivered. There can be no spiritual renewal without that vital ingredient. Acknowledging the truth of God's assessment, they wept and offered sacrifices. That was good, as far as it went. Unhappily, as the book unfolds, we shall see that it did not go nearly far enough. The fact that the change of heart expressed was only temporary indicates that theirs was a superficial response of remorse, rather than a life-changing repentance. True repentance (*metanoia*) is a change of mind about God and about my relationship with him. It issues in a change of action and direction but the mind has to be convinced if ever that is to happen. That is why the message of God's Truth is so crucial for our continuing spiritual health. If we want a strong church of maturing believers, we must teach the whole counsel of God as the very core of our ministry. God responds to true repentance, but there is something even better. "To obey is better than sacrifice, and to heed than the fat of rams" (1 Sam. 15:22).

Incomplete victories are always dangerous because they so easily lead to complacency and compromise. Many an army that has not pressed home its initial advantages has been cut off in the rear by the pockets of resistance it failed to mop up. Old sins dog our footsteps and many of today's worries and pressures can be traced back to yesterday's disobediences. We need to set our hearts on the course of wholehearted obedience. It's a matter of daily, detailed discipline. Yet God's commands are not a burden (1 John 5:3) any more than are wings a burden to a bird! As we trust and obey, we find the Spirit within molding us more and more into the image of the beloved Son, the only one whose obedience was perfect. "When Christ came into the world, he said, . . . 'I have come to do your will, O God'" (Heb. 10:5–7 NIV). That is what pleases the Father's heart. Praise God that there is forgiveness through the blood of Jesus, that the price of our peace has been fully paid and our enemy totally routed. But we need to warn ourselves that sometimes we have to live with sin's consequences a long, long time. We dare not be satisfied with an incomplete conquest.

CHAPTER TWO

Uncovering the Meaning of the Book

Judges 2:6–3:6

This passage constitutes the second part of the introduction to the Book of Judges. Instead of moving on chronologically from the events at Bochim, it runs parallel to the first chapter of the book but with a focus on the spiritual reasons for the predicament Israel faced. Both parts take us from the high hopes of the total conquest of the land in Joshua's day to the harsh realities of despair, as God pronounces that he will no longer drive out the tribes. Just as the first two chapters of Genesis present not two contradictory accounts of creation, but two complementary perspectives of the one event, so Judges opens with a similar literary style and pattern. In Genesis 1, man is viewed as the apex of the chronological process of creation, whereas in Genesis 2 he is the center of the created order around which and to which everything else relates. In Judges 1, we see Israel's failure and God's judgment depicted largely in chronological and physical terms, through their own laziness and compromise. But in chapter 2 the focus is much more clearly spiritual, as the root problem is seen to be their idolatry. They are complementary accounts of the same reality.

As chapter 2 traces the recurring pattern of apostasy, oppression, distress, and deliverance, we are introduced to some phrases that will become increasingly familiar as the narrative unfolds. Israel "did what was evil in the eyes of the Lord," so he "handed them over to" their enemies, who oppressed them.

The Peril of the Second Generation

6 And when Joshua had dismissed the people, the children of Israel went each to his own inheritance to possess the land.

7 So the people served the Lord all the days of Joshua, and all the days of the elders who outlived Joshua, who had seen all the great works of the Lord which He had done for Israel.

8 Now Joshua the son of Nun, the servant of the Lord, died when he was one hundred and ten years old.

9 And they buried him within the border of his inheritance at Timnath Heres, in the mountains of Ephraim, on the north side of Mount Gaash.

10 When all that generation had been gathered to their fathers, another generation arose after them who did not know the Lord nor the work which He had done for Israel.

Judg. 2:6–10

Our relationship to the past is a fascinating theme of the Scriptures. In one sense, we are all its prisoners—through our genetic inheritance, through transmitted family values over several generations, as well as through the movements of nations in world events. As Christians, we are also and more importantly the privileged heirs of all that God has done in salvation in history and in the church down the millennia. We have a glorious past of God's faithfulness from which to draw inspiration and strength.

Yet sometimes we allow our dependence on the past to be too great a conditioning factor in the present, as when we limit ourselves to what we have already learned or experienced. We forget that the unchanging and eternal God is not trapped in our time warp, that his dependability is not merely a commitment to the past, but equally an assurance for the future. His eternality places him outside our temporal limitations. So, while we look back with thanksgiving and treasure our spiritual heritage, only through the conviction that the Holy Spirit is always doing something new and that God is never out of date shall we look up in faith for today and forward with vision for tomorrow. The mark of our spiritual appreciation of the past is that we cleave to the God of history with a living faith and present obedience. The cynic may claim with some truth that history teaches us nothing, but that is hardly history's fault. Those who do not learn its lessons usually find themselves compelled to relive them!

That was Israel's problem. Each new generation has to prove God in its own time and in its own unique environment—learning from the past without becoming dependent on it. But when Joshua's generation died out, the next generation lacked that personal knowledge of God which is the heart of biblical faith and quickly forgot all that he had done for their nation. This is a "generation gap" of the most profound and challenging kind, and, as usual, both sides were to blame. There is always a parental responsibility to pass on a living testimony of the reality of God's grace and power to our children. They have the right not only to be taught the truth but to see it embodied in godly leadership and example, both within the family and the church. That magnificent challenge in Deuteronomy 6:4–9 to make the commandments of the Lord the very fabric of family life is one that contemporary Christian families would do well to take more seriously. Somehow the Joshua generation, though they had personally experienced so much of God's goodness, failed to keep the record of his mighty acts alive. If we do not tell what God has done and keep the memory fresh and vibrant, the past will die and its lessons with it. This is even more the case in a generation like ours, when the amazing technological developments of the recent past and present lull us into a false arrogance, as though we were the only generation ever to have lived on the face of the earth. All who are parents or pastors need to be thoroughly convinced of the link between loving the Lord and knowing what he has done. If our love is not generated by a growing, deepening awareness of God's commitment to us, in Christ, in his mighty acts of salvation, it will not last longer than morning dew. If we do not build our younger generation's faith in what God has done on our planet, in our history, and what those interventions mean to us (and that surely is biblical theology), we shall not teach them properly to love the Lord, whatever emotional experiences they may have or seek.

For it is the presumption of the second generation to live on their parents' capital, spiritually. The old saying is that "God has no grandchildren," and it's true. But pastors know within their own families and churches how easily the opposite assumption is made. I live in a nation where Christian values are accepted. I attend a lively church. My parents are Christians. The danger is to assume continuity of faith without God necessarily being real to me personally. We cannot learn Christ by osmosis! There has to be personal faith.

The point is well made, in a different context, by the British writer Norman Lewis in his autobiography, *Jackdaw Cake*. Writing about his childhood in north London under parents who were avidly committed to "spiritualism," he comments: "like many people steered by the pressure of custom to profess a religion to which in reality they have hardly given a thought, I neither believed nor disbelieved these things. It gave my mother and father great pleasure when I offered lip service to their convictions, but at heart the best I could manage was indifference, coloured with scepticism."[1] That was Israel's problem. It is for every second generation, as the derelict chapels scattered across Britain and now being converted into art studios or domestic homes eloquently declare. We must never presume that the blessing of God yesterday guarantees the same reality today. Unless we have a lively faith and communicate that in every way possible to our children there is no guarantee of their continuance spiritually, let alone of progress for the gospel in their lifetime. No creed is alive that is not embraced; no virtue is safe that is not enthusiastic.

The Downward Spiral

11 Then the children of Israel did evil in the sight of the Lord, and served the Baals;

12 and they forsook the Lord God of their fathers, who had brought them out of the land of Egypt; and they followed other gods from among the gods of the people who were all around them, and they bowed down to them; and they provoked the Lord to anger.

13 They forsook the Lord and served Baal and the Ashtoreths.

14 And the anger of the Lord was hot against Israel. So He delivered them into the hands of plunderers who despoiled them; and He sold them into the hands of their enemies all around, so that they could no longer stand before their enemies.

15 Wherever they went out, the hand of the Lord was against them for calamity, as the Lord had said, and as the Lord had sworn to them. And they were greatly distressed.

16 Nevertheless, the Lord raised up judges who delivered them out of the hand of those who plundered them.

17 Yet they would not listen to their judges, but
they played the harlot with other gods, and bowed
down to them. They turned quickly from the way in
which their fathers walked, in obeying the commandments of the Lord; they did not do so.
18 And when the Lord raised up judges for them,
the Lord was with the judge and delivered them out
of the hand of their enemies all the days of the judge;
for the Lord was moved to pity by their groaning because
of those who oppressed them and harassed them.
19 And it came to pass, when the judge was dead,
that they reverted and behaved more corruptly than
their fathers, by following other gods, to serve them
and bow down to them. They did not cease from their
own doings nor from their stubborn way.

Judg. 2:11–19

The previous paragraph has not only posed the problem which Israel faced. It expresses the dilemma in spiritual terms, by drawing attention to the evil that was involved in the second generation's rejection of Yahweh. It was against the background of his mercy and faithfulness that they chose to drift into rebellion. Implicit in the whole chapter is the covenant relationship which the angel of the Lord invokes in 2:1–5. We are not surprised therefore that this section, which is so important for our understanding of the book as a whole, expresses the issue from God's point of view. Yahweh is depicted as responding to their idolatry with anger (vv. 12b, 14), to their distress with compassion (v. 16), and to their further rebellion with stronger anger (v. 20). Obviously the terms are anthropomorphic, but the emotion is stressed in order to underline the covenant relationship that is at stake. God cares so deeply because he is committed by covenant to his people.

These verses describe a cycle that will become increasingly familiar as the book proceeds. Broadly there are four stages. (1) The people of Israel fall away into idolatry (vv. 11–13). (2) The Lord's anger is kindled so that he hands them over to their enemies, who plunder and oppress them until they are greatly distressed (vv. 14–15). (3) They call to the Lord who raises up a judge to deliver them (v. 16). (4) After a period of return to God and relative prosperity during the lifetime of the judge, they go back to an even more corrupt and idolatrous life-style (vv. 17–19).

What we have to realize is that this is not merely a cycle of events; it is a vortex or downward spiral. Each successive rebellion is deeper; its consequences are longer lived and more difficult to counteract. We are locked into a pattern of progressive deterioration.

The root problem is the foreign gods, whose altars had not been destroyed (2:2). Baal was the male deity worshiped throughout the land of Canaan, but the great diversity of his images and the appropriation of him by many tribal groups as their particular local deity enables the writer to refer to *"the Baals"* (plural) in verse 11.

Idolatry is usually polytheistic because it can never be sure that any contact has been made with reality or that the worshiper has ever done enough. Ashtoreth (v. 13b) is the equivalent female deity, representing Mother Earth, the goddess of fertility. Canaanite religion was very earthy. It was a matter of survival economics. In an agrarian society everything depends on good harvests. So the aim of religion was to produce fertility by means of sympathetic magic, hence the male and female god forms. All false religion is based on works, on what the worshiper does, or gives, or achieves, to persuade the deity to grant his request. The concept of grace is totally foreign, because that is the centerpiece of the revelation of the living God. Man would never have thought that up! Canaanite religion sought through its ritual prostitutions, its child sacrifices and mutilations, to persuade the deities to grant fertility to man, to beasts, and to crops. Nothing could have been further from the revelation of Yahweh in the Torah.

There is still the attraction of false religion and all the distortions of Christianity that abound today. At base, all are saying, "You can make it with God. You can get what you want from him, if only you follow these rules." The outward forms and expressions may be immeasurably more sophisticated now, but the same basic mechanism is at work. That will always appeal far more to the naturally sinful human heart, because it requires no submission to God, no dying to self. That's the attraction of religion! Instead of making me utterly dependent on God's grace it boosts my ego by pretending that I can actually manipulate God into giving me what I want by my devotion, commitment, sacrifice, or whatever.

Just one way in which this idolatry surfaces, for example, is the tremendous emphasis on "having faith." Many Christians are on a perpetual inner quest to discover or dredge up a greater subjective feeling of faith, in order to present this to God so that he will be forced to grant their particular requests. In this way we make faith our idol, and we actually start to put our faith in having faith rather than in God. You can see it in the "name it and claim it" philosophy, to quote just one example. When we start to justify this pragmatically by the fact that "it works," we show how far we have drifted from the New Testament revelation, which recognizes faith as God's gift and salvation as his grace, from start to finish. Our reaction to this may initially be that we regard it as an over-subtle interpretation of Judges, but I don't imagine for one moment that the proponents of Baal worship came knocking on the door, selling little idols for the Israelites to worship. The devil knew he wouldn't be able to hook them that crudely. It *was* subtle. And it is still so in our day. If the wolves are not disguised as sheep they will never stand a chance of entering the fold. Often they are very woolly "sheep" indeed!

And is God's response an overreaction? Isn't he made to sound like a jealous, jilted lover (v. 14a)? But that is precisely what he is! He loves these people everlastingly. That is why he has entered into covenant relationships with them. It is as though they are married to him, which is why their idolatry is so often referred to as spiritual adultery in the Old Testament. God's love is possessive in the righteous sense, in which the love of every husband and wife is possessive. If it is true love, it will never be content with second place. The marriage relationship is exclusive, by its very nature.

Many situations exist in life where to come second and express our feelings in terms of jealousy simply reveals our wounded pride. The sports player who cannot admit to being fairly beaten, or the executive passed over in the promotion race spring to mind. But the marriage partner where love is spurned has a right to be jealous; it is the nature of the relationship. How he or she handles that jealousy is of course all-important, and sadly that is often as sinful as the original unfaithfulness that prompted it. But God's jealousy for Israel was pure and righteous, as we can see by the fact that it is his love which motivates his action. Real love always works for the total good of the loved one, however hard that may be and at whatever personal cost. There is no suggestion here of the bad temper or petulance, which so often characterizes our human anger, but rather a dedicated, holy love that determines to discipline his beloved Israel until the people's hearts are turned back to him.

The demands of our New Covenant relationship are not less stringent. The righteousness of God is seen in his demand that we should be faithful exclusively to him, for that is to our own good. He is working for our best. What kind of husband would he be who didn't care where his wife was or how she spent her life? What kind of God would he be if we were allowed to continue worshiping our manmade idols? Like Israel, we sometimes experience God's discipline in terms of defeat, which is intended to lead us to despair, in order to bring us in turn to repentance.

However, not all of God's activity is to be seen as disciplinary. With the people in great distress (v. 15b), he raised up *"judges"* (v. 16a). His activity of love also delivers. It is interesting and instructive to note here that there is no reference to the people's repentance motivating God to act in this way. Rather, the motivation explicitly identified in verse 18 is the Lord's compassion. This is in keeping with what we have already noted. The judges were given because God loved his people, as an expression of his compassion, and because he longed for them to return to a close relationship of love with him. They were not a reward given because of the people's works of repentance (though that often preceded the deliverer's appearance), but a gift of God's grace. How good it is to know that there is always more grace. So, God raised up a man (and at least one woman) with the right gifts and abilities, in the right place and at the right time to meet his people's deepest needs. In this way, the nation was being taught how totally dependent on God they actually were. This seems to be the major lesson of verses 18–19. As long as the particular judge, the agent of God's grace, was alive, the people were delivered; but with his death the downward spiral took over again. It is as though God is pointing out that the human leaders he gives are, at their best, only temporary expedients. They are only pointers to the limitless resources of divine grace, which would be so readily at the disposal of a people whose hearts truly loved God.

The vacuum following the departure of the great national leaders, Moses and Joshua, was only partially filled by the judges. If God was teaching the people to depend more completely on him, it is nothing short of tragedy that the judges' period ends with the demand for a king, "like all the nations" (1 Sam. 8:5). And what a king Saul would prove to be! But then the 350 years of the judges prove over and over again the truth of the Lord's response to Samuel about Israel's demand. "It is not you they have rejected as their king, but me. As they have done from the day I brought them up out of Egypt until this day, forsaking me and serving other gods . . ." (1 Sam. 8:7b–8 NIV). God wants us to learn to trust in him alone, not even in the most gifted of his servants.

In application, we may well draw parallels to the contemporary danger of relying over-heavily on human leaders in spiritual matters. After a much-used and greatly loved pastor retires or moves, many a church has faced a vacuum, which has provided a sterner test of its spiritual reality than had ever been anticipated. Has the church been gathered around the man, or around his Lord? The temptation to Christian leaders is to the wrong use of authority, to lord it over the flock of God. It can be very flattering to have people hanging on our words, waiting for our advice, following our suggestions. For many it is only a few steps into a heavy-handed shepherding, which actually interposes the pastor between the individual and Christ. Plenty of Christians are looking for someone else to carry the responsibility for their decision making, and a well-motivated pastor can easily fall into the error of making his people too dependent on him. They will want to put him on a pedestal, and he may want to let them. Perhaps the reason many great men of God have seemed to have no successor ready to step into their shoes, and why attempts of the sort when made have so often failed, is that God is teaching his church not to rely on human leaders, but on him alone. The lesson may prove a painful one to learn, but it is of the utmost spiritual value.

The Mercy of Judgment

20 Then the anger of the Lord was hot against Israel; and He said, "Because this nation has transgressed My covenant which I commanded their fathers, and has not heeded My voice,

21 "I also will no longer drive out before them any of the nations which Joshua left when he died,

22 so that through them I may test Israel, whether they will keep the ways of the Lord, to walk in them as their fathers kept them, or not."

23 Therefore the Lord left those nations, without driving them out immediately; nor did He deliver them into the hand of Joshua.

> 3:1 Now these are the nations which the Lord left, that he might test Israel by them, that is, all who had not known any of the wars in Canaan
>
> 2 (this was only so that the generations of the children of Israel might be taught to know war, at least those who had not formerly known it),
>
> 3 namely, five lords of the Philistines, all the Canaanites, the Sidonians, and the Hivites who dwelt in Mount Lebanon, from Mount Baal Hermon to the entrance of Hamath.
>
> 4 And they were left, that He might test Israel by them, to know whether they would obey the commandments of the Lord, which He had commanded their fathers by the hand of Moses.
>
> 5 Thus the children of Israel dwelt among the Canaanites, the Hittites, the Amorites, the Perizzites, the Hivites, and the Jebusites.
>
> 6 And they took their daughters to be their wives, and gave their daughters to their sons; and they served their gods.
>
> *Judg. 2:20–3:6*

The repetition of the anger of the Lord, expressed here even more intensively, introduces us to a further theological reflection on the whole situation. We have watched the downward spiral in action as rebellion leads to judgment, judgment to contrition and deliverance, only to be followed by further rebellion. So what is the end of this to be? Can this process continue indefinitely? Is God actually going to cast Israel aside? The answer provided in verses 20–22 is not directly addressed to the nation at all, but is God's judicial sentence on them. It is an amazing blend of judgment and mercy.

There is a distance, created by God, as he ceases to call Israel "my people" and refers to them as *"this nation"* (v. 20). If the covenant is violated, the relationship is in deadlock. There came a point at which all God's stratagems of grace seemed to have failed. In spite of his often-repeated compassion in raising up the deliverers, the heart of the nation remained stubbornly unchanged. Therefore God chooses a different policy. Indeed, one may almost say it is forced upon him by the terms of the covenant. As Israel has refused to know her covenantal obligations, she must forfeit her covenant privileges. God is equally released from his obligations toward her. So he resolves not to drive out the Canaanite tribes before them (v. 21).

But lest we should interpret this merely as a judicial action of punishment, the next verse shows us how mercy always blends with justice in the heart and activity of the God who is love. God is not breaking off relations with Israel. His discipline is always with a view to restoration. It is never vindictive.

These are principles we need to build into the foundations of our church and family life today. The Canaanite tribes that remained at the death of Joshua will still remain, and they will become a test of Israel's covenant intentions. God's plan had been to remove the opposition gradually, a stage at a time, because the land would not otherwise have been able to tolerate the vacuum, but now that plan is on "hold." Everything will depend on whether or not the people turn to the Lord and seek to walk in his ways.

The practical lessons for our Christian lives today are not difficult to draw. We never sin and get away with it. Every action of disobedience produces a consequence which affects our relationship with God. While God's forgiveness is always available to those who turn to him in true repentance and sincere faith, we must never forget that it cost the lifeblood of God's Son to open the way into his holy presence. That blood does go on cleansing us from every sin (1 John 1:9), but it does not separate us from sin's consequences. The classic New Testament passage, Hebrews 12:4–11, explains the disciplinary treatment which God permits in our lives as a mark of his fatherly care. He loves us enough to bother with us. We have all met young people who have never experienced discipline because their earthly parents had no real love or concern for them. But not so God! His love always puts our ultimate, greatest good at the top of the agenda. That is why the tests he permits are in fact his votes of confidence in us. They are sent "for our profit, that we may be partakers of his holiness" (Heb. 12:10).

A further and more specific reason for this merciful judgment is outlined in Judges 3:1–2. The remaining tribes still have to be conquered and the method has not changed. As they had no first-hand experience of Yahweh as a god of battle and victory, they had missed out on the greatest stimulus of their fathers' faith. So God will teach them to know war in the hope that this will develop their dependence upon him in every situation of need. It may be the trigger that is needed to fire their obedience so that the new generation will be able to see God at work on behalf of his people. The greatest battle in this book is that fought by Yahweh for all the whole-hearted allegiance of his people. But to be forced to fight physical battles would at least remind Israel of who the real enemies were. The tribes could yet be a hidden blessing if they brought the people of God to their knees.

It is not so much the circumstances of life themselves, but how we react to them which determines whether we are blessed or buffeted. If God allows the lingering consequences of past rebellion to dog our footsteps it is not because he loves us less, but because he is keeping us on that short lead of dependence on him to get through each day, which is actually our position of greatest strength. That's why James can write,

> My brethren, count it all joy when you fall into various trials, knowing that the testing of your faith produces patience. But let patience have its perfect work, that you may be perfect and complete, lacking nothing.
>
> *James 1:2–4*

When we see what the trials are designed to do we begin to thank God for them and to trust where we cannot see. So often we want to give our problems to the Lord because we think that what we need most is to have them solved. So we are happy to give them to God, forgetting that Psalm 55:22 teaches us, "Cast your burden on the Lord, and He shall sustain you. . . ." He is never so interested in solving the problem as in deepening our relationship with him. To deal with the Canaanite nations was no problem to God. It simply required a small exercise of his almighty power. But to win Israel's heart to trustful obedience drew upon all the resources of almighty love. It is a great lesson to learn to look through the circumstances to the Lord, beyond the scenery to the designer, and then to let the present pressures drive us to a fresh, personal commitment to his omnipotent love.

A little girl in England was waiting for her father to return from the stores, where he had gone to buy a special present for her mother's birthday. She had not accompanied him because she was crippled and hardly able to walk. But when the car drew up she struggled out to greet him. The box was large, much larger than she was, but the little one was insistent.

"Give me the box, Daddy, so that I can take it to Mummy!" Her father could see all the difficulties.

"But you won't be able to manage it, dear. It's too big and heavy. You'll never be able to walk with it." Still, she insisted, "Give me the box, Daddy," adding, "I have a plan!" So eventually her father handed the box to the excited little girl.

"Now," she said triumphantly, "I'll carry the box and you can carry me!" God takes the load of our burdens from our aching shoulders, but what he really wants to do is to carry us, to put his great resources at the disposal of those who, by faith, commit their ways to him.

But our passage closes with a sad epilogue. Verse 3 lists the peoples who lived to the southwest (Philistines) and to the north, the border areas where Joshua had not penetrated. But verse 5 includes the peoples whom Joshua had subjected, but who had obviously been left with considerable numbers of survivors. The depressing fact recorded is that Israel totally failed the test. Far from proving God in battle, they lived among the pagan peoples of Canaan, intermarried with them and *"served their gods"* (3:6) This is the background against which the story of the twelve deliverers now begins to be told. We are alerted to the fact that it will be a story blending mercy with judgment, occasional obedience with prevailing unfaithfulness. Yet through it all Yahweh is calling his people to enjoy his love, through their trustful obedience. That is what he wants more than anything else.

> If you keep My commandments, you will abide in My love.
> *John 15:10a*

NOTES

1. Norman Lewis, *Jackdaw Cake* (London: Hamilton, 1985), 41.

CHAPTER THREE

Patterns of Unpredictability

Judges 3:7–31

One of the dangers we fall into most readily is that of imagining that God somehow has to ask our permission before he can act. Of course we would never express it that boldly, but many of us only recognize the hand of God, in practice, in the things that we expect and approve. I remember an honest moment at the end of a rather tedious conversation with a Christian leader, whose theological position was somewhat different from my own, when he turned to me and confided, "Well, according to my theology God ought not to be working in your church, but I suppose I have to admit that he seems to be. . . ." The tragedy is that "my theology" can become the yardstick by which everything and everyone (including God) is measured. Yet we would be the first to defend the inscrutability and infinity of God. Why should we imagine we can box him up in our theology? We all have our blind spots, however sound our theological position—and I am all for us being the best biblically educated theologians we can be! However, God *does* move in mysterious ways "his wonders to perform." William Cowper went on to write:

> Judge not the Lord by feeble sense, but trust Him for His grace;
> Behind a frowning providence He hides a smiling face. . . .
> Blind unbelief is sure to err and scan His work in vain;
> God is His own Interpreter, and He will make it plain.

The first three of the judges whose stories are related in this chapter are each in their way illustrations of this truth, that God is not bound by human restrictions or expectations. If "God is able to raise up children to Abraham from these stones" (Matt. 3:9), then we should beware of ever being trapped into declaring "God cannot" or "God would not." We dare not judge by what we have already seen or experienced. Not that God is capricious or unpredictable in his character. Nor that he ever acts out of character, or contrary to his self-revelation in the Scriptures.

The revelation of the Bible is indeed truth that endures for ever; that is why we give ourselves to its study and proclamation. But we cannot train or domesticate the living God. As soon as we begin to think that we have him buttoned up in our pockets, encompassed by our tiny minds, we have lost God and begun to empty the very name of its meaning.

It is always a trap for those of us who believe in the infallibility of Scripture to be tempted to transfer its inerrancy to our own particular interpretation. Few would have had a higher doctrine of the inspiration and authority of the written word in Jesus' day than the Pharisees, but we hardly want to take them for our model! They stand as a permanent warning to us. What we can and must hold on to is the unchanging character of God, but that does not mean that we will always be able to understand, much less predict, what he is doing in our lives. We should not expect to. The God of order and unchanging faithfulness never descends to human predictability. He loves to demonstrate his deity by transcending our finite thought patterns (see Isaiah 55:8–9). Isn't that why sometimes the very people who have earnestly prayed for revival have failed to recognize God's answer when it came? A different cultural clothing can so easily blind us to God's reality.

Othniel—The Man for the Job

7 So the children of Israel did evil in the sight of the Lord. They forgot the Lord their God, and served the Baals and Asherahs.

8 Therefore the anger of the Lord was hot against Israel, and He sold them into the hand of Cushan-Rishathaim king of Mesopotamia; and the children of Israel served Cushan-Rishathaim eight years.

9 When the children of Israel cried out to the Lord, the Lord raised up a deliverer for the children of Israel, who delivered them: Othniel the son of Kenaz, Caleb's younger brother.

> 10 The Spirit of the Lord came upon him, and he judged Israel. He went out to war, and the Lord delivered Cushan-Rishathaim king of Mesopotamia into his hand; and his hand prevailed over Cushan-Rishathaim.
> 11 So the land had rest for forty years. Then Othniel the son of Kenaz died.
>
> *Judg. 3:7–11*

The way has been prepared for the sad statements of verse 7, by the descriptions of verses 5–6. The pattern of compromise was beginning to become well established. The Israelites were now being tolerated by the pagan tribes to whom they had at one time posed such a threat. A church that domesticates its God will soon become dull, boring, and ultimately irrelevant to the world outside. What began as a workable pattern of coexistence soon degenerated into a loss of Israel's distinctive identity. This was the inevitable fruit of the increasing intermarriage, so that the tribes of Jacob brought out of Egypt began to lose their family identity and unity. Naturally, with the loss of their identity as God's special people came their loss of commitment to their special God, the one true and living God. That was why idolatry flourished, and all in a generation. The spiritual capital of the past very quickly ran out.

The empty churches of Western Europe provide a contemporary example of that unchanging principle of spiritual life. Once God is accommodated to the principle of human rationality, he is soon dethroned from his sovereignty. A culture in which Reason reigns supreme can afford to demythologize the Bible and reject God as an unnecessary hypothesis. But those who sow the wind, reap the whirlwind (Hos. 8:7). A world without God becomes a world without absolutes. The death of God carries implicit within it the death of man also. A hundred years ago atheistic philosophers such as Nietzsche were proclaiming they had killed God, that the stench was over Europe, and that from then on nothing would be forbidden. But at the other end of the twentieth century we are able to look back and see what a horrifying prophecy that really was. Out of that militant atheism have come two global wars, innumerable other conflicts, and the specter of 40 percent of the world's population living under Marxist dictatorships. The history of Europe in our century is a history of spiritual crisis created by the vacuum of atheism until, in 1988 in Poland, the British prime minister was greeted by hundreds of workers chanting, "Plague is better than socialism." That is where we get to when God is dethroned. No wonder the churches are empty in the West. The equally tyrannous effects of sheer materialism have yet to bite so deeply in the Western democracies, as have the dictatorships of the Eastern bloc. But both systems are equally bankrupt spiritually, since their "gods" are totally illusory.

Undoubtedly the Israelites of Othniel's day could have rationalized their evil actions as cleverly and persuasively as do the media pundits of our own generation. Perhaps they didn't really see anything wrong in what they were doing. The laws that had been laid down about not marrying foreigners were all well and good in that context, for that time—but times had changed, they could have argued. "Actually, these Canaanites are very pleasant people, not the monsters that they have been made out to be. They make very good, devoted wives. Often if you marry a girl who's been brought up a bit differently from yourself you've got to allow her to bring her gods along with her. It's part of her culture, isn't it?" You can imagine how the argument would run.

We are all very good at arguing our way around God's commands. It seems to be a natural talent of our fallen human nature. But verse 7 underlines that to break God's laws is to do evil *"in the sight of the Lord,"* whatever we or others may think about it. You see, we don't write the rules, do we? We cannot define good and evil. That's the predicament of the modern atheist. Once he has dismissed God he is forced down the road of totalitarianism if he is going to preserve any sense of order and responsibility in human society. It is God who gives the knowledge of what is good and what is evil, and that is entirely dependent on whether or not something is in accordance with his will and character.

This explains why God's response to Israel's sin is that his righteous anger burns against it (v. 8). So he gives his misguided, but still loved, people a sentence of punishment that fits the crime. They will serve eight years under a foreign tyrant, Cushan-Rishathaim, whose name can probably best be translated "Cushan the archvillain."[1] If you serve foreign gods you can expect to be tyrannized by them. If you give yourself to sin, it will dominate and conquer you. As with Cain (Gen. 4:7), it always crouches at the door ready to overpower the unwary. The roaring lion is always on the prowl looking for his next meal (1 Pet. 5:8). It is worth underlining, however, that what Israel saw superficially as a tyrant overlord was a man completely under the control of Yahweh.

It is the reflex action of God's people to cry out to him whenever we are in trouble, even though we may feel far from him. Sometimes it takes us a long time to become aware of how much we need him. We express this, unconsciously, whenever we come to the end of our tether and say with resignation, "Well, the only thing we can do now is to pray." It is as though prayer is the last desperate throw, whereas it is, in fact, the only resort we have at any time. Prayer should be our first reaction because it is so much more powerful and effective than anything we could put together (see James 5:16b).

Here, at last, these sinful people turned back to their God and begged him to deliver them. It was not that he needed to be persuaded to show mercy, but that their repentance opened the channels through which his covenant compassion was always ready to flow. *"He raised up a deliverer . . . who delivered them"* (v. 9).

God did this by empowering a man called Othniel with his Spirit, breathing his life and power into him to equip him to act in a way which he could never have done unaided. In that power Othniel leads the people; he goes out to war against the tyrant oppressor, and the Lord gives the victory (v. 10). The historian is short on details but strong on the facts. The power of Othniel is God-given, as are the victory of Israel and the forty years' peace which follow.

But what do these facts teach? Supremely that Yahweh is in sovereign control the whole time. The oppression of Cushan is as much the sovereignty of God in chastisement for sin, as the deliverance through Othniel is the sovereignty of God in salvation. Even when his people funnel all their energies into rebelling against him, God is in total control. It is he who makes sin bitter to their taste; he who generates repentance; he who intervenes to save and restore. This is the true meaning of that favorite text, Romans 8:28. All things *do* work together for good to those who love God, but not in an easy way or by an effortless avoidance of difficulties and troubles. God is at work in all our circumstances to work for our good, in using them to help fashion us that little bit more into the likeness of Christ (Phil. 1:6). Our God is so much in command that even Satan finds out in the end that all he has done has simply promoted God's cause.

Josef Tson, president of the Romanian Missionary Society, was exiled from his native Romania from 1981–1990. Before his exile he was the pastor of the Second Baptist Church in Oradea, now probably the largest Baptist church in Europe, with a membership of 2,500. He was exiled by the Romanian government after many months of interrogation. In an article entitled "Thank You for the Beating," published in *Christian Herald* magazine,[2] Tson explains how he survived all the pressures the Romanian police brought upon him to try to destroy him. He says that he saw those actions not as an encounter between himself and the authorities, but between himself and God. The experience of interrogation he identified as a means by which God was teaching him, which assured him that the secret police could not go one inch further than God permitted them. They were simply instruments of God or, as Tson described them, "my Father's puppets." Behind them stood the roaring lion, the enemy of souls, but as the first chapter of the Book of Job so vividly makes clear, this enemy is on a leash that is firmly held by God's all-wise and all-loving hand.

But why did God choose Othniel? It would be tempting to say that he was just the right man for the job. Indeed, it would be hard to imagine a more suitable candidate. Chapter 1 revealed his impeccable pedigree (see v. 13). He seems to have been a born leader, an irrepressible volunteer, who had inherited the go-getter spirit of his uncle Caleb. He captured a city in order to win his bride Achsah, and she was no less a person than the daughter of Caleb himself, one of Israel's greatest heroes. Of course, Othniel was the obvious candidate. He had it all—breeding, background, track record, guts. We could be forgiven for thinking what a good thing it was for Yahweh and for Israel that a man of such stature was available. But we would be entirely wrong. That would be putting God in our box.

Natural gifts of temperament and background are not to be despised, and we certainly need to beware of the inverted snobbery that excludes someone from a spiritual task just because he or she is so able. But such persons do not achieve God's purposes unless he takes and uses them. If we think we know why God acted as he did in choosing Othniel, and build our pattern of expectation on that one example, we are in for a surprise, as the rest of the chapter shows. It is not the script we would have written.

EHUD—ONE OF GOD'S "IRREGULARS"

12 And the children of Israel again did evil in the sight of the Lord. So the Lord strengthened Eglon king of Moab against Israel, because they had done evil in the sight of the Lord.
13 Then he gathered to himself the people of Ammon and Amalek, went and defeated Israel, and took possession of the City of Palms.
14 So the children of Israel served Eglon king of Moab eighteen years.
15 But when the children of Israel cried out to the Lord, the Lord raised up a deliverer for them: Ehud the son of Gera, the Benjamite, a left-handed man. By him the children of Israel sent tribute to Eglon king of Moab.
16 Now Ehud made himself a dagger (it was double-edged and a cubit in length) and fastened it under his clothes on his right thigh.
17 So he brought the tribute to Eglon king of Moab. (Now Eglon was a very fat man).
18 And when he had finished presenting the tribute, he sent away the people who had carried the tribute.
19 But he himself turned back from the stone images that were at Gilgal, and said, "I have a secret message for you, O king." He said, "Keep silence!" And all who attended him went out from him.
20 And Ehud came to him (now he was sitting upstairs in his cool private chamber). Then Ehud said, "I have a message from God for you." So he arose from his seat.
21 Then Ehud reached with his left hand, took the dagger from his right thigh, and thrust it into his belly.
22 Even the hilt went in after the blade, and the fat closed over the blade, for he did not draw the dagger out of his belly; and his entrails came out.
23 Then Ehud went out through the porch and shut the doors of the upper room behind him and locked them.
24 When he had gone out, Eglon's servants came to look, and to their surprise, the doors of the upper

room were locked. So they said, "He is probably attending to his needs in the cool chamber."
25 So they waited till they were embarrassed, and still he had not opened the doors of the upper room. Therefore they took the key and opened them. And there was their master, fallen dead on the floor.
26 But Ehud escaped while they delayed, and passed beyond the stone images and escaped to Seirah.
27 And it happened, when he arrived, that he blew the trumpet in the mountains of Ephraim, and the children of Israel went down with him from the mountains; and he led them.
28 Then he said to them, "Follow me, for the Lord has delivered your enemies the Moabites into your hand." So they went down after him, seized the fords of the Jordan leading to Moab, and did not allow anyone to cross over.
29 And at that time they killed about ten thousand men of Moab, all stout men of valor; not a man escaped.
30 So Moab was subdued that day under the hand of Israel. And the land had rest for eighty years.

Judg. 3:12–30

In the story of Ehud the same basic sequence of events unfolds. Apostasy (v. 12a) leads to punishment (v. 12b), this time in the form of King Eglon of Moab, under whose tribute Israel suffers for eighteen years (v. 14). Once again there is an appeal, a cry of anguish to God, and again God raises up a savior who single-handedly removes the oppressor and brings in a period of peace for eighty years (v. 30). So whom does God choose this time? We might imagine it should be the son of Othniel and Achsah. What a pedigree, what breeding he would have! In reality, the contrast could hardly be more pronounced. Instead of a five-star general, God selects a left-handed assassin (v. 15).

This gives the story an unexpected twist at the start, which continues in a highly ironic, even satirical, vein which is clearly intentionally humorous. Many writers comment on the masterly style of this unknown wry narrator, and it is certainly one of the most memorable short narratives of the Old Testament. The principal target of the irony is the tyrant king, Eglon, whose physique would presumably have done credit to a sumo wrestler (v. 17). He had kept Israel in his iron grip for so long and no one had any answer to his tyranny. No one, that is, except Yahweh, and he selects a most unlikely deliverer. Eglon has grown fat, very fat on the tribute he has been extracting from Israel. But his greed makes him vulnerable. Certainly there was no shortage of target for Ehud to aim at, as the deliberately grotesque description of verse 22 makes clear.

Eglon is also very gullible. His absurd pride cannot resist the "*secret message*" offered him by Ehud. The pompous monarch first seals his fate by dismissing his servants and then receives the message—the sword of God's judgment, delivered by Ehud. The servants are equally gullible (vv. 24–25), the object of the narrator's irony, and by the time they get themselves together and discover their murdered master, the assassin has fled.

The left-handed, sinister motif runs throughout Ehud's actions. He appears to come to deliver the tribute, but actually he has planned the assassination in detail. He appears to be unarmed, but actually he carries a specially made dagger, just the right length, strapped to his right thigh so that he can draw it with his left hand without unduly arousing suspicion. He appears to offer a special sign of God's favor (an oracle), but actually kills the bemused king. It is a strategy built entirely on things being the opposite of what they seem to be.

As a result, the ethical implications of Ehud's plot have often been questioned. The significant factor to bear in mind is that he has already been called and appointed as God's deliverer before the incident occurs. That is why the tribute is sent to Moab by him (v. 15). So this is not a case of one individual taking the law into his own hands, and it cannot therefore be used to justify any similar acts of political murder. In principle, this is a judicial sentence carried out by Yahweh's appointed representative on one of the major enemies of Israel. In essence, it is not different from the destruction of the Canaanites under Joshua. Personal motives are not referred to in any way. Goslinga summarizes this well when he comments:

> Ehud came forward to uphold the rights of God and to take vengeance on His behalf against the Moabites and their king, and it is in this light that his actions have to be judged. Even though the Moabites were the Lord's instrument for punishing Israel, they still remained His enemies and had no right to occupy His sacred land and oppress His sacred people.[3]

Ehud was a man who led Israel into a great national victory on the basis of a personal victory carved out with not a little daring, ingenuity, and courage. In verse 27, he seizes on the vacuum of leadership in Moab to rally Ephraimites in a military operation against their oppressors, driving home their tactical advantage. His confidence in the Lord's ability to provide victory for his people illustrates the faith which made him a leader. Doubtless his own victory over Eglon revived the sagging faith and limitless spirits of the Israelites. So they rallied to their new deliverer, taking control of the fords of the Jordan in order to cut off the occupying army's retreat to their home land. The historian underlines in verse 29 that the ten thousand Moabites who were slaughtered were *"all stout men of valor,"* literally fat or well-fed, like their murdered king. He is making the point that they prospered at Israel's expense, but that this was Israel's own fault (see verse 12). To do evil in the eyes of the Lord only serves to prosper the enemies of the people of God.

In applying the story we do well to draw attention to the fact that God's ways are not ours. The apparent unsuitability of the great men of God in Scripture is a recurrent theme which finds its peak in the selection of the twelve by Jesus. Their references would hardly have been impressive, either from the point of view of their character or their track record. No management consultant would have recommended their appointment. Peter with his impetuous unstable nature, James and John—sons of thunder, Matthew the tax collector, Simon the political extremist; none of them were likely material. They had none of the pedigree or accomplishments which today would be considered absolute necessities.

They were different times, of course, and we must beware of making oversimplistic comparisons. But are we not in danger of supposing that a doctorate is needed to pastor a church? Do we not run the risk of spending so much time in pursuing paper qualifications that we produce a generation of eternal students of ministry rather than skilled practitioners?

God has many surprises. One in the last century was Charles Haddon Spurgeon, the "prince of preachers," who began his ministry in his late teens with no formal preparation, but on whom the Spirit of God rested in power. Certainly, he was exceptional in every way, but today would we not be inclined to package him up and send him off to college and seminary, then to complete his doctoral thesis before pronouncing him ready to minister? I wonder whether he would be the better preacher for that! We need to be aware that God has his "irregulars," who can do great service for him in highly unusual ways. They do not fit neatly into our systems and controls; they are left-handers. But the danger is that we organize the Holy Spirit out of office by our patterns and assembly lines. Ehud is a salutary reminder that

> not many wise according to the flesh, not many mighty, not many noble, are called. But God has chosen the foolish things of the world to put to shame the wise, and God has chosen the weak things of the world to put to shame the things which are mighty; and the base things of the world and the things which are despised God has chosen, and the things which are not, to bring to nothing the things that are, that no flesh should glory in His presence.
>
> *1 Cor. 1:26–29*

The last verse of Judges 3 makes that principle even more clear and plain.

Shamgar—A Rank Outsider

> 31 After him was Shamgar the son of Anath, who killed six hundred men of the Philistines with an ox goad; and he also delivered Israel.
>
> *Judg. 3:31*

This one verse, which ends the chapter, comes, as it were, to emphasize the surprise. Here again is a most unlikely hero. Not only does he defeat one of Israel's most persistent and technically competent enemies, the Philistines, but he makes them look completely ridiculous, in the bargain. Six hundred skilled warriors fall to Shamgar's virtuoso performance, with an ox goad. It isn't even a weapon built for that purpose. Presumably, it just happened to be the first thing he laid his hands on. The implication is that Shamgar was not a trained warrior at all, but a farmer who in the strength supplied by God performed this superhuman feat. Although this is the only event associated with Shamgar, the implication of the phrase used in

5:6, "in the days of Shamgar," is that he functioned as a judge for some period of time and became known as a leader of significance and authority. This is supported by the concluding clause of the verse *"and he also delivered Israel."*

The major thrust of this tantalizingly brief reference seems to be to underline again the unexpected and humanly unlikely identity of both the man and the weapon. Barry G. Webb comments: "The weapon used . . . is makeshift rather than purpose-made, and it marks its bearer even more clearly as a non-professional, a makeshift warrior."[4] He goes on to suggest that although the *"also"* of verse 31 clearly links Shamgar to Ehud, in the sense of him being another rescuer raised by Yahweh, the surprising thing is that we are not provided with any details of his tribal background or place of residence, though it would not be unreasonable to suppose this was in the country bordering the Philistines. Perhaps this was the only area that experienced his deliverance, since 5:6 indicates that conditions elsewhere in Israel were exceedingly grim during his time. Webb's suggestion is that "his name only adds to the mystery surrounding his person, leaving open the possibility that he was not even an Israelite." If that is so then here is an even more startling illustration of the principle that God selects those whom others would never even have thought of.

Throughout this fascinating chapter we are being told, "Don't think that you can predict God." He will break out of all our boxes and categories. The wayside pulpit I once saw outside a church was only partly true. "You need God and God needs you." The latter half of that statement is totally misleading. He may graciously choose to catch us up in his plans and share with us the inestimable privilege of playing some small part in his sovereign purposes, but he does not need any of us. It is a healthy corrective to our all too pervasive habit of asking God to rubber-stamp our carefully worked out plans. We cannot dictate to God; yet that is precisely what our sinful human hearts will always try to do.

Let us remember that Israel's flirtation with other gods came from their overdomestication of the living Lord. It was because they thought they had God sewn up, in their pockets, that they reduced his omnipotence to the level of all the other "godlets" around them—the pagan deities which were the product of rebellious human imagination. That was the danger of being the covenant people. The agreement which God had concluded with his people, in confirming them as his own and binding himself to them by unbreakable promises, led them to presume upon his mercy to the point of indulgence. The love that God required of them degenerated into mere sentimentality. They thought they had God in a box, that he would always be there to deliver irrespective of their neglect of the covenant obligations he had imposed on them. They thought they had trained God. That is always the essence of idolatry. The making of graven images, however much it may be protested that they are merely symbolic, inevitably has the effect of reducing the invisible, infinite, sovereign Creator to a man-sized, predictable representation. That is why the Decalogue so expressly forbids it. The next step is to equate the living God with all the false idols and to incorporate him into the pantheon, even albeit as its head, which is an abomination to the Lord. It is not so surprising, then, that God teaches his rebellious people their total dependence on omnipotence by breaking out of their predictable boxes to use methods and men that no one could have imagined.

On the one hand, this emphasizes God's power. If he so wishes, it is not the slightest problem to God to deliver his people through one man and a piece of farm equipment. If that man is under divine authority and relying on the divine enabling, nothing and no one can stop him. One man with God is thus a majority.

But, on the other hand, the chapter emphasizes God's inscrutability. Why the weapons of deviousness and deception of Ehud? Why choose a Benjamite when they were the very Hebrew tribe that had failed to take Jerusalem? Why the secrecy? And, with Shamgar, why this man with no pedigree or background, using such a bizarre weapon? Surely part of the answer is that in every generation covenant people face the same dangers and need to learn the same lessons. We are just as prone to domesticate the awesome power and majestic authority of God to fit into our little minds and pockets. We still want to control the omnipotent, to predict the infinite. We feel more comfortable that way. What we do not realize is that this is a quick route to spiritual disaster. Any god who can be encompassed by our puny finite minds and accommodated within our feeble systems is not worthy of the name. We have effectively emptied the word *God* of its meaning. Unless we recover a healthy fear and awe of the inscrutable power and sovereignty of God, we shall end up as idolatrous as everyone else. That is why God is constantly surprising us. No situation, however desperate, is beyond his retrieval. No individual can ever be written off in God's providence, or written out of God's script. God has not finished with any of us yet and he is still a specialist in the most unlikely interventions of deliverance. Do you recall the old chorus?

> Got any rivers you think are uncrossable?
> Got any mountains you cannot tunnel through?
> God specializes in things thought impossible!
> He knows a thousand ways to make a way for you.

Let us make sure we are worshiping the real, the living God, and not being duped by all the substitutes offered in the religious supermarkets of our culture and generation. "Little children, keep yourselves from idols" (1 John 5:21).

NOTES

1. Goslinga, *Judges*,p. 278, quoting Noordtzij, "God's Woord," 362.
2. *Christian Herald*, April, 1988, Address: 40 Overlook Drive, Chappaqua, New York 10514.
3. Goslinga, *Judges*, 284.
4. Webb, Barry G., "The Book of the Judges—An Integrated Reading," *Journal for the Study of the Old Testament*, Supplement Series 46, 1987.

CHAPTER FOUR

A Famous Victory

Judges 4:1–5:31

These two chapters comprise a unique unit within the total scheme of the Book of Judges, each dealing with the same event but from the very different perspectives of the historian in chapter 4 and the poet in chapter 5. The song of Deborah and Barak was obviously written first, since it was composed in the full flush of this great victory.

Commentators are not slow to describe this poem of praise as one of the great literary achievements of the ancient world. It would make a splendid dramatic reading in a congregational context, but is equally a delight to read and savor privately. The directness of its expression matches the simplicity of its theme. It is full of vivid word pictures, daring imagery, and rhythmic subtleties (look at 5:27 for example!).

The exultation of victory throbs throughout the poem and we are never allowed to forget that its purpose is primarily to bring worship and thanksgiving to the Lord, the God of Israel, to whom this famous liberation belongs. By contrast, chapter 4 is literally a more prosaic, and therefore factual and historical, account. It was probably written after the period of the judges had ended, in order to explain the background to the great victory poem. Putting them together affords us a fascinating blend of fact and emotional response that can carry us into the heart of these events and what it was like to be living through them.

Such a wealth of material poses particular challenges for the contemporary communicator. To deal with the two accounts separate from each other is to reduce the power and effectiveness of each of them and is liable to be repetitious and pedestrian. To divide the material into its different historically sequential elements is to lose the thrust of the whole in the detail of the parts. My proposal is, therefore, to take the two chapters as one integrated unit and to analyze and expound their message thematically, so as to draw out the theological understanding of the event, which everywhere underlies the history and drama. In this way, hopefully, those to whom we communicate can share the excitement of the text while also recognizing some markers which serve to guide the reader to its contemporary application and unchanging spiritual truth.

A Desperate Situation

4:1 When Ehud was dead, the children of Israel again did evil in the sight of the Lord.

2 So the Lord sold them into the hand of Jabin king of Canaan, who reigned in Hazor. The commander of his army was Sisera, who dwelt in Harosheth Hagoyim.

3 And the children of Israel cried out to the Lord; for Jabin had nine hundred chariots of iron, and for twenty years he had harshly oppressed the children of Israel.

5:6 "In the days of Shamgar, son of Anath,
In the days of Jael,
The highways were deserted,
And the travelers walked along the byways.
7 "Village life ceased, it ceased in Israel,
Until I, Deborah, arose,
Arose a mother in Israel.
8 "They chose new gods;
Then there was war in the gates;
Not a shield or spear was seen among forty thousand in Israel.
9 "My heart is with the rulers of Israel
Who offered themselves willingly with the people.
Bless the Lord!
10 "Speak, you who ride on white donkeys,
Who sit in judge's attire,
And who walk along the road.

11 "Far from the noise of the archers,
among the watering places,
There they shall recount the righteous acts of
the Lord,
The righteous acts for his villagers in Israel;
Then the people of the Lord shall go down to
the gates.
12 "Awake, awake, Deborah!
Awake, awake, sing a song!
Arise, Barak, and lead your captives away,
O son of Abinoam!"

Judg. 4:1–3, 5:6–12

The opening verses of chapter 4 are very clear about the historical background situation. Following the death of Ehud, the cycle of apostasy and judgment is being repeated yet again. It seems that on this occasion the problem began among the northern tribes where Ehud's oppressor is introduced onto the scene in the person of Jabin, king of Hazor—a city which Joshua had captured and burned (Josh. 11:10–13). Because of the lethargy of Naphtali (1:33) the Canaanites seem to have been allowed to resettle and build a new city there. We are back with the earlier lesson that incomplete victories are a sure recipe for future defeats. This reinforced pagan city had by now produced a powerful and fearsome war machine, in the shape of nine hundred iron chariots, to which the Israelites had no answer at all. As verse 2 alerts us, the focus of the story is Sisera, the tyrant general of the Canaanite forces. By this time he and his chariots were in control of the whole northern plain. It was to be twenty years before God's people came to their senses and cried to the Lord for further deliverance.

This matter-of-fact account is enormously enlivened by the vivid picture of what life in Israel was like during this period (which included the judgeship of Shamgar), drawn for us in the poem, 5:6–12. No one used the major highways for fear of being robbed or killed. It was safer to use winding detours and secret paths, but even these would have been vulnerable (v. 6). Public life in Israel was governed by fear; the whole community seemed paralyzed and helpless (v. 7a). There was an absence of any viable leadership, so that when Israel's enemies attacked, there was no resistance (v. 8b). The people were so demoralized that they did not even bother to make weapons. The situation looked utterly hopeless. One cryptic sentence sown in the middle of this depressing picture (v. 8a) gives the reason for the nation's plight—*"they chose new gods."* That, as always, is the root of the problem.

In the contemporary application of these verses it is all too easy for us to be thinking in material rather than spiritual terms. Of course, it is true that when absolute standards of morality which depend for their authority on the existence of an infinite, yet personal, Creator God are rejected, then a nation begins to slide into an abyss of moral chaos in which personal safety and the rule of law are eventual casualties. But, remembering that the New Testament paradigm of interpretation sees the role of the old covenant people of God transferred now to the church of all races and generations, we cannot be content to stop there. These lessons relate powerfully to our spiritual state, both as the new covenant community and as individuals within it. The simple lesson is that when God is marginalized in our lives, decline and disintegration inevitably follow. They may show up at first in terms of depression or frustration, a spirit of dissatisfaction and rebellion, corporately or personally. These symptoms usually indicate that God no longer has his rightful place in our thinking and affections. Rival gods have usurped his throne. The subtlety for us to be aware of is that, like the gods of Canaan, our modern idols are very acceptable socially and even masquerade as being in the service of the Lord. Indeed, is it not the case among us Christians that our very service for God displaces the God whom we profess to be serving?

Every pastor knows what it is to wrestle with the temptation to use his ministry to minister to self rather than to God and, through him, to his world. Ministry can become an idol. Nor do the lay members of our churches possess a natural immunity from this infection. We have all met office bearers who cling to their little area of petty power and influence with a tenacity that would do credit to a barnacle. We all know how easy it can be to accept a task nominally for God's glory but actually for our own kudos, or status within the group. Then because our identity is bound up with it we cease to keep that position or work on an open palm, before God, conscious that he who gave it may also take it away. Instead, we grasp it to ourselves, resist every approach to change or modify our stance and end up enslaved by an idol erected to our own ego. Whenever service or ministry becomes a front for selfish ambition, having things done the way *we* want, we are in a desperate situation.

Before we move on to look more closely at God's answer, we need to take in the content of 5:9–11, noting how it contrasts with the description of the situation outlined earlier in the chapter. Now, Deborah looks back on what God has achieved and sees the current situation is so very different from the way things were. Responding to her call, through Barak, the leaders of Israel had offered themselves willingly for the task of defeating their oppressors. Now, instead of insecurity and violence, peace and prosperity will characterize the country. The rare *"white donkeys"* are symbolic of the return of civil order and freedom of movement, essential for economic well-being (v. 10). Shepherds at the watering holes with their flocks are no longer subject to marauding invaders or the skirmishes of war. The villages are restored to tranquility and town life is no longer under constant threat (v. 11). All this has been possible because Deborah and Barak were awake and alert to take up God's call and fight in God's cause (v. 12). And this is the beginning of the answer to the problem. God has a man—or, in this case, a woman!

A Remarkable Woman

5:7 Village life ceased, it ceased in Israel,
Until I, Deborah, arose,
Arose a mother in Israel.

4:4 Now Deborah, a prophetess, the wife of Lapidoth, was judging Israel at that time.

5 And she would sit under the palm tree of Deborah between Ramah and Bethel in the mountains of Ephraim. And the children of Israel came up to her for judgment.

6 Then she sent and called for Barak the son of Abinoam from Kedesh in Naphtali, and said to him, "Has not the Lord God of Israel commanded, 'Go and deploy troops at Mount Tabor; take with you ten thousand men of the sons of Naphtali and of the sons of Zebulun;

> 7 "'and against you I will deploy Sisera, the commander of Jabin's army, with his chariots and his multitude at the River Kishon; and I will deliver him into your hand'?"
>
> *Judg. 5:7, 4:4–7*

Deborah describes herself as "a mother in Israel." We have become so used to that term being used to describe someone of outstanding care and pastoral concern that we can easily forget that it is first and foremost a statement of facts. Deborah was a wife and a mother. In that sense, she stands in the line of Ehud and Shamgar, among the most unlikely of candidates for God to select. But in another sense, she was an obvious choice because of the gifts of wisdom, judgment and pastoral direction which she was already exercising to the great benefit of God's people (4:4–5). She was serving as mother to the whole nation at a time when male leadership was conspicuous by its absence. She took the needs of the people to heart, watched over them, and worked things out for their best interests.

But we must notice that this role was not one which she had chosen for herself. She was a prophetess. In other words, God had marked her out for a special task by giving her this gift of his grace, through which she was able both to receive and to pass on his word of truth to his people. So, when Deborah sent for Barak (4:6), it was not because she had just thought up a bright idea of a new and clever strategic initiative, but because she had received a command from God. This was how she regularly operated as a judge in Israel. Now her general work is given a particular focus at a particular point in time, according to the will of God. The old liberal idea that prophecy is a special intellectual endowment by which the prophet had a little extra insight or long sight beyond the normal is so untrue to the Bible in its plain sense. Deborah was not a more brilliant tactician than had been seen for a couple of decades in Israel; she was a channel of divine revelation, the leader specially raised up by God for this time. As with every true spiritual gift, this was recognized, not because she wore a badge, or carried a diploma or even announced herself as possessing it, but just because people were so consistently and regularly helped by her ministry. That is the biblical way a gift has to be tested and proved.

Deborah's uniqueness lies in this, that she was the first and only woman revealed as having exercised civil authority in Israel, at God's direction. This is not the place for a detailed discussion of the role of women in the purposes of God, either in Scripture or the church. Sadly, the issue has become clouded and contentious in many areas today due to the incursions of a militant feminism, the roots of which are often found to be in materialistic atheism. In the pages of both testaments a gloriously rich diversity presents itself in the array of women taken up and used by God, from the apparently insignificant slave girl who waited on Naaman's wife (2 Kings 5) to the hugely influential and powerful Queen Esther. In the life and ministry of our Lord Jesus Christ women are first elevated to the dignity and respect which is their birthright; and in the apostolic teaching the implications of equality are fully spelled out. However, equality of status is not the same as identity of role. The New Testament is clear that while the variety of gifts and abilities given to women are many and far-reaching, they are not without limit (1 Tim. 2:12). God has often chosen to raise up godly women as agents of change in the history of his church, especially through their perception, their prayers, and their pastoral service. But the significant factor about Deborah, under the influence of the Lord and as his channel of revelation, is that she did not usurp the man's role. She did not lead the army. That was God's summons to Barak, through her, and she would not step beyond the task which God had given her to do. Deborah was content to remain as the Lord's mouthpiece through whom he revealed the divine strategy by which Sisera and his chariots would eventually become bogged down. It is said that behind every successful man there is a powerful and determined woman, but behind this remarkable woman we see. . . .

A Hesitant Man

> 8 And Barak said to her, "If you will go with me, then I will go; but if you will not go with me, I will not go!"
>
> 9 So she said, "I will surely go with you; nevertheless there will be no glory for you in the journey you are taking, for the Lord will sell Sisera into the hand of a woman." Then Deborah arose and went with Barak to Kedesh.

> 22 And then, as Barak pursued Sisera, Jael came out to meet him, and said to him, "Come, I will show you the man whom you seek." And when he went into her tent, there lay Sisera, dead with the peg in his temple.
>
> *Judg. 4:8–9, 22*

God chooses a leader from among the tribe of Naphtali which had allowed the Canaanites to repossess the ground from which he had driven them. To Barak came both the divine command and the divine strategy, and with them, perhaps most importantly of all, the divine promise, *"I will deliver [Sisera] into your hand."* Obedience is therefore, as always, the product of faith. In Scripture, it is by believing the promises that we are enabled to obey the commands. In the mercy of God, the two always run together. So here, Barak is the privileged recipient of both; but while he seems to have answered Deborah's summons readily enough, the succeeding verses sadly show that he did not match up to her faith. This must surely be the reason why God did not entrust him with the civil leadership of the nation.

The real flaw in Barak's character is shown in the fact that having received God's call through Deborah, he tried to make his obedience conditional (4:8). Whenever we start to bargain with God about the clear terms of his word which demand our obedience, we are bound to be wrong-footed. "If . . . then . . . but if not, then I will not . . ." is a formula which is always an affront to God in his dealings with us. There can be no "if" in a response of obedient faith. In fact, Barak seems to have more confidence in the presence of Deborah than in the word of the Lord, so it is not surprising that his lack of real trust precludes him from sharing the glory of the victory. Instead, he will suffer the huge indignity for a military leader of his task being fulfilled by a woman, Deborah prophecies (v. 9). The fulfillment comes at 4:22 where Barak, pursuing Sisera from the field of battle, arrives too late and simply becomes a spectator of the scene, the general having been murdered by Jael, Heber's wife. God is in control. Barak must learn that what the Lord says will infallibly happen.

We need to learn that also. Our sovereign God, who reigns over all, is going to accomplish his purposes, with or without us. When the call of God comes to us through Scripture to some fresh or renewed obedience, if through lack of faith we fail to obey, we will not hold up God's work. He will simply drive round us and give the honor of being his agent to another of his servants. It is a salutary reminder that we cannot hold back God's work by our little faith. All we achieve is to disqualify ourselves from sharing in its blessings. When rightly understood, this provides a powerful impetus for us to discover and work with God's purposes. Of course it remains true that in his total sovereignty God may choose to limit his activity until his people repent of their lack of faith or obedience, but then that is a sovereign choice of divine and infallible wisdom, not an inevitable consequence of human foolishness. Some promises are conditional upon our obedience, such as 2 Chronicles 7:14:

> "If My people who are called by My name will humble themselves, and pray and seek My face, and turn from their wicked ways, then I will hear from heaven, and will forgive their sin and heal their land."

But it is God who sets the conditions, not Barak. It is God who addresses us "if . . . then," not we who address him. The parallels of a parent's relationship to a child illustrate the point.

Eventually, Barak did go ahead; but only with Deborah holding his hand (4:9). Significantly enough, even when they arrive at the scene of the battle and confront the forces of Sisera, it is Deborah who fires the starter's gun (4:14). Yet one cannot escape the impression throughout these verses that she was anxious not to take over. She was all the time the servant of the Lord and therefore of Israel, who wanted to encourage Barak to fulfill his proper role. Although married to Lapidoth, not Barak, she nevertheless fulfilled the helper role of Genesis 2:18, in a difficult situation which undoubtedly required great self-restraint, godliness and above all faith. It is to Deborah's credit and Barak's shame that things turned out that way. The danger is that while plenty of Christian men may set to emulate Barak, there are not many women who show both the positive qualities and the restraint of Deborah.

We still live with the results of the Fall, one of the most far-reaching of which seems to be the distorting of the divinely given relationships and roles of men and women. Part of the judgment of God, spoken of in Genesis 3:16, has to do with the tyranny by which unregenerate human nature in the man rules over the woman, exploiting and inhibiting her, as is still evident today in many non-Christian societies. But the opposite distortion seems to be particularly prevalent in Christianized cultures, where the man is often only too ready to concede his responsibilities in leadership to his wife, whether within the family or the church, and the wife is often equally ready to take them over. There is a danger in some Christian circles today of confusing wimpishness with sanctity and weakness with meekness. "Moses was very humble, more than all men who were on the face of the earth" (Num. 12:3), but I do not get the impression that he was a pushover!

A Divided Nation

4:10 And Barak called Zebulun and Naphtali to Kedesh; he went up with ten thousand men under his command, and Deborah went up with him.

5:13 "Then the survivors came down,
The people against the nobles;
The Lord came down for me against the mighty.
14 "From Ephraim were those whose roots were in Amalek.
After you, Benjamin, with your peoples,
From Machir rulers came down,
And from Zebulun, those who bear the recruiter's staff.
15 "And the princes of Issachar were with Deborah;
As Issachar, so was Barak
Sent into the valley under his command;
Among the divisions of Reuben
There were great resolves of heart.
16 "Why did you sit among the sheepfolds,
To hear the pipings for the flocks?
The divisions of Reuben have great searchings of heart.
17 "Gilead stayed beyond the Jordan,
And why did Dan remain on ships?
Asher continued at the seashore,
And stayed by his inlets.

18 "Zebulun is a people who jeopardized their lives
to the point of death,
Naphtali also, on the heights of the battlefield."
Judg. 4:10, 5:13–18

This section takes up the Barak theme and reinforces its lessons. Ten thousand men from Zebulun and Naphtali were prepared to rally to Barak (4:10), coming down out of the hills where they had judged themselves safe from Sisera's chariots. Now they respond to the call to do battle with Sisera, but it must be on his home ground, the plain, where Sisera has the undoubted and massive advantage. Otherwise, the tyrant king would not be so foolish as to risk his troops in an engagement. It says much for the faith of these men that they were prepared to take Sisera on in a context where he was undisputedly master. But then they reckoned on God, and Sisera did not. So they came from Ephraim and Benjamin, from Machir (the half-tribe of Manasseh living west of the Jordan), and from Zebulun and Issachar, tribes that had suffered great hardship under Jabin. Leaders and men, they rallied to Deborah and Barak, moved by the Spirit of the Lord.

But others declined (5:15b–17). There is a poignant irony about the description contained in these verses. Across the Jordan, Reuben went in for endless committee meetings around the campfires. There was much heart-searching, even *"great resolves,"* but they actually did precisely nothing. What a contemporary ring Deborah's chiding has! Discussion and resolutions are never a substitute for faith and obedience. There was no real motivation to come to help their brothers. They wanted to hear the shepherd's pipe in their undisturbed rural setting, rather than the war trumpet. They did not want to be disturbed. Supporting the initiative against Sisera was, after all, too costly to contemplate.

How often the church of our day reacts in exactly the same way! "Lord here am I; please send somebody else."

Gilead (the other half-tribe of Manesseh) was indifferent. They were not directly affected, so they had no interest. Theirs is a very different attitude from that enjoined on us by Paul in Philippians 2:4, "Let each of you look out not only for his own interests, but also for the interests of others." But it commonly affects Christians. When William Carey, the English Baptist pioneer missionary to India, first began to share his sense of God's call to evangelize the heathen in the 1790s he was told by senior pastors of his acquaintance that it was none of his business. When God wanted to evangelize the pagan world he would do so without resorting to human channels or methods.

Dan and Asher were too busy trading with the Phoenicians along the coastal routes. They did not have time to obey God's call. After all, they did have a living to make—wife and 2.4 children to support! Once again, self-interest proved to be the hindrance to their involvement in God's campaign. If you doubt the contemporary relevance of this, try calling the local church to a prolonged and consistent obedience in the matter of prayer. For that is surely where the spiritual battle is joined now. But how good we are at finding other more important things to occupy our precious hours! Of course, it *is* tough very often obeying God, as 5:18 reminds us. What we have to realize is that the only way to share in the enjoyment of God's blessings is to get involved with him in fighting his battles. Too much of our contemporary Christianity is boring and useless because we have become so adept at side-stepping God's challenges.

Our spectator culture is profoundly challenged by the gospel of a God of grace who acts in the arena of human history. Today we are so used to watching—before the TV set, at the ball game, even in the worship service. We become expert analysts of the action replay, brilliant strategists, great talkers; but all from the comfort of our spectator's seat. We have lost the thrill of being in the rough and tumble, amidst the ups and downs of the team commitment to putting things together and achieving results against the odds. We forget what it is like to be on the inside, with all its heartache but with its exultation too. Our highs and lows are experienced vicariously. We are shadows of our real selves.

Surely within the church of Christ we need to, and can, regain the commitment to the adventure of faith, to prove God's power, to lift our lives beyond the mundane and the ordinary and embrace a cause that is greater than our own little private world. Our young people especially need to see the privilege of living for Christ rather than self in an alien world. But they will only begin to believe it when they see that Spirit exemplified in their elders and leaders. I love that old warrior Caleb who declared at the age of eighty-five, "I am as strong this day as I was on the day that Moses sent me [to spy out the land]; just as my strength was then, so now is my strength for war, both for going out and for coming in. Now, therefore, give me this mountain of which the Lord spoke in that day . . ." (Josh. 14:11–12a). Who needs to go quietly downhill when he can go storming on to glory? It depends on whether we believe the promises and obey the commands. As then the nation, so now the church is divided between those who do and those who prefer a softer option.

A Miraculous Intervention

4:11 Now Heber the Kenite, of the children of Hobab the father-in-law of Moses, had separated himself from the Kenites and pitched his tent near the terebinth tree at Zaanaim, which is beside Kedesh.

12 And they reported to Sisera that Barak the son of Abinoam had gone up to Mount Tabor.

13 So Sisera gathered together all his chariots, nine hundred chariots of iron, and all the people who were with him, from Harosheth Hagoyim to the River Kishon.

14 Then Deborah said to Barak, "Up! For this is the day in which the Lord has delivered Sisera into your hand. Has not the Lord gone out before you?" So Barak went down from Mount Tabor with ten thousand men following him.

15 And the Lord routed Sisera and all his chariots and all his army with the edge of the sword before Barak; and Sisera alighted from his chariot and fled away on foot.

16 But Barak pursued the chariots and the army as far as Harosheth Hagoyim, and all the army of Sisera fell by the edge of the sword; not a man was left.

5:19 "The kings came and fought,
Then the kings of Canaan fought
In Taanach, by the waters of Megiddo;
They took no spoils of silver.
20 "They fought from the heavens;
The stars from their courses fought against Sisera.
21 "The torrent of Kishon swept them away,
That ancient torrent, the torrent of Kishon.

O my soul, march on in strength!
22 "Then the horses' hooves pounded,
The galloping, galloping of his steeds.
23 "'Curse Meroz' said the angel of the Lord,
'Curse its inhabitants bitterly,
Because they did not come to the help of the Lord,
To the help of the Lord against the mighty.'"
Judg. 4:11–16, 5:19–23

The scene is set; the battle lines are drawn. The significant unseen factor is found in 4:14, *"Has not the Lord gone out before you?"* Note the importance of the divine word again as his people go forward into the fight. We cannot expect to be strong if we are not nurtured on the word of God. It is the people who know their God who are made strong and who carry out great exploits (Dan. 11:32). Yet the outcome, which is the climax of an initiative which is truly God's from beginning to end, is far beyond anything that his people could ever have imagined. The prose account (4:15–16) simply states the cold facts, with an economy of words that is breathtaking in itself. It was a rout. There was the advantage to Israel of the element of surprise since Sisera is unlikely to have imagined that the battle would be carried to him. In fact, there never was an organized military engagement as such, yet Israel's victory was total. So, how did it happen?

Verses 19–23 of chapter 5 provide us with the answer. Jabin's alliance of Canaanite kings came ready to fight in the valley of the Kishon near Megiddo, ready to seize the advantage with their military hardware—only to find that Heaven was fighting against them (v. 20). Sisera's army crossed the river and then a cloudburst occurred causing a flash flood so that the Kishon rushed down upon the army. The chariot wheels became embedded in the silt and mud. Many of Sisera's men were swept away by the current and drowned. Verse 22 is a graphic verbal picture of any army in frenzied panic, trying desperately to escape, but to no avail. It was an outcome that none of the expert military analysts appearing on Canaanite breakfast television could ever have predicted. It left Sisera's forces decimated and their commander-in-chief running away on foot. No one can predict what God will still do today to support a people who are obedient to his detailed commands. It is a curse not to be on the side of the Lord (5:23). "He who is not with Me is against Me, and he who does not gather with Me scatters abroad" (Matt. 12:30).

Both accounts serve to underscore very powerfully that the battle was entirely the Lord's. The incident provides one of the clearest Old Testament illustrations of the principle spelled out with unmistakable clarity in the New, particularly in Paul's second letter to the Corinthians. "My strength is made perfect in weakness" (2 Cor. 12:9).

Israel could hardly have been in a weaker position. Outwardly, she had been under the tyrant's yoke for twenty years. Inwardly, disillusionment and disintegration reigned. There were no leaders, no armaments, no vision. It was a classic no-win situation. But *"Israel cried out to the Lord"* (4:3) and God answered by revelation through the prophetess, which stirred the hearts and resolves of some of his people and which provided the strategy for victory. Yet even that victory was not won by their blows but by heavenly intervention. Israel began in weakness and ended in weakness. What we have to grasp is that this is not an unfortunate oversight or accident, but the very heart and kernel of God's plans. In Pauline terms again, "We have this treasure in earthen vessels, that the excellence of the power may be of God and not of us" (2 Cor. 4:7). To use frail, weak, easily smashed clay pots to carry the light of the gospel into the world is an essential ingredient of the divine strategy. That way, as here in Judges, everybody knows that the power is superhuman. In Corinth, little clay jars used to contain oil or to carry a light were cheap and expendable, almost the equivalent of our paper cups and plastic cartons. And that is what we are like, says Paul. We are disposable, but the power of God will go on being demonstrated through our human weakness.

Sometimes we find that hard to accept, especially in our world that is devoted to power and success, impressiveness and influence. It runs counter to all that our materialistic culture holds dear. That is why it is so much needed—to challenge the culture's presuppositions and expose its false values, from the perspective of eternity. The problem is that we Christians are all too often conformers rather than transformers. We let the world squeeze us into its mold rather than allowing the Spirit of God to renew our minds daily through the truth of his word (Rom. 12:2). So we tend to be very impressed by the outward trappings of success, by size and wealth and breadth of influence, in our churches and organizations. What we have to stop and ask ourselves is how much of all that is really biblical. And the honest answer is, "not much."

There is a hidden but inescapable logic behind this. How can the messengers of the gospel expect to be outwardly impressive, widely acclaimed and financially successful when the message they are commissioned to preach and live concerns a suffering Servant-King, who was and is despised and rejected by men, who died a criminal's death and was buried in a borrowed tomb? The very message of the gospel stands in direct contradiction of many of its modern messengers. No wonder the world thinks the church lacks credibility.

Now this does not mean that we do not use all the resources available to us via material means to get the gospel out. Nor does it mean that we settle for a mediocre level of presentation or a self-consciously ascetic life-style. There are equal and opposite snares at the other end of the spectrum. But it *does* mean that we do not rely on these human resources. Rather, we recognize that power belongs to God alone, that his is the battle and his is the glory; so we put no confidence in the flesh (Phil. 3:3). In practice, this means that we can with Paul "boast in [our] infirmities, that the power of Christ may rest upon [us]" (2 Cor. 12:9b). His strength is made perfect in weakness, provided that weakness is put into God's hands. We are made to feel and know our weakness in order to drive us to a fresh dependence on Christ.

An Unexpected End

4:17 However, Sisera had fled away on foot to the tent of Jael, the wife of Heber the Kenite; for there was peace between Jabin king of Hazor and the house of Heber the Kenite.

18 And Jael went out to meet Sisera, and said to him, "Turn aside, my Lord, turn aside to me; do not fear." And when he had turned aside with her into the tent, she covered him with a blanket.

19 Then he said to her, "Please give me a little water to drink, for I am thirsty." So she opened a jug of milk, gave him a drink, and covered him.

20 And he said to her, "Stand at the door of the tent, and if any man comes and inquires of you, and says, 'Is there any man here?' you shall say, 'No.'"

21 Then Jael, Heber's wife, took a tent peg and took a hammer in her hand, and went softly to him and

drove the peg into his temple, and it went down into the ground; for he was fast asleep and weary. So he died.

5:24 "Most blessed among women is Jael,
The wife of Heber the Kenite;
Blessed is she among women in tents.
25 "He asked for water, she gave milk;
She brought out cream in a lordly bowl.
26 "She stretched her hand to the tent peg,
Her right hand to the workmen's hammer;
She pounded Sisera, she pierced his head,
She split and struck through his temple.
27 "At her feet he sank, he fell, he lay still;
At her feet he sank, he fell;
Where he sank, there he fell dead.
28 "The mother of Sisera looked through the window,
And cried out through the lattice,
'Why is his chariot so long in coming?
Why tarries the clatter of his chariots?'
29 "Her wisest ladies answered her,
Yes, she answered herself,
30 "'Are they not finding and dividing the spoil:
To every man a girl or two;
For Sisera, plunder of dyed garments,
Plunder of garments embroidered and dyed,
Two pieces of dyed embroidery for the neck of the looter?'"

Judg. 4:17–21; 5:24–30

The prose account of chapter 4, embroidered by the superb pathos and drama of the poem in chapter 5, together show how Deborah's prophecy was fulfilled, as Sisera met his death at the hands of a woman, Jael, wife of Heber. Again there is an emphasis upon the inscrutability that led to Sisera's death, but the Word of the Lord was most certainly fulfilled. Like Shamgar before her, Jael used the implements which were near to hand, tent peg and hammer, to dispatch the enemy of God's people.

Scholars comment that among the Bedouin pitching the tent is regarded as the women's task, so that Jael was not performing an unfamiliar action, even if its purpose was unique. In our times, the treachery involved has often been noted and condemned. Verse 11 (chap. 4) has prepared us for the fact that the descendants of Hobab, Moses' father-in-law, in which line Heber stood, had already separated themselves out from Israel again and thereby enjoyed much more favorable relations with Jabin (4:17b). So, as Sisera enters Jael's tent, he imagines that he is entering a friendly environment, a conclusion which the provision of milk and the offer of rest only confirm. He even asks her to stand guard over him while he sleeps. For this trusted hostess to murder her guest is surely a crime of the worst sort.

Yet we cannot escape the biblical fact that Deborah, inspired by the Spirit in her victory song, pronounces Jael *"most blessed among women"* (5:24). In context, there seems to be a deliberate contrast between the curse on Meroz (5:23), who did not help Israel in the pursuit of the fleeing Canaanites. They were Israelites who should have been identified with God's cause; but instead their lethargy condemned them and their city is never heard of again and has never been located. But Jael, who was not a true Israelite, was the agent of the Lord's vengeance on the tyrant oppressor, and for that reason her action is praised, even though we may not approve of the method. We need to remember C. J. Goslinga's comment that "Deborah's blessing does not make Jael into a Saint."[1]

However, the overall thrust of these dramatic verses is to remind us that the way of sinners is hard (Prov. 13:15). Sisera may be shown to us, from the divine perspective of revelation, as the agent of God's judgment upon his rebellious people, but that does not exonerate him from the moral responsibility of his oppressive and cruel exploitation. There was that mysterious blend of divine sovereignty and human responsibility in Sisera's actions and life-style which so often surfaces in the Old Testament. The pharaoh whom God raised up so that he might show his power in him, and so that God's name might be declared in all the earth (Exod. 9:16) nevertheless exalted *himself* against God and his people in refusing to let them go from the land of Egypt (Exod. 9:17). Thus, the pharoah whose heart God hardened was a man who had already hardened his heart.

Or, one can think of the burden of the Book of Habakkuk, in which God declares, "I am raising up the Chaldeans, a bitter and hasty nation" (Hab 1:6) as an instrument of judgment. Yet they will not escape that same judgment. "Because you have plundered many nations, all the remnant of the people shall plunder you" (Hab. 2:8). The death of Sisera reminds us that he met his nemesis just when he thought he was safe. And the echo from the New Testament is that "the day of the Lord so comes as a thief in the night. For when they say 'Peace and safety!' then sudden destruction comes upon them. . . . And they shall not escape" (1 Thess. 5:2–3). It reminds us that whether through death or Christ's return we all have an appointment to keep with God; and we cannot put it into our diaries. The timing belongs to God alone.

Sisera's mother may comfort herself that her son's homecoming has been delayed by the size of the victory and the quantity of the booty to be divided, but the reality is that God has called him up for judgment. The poignancy of 5:28–30 depends on the fact that we, the readers, know of the grief that is about to break on the unsuspecting mother. It sharpens our sense of human vulnerability, of the uncertainty of this short and transitory life. That is a message which the present generation badly needs to hear, as we do everything in our power to distance death and pretend it does not happen.

A Challenging Contrast

1 Then Deborah and Barak the son of Abinoam
sang on that day, saying:
2 "When leaders lead in Israel,
When the people willingly offer themselves,
Bless the Lord!
3 "Hear, O kings! Give ear, O princes!
I, even I, will sing to the Lord;
I will sing praise to the Lord God of Israel.
4 "Lord, when You went out from Seir,
When You marched from the field of Edom,
The earth trembled and the heavens poured,
The clouds also poured water;
5 "The mountains gushed before the Lord,
This Sinai, before the Lord God of Israel. . . .

31 "Thus let all Your enemies perish, O Lord!
But let those who love Him be like the sun

When it comes out in full strength."
So the land had rest for forty years.
Judg. 5:1–5, 31

We return to the beginning of the song to catch again the note of exultation and triumph which permeates the whole composition. It is the celebration of a great day, a famous victory. The names of Deborah and Barak do feature in the poem; they were God's channels. The tribes that gave themselves to the conflict are faithfully recorded, as indeed are those who had no stomach for the fight. But the focus of rejoicing is the Lord, Yahweh the God of Israel. It begins and ends with God. He is to be praised (v. 2) because it was his word and power that moved the otherwise ineffective leaders of the people to fulfill their role and the people to follow them. As has been said, "He who thinks he leads when no one follows is merely going for a walk!" The change was made, however, not by human endeavors but by responding in faith to a new word from God. So, as Deborah leads the Song of Thanksgiving, it is not surprising that her focus is entirely on God and his activity.

She depicts God as marching out in all the splendor and majesty of an oriental monarch to meet with Jabin and Sisera, in words that deliberately recall his meeting with his people at Sinai after the Exodus. This was not just the historic foundation of the covenant between Yahweh and his people, but the constant reminder to the present generation of his faithfulness and dependability so graphically demonstrated again in this miraculous deliverance. This same God who delivered from Egypt has led into Canaan and will deliver his people there. Then he came in fire and thunder. Now he has come in the heavy storms and cloudbursts by which Sisera's army was literally washed away. Before this God who has such total creational authority over the elemental force of the universe, no army of mortal men can hope to stand. Thus thanksgiving for deliverance leads to adoration and worship of such a glorious Being, "perfect in power, in love, and purity."

Not surprisingly then, the poem ends by reminding its reciters and readers that everything depends upon one's relationship to this great and glorious Sovereign Lord. The last verse shows Deborah addressing the Almighty directly. She sees the great divide in humanity established according to whether we use the life and breath that God grants us to fight him or to love him. She voices her certainty that those who oppose him can expect eventually to share Sisera's fate, perishing under his judgment. It is a solemn warning to a nation which, while currently celebrating God's goodness, has all too often in the past put itself under his wrath, through its rebellion and idolatry. Each successive deliverance carried on its reverse side the warning of inevitable judgment on God's enemies. The sad history of the period of the judges is that this lesson was never learned at a deep enough level, or beyond a single generation. But the contrast is wonderful! Those who stand on God's side because they love him are like the sun coming out in its *"full strength."* They are a light to the entire world, experiencing the light of God within their own lives, firstly, to dispel the inner darkness of sinful disobedience, and then reflecting that light throughout the world, in the proclamation of God's truth and the living of holy lives.

As this strong biblical theme develops it takes an increasingly pronounced Messianic content. We see it in Isaiah 9:2, 6.

> The people who walked in darkness have seen a great light; . . .
> For unto us a Child is born,
> Unto us a Son is given;
> And the government will be upon His shoulder.
> And His name will be called
> Wonderful, Counselor, Mighty God,
> Everlasting Father, Prince of Peace.

The Old Testament ends with the same note of promise—"To you who fear My name the Sun of Righteousness shall arise with healing in His wings" (Mal. 4:2)—and the Gospel takes it up in the Song of Zacharias: "The Dayspring from on high has visited us; to give light to those who sit in darkness and the shadow of death, to guide our feet into the way of peace" (Luke 1:78–79). This promise comes to its glorious climax when the Lord Jesus declares, "I am the light of the world. He who follows Me shall not walk in darkness, but have the light of life" (John 8:12). Those who love him will become like him. So, Deborah's ancient song points us forward to the Christ in whom all the promises of God find their "yes" and their "Amen" (2 Cor. 1:20), the Christ of all the Scriptures, the true light of the world. And God's victory through her provides us with a most powerful reminder of one thing that no human being can do. However powerful he may imagine himself to be, no one can resist the sun rising.

NOTES

1. Goslinga, *Judges*, 318.

CHAPTER FIVE

Gideon: In God's Base Camp

Judges 6:1–32

For the first time in the book a major character now appears on the stage, one with whose life the next three chapters of Judges will be entirely concerned. Gideon and Samson are undoubtedly the best known of the figures within Judges, not only because of the amount of detail given to their exploits, but also because we find it easier to identify ourselves with them. This is certainly true of Gideon, the hero of many a Sunday school lesson. But for serious communicators of the Bible this can pose the problem of overfamiliarity within the ingredients of the story, so that we miss the wood by a detailed examination of the trees.

As a corrective, we need to recall the overall context. If we were to do away with the chapter division and simply move on, from the exultation of Deborah's praise poem to the bald statement with which chapter 6 opens, we would at least be shocked into seeing the spiritual perspective in which Gideon appeared. We cannot divorce him from his time. While the lessons he had to learn we must learn, too, if our lives are to count for God, there is a particularity about Gideon's story which should warn us against simply transposing ingredients of the narrative into our world and making too quick and easy an application. If we do not understand why Gideon was raised up then, and why God's dealings with him were recorded in the form we have them, we shall not make much progress in understanding their relevance to us today.

There is a sense in which most books of the Bible have an internal movement which helps us to grasp their construction and then their message. Thus the Gospel of Mark is divided into two roughly equal halves around the pivotal question of Jesus, "Who do you say that I am?" The first half, up to Peter's confession at Caesarea Philippi (8:29), constantly poses the question of the identity of Jesus as he demonstrates his power over all the hostile forces that oppose him. Once the disciples came to the key realization that he is the Christ, the rest of the Gospel incredibly shows that the king will only come into his inheritance through suffering and death. We climb a steep slope to the mid-way point, only to realize that on the other side is a totally different vista leading to Calvary.

The First Letter of John I have likened to a spiral staircase ascending round the themes of light and love, carrying us further and further upward and giving new views of familiar truths all the way.

But Judges has a different movement. At first it seems to be circular. Israel sins; God disciplines; Israel repents; God delivers. But that is only part of the story. The movement is actually a downward spiral, an ever-deepening vortex, for with each fresh apostasy the oppression seems to deepen, either in length or intensity, or both. And each time a leader is raised up he seems to be more flawed than the last one; a process which develops through Jephthah to reach its peak in Samson.

Things are not just repeated in Scripture, and to read each successive story as a rerun is too simplistic. We know from our own experience in the Christian life that we do not stand still. We move in one direction or another. The only body that is perfectly still is a corpse. So, although Gideon becomes a man of great faith (Heb. 11:32), he is always a fallible human being, whose end is not as glorious as his beginning. "It is better to travel hopefully than to arrive," the saying goes. Certainly for Gideon "arrival" was ultimately much more testing than the journey. The tests of his success were what found him lacking, as we shall see. But we begin with him as a raw recruit in training camp.

God Chastises

1 Then the children of Israel did evil in the sight of the Lord. So the Lord delivered them into the hand of Midian for seven years,

2 and the hand of Midian prevailed against Israel. Because of the Midianites, the children of Israel made for themselves the dens, the caves, and the strongholds which are in the mountains.
3 So it was, whenever Israel had sown, Midianites would come up; also Amalekites and the people of the East would come up against them.
4 Then they would encamp against them and destroy the produce of the earth as far as Gaza, and leave no sustenance for Israel, neither sheep nor ox nor donkey.
5 For they would come up with their livestock and their tents, coming in as numerous as locusts; both they and their camels were without number; and they would enter the land to destroy it.
6 So Israel was greatly impoverished because of the Midianites, and the children of Israel cried out to the Lord.

Judg. 6:1–6

If ever we are prone to be depressed by the repetition of the cycle of sin and failure, surely we need to look into our own hearts and see how endemic it is to our fallen human nature. We cannot point the finger of accusation at Israel when we know our own depravity. Indeed, we have so much more in terms of the full revelation of God in Christ and in the completed Scriptures, as well as the gracious indwelling of the Spirit in every believer, that we are the ones who should be ashamed. If we can feel something of the irritation of Israel's continual stubborn rebellion, how must God feel about my ungrateful, sinful heart? Such continued mercy drives us to our knees, "lost in wonder, love, and praise." However, we do need to learn the lesson that repeated sin brings its own consequences, not because God is cruel and vindictive, but because he has our best interests at heart and loves us too much to let us get away with our sins. That is why he chastises his children.

The principle is fully explained in Hebrews 12:5–11, an important control passage for understanding God's dealings with Israel, and one that is worth quoting selectively here:

"For whom the Lord loves He chastens,
and scourges every son whom He receives."
If you endure chastening, God deals with you as with sons; . . .

> but if you are without chastening . . . then you are illegitimate and not sons. . . . [our human fathers] for a few days chastened us as seemed best to them, but He for our profit, that we may be partakers of His holiness. Now no chastening seems to be joyful for the present, but painful; nevertheless, afterward it yields the peaceable fruit of righteousness to those who have been trained by it.

God's discipline is a feature of his love, and it is only by allowing us to taste the consequences of our sin that God teaches us to hate it. He has the long-term gains always in view—holiness and righteousness. The mark of being in a family is that the father is always working for our greatest good, though it may grieve him at times, and us, frequently. But we all know that undisciplined kids are no credit to their parents. It is not love to allow them always to have their own way or to run wild—quite the opposite in fact. Children who rebel often do so with increasing outrageousness just because they are desperately pleading for the line to be drawn somewhere; for someone to love them enough to say no. That is how God's motivation of love often works out in the lives of his immature children. Of course, we need to be careful not to make too easy an equation between adversity and God's chastisement, for not all suffering has that source. But, when as God's people we face a prolonged period of difficulty, such as the seven years of verse 1, it should at the very least make us stop and examine our ways. "Is this God's discipline?" we need to ask.

For Israel, God's chastening came in the form of oppression by the Midianites (v. 2). The people who had been given the land by the Lord who created and owned it all were reduced to hiding themselves in caves in the barren and inhospitable hill country. Even there they felt insecure and were forced to build fortified strongholds because they had no answer to the marauding forces of Midian. This reminds us that there is no real answer to God's discipline apart from the spiritual one of repentance and renewal. The very lives of the Israelites were conditioned by the annual invasion, of which the passage provides us with a most graphic description. Living in dens and caves like animals themselves they lost their crops and their own livestock without any hope of redress because the enemy was as numerous as a locust plague, and as highly mobile, traveling on their numberless fast camels to penetrate and devastate every corner of the land. We do not need much imagination to grasp what wave after wave of this sort of total destruction, year after year, would do to the Israelites' morale. When the invasion was over the rest of the year was lived out in poverty which it had caused. Not only materially, but emotionally and psychologically the people of God were reduced to utter destitution. Only then, after seven years of this treatment, did they humble themselves sufficiently to call upon the Lord. How stubborn and rebellious human will really is!

The immaturity of childish behavior provides us with so many illustrations, for its spiritual equivalent is where all sin finds its roots. It is the height of folly to be found fighting against God, but we become so mesmerized by our own ideas of what is best for us that we risk anything rather than give them up. "I may make a mess of my life," a rebellious teenager once told me, "but at least it will be my own mess!" Or I think of the little girl, justly disciplined by her mother for her misbehavior, stubbornly refusing to admit that she was wrong. When it came to prayer time at the end of the day, her mother suggested they should find something to thank God for, only to be met by blank and determined silence. Exasperated, her mother replied that there were many things to thank God for and that she was prepared to sit it out until junior mentioned at least one. The minutes ticked by, until eventually out it blurted. "Thank you, God, for nice me!" Yes, that's the human heart, whatever time, whatever place.

God Convicts

> 7 And it came to pass, when the children of Israel cried out to the Lord because of the Midianites,
>
> 8 that the Lord sent a prophet to the children of Israel, who said to them, "Thus says the Lord God of Israel: 'I brought you up from Egypt and brought you out of the house of bondage;
>
> 9 and I delivered you out of the hand of the Egyptians and out of the hand of all who oppressed you, and drove them out before you and gave you their land.
>
> 10 'Also I said to you, "I am the Lord your God; do not fear the gods of the Amorites, in whose land you dwell. But you have not obeyed my voice."'"
>
> *Judg. 6:7–10*

God answers prayer, even that of the worst rebellious children when at last they begin to cast themselves on his grace. "God be merciful to me a sinner!" (Luke 18:13) is the one prayer that always gets through. But the answer is not always in the form that we might expect. On this occasion, a prophet appeared, just as Deborah had done in chapter 4; but this time the prophet's task is not to set the wheels of deliverance in motion. The downward spiral effect is operating. His message from the Lord is that the people have forfeited any right to Yahweh's help because of their persistent idolatry.

Far from offering the hope of deliverance, he is sent by God to serve an indictment on his rebellious people in the form of a triple accusation. First, they are charged with *ingratitude* as God recounts all that he has done for them in delivering them from Egypt and giving them the land. They have effectively thrown his gracious provision back in his face. Next, God reminds them that although he had forbidden them in the clearest possible terms to worship other gods, they have run into *idolatry*, by choosing not to hear and not to bother with his commands. Lastly, all this has been worsened by their *impenitence*, since up to this point they have deliberately chosen not to change their ways in spite of the seven-year Midianite oppression. The charges are detailed and specific.

Israel is being taught the lesson that where these sins are not recognized, they cannot just call upon God when circumstances become tough and expect him to deliver them, like a piece of automatic machinery. For the ground of their appeal was not their humanity, but their covenant relationship with the Lord. What they had forgotten was that covenant privileges presuppose the fulfillment of covenant obligations, which Israel had not only failed to keep but vigorously transgressed. There is therefore a real controversy between God and his people, and at this point in the narrative we do not know what decision God will take in answer to their cry.

Presumption is a particular danger for those who believe their membership in the new covenant community is assured. The more involved we are in the work of God, the more we can be tempted to think that God will be indulgent toward our failures and even our sins. We can develop our own familiarity with God which overlooks his strongest holiness by emphasizing his friendship with us, almost to the point of "mateyness." This is always a perilous path to travel down. We need to remember that no amount of past faithfulness in service buys us the right to bend the rules in the present.

Or, as John Chapman, the Australian evangelist, once told a group of ministers in my hearing, "You've got to remember that just because you're a minister, doesn't let you off being a Christian." Whatever our position or role within the church, we all need the reminder that we have only to tie a loose knot of faith around the bollard and the tide will do the rest. The prevailing current will do all that is needed to sweep us out to sea unless we are making constant and vigorous efforts to be anchored, by faith and obedience, to Christ himself. No belief is secure that is not wholehearted, and no virtue is safe that is not enthusiastic.

When we are convicted of our sin and do turn to God, we begin to realize that his response is not on the basis of our need, or even of our repentance, but solely because of his grace. It took Israel seven years to reach that point. It takes some of us a long time to come to a repentance that is deep and real. So, we ought not to be discouraged if in our increasingly godless climate people do not instantly respond to God's call to repent and believe the good news. We must not give up because so little seems to be happening on the surface. We must pray and persevere, because it can take a long time to turn and trust.

God Conscripts

> 11 Now the Angel of the Lord came and sat under the terebinth tree which was in Ophrah, which belonged to Joash the Abiezrite, while his son Gideon threshed wheat in the winepress, in order to hide it from the Midianites.
>
> 12 And the Angel of the Lord appeared to him, and said to him, "The Lord is with you, you mighty man of valor!"
>
> 13 Gideon said to Him, "O my lord, if the Lord is with us, why then has all this happened to us? And where are all his miracles which our fathers told us about, saying, 'Did not the Lord bring us up from Egypt?' But now the Lord has forsaken us and delivered us into the hands of the Midianites."
>
> 14 Then the Lord turned to him and said, "Go in this might of yours, and you shall save Israel from the hand of the Midianites. Have I not sent you?"

> 15 So he said to Him, "O my Lord, how can I save
> Israel? Indeed my clan is the weakest in Manasseh, and
> I am the least in my father's house."
> 16 And the Lord said to him, "Surely I will be with
> you, and you shall defeat the Midianites as one man."
>
> *Judg. 6:11–16*

The answer to the impasse is now provided in the form of God's initiative in selecting and conscripting his man. Gideon did not choose himself. No true servant of God ever does that. In fact, his reaction to the angelic visitor is almost standard in the Bible, "You must have got the wrong number."

Indeed, on the surface, there is nothing special whatsoever about the man of God when he is called. All the external signs would seem to point in quite the opposite direction. His faith is far from robust, his courage is minimal, and his credentials in terms of family background and preparation are almost nonexistent. Somehow, Gideon's family had managed to save a little of the wheat crop from the Midianites. Hidden away in the wine press, which would be sunk in the earth, this youngest son is threshing the grain when the angel of the Lord appears.

In many ways, Gideon embodies within himself and his situation the fate of the whole nation—defeatist and negative without hope or vision, under Midian's heel. But God sees the man that he will make and it is on that basis that he greets Gideon. It seems to be all wrong. The "mighty man of valor" is timid and inexperienced, is hiding from the enemy, and working for his father Joash, who is actually a priest of a pagan shrine. Again, the Bible is stressing the ingenuity and sublime resourcefulness of God. He loves to take the most unlikely clay to mold his choice vessels. There is great encouragement in this for young Christians, like the young man in my own congregation who sported a sweatshirt which bore the message "Be patient! God isn't through with me yet!" How we need to encourage one another not to judge by outward appearances or by human assessments, not to label and catalogue particularly young people. God saw what he was going to do with Gideon, so that everyone would know whose power it was at work. He still chooses some of his ugliest ducklings to be his swans!

For Gideon, however, there were plenty of questions, not to say objections. He was certainly a child of his time. He takes up the very issue addressed by the prophet earlier and demonstrates his spiritual receptivity by recognizing the correctness of its diagnosis, but in the context of a hopeless fatalism. *"All this"* has happened because God has abandoned his sinful people, so how can the Lord be with him (v. 12)? What has happened to all his miracles, if he still really cares for Israel? Actually, the next two chapters will be full of them—fire from the rock consuming the bread and meat Gideon will prepare (v. 21), the wet and dry fleece, and God's actual deliverance accomplished with only three hundred men. But all of that is in the future. At present, just like us, Gideon is busy limiting God's future by his own past. We are like children who refuse to eat a new dish served at the family table on the grounds that "we don't like it," before we have even tasted it! When pressed further, the illogicality of the argument is usually compounded by, "Well, I didn't like the last new one!"

There is an additional factor in verse 14, for God knows the power he will grant. When he conscripts, he enables. When he sends, he equips. That's why it would be sheer stupidity to call ourselves into God's service, or to venture out into the spiritual battle without his clear commissioning. Even then there will be plenty of good reasons why we shall think God has the wrong person for the job. Gideon has his disqualifications all lined up as Moses did before him and Jeremiah after him; but these are all swept away by the Lord's majestic assertion, *"Surely I will be with you, and you shall defeat the Midianites as one man"* (v. 16). This is what the Lord meant when he referred to *"this might of yours"* (v. 14). We are back to the theme of Ehud and Shamgar, Deborah and Barak, that God delights to manifest his sovereign power in the very midst of human weakness. Far from being a barrier to God, human weakness is the first necessity for spiritual usefulness, provided only that it leads to obedience, in total dependence on him. No human power could possibly fulfill this mission, as Gideon must have been well aware, so that his trust has to be in God alone. We should learn to be thankful to God for everything that brings us back to that bedrock of spiritual reality.

God Confirms

> 17 Then he said to Him, "If now I have found favor in Your sight, then show me a sign that it is You who talk with me.

18 "Do not depart from here, I pray, until I come to
you and bring out my offering and set it before You."
And He said, "I will wait until you come back."
19 So Gideon went in and prepared a young goat,
and unleavened bread from an ephah of flour. The
meat he put in a basket, and he put the broth in a pot;
and he brought them out to Him under the terebinth
tree and presented them.
20 The Angel of God said to him, "Take the meat
and the unleavened bread and lay them on this rock, and
put out the broth." And he did so.
21 Then the Angel of the Lord put out the end of the
staff that was in His hand and touched the meat and
the unleavened bread; and fire rose out of the rock
and consumed the meat and the unleavened bread. And
the Angel of the Lord departed out of his sight.
22 Now Gideon perceived that He was the Angel
of the Lord. So Gideon said, "Alas, O Lord God! For I
have seen the Angel of the Lord face to face."
23 Then the Lord said to him, "Peace be with you;
do not fear, you shall not die."
24 So Gideon built an altar there to the Lord, and
called it The-Lord-Is-Peace. To this day it is still in
Ophrah of the Abiezrites.

Judg. 6:17–24

Many of us Christians can relate well to Gideon because we too find our lack of resources all too obvious. The danger is that we develop a false modesty which can soon lead to a total lack of vision. When God conscripts, we had better take him seriously because he does know what he is doing. In applying this story to the lives of our congregations, we need to remind them that we are together as a body because God has put us here. He calls not only the pastor, but the members to that particular local manifestation of the universal body of Christ. We can all spend plenty of time analyzing one another's weaknesses and inspecting our deficiencies, but in the end that's a useless waste of energy. If God has called us, he is with us. If he is with us, then Midian will be knocked out *"as one man."*

But it takes some believing, doesn't it? That's why I'm so glad this paragraph is here. God knows the weak state of Gideon's faith only too well, so he accommodates himself perfectly to that situation. For

Gideon the implications are overwhelming, life-changing in a total way. Not unreasonably he wants to know that what he has heard is really the voice of God (v. 17). He needs to be sure, and God doesn't write him out of the script for that, or accuse him of unbelief. There is a healthy skepticism that we need to learn. How many of us Christians today assume that every bright idea that comes into our heads must be the Lord's Word? How many "visions" and "clear calls" have come to nothing because they relied on human enthusiasm rather than the divine initiative? We do better to take time to be sure, because God loves to confirm his will when we ask him, provided it is an asking in faith, not just a stalling through unbelief. Gideon asked and so may we, *through prayer.*

Meanwhile, the young man prepares a generous meal for the stranger. He describes it as *"my offering"* (v. 18), desiring to honor the messenger of God with a gift, which, in a time of famine such as they were experiencing, was in itself a considerable sacrifice of faith. But the rock that was to be a meal table actually becomes an altar (v. 21). The fire of God consumes the offering and the angel disappears. Thus God confirms his will with power. It is as though he is teaching Gideon that the very best he can offer from his meager resources is not needed by God, but is accepted by grace. This is a lesson he will learn again in chapter 7. Such an unexpected response terrified Gideon, since it confirmed to him beyond doubt that he had been speaking with the angel of the Lord. Remembering that no one can see God and live (Exod. 33:20), the frightened and reluctant servant finds God's will further confirmed to him in *"peace."* He will not die, because God has called him for a specific purpose. God's peace is upon Gideon and so he worships, calling his altar Yahweh-Shalom, *"the-Lord-Is-Peace"* (well-being).

In applying this paragraph, we need to help our congregations distinguish between objective confirmation and subjective feelings, in guidance issues. We are right to expect evidences of God's power to be at work as we move forward in his will, but we cannot dictate to God what they should be; they are never given to satisfy our curiosity but to confirm our obedience. Under the old covenant, signs were among the ways in which God revealed himself to his people. But signs and wonders usually cluster around periods of verbal revelation, as in the wilderness, or with the first great prophets Elijah and Elisha, or supremely in the ministry of the Word made flesh. For us, the completed canon of the Scriptures provides the objective touchstone by which all our inner inclinations must be tested. "Feeling at peace" may well accompany living in God's will, but it is not the proof of having discovered it. Many an anaesthetized conscience has been happy enough to plunge into sin while feeling perfectly peaceful about it. We can so easily fool ourselves. We need to underline that Gideon's peace came as a direct result of a word from God and was not generated by his own wishful thinking. He was terrified (v. 23).

God Challenges

25 Now it came to pass the same night that the Lord said to him, "Take your father's young bull, the second bull of seven years old, and tear down the altar of Baal that your father has, and cut down the wooden image that is beside it;

26 "and build an altar to the Lord your God on top of this rock in the proper arrangement, and take the second bull and offer a burnt sacrifice with the wood of the image which you shall cut down."

27 So Gideon took ten men from among his servants and did as the Lord had said to him. But because he feared his father's household and the men of the city too much to do it by day, he did it by night.

28 And when the men of the city arose early in the morning, there was the altar of Baal, torn down; and the wooden image that was beside it was cut down, and the second bull was being offered on the altar which had been built.

29 So they said to one another, "Who has done this thing?" And when they had inquired and asked, they said, "Gideon the son of Joash has done this thing."

30 Then the men of the city said to Joash, "Bring out your son, that he may die, because he has torn down the altar of Baal, and because he has cut down the wooden image that was beside it."

31 And Joash said to all who stood against him, "Would you plead for Baal? Would you save him? Let the one who would plead for him be put to death by morning! If he is a god, let him plead for himself, because his altar has been torn down!"

32 Therefore on that day he called him Jerubbaal, saying, "Let Baal plead against him, because he has torn down his altar."

Judg. 6:25–32

Without any further delay, the program begins. Before the battle with Midian there has to be a battle with Baal. The altar that exists in Gideon's own backyard has to come down. You cannot have an altar to Yahweh-Shalom and an altar to a false god on the same property. The Lord is a jealous God. He will not share his territory or his glory with any other. Syncretism is an impossibility.

This is an important lesson to learn in a climate that is increasingly hostile to the exclusive claims of the Christian gospel. Many people today are happy enough to affirm the opening clauses of John 14:6, "I am the way, the truth, and the life." But what they really mean is *a* way. Their tolerant social views and rejection of any concept of absolute truth mean that they are very comfortable with Jesus as one of many ways up the mountain to God. We each have to choose the one we find most conducive. In the words of the British writer Rudyard Kipling, "Many roads thou hast fashioned; all of them lead to the light." But quote the second half of Christ's claim in John 14:6, "No one comes to the Father except through me," and a very different reaction is produced. That is intolerant, arrogant, narrow-minded, divisive. There is a whole repertoire of swear words available!

Recently, in Canterbury Cathedral, the very cradle of English Christianity, a multifaith festival was held over a whole weekend in which was included a "service" in which representatives of all the world's major religions contributed and "worshiped" together, on equal ground. When a group of Anglican evangelicals from that diocese tried to gain entrance to their own cathedral to distribute a biblical statement about the abhorrence of such events in the eyes of God, they were forbidden by the stewards and castigated for their intolerant divisiveness. "Start at home" is usually God's first challenge. Battles have to be won in the heavenlies before they can be translated into victories on earth. Baal has to be broken down before Midian can be overcome.

The personal application is that none of us can be useful to God in the public sphere if we are not putting him first in our private lives. Isn't it true that many of us Christians are far less effective for God than we should be in our society, in spite of our gifts and training and experience? Could it be that many of us have secret altars hidden in our backyards that need to be pulled down before we can do anything for the Lord? Perhaps we need to ask ourselves and our people where we actually worship most. Is it at the altar of popularity, or fashion; of money, or status; of self-image and personal kudos? *"Tear down the altar . . . and cut down the wooden image."* They may well still be God's instructions to us, which need to cut through the pseudo-sophistication of much of our evangelical life, like a knife through butter.

Gideon had to learn to follow instructions, as does every servant of the Lord (v. 27). He did what God told him to do. He did it in great fear, under cover of night, but he got together a working party and did it.

It was the same lesson Mary passed on to the dumbfounded servants at the wedding reception in Cana (John 2:5): "Whatever he says to you, do it." You won't see the miracle until you fill the waterpots. You won't defeat Midian until you smash Baal. When God shows us a step, we must take it, for the next door will not open until we have gone through the one already in front of us. And in order to do that, we have to learn to trust God with the consequences.

The next morning there was great indignation (vv. 28–30). These Israelites were very committed to their false idol even after seven years of devastation. Idolatry roots itself deeply in the human psyche. But God was in control and support for Gideon came from the most unlikely source, his father. Was he simply standing up for a member of the family? Or had he merely followed the prevailing fashion in erecting an altar to a god he knew was ultimately powerless? Either way, his argument in verse 31 is one that torpedoes all idolatry. If your god cannot defend himself, what is the point of worshiping him? It's unanswerable. Clearly the people expected Gideon to be struck down (v. 32); but instead, the false god's altar lay shattered.

The Lord looked for a fearful young man who acted obediently in faith. Gideon has struck the first blow against idolatry, not just by an outward act of courage, but by throwing down a spiritual challenge to the false god to prove himself. This has the potential not only of discrediting Baal, but of changing men's hearts toward the true and living Lord.

CHAPTER 6

Proving God

Judges 6:33–7:8

There is no doubt that the Bible regards Gideon as an outstanding man of faith. He receives an admirable mention in Hebrews 11:32 among those who believe God to fulfill his Word, in bringing about realities which they do not yet see. The danger, however, is that we are tempted to put him on a pedestal as though he lived in another world and breathed a different air from ourselves. That is a big enough danger even within our own churches. Many a congregation would like to put their minister on a pedestal, and many a minister is only too eager to allow them to do so! It is hardly surprising, therefore, if we tend to underestimate the difficulties which biblical characters faced in their own pilgrimages of faith.

The narrative here in Judges emphasizes Gideon's ordinariness. He was quite right to exclaim, *"O my Lord, how can I save Israel?"* (6:15). We have already been shown that the answer is that he could not do it, but that God chose to do it through him. If the angel of the Lord had not come to commission Gideon, he would still have been threshing wheat in the winepress, and the altar of Baal in his own backyard would never have been broken down.

This reminds us that God was not looking for the most courageous man in Israel, the greatest warrior, or the most accomplished strategist. He was looking for a man who, knowing his own weakness, would depend all the more upon God for divine strength. Such a man was one whose faith could grow. God is always looking for men and women who are available to him in that way. Indeed, if we look at the record of God's mighty deeds in history, more often than not he has used very ordinary people through whom God has done so much simply because they were so dependent upon him. Perhaps one of our dangers today is that we tend to look for men and women who have already been proved before we allow them any sort of responsibility. Charles Haddon Spurgeon, the great Baptist preacher of the nineteenth century, was pastoring a church at the age of seventeen. Today he would have to wait another six years before being admitted to most theological seminaries. We may have become too structured in our church organization to allow for the initiative of the Holy Spirit in picking up a young and inexperienced man like Gideon and using him in transforming the situation. God's promise *"surely I will be with you"* (6:16) was what made all the difference in the situation. And that is the note which is sounded again in the next paragraph.

The Transforming Factor

> 33 Then all the Midianites and Amalekites, the people of the East, gathered together; and they crossed over and encamped in the Valley of Jezreel.
>
> 34 But the Spirit of the Lord came upon Gideon; then he blew the trumpet, and the Abiezrites gathered behind him.
>
> 35 And he sent messengers throughout all Manasseh, who also gathered behind him. He also sent messengers to Asher, Zebulun, and Naphtali; and they came up to meet them.
>
> *Judg. 6:33–35*

There are the Midianites and the Amalekites; it is business as usual, as it had been for the past seven years. They have crossed the Jordan and prepared to ravage the land again. But, unknown to them, this time things are different. It is a hidden difference which they could never have predicted. Israel has cried to the Lord and God has already commissioned his deliverer. Entirely unaware of this, the enemy basks in a false security. No armies have been raised. There has been no rearmament program. No scouts are seen out on maneuvers. God's work usually begins unobserved and silently.

One of the most instructive ingredients in the teaching of Jesus is the metaphors that he uses for the church. Christians are to be the light of the world and the salt of the earth (Matt. 5:13–14). The kingdom will spread and yeast will penetrate the dough (Luke 13:21). What these processes have in common is that they are unheralded, pervasive, and irresistible. So it is here with God's work through Gideon. Very few people know anything about it. The man himself is characterized by weakness, inexperience, faltering faith, and uncertainty. But he is God's man. That is what matters. In the same way, the apostles dealt with the dangers which beset the early church. They had a deep confidence that error could only be undermined by steady proclamation of the truth. There were comparatively few large gatherings or important decisions such as the Council of Jerusalem (Acts 15). Rather, there is an emphasis in the Pastoral Epistles on the unspectacular business of teaching the truth systematically, week in, week out. This is largely hidden and undramatic work, but it is the only way that the church will grow strong and that error will eventually be destroyed.

The key to these verses is the experience of verse 34. Although he is already commissioned, there is no way in which Gideon can assume leadership without the personal experience of the power of God in his life. His only credentials were the destruction of Baal's altar, and that was hardly enough to gather an army; but verse 34 is the turning point of the whole story. At this point of acute need, with the enemy poised to attack yet again, the call to Gideon becomes a divine enabling. The verse reads literally, "the Spirit of the Lord clothed himself with Gideon." It is an arresting and instructive picture. We are told that the Holy Spirit put on Gideon like a suit of clothes, much as we might dress up for a special occasion, such as a wedding, or put on overalls to crawl under the car. Gideon is the clothing in which God is going to appear, the instrument that he is going to use. The stress is therefore entirely on the power of God and not on the faith of Gideon. He was capable of the great deeds that follow *only* because the Spirit of the Lord took hold of his life and gave him power.

This is the same "power" promised to the church by the risen Lord and fulfilled on the day of Pentecost. The Greek word translated "power" in Acts 1:8 (*dunamis*) has as its root meaning the ability to get the job done. Some translations render it "enabling." Certainly, this was the effect of the Holy Spirit upon Gideon at this time. He could now begin to do the job. This explains why he was able to summon an army of 32,000 men. Beginning with his own clan, his call extended to the other clans in Manasseh who lived south and west of the Jezreel Valley. The summons was then heard and received also by the tribes to the north—Asher, Zebulun and Naphtali. They too mustered their men and came to meet with Gideon's force. It was the Spirit of the Lord who gave Gideon this credibility and who stirs the men to respond to his call. God is taking the initiative and, as we shall see later, he has his own plans as to how the victory is to be achieved.

What are we to learn from this? Historically, it is true to say that it is often when things are at their lowest ebb morally and spiritually that God has raised up men specially empowered by him to transform the situation. Usually this has been preceded by a period of increasingly intensive prayer on the part of those who have seen that only direct intervention from God could turn the tide. I can think of the great evangelical awakenings of the eighteenth and nineteenth centuries as evidence of this pattern. But it is true on a much smaller scale, as well. We need to inspire ourselves and our congregations to realize that in a town or a business, a school or a hospital, a street or a family, God can raise up the most unlikely people, to change the situation for good when the Spirit of the Lord comes upon them in power. We may regard ourselves as the most unsuitable suit of clothes, but if we are prepared to put ourselves at his disposal and be obedient, there is no telling what God may do through our lives.

But another important point, concerning the qualitative difference between the Old and New Testaments, must be recognized here. In the Old Testament, the Holy Spirit came upon an individual to empower him or her for a particular task. This was the symbolic significance of the anointing of the king or of the high priest. Exodus 31:2–3 tells us that the Spirit of God filled Bezaleel "in wisdom, in understanding, in knowledge, and in all manner of workmanship" in order that the Tabernacle might be built according to God's pattern.

But the Holy Spirit could also depart, which explains why David in his prayer of penitence pleaded with God, "do not take Your Holy Spirit from me" (Ps. 51:11).

This is also the explanation of the great promise of our Lord Jesus in John 7:38–39. Anyone who comes to Christ in faith, like a thirsty person taking a drink of water, becomes in himself a source of living water to others. As we drink deeply of Christ, so we are filled with his Spirit and overflow the life of God to others all around us. But

John explained that this was only possible following the death and resurrection of the Lord Jesus. It was by the giving of the Holy Spirit that the new birth became possible for men and women of all nations (Acts 2:38–39). As Christians, we rejoice in the indwelling of the Holy Spirit in every one of God's people (Rom. 8:9). What he chooses to do with each life is subject to God's sovereign choice, and there will always be mystery in this. Some will be chosen to a more public ministry than others, but that does not make them better. Their responsibilities may be greater, but the same resources are available to all who trust in Christ, and all of us are to be available to the Holy Spirit for him to take up and use wherever and however he chooses.

We need to remember that what he calls us to do is not as important as the faithfulness in doing it. That is why we need to be living each day in the fullness of the Holy Spirit's power and why we need to settle once and for all that without him we can do nothing of lasting spiritual value. When Paul called upon the Ephesian Christians to let the Holy Spirit fill them (Eph. 5:18) he was underlining that very point. We need every day to ask God to fill us afresh with his life, his love, and his power. A church living like that will be unstoppable.

THE CONFIRMING FACTOR

36 So Gideon said to God, "If you will save Israel by my hand as you have said—

37 "look, I shall put a fleece of wool on the threshing floor; if there is dew on the fleece only, and it is dry on all the ground, then I shall know that You will save Israel by my hand, as You have said."

38 And it was so. When he rose early the next morning and squeezed the fleece together, he wrung the dew out of the fleece, a bowlful of water.

39 Then Gideon said to God, "Do not be angry with me, but let me speak just once more: Let me test, I pray, just once more with the fleece; let it now be dry only on the fleece, but on all the ground let there be dew."

40 And God did so that night. It was dry on the fleece only, but there was dew on all the ground.

Judg. 6:36–40

Although the Holy Spirit had come so powerfully upon Gideon, he was still very weak in faith and clearly daunted by the prospect before him. Who would not be? This is a reminder to us that grace does not delete or destroy nature. When God comes into our lives he takes the temperament which he has created and begins to refine and empower it. But we must be careful that when we speak about the new creation in Jesus we do not imply that all our psychological characteristics are erased or that God somehow bulldozes us into a Christian conformity. He wants to maximize our effectiveness and deal with our weaknesses, but it is often his way to keep us conscious of the fact that those weaknesses do exist, so that we depend on him and not on ourselves. He knows how readily we lean on our own imagined resources and think that we can cope without total dependence on him. This may be the very reason why he allows us to feel our weakness more and more. When I think I am such an experienced sailor that I no longer need to wear a life jacket in a stormy sea, I am actually in the greatest danger of being swept overboard and lost.

Doubtless, Gideon reflected on the situation. There would be no shortage of people to point out that all the odds were stacked against them. His men were not used to war, had received no training, and were in a grossly inferior position with regard to weapons. Undoubtedly it was the consideration of these outward circumstances that led to the inner doubts expressed in verse 36a. Could he really be certain that he was following God's call, or was he imagining it all?

Gideon was going through agonizing self-doubt, produced by the fear that he might be a victim of his own bright ideas or grossly inflated illusions. Objectively, he had the angel visit, confirmed by the fire consuming his offering. There was also the divine enabling by which the army was gathered together. But at that moment, neither of these was enough. In spite of God's Word and God's power, Gideon wanted to be really sure, and so he hit upon the idea of the fleece.

The details of the event are comparatively simple and clear, but the question all our congregations will be asking is whether this is a pattern we ought to follow. We all know Christians who have done so with apparent success. It is a very tempting procedure because it seems to offer a certainty which makes faith redundant. Most of us have probably tried it at some time or other. "Lord, if I see a new car of the particular model I like, on the way to work, then I will know that it's right to change the car." Or perhaps, "If something comes on TV about Ethiopia this evening, then it must be right to send money to that missionary." Or again, "If you want me to follow 'plan A' then please let the phone ring by 9:30." Is the lesson we are to learn from Gideon that we should live by dependence on fleeces? I think not.

In a very helpful analysis of the passage contained in Garry Friesen's provocative and stimulating book *Decision Making and the Will of God,* the author points out that Gideon's requests were the fruit of doubt and unbelief, rather than faith. There are also other crucial differences between his situation and ours. Friesen reminds us that Gideon was seeking a miraculous sign, not a circumstantial one. What he wanted was supernatural and therefore divinely given proof of his call. It could have no other explanation, unlike the "fleeces" to which many of us are addicted.

Also, he was not using the fleece to obtain guidance, but to confirm guidance already given. Note the phrase in verse 36, *"as You have said,"* repeated in verse 37. He was not looking for a right decision, but for enough faith to believe that God would do what he had promised through him. Furthermore, he was putting God to the test, rather than trusting him. Gideon is himself aware of that and his remarks in verse 39, *"Do not be angry with me, but let me speak just once more . . . ,"* surely revealed this. This is hardly a robust faith. Rather than wanting to do God's will, he betrayed his reluctance to follow God's guidance because of his own doubts.

When we look at the incident in this light we can identify very readily with Gideon's problem. For us, too, finding God's guidance is not so difficult. Our problem is in obeying what he tells us to do. We want to find all sorts of circumstantial reasons why we can navigate around the clear instructions of Scripture. So it does not seem that we are being encouraged to follow Gideon's example. In cases where it is argued that it has "worked" we need to look carefully at the sign that was chosen. We are perhaps more ready to believe self-fulfilling prophecies than we are willing to recognize the fact. Yes, God did stoop to Gideon's need and graciously confirmed his call and promise, by two supernatural occurrences. But then Gideon did not have the written Scriptures and the Holy Spirit had only recently come upon him. Clearly the way of wisdom is to seek God's will through the Scriptures, in dependence on the Spirit, by using a renewed mind to work out God's priorities and a renewed will to carry them out in his strength.

Having said all this, however, we do not want to leave our hearers with the implication that God is not able to work through circumstances to confirm his revealed will. It will be helpful to illustrate this from some of our own experiences.

My wife and I still look back on a particular evening when we had a major decision to make about our children's education, with very considerable financial implications. We spent a good deal of time in prayer and thorough discussion, concluding that God was leading us in a particular direction, which would involve us in trusting him for financial resources way beyond what we currently had. On our way to bed that night we discovered an envelope that had been slipped under the door. In it was a very substantial gift from a couple within our church congregation who had never given us anything before, nor have they since. To us this was God's confirmation that we were on the right track, but it was not his means of guidance. However, when we rang the couple next day to thank them for this gift they asked us why it had been necessary to get it to us that evening. They had had an overwhelming compulsion that what they had planned several weeks earlier to do had to be carried out that night. We were able to share the Lord's timing with them and together we rejoiced in his guidance. Things like that don't often happen in my life, and there is, of course, a danger of looking for the 'special' at every turn of the way. However, many of our people will have experiences like that that we can encourage them to thank God for, and they should in turn be a stimulus to our faith for future decision making.

The Reduction Factor

> 1 Then Jerubbaal (that is, Gideon) and all the people who were with him rose early and encamped beside the well of Harod, so that the camp of the Midianites was on the north side of them by the hill or Moreh in the valley.
>
> 2 And the Lord said to Gideon, "The people who are with you are too many for Me to give the Midianites into their hands, lest Israel claim glory for itself against Me, saying, 'My own hand has saved me.'
>
> 3 "Now therefore, proclaim in the hearing of the people, saying, 'Whoever is fearful and afraid let him

> turn and depart at once from Mount Gilead.'" And twenty-two thousand of the people returned, and ten thousand remained.
>
> 4 And the Lord said to Gideon, "The people are still too many; bring them down to the water, and I will test them for you there. Then it will be, that of whom I say to you, 'This one shall go with you,' the same shall go with you; and of whomever I say to you, 'This one shall not go with you,' the same shall not go."
>
> 5 So he brought the people down to the water. And the Lord said to Gideon, "Everyone who laps from the water with his tongue, as a dog laps, you shall set apart by himself; likewise everyone who gets down on his knees to drink."
>
> 6 And the number of those who lapped, putting their hand to their mouth, was three hundred men; but all the rest of the people got down on their knees to drink water.
>
> 7 Then the Lord said to Gideon, "By the three hundred men who lapped I will save you, and deliver the Midianites into your hand. Let all the other people go, every man to his place."
>
> 8 So the people took provisions and their trumpets in their hands. And he sent away all the rest of Israel, every man to his tent, and retained those three hundred men. Now the camp of Midian was below him in the valley.
>
> *Judg. 7:1–8*

While Gideon was worrying about whether he would have enough troops, God was preparing to reduce the numbers drastically. He knew the pride and stubborn hearts of his people and how they would very readily attribute any victory to their own strength if they were too numerous. Even at the practical level, they were probably better off without the twenty-two thousand fearful warriors who seemed only too pleased to have left the scene of battle when given the opportunity (v. 3). Soldiers as scared as that are hardly likely to lift morale and think in terms of victory. God doesn't need the tremblers. Nor does God need the ninety-seven hundred whose interest is in their personal comfort and safety, rather than in getting on with fighting the enemy. The water test of verses 5 and 6 seems to have been designed to identify those who were committed to civilian ease rather than fighting efficiency. In the end, only three hundred are left (vv. 7–8).

We do not need too much imagination to know what Gideon must have felt like then. If he needed the double fleece sign with an army of thirty-two thousand, what state is he likely to be in when God has reduced that to three hundred and when the enemy now outnumber them four hundred to one? But God, in his mercy, had explained to Gideon why this process has been happening. Back in verse 2, we are reminded that the real battle is not with Midian at all. They are only a problem because God has raised them up as his instrument of discipline for Israel. He can deal with Midian any time. The problem is with Israel's attitude of self confidence and pride which would take all the credit to themselves and refuse to give God the glory. From there it is only a short step to idolatry—the sin of putting themselves in the place of God.

That, after all, is the attraction of idolatry, isn't it? We imagine that we are in control and that the God whom we have set up to worship is there to indulge our whims and fancies. So we exalt our wills above God's and refuse to let him be God in any practical way in our circumstances. This was the problem Israel had encountered over and over again. The only remedy is to have printed indelibly on our minds and hearts that it is not our own strength that has saved us. The verbs in verse 7 are highly significant. *"I will save . . . deliver. . . ."* So, what is the parallel for us today?

Wherever there is a clear command in Scripture, we are to seek to obey it in every detail in our lives. But God may well reduce our resources to almost nothing in order to prove that it is by his power alone that we can be victorious and that his strength is made perfect in our weakness (2 Cor. 12:9).

Gideon's story proves that when we are at our least, God can be at his greatest. Like Gideon, we may think that we are proving God, but actually he is proving us. Yet all the while, in grace and mercy, he is giving us far more than we could legitimately ask for or expect, because he knows and understands our needs and because he sympathizes with our weaknesses.

Fiction abounds with stories of the little guy who goes out and against all the odds kills the giant. History even has some real-life examples which show that has happened. Huge armies have been turned to flight by comparatively under-resourced opponents. But behind such stories there nearly always lie either events of incredible good fortune or of low-down cunning. As with the story of David and Goliath, we are not to take away from this passage of Scripture the idea that it is always worth the little guy having a go because he may land a stone on target! Rather, we are to take seriously the words of Jesus when he said to his disciples, "without me you can do nothing" (John 15:5). If we truly identify with Gideon, it should drive us to our knees, seeking from God to rightly discern what he is calling us to do and, secondly, that we might have the faith to believe that he will do it through us. There is all the difference in the world between writing our own agenda and striving to do it for God as best we can and, on the other hand, allowing him to pick us up and use us in whatever way he chooses.

CHAPTER 7

Divine Strategy

Judges 7:9–25

To live, as we do, in a highly sophisticated, technological society brings with it many benefits. But we also have our own peculiar blindnesses. Because there is so much interest in how things work, we are often at a loss to explain why they are there in the first place. The scientific revolution which has been so successful in explaining mechanisms is unable to help us when it comes to an explanation of meanings. It is not surprising, therefore, that all sorts of esoteric philosophies and religions are gaining ground in our society, since man, made in the image of God, must have a spiritual explanation for his own existence.

There must be a place for mystery in our experience of human life. The Bible recognizes this and affirms that "the secret things belong to the Lord our God, but those things which are revealed belong to us and to our children forever, that we may do all the words of this law" (Deut. 29:29). Biblical faith affirms that God has revealed all that is necessary to bring us into a living relationship with himself and to enable us to travel through this world into his presence.

But this does not mean to say that we can shut up God in a box or that we can predict his every action. While he always acts consistently with his character, his infinite wisdom means that we cannot always tell why he is taking a particular course of action or what his long-term purposes may be. It is at the point where the inscrutability of God crosses our experience of life that the Christian faith presents us with certain essential paradoxes. For example, Jesus tells us that "whoever desires to save his life will lose it, but whoever loses his life for My sake will save it" (Luke 9:24). This cuts right across everything that we naturally assume about the value and purpose of our existence.

Or again, he points out another contrast in telling his disciples, "'the kings of the Gentiles exercise lordship over them, and those who exercise authority over them are called "benefactors." But not so among you; on the contrary, he who is greatest among you, let him be as the younger, and he who governs as he who serves'" (Luke 22:25–26). To say that the way *up* in the kingdom of heaven is *down* is to present a paradox that appears to contradict all our normal human experiences. In the same way, the apostle Paul affirms that "I take pleasure in infirmities, in reproaches, in needs, in persecutions, in distresses, for Christ's sake. For when I am weak, then I am strong" (2 Cor. 12:10).

You will not find any of these sentiments in modern psychology where the emphasis is all upon feeling good, looking great, living it up, and generally imposing your will on everybody else around you. Perhaps what is why G. K. Chesterton once said that the problem with Christianity is not that it has been tried and found wanting but that it has been found difficult and not tried.

We have seen how this paradox runs through the whole story of Gideon. Indeed, God reduces his strength to such ridiculously tiny proportions that this must be a major reason why the whole story has been included in the Scriptures. The strategy by which God will win the battle against the Midianites is not as fascinating as the strategy by which he is teaching Gideon lessons of faith. Nor is this simply a private tuition course for one man. Through Gideon the whole nation will learn that only God can deliver them from the power of their enemies and that only God can keep them. They have no strength of their own to keep in God's way and no resources of their own to deliver them from the perils of their rebellion. The lesson is that divine strength is only possible in the context of human weakness.

When we are at our least, God can begin to do his most. Sometimes he has to bring us down to the dust in order for us to recognize that. At other times it is the expression of a heart attitude which enables an individual to be useful to God. Thus, John the Baptist, of whom Jesus said none greater was born of woman (Matt. 11:11), is on record as describing his own ministry in these terms: "he must increase, but I must decrease" (John 3:30). Yet Jesus told his disciples that "he who is least in the kingdom of heaven is greater than John." This must be because the kingdom is all about God's power made perfect in human weakness. When Paul reminded the Corinthian Christians that "we have this treasure in earthen vessels, that the excellence of the power may be of God and not of us" (2 Cor. 4:7), he was simply highlighting the divine strategy. It is not that God is unable to find powerful and impressive people to serve him, but that he delights to take the weak and fearful in order to demonstrate that the power at work is divine and not human.

From Fear to Faith

9 It happened on the same night that the Lord said to him, "Arise, go down against the camp, for I have delivered it into your hand.

10 "But if you are afraid to go down, go down to the camp with Purah your servant,

11 "and you shall hear what they say; and afterwards your hands shall be strengthened to go down against the camp." Then he went down with Purah his servant to the outpost of the armed men who were in the camp.

12 Now the Midianites and Amalekites, all the people of the East, were lying in the valley as numerous as locusts; and their camels were without number, as the sand by the seashore in multitude.

13 And when Gideon had come, there was a man telling a dream to his companion. He said, "I have had a dream: To my surprise, a loaf of barley bread tumbled into the camp of Midian; it came to a tent and struck it so that it fell and overturned, and the tent collapsed."

14 Then his companion answered and said, "This is nothing else but the sword of Gideon the son of Joash, a man of Israel! Into his hand God has delivered Midian and the whole camp."

15 And so it was, when Gideon heard the telling of the dream and its interpretation, that he worshiped. He returned to the camp of Israel, and said, "Arise, for the Lord has delivered the camp of Midian into your hand."

Judg. 7:9–15

One of the sillier things we Christians do is to imagine that God cannot see us as we really are. We have probably all had the experience of playing with young children who will run away to hide. But instead of concealing themselves from our view the child simply puts his hands over his eyes and shouts out, "You can't see me!" Because the child cannot see, he or she assumes that we cannot either. How like that we are in our attitude to God.

So often we think, "first of all, I must get myself sorted out. I will make my faith grow and then I will be in a position to present my problems to God." I have sometimes had to counsel Christians who felt that they could not come to God with their problem because they could not be sure that their motives were pure enough. God knew exactly what Gideon's problem was. He was still afraid! We need to remember that the problems we face which we are unwilling to confess and lay out before God are equally transparently obvious to him. After the episodes with the fleece, Gideon may well have felt that he dare not ask God for anything more. The lovely touch in this passage is that God takes the initiative and comes to speak to Gideon. He meets the man of faith as his knees are knocking in order to minister his grace and encouragement to him. So, how does God move us from fear to faith?

God's Promise Is Renewed

At its simplest, this can be said: God came to speak to Gideon. The movement from fear to faith always begins with a fresh hearing of God's Word. That is one reason why daily, personal Bible reading is such an essential ingredient for a healthy Christian life, and why the weekly preaching ministry of the church is so central to a strong congregational development. For "faith comes by hearing, and hearing by the word of God" (Rom. 10:17).

One of the saddest features of contemporary church life is that while we have so many aims and incentives to Bible study we are probably less well grounded in the Scriptures than many previous generations. Our busy lives tend to mean that we never get out of the fast lane long enough to let God speak to us through his Word, and that our understanding of the Scriptures remains therefore comparatively superficial.

Our generation needs to take heed to Peter's word when he says, "we have the prophetic word confirmed, which you do well to heed as to a light that shines in a dark place, until the day dawns and the morning star rises in your hearts" (2 Pet. 1:19). The Scripture is full of commands and promises to guide our lives, and that is what we have in God's dealings with Gideon here. There is a command, *"Arise, go down against the camp,"* and with it there is the promise, *"for I have delivered it into your hand"* (v. 9).

To Bible students, this is, of course, a familiar pattern. God does not command us without giving us reasons, but the reasons are usually promises that have to be claimed in faith if the command is going to be obeyed. So often we fail to obey because deep down we refuse to believe. Our fears paralyze the development of our faith. Sometimes the problem gets worse as we become more experienced. Little children who are learning to swim find it comparatively easy to trust the instructor and to lean all their weight on him. But if you see an adult in the same situation, the degree of trust is usually very much less. Some of us have habits of practical unbelief which we need to overcome if ever we are going to make progress in the Christian life. So how did God lead Gideon onward?

God's Providence Is Revealed

Notice that he neither compromises his command nor accommodates himself to our weaknesses, but God does meet us with what he sees we need most. What Gideon needed at that moment was for his doubts to be removed, his perplexity about how this victory could ever come about to be solved. So God in his love and grace came right down to where his reluctant servant was (v. 10). How much like Gideon we are! We, too, measure what God can do by our own reasoning and by our experience of God up to this point in time, and so we effectively limit him. Do we not often discover ourselves saying, "Lord, I can't see how this situation will ever work out," and so we stop believing that it will. Doubt suffocates faith and the devil wins again. But what Gideon and we have to learn is that God's hidden providence is working out his sovereign will all the time, even though it is unseen.

There is a very important lesson to be learned here. "Faith is the substance of things hoped for, the evidence of things not seen" (Heb. 11:1). Living in a world that puts all its emphasis on what can be seen, touched and experienced now makes it difficult for us to grasp the New Testament emphasis on the unseen realities which are eternal.

The apostles affirm that God has broken into our world at a particular point in time and in a specific geographical location, in the person of the Lord Jesus Christ. The invisible, eternal God has revealed himself to man in terms that we can all understand—a perfect human life. "The Word became flesh and dwelt among us" (John 1:14). The life was manifested and it (he) could be heard, seen, and touched (1 John 1:1–2). There has been a making visible of the invisible, as the kingdom of the heavens has broken into our world in the power of the King.

But the "now" of that revelation is balanced by the "not yet" of its full realization. There is sufficient evidence for faith today, but such faith moves on and out into the hope of the glory of what will one day be ours. The best is yet to be, and our future is as bright as the promises of God. So we are called to walk by faith rather than by sight. "'Blessed are those who have not seen and yet have believed'" (John 20:29).

To teach Gideon and us that lesson, God graciously lifts the veil covering his unseen purposes and allows us a peep behind the scenes. He arranges for his fearful servant to hear a most significant conversation right there in the enemy's camp. No one could have invented the script. This was so entirely of God that it was impossible for Gideon to doubt any longer. It was God who provided the dream for the Midianite guard (v. 13). It was God who directed Gideon's path to this man's tent at the precise moment when he was telling his friend about the dream. It was God who protected Gideon and Purah from being observed or captured. And most significant of all, it was God who is revealed to have been already at work among the Midianite troops, lowering their morale, making them afraid of Gideon, and bringing them to realize that Israel's God was about to secure their destruction. They did not know how that was to happen. They had no idea who was listening to them. But in his sovereign wisdom and control, God uses the enemy to encourage his reluctant general. The visible reality is still verse 12, a totally impossible situation. But the hidden certainty is seen in verse 14. Is anything too hard for the Lord?

If we insist on trying to pull the future victory into the present and having everything proved to us now before we are willing to venture out in faith, we shall deprive ourselves of the greatest spiritual challenges, which are the only way real faith can grow. We need to focus on the far horizon, not judge by "feeble sense." All the time there is an omnipotent providence working all things together for the good of his loved ones (Rom. 8:28). The purpose of that love is often to bring us to the rock bottom of our fears so that he can build our faith on his unchanging word, rather than our feelings or our circumstances. This is the mark of all true spirituality.

God's Person Is Revered

Gideon *"worshiped."* This is the expression of faith because it is worship that turns us away from ourselves to the God who is immeasurably greater than our minds can imagine or our hearts encompass. And we rejoice in him, for himself. Thanksgiving motivates Gideon to prostrate himself before God, in worship.

Signs like that will not happen every day; they do not need to. But there are everyday touches of God's providential care and sovereign overruling in all sorts of little things, in even the darkest days. So, when the large decisions present themselves, we can be sure of sufficient help and guidance to enable us to move out from fear to faith.

From Faith to Fulfillment

16 Then he divided the three hundred men into three companies, and he put a trumpet into every man's hand, with empty pitchers, and torches inside the pitchers.

17 And he said to them, "Look at me and do likewise; watch, and when I come to the edge of the camp you shall do as I do:

18 "When I blow the trumpet, I and all who are with me, then you also blow the trumpets on every side of the whole camp, and say, 'The sword of the Lord and of Gideon!'"

19 So Gideon and the hundred men who were with him came to the outpost of the camp at the beginning of the middle watch, just as they had posted the watch; and they blew the trumpets and broke the pitchers that were in their hands.

> 20 Then the three companies blew the trumpets and broke the pitchers—they held the torches in their left hands and the trumpets in their right hands for blowing—and they cried, "The sword of the Lord and of Gideon!"
>
> 21 And every man stood in his place all around the camp; and the whole army ran and cried out and fled.
>
> 22 When the three hundred blew the trumpets, the Lord set every man's sword against his companion throughout the whole camp; and the army fled to Beth Acacia, toward Zererah, as far as the border of Abel Meholah, by Tabbath.
>
> 23 And the men of Israel gathered together from Naphtali, Asher, and all Manasseh, and pursued the Midianites.
>
> 24 Then Gideon sent messengers throughout all the mountains of Ephraim, saying, "Come down against the Midianites, and seize from them the watering places as far as Beth Barah and the Jordan." Then all the men of Ephraim gathered together and seized the watering places as far as Beth Barah and the Jordan.
>
> 25 And they captured two princes of the Midianites, Oreb and Zeeb. They killed Oreb at the rock of Oreb, and Zeeb they killed at the winepress of Zeeb. They pursued Midian and brought the heads of Oreb and Zeeb to Gideon on the other side of the Jordan.
>
> *Judg. 7:16–25*

Perhaps the most immediate lesson to note and learn from here is that the battle still had to be joined, and Gideon had to fight it. There had to be a readiness on his part to obey God's orders, to go down to the Midianite camp and show by this action his faith that God would deliver it into his hands.

Sometimes we become so taken up with our own personal experiences of God and of our own faith growing and being stretched that we are prone to forget his wider purposes. All that God is working in us he wants to work out, in the world. Too often our Christian gatherings and activities are wrongly introspective. God's heart is for the lost world, and he wants to turn us loose in it, as people who are constantly in touch with him, so that we can be channels of his love and truth. But like secret agents in wartime, infiltrating enemy territory, the success of our operation depends on excellent communications links with home base and detailed obedience to instructions. The world will be hostile to God and to us as his people. Like the Midianites, they will always greatly outnumber the forces of the Lord. But also like the Midianites they are often much more fearful and demoralized than we would ever guess.

Sometimes when we consider the violent anti-Christian sentiments and behavior of those who oppose God's Word, as for example on the abortion issue, we are tempted to think of their ranks as unassailable. But we also know that those who shout longest are often the most unsure, and that all "opponents" of God's truth are people who matter to him, created in his image to find their fulfillment in fellowship with him, for whom his heart aches. "You have made us for yourself, and our hearts are restless, until they find their rest in you," said Augustine. The church is therefore not to be a tight circle of people, turned in to look on themselves, holding hands in a desperate attempt to ward off the wicked world. Rather, it is to be a circle of people facing out in love, with arms outstretched, in their Lord's name, to welcome all who will come to him. So, how can we move from faith to fulfillment, from theory to action?

Courage in Obedience

Gideon returns to the three hundred, his faith renewed, able now to relay what God has said to him with real conviction. His leadership in the whole enterprise is crucial, which is why the biblical text has spent so much time on the preparation of the man, and spends comparatively little on the actual victory. The leadership of any group or local church can be either its greatest enabling factor, under God, or equally its most conditioning and inhibiting factor. We cannot lead others beyond where we are ourselves. *"Look at me and do likewise"* (v. 17a) is something that every Christian leader must be able to echo. In one of Gilbert and Sullivan's comic operas, *The Gondoliers,* the Duke of Plaza-Toro sings:

> In enterprise of martial kind,
> When there was any fighting,
> He led his regiment from behind—
> He found it less exciting.

That is not an option for the would-be biblical leader! Leadership is a call to be an example to the people of God, and indeed to the watching world. Is that not why the qualities required of local church elders in the Pastoral Epistles are almost all qualities of character, and the only spiritual gift mentioned is that of teaching, which is how the church is to be governed and led (1 Tim. 3:1–7). Paul continues to instruct the young pastor, "Let no one despise your youth, but be an example to the believers in word, in conduct, in love, in spirit, in faith, in purity" (1 Tim 4:12). In similar vein, Peter exhorts the elders to "shepherd the flock of God . . . [not] as being Lords over those entrusted to you, but being examples to the flock" (1 Pet. 5:2–3). Such a charge requires courage to go forward in obedience to God's Word, trusting him to keep his promises.

It may help our hearers if we make the point deliberately that obedience nearly always does require courage. There is usually sufficient evidence to inspire faith, but also sufficient uncertainty to stretch it. That is the way God works for our good. He doesn't hand things to us "on a plate," but he makes us dependent on him step by step, stage by stage, so that we gradually learn to trust him continuously. Have you ever tried to coax a frightened animal out of its cage? You tempt it with some particularly appetizing and well-loved food treat. Inch by inch, the animal moves forward. Fear gives way to faith. Desire gradually overcomes timidity. But all the time the animal is making the moves. Some of our Christians stay cooped up for years because we are so unwilling to move from an intellectual acceptance of God's truth into a sharp-edge daily experience of putting that faith into practice, by obedience. Gideon teaches us that being prepared to launch out with God is an essential for vital Christianity. Otherwise, we shall get stuck in the concrete!

Wisdom in Action

Gideon's strategy was brilliant, both in its simplicity and its ingenuity. The dream seems to have alerted him to the realization that God would deliver the Midianite camp into his hands without elaborate military preparation or superior battle power. In fact, he had no time for the former and God had deliberately removed any hope of the latter. Undoubtedly, the plan was divinely given, although it is interesting that the text does not mention that, but attributes the tactics directly to Gideon. His aim was to frighten the already demoralized enemy and provoke a panic rather than to rush the camp on any sort of suicide mission.

In developing a strategy full of sound common sense, Gideon accepted God's limitation of his forces to three hundred, believing this to be the way in which the Lord would bring greater glory to his name. He used what he had at hand, both in terms of men and materials.

Everything worked to plan. He attacked totally unexpectedly, in the middle of the night, before the newly posted guards had become accustomed to their task (v. 19). The combination of the sudden light, the trumpets blowing, and the shouting stampeded the Midianites. Gideon did what he could with his limited numbers, and trusted God to do the rest. He did not fail his obedient servant! The Midianites imagined they were being attacked by a huge army (they had probably heard of the thirty-two thousand).

C. J. Goslinga catches it well in his commentary, and the more vividly we can "see" the event the more firmly we shall learn and be able to recall its spiritual lessons.

> The torches flickering on all sides told [the Midianites] they were surrounded. The pandemonium of shattering jars deluded them into thinking that the Israelites had already entered the camp and were creating havoc there. And the battle cry with the dreaded names of Yahweh and Gideon did the rest. The enemy was thrown into a panic. While Gideon and his 300 men merely held their positions, waving their torches and blowing their trumpets, the camp rushed about in wild confusion.[1]

That is always happening in the devil's camp, when the people of God obey him, in faith. In application, we need to stress that the fulfillment of spiritual vision will always require courage, coupled with careful planning and sound tactics. But we also need to note the final, essential ingredient.

God in Control

"The Lord set every man's sword against his companion throughout the whole camp. . . ." Gideon and his men frightened Midian, almost "to death" as we might say; but God destroyed them. The terror in the

darkness and the sheer blind panic engendered in the hearts by God led the Midianites to massacre one another as they fought to escape from Gideon's "army." Their vast numbers were actually used against them, in this way, increasing their own destruction. So God did what he had promised. Just as with Deborah and Barak in chapter 4, there was no battle; there were mopping-up operations, which are the concern of the end of this chapter into chapter 8. But this was clearly not Israel's victory (cf. 7:2), but God's. From beginning to end, it was conducted on his terms, following his instructions, for his glory.

The divine strategy is often to allow the forces hostile to God to bring about their own destruction. Because he rules in sovereign authority over the whole world, all temporal power is subject to God. The Old Testament often reminds us of this, in passages like Proverbs 8:15–16, where wisdom says,

> By me kings reign, and rulers decree justice. By me princes rule, and nobles, all the judges of the earth.

The fatal flaw in the thinking of those powers hostile to God, whom he chooses to raise up, is that by their own strength and ability they have achieved power and influence. But even a world conqueror like Cyrus the Persian is "my shepherd, and he shall perform all my pleasure" (Isa. 44:28). His military conquests are directly attributable to the Lord's anointing, to the fact that God has strengthened his right hand "to subdue nations before him" (Isa. 45:1).

That is the hidden reality which enables a New Testament believer to affirm with Paul, "If God is for us, who can be against us?" (Rom. 8:31). What we have to grasp, in our secular culture, is that the unseen things are the eternal realities, and the order of things as we see them is purely transient.

Who would have predicted the changes in the Soviet Union a decade ago? It seems likely that we have only begun to witness the social, economic, and political upheaval which, under *glasnost* and *perestroika,* must inevitably multiply. Yet for decades the Marxist system seemed an impregnable fortress. What we failed to realize was that it had the seeds of its own decline already planted in its atheistic philosophy. The same was true of Hitler's Nazi Germany earlier in the twentieth century. And the same is true of our western materialism, on both sides of the Atlantic, in so far as our headlong pursuit of wealth and pleasure sets us in opposition to the living God.

The God who raised up Midian, in order to discipline his people Israel, still rules the world for the good of his church. That does not mean a cosy, comfortable existence is guaranteed, as both Scripture and history bear witness. One of the most sobering insights gained during my visits to Eastern Europe and contacts with church leaders there has been to hear them speak of God permitting the Marxist tyranny to discipline and purify the church. If we in the West refuse to listen to his gracious, gentle warnings, if we continue to turn our backs on the spiritual heritage God has given us and turn to idols, we can expect Midian to appear. Yet ultimately God is working only for our good, and if we really allow him his rightful place, we shall witness his control and be humbled by his victories.

Christopher Idle sums it up for us in the opening stanza of his contemporary paraphrase of Psalm 37.

> When lawless people succeed
> and wrong suppresses right,
> remember they will fade away
> and wither overnight.
> Commit your life to God,
> and trust the Lord to make
> the justice of your righteous cause
> shine clear for his name's sake.[2]

NOTES

1. Goslinga, *Judges*, 340.
2. Quoted from *Psalm Praise* (London: Falcon Press, 1973).

CHAPTER EIGHT

The Test of Success

Judges 8:1–35

Burnout is a phenomenon currently attracting plenty of media attention. In the financial capitals of the world, it is not uncommon to find young executives, in their early thirties, who have made a great amount of money in comparatively few years and who are now being moved on and out by the companies that have exploited their talents. They no longer have quite the "edge" that is needed. Success is not always so easy to handle. Today's gold medalist is tomorrow's quaint archive film. This month's pop star is next month's wreckage. No wonder Thomas Carlyle wrote that "only one in a hundred passes the test of prosperity."

Gideon, sadly, belonged to the ninety-nine, as do probably most of us. The contrast between the man we are introduced to in chapter 6 by the sudden visit of the angel of the Lord and the man we see as judge of Israel, at the end of chapter 8, is stark and alarming. The first is a reluctant conscript who deeply distrusts his own competence and is only gradually persuaded to believe God's Word and act upon it. The second is an empire builder who, if not setting up a dynasty, is prepared to create his own memorial and pursue advantage for his own family, rather than for the glory of God.

Gideon found success very difficult to handle. When his 300 men were used by God in the destruction of a good part of the Midianite army and in sending the rest of the 135,000 flying back over the Jordan, Gideon, not unnaturally, became a national hero overnight. The tragedy was that he could not cope with it. He forgot that he was a weak man, made strong only by the Spirit of the Lord; he began to believe his own press releases!

It is so easy to forget God as you climb the ladder. The nation had been warned of the dangers of prosperity (Deut. 6:10–12, 8:8–14) before they entered the land, but they fell into the trap of stubborn pride time and time again. Now Gideon exemplifies the same danger, in spite of all his splendid qualities.

Perhaps we are preaching not so much to demoralized people, as to a congregation which is prosperous materially and spiritually "successful," at least outwardly so. Church growth, the development of plant and staff, and respect in the community can all be marks of spiritual health, for which to praise God. But they will bring their own tests, and we would be foolish and short-sighted not to learn God's lessons from this last chapter of the Gideon saga.

The Test of Criticism

> 1 Now the men of Ephraim said to him, "Why have you done this to us by not calling us when you went to fight with the Midianites?" And they reprimanded him sharply.
>
> 2 So he said to them, "What have I done now in comparison with you? Is not the gleaning of the grapes of Ephraim better than the vintage of Abiezer?
>
> 3 "God has delivered into your hands the princes of Midian, Oreb and Zeeb. And what was I able to do in comparison with you?" Then their anger toward him subsided when he said that.
>
> *Judg. 8:1–3*

Without doubt, criticism is one of the Lord's regular methods of keeping his servants humble. We can marvel at Spurgeon's spiritual presence of mind when he was approached by an over-effusive admirer, following a particularly brilliant sermon. "Mr. Spurgeon, you were wonderful," she crooned. To which the reply came, "Madam, the devil whispered those same words in my ear, as I left the pulpit." Most of us could probably cope with a few more problems of that sort! We are more likely to walk out of the pulpit into criticism about how a business meeting was handled, or a comparatively trivial issue was overlooked, or why an individual was passed by or remained unappreciated.

The latter struck Gideon straight in the face as he pursued God's victory, to force home the advantage. He had called the Ephraimites into action, late in the campaign, to occupy the crossing points of the Jordan and cut off as many as possible of the retreating army. They had done this successfully, even killing two Midianite princes, Oreb and Zeeb (7:24–25). But what galled them was their comparatively late involvement. Why should Gideon and the men of Manasseh have all the glory? It was a deeply felt and bitter exchange. This provided a new test for Gideon, but it was also demonstrating their own failure. For the test they faced was whether they could cope with someone else's success.

On any Sunday, in any church, there will be "Ephraimites" in the pews. They are the people who feel they are constantly put upon. They work hard for the church, but never get any of the credit. They get called in to cope with the last-minute emergencies, to field the loose balls, but they rarely if ever get up-front recognition, or even thanks. At least that is what they feel, and often with good reason. Assistant ministers, directors, and managers are particularly open to Ephraimite tendencies by virtue of their roles. The danger is that of wounded pride, degenerating into self-pity. It can become the "poor old me" syndrome, so it needs to be dealt with sensitively and directly.

Gideon's response is both measured and modest. He is able to deal with their criticism by directing their attention away from what they or he did and reminding them that it was *God* who gave the Midianites into their hands (v. 3). Either side could have been jealous of the other. At this point, Gideon has not killed any of the enemy commanders as the Ephraimites had. So he encourages them to see that what they call the leftovers are actually a much better vintage than anything he, representing the clan of Abiezer, has achieved. This successful response reminds us of the importance of dealing with criticism in a positive way and not allowing it to fester. If Gideon had reacted angrily or refused to bother, the grievance could easily have smoldered into a time-consuming controversy or even presented a threat of intertribal, civil war. The quality of Gideon here is that he did not allow the criticism to wound his pride, as the Ephraimites' own pride had been deflated. So, no conflict situation was able to develop. To deal with such problems openly and quickly in church life can prevent a totally disproportionate amount of time being spent on comparatively minor matters.

The Test of Noncooperation

4 When Gideon came to the Jordan, he and the three hundred men who were with him crossed over, exhausted but sill in pursuit.
5 Then he said to the men of Succoth, "Please give loaves of bread to the people who follow me, for they are exhausted, and I am pursuing Zebah and Zalmunna, kings of Midian."
6 And the leaders of Succoth said, "Are the hands of Zebah and Zalmunna now in your hand, that we should give bread to your army?"
7 So Gideon said, "For this cause, when the Lord has delivered Zebah and Zalmunna into my hand, then I will tear your flesh with the thorns of the wilderness and with briers!"
8 Then we went up from there to Penuel and spoke to them in the same way. And the men of Penuel answered him as the men of Succoth had answered.
9 So he also spoke to the men of Penuel, saying, "When I come back in peace, I will tear down this tower!"
10 Now Zebah and Zalmunna were at Karkor, and their armies with them, about fifteen thousand, all who were left of all the army of the people of the East; for one hundred and twenty thousand men who drew the sword had fallen.
11 Then Gideon went up by the road of those who dwell in tents on the east of Nobah and Jogbehah; and he attacked the army while the camp felt secure.
12 When Zebah and Zalmunna fled, he pursued them; and he took the two kings of Midian, Zebah and Zalmunna, and routed the whole army.
13 Then Gideon the son of Joash returned from battle, from the Ascent of Heres.
14 And he caught a young man of the men of Succoth and interrogated him; and he wrote down for him the leaders of Succoth and its elders, seventy-seven men.
15 Then he came to the men of Succoth and said, "Here are Zebah and Zalmunna, about whom you ridiculed me, saying, 'Are the hands of Zebah and

Zalmunna now in your hand, that we should give bread to your weary men?'"

16 And he took the elders of the city, and thorns of the wilderness and briers, and with them he taught the men of Succoth.

17 Then he tore down the tower of Penuel and killed the men of the city.

18 And he said to Zebah and Zalmunna, "What kind of men were they whom you killed at Tabor?" So they answered, "As you are, so were they; each one resembled the son of a king."

19 Then he said, "They were my brothers, the sons of my mother. As the Lord lives, it you had let them live, I would not kill you."

20 And he said to Jether his firstborn, "Rise, kill them!" But the youth would not draw his sword; for he was afraid, because he was still a youth.

21 So Zebah and Zalmunna said, "Rise yourself, and kill us; for as a man is, so is his strength." So Gideon arose and killed Zebah and Zalmunna, and took the crescent ornaments that were on their camels' necks.

Judg. 8:4–21

Gideon's vigorous pursuit of the Midianites had a very practical purpose, besides relieving the pent-up frustrations of seven years' suffering under their tyranny. Only if the attack was pressed into their own territory, with the execution of their leaders, would the Midianites be permanently restrained from invasion. But the band of three hundred, by now hungry and not far from exhaustion, first had to meet with sullen noncooperation tactics from two Israelite settlements across the Jordan, at Succoth and Penuel.

On the level of expediency, we should not be too surprised at the attitude in these settlements. Living as near as they did to the marauding Midianite armies, they had probably borne the brunt of their oppressive tactics for the past seven years. They wanted to be sure that the kings Zebah and Zalmunna were dead before they could assure Gideon of assistance in the provision of food (v. 6). However, as the judge of Israel, Gideon formally pronounces punishments on the cities and especially their elders, which he later returns to execute in full. His reasons seem to be these: They were denying their ties of blood and nationhood by being more concerned about their own skins than in helping Gideon and his men, and they were actually assisting the enemies of Israel and of the Lord by their noncooperation. Thereby they demonstrated their lack of faith in the Lord's power and protection, which unbelief had led the nation into its perilous condition. It is probably correct to see the beating of the elders of Succoth (v. 16) and the destruction of the tower of Penuel—which was probably occupied in defense of the city (v. 17)—as judicial sentences carried out by Gideon as judge, rather than as indicating a personal vendetta or a fit of revenge.

But in Gideon's dealings with the Midianite kings, there is a stronger personal and family ingredient. Verses 10–12 describe how Gideon came to capture them. We cannot but admire his determined perseverance. He has to travel another 150 miles or so to Karkor before he catches up with the retreating decimated army, now numbering only 15,000 of the original 135,000. Their swift camels would have enabled them to gain ground in fleeing from Gideon, and now, well inside their own territory, they do not expect the more parochial Israeli farmers to follow. The unsuspecting army seems not to have bothered to set a guard on their camp, and so Gideon is again able to use the weapon of surprise, using a desert track, to approach them unnoticed. The army is routed, but more importantly the two kings are captured.

After punishing Succoth and Penuel, to whom he showed the kings as the proof of his conquest, Gideon seems to have returned to his family home at Ophrah. His eldest son, *"still a youth,"* was present and he would clearly not have been a member of the three hundred (v. 20). Most probably Zebah and Zalmunna were executed in front of the whole family or clan as retributive justice for their murder of Gideon's brothers at Tabor (v. 18). Unfortunately, we do not know any details of this event, which is mentioned here for the first time. But if the event had happened comparatively recently and if Gideon's family was reasonably prominent (the presence of the city altar to Baal on their property seems to suggest this), some of the otherwise hidden background to the visit of the angel of the Lord to "the least in my father's house" (6:15) is apparent.

Another problem here is why Gideon should ask his firstborn son Jether to kill the kings, in view of his youth. There cannot have been any lack of courage or ability on Gideon's part, as verse 21 makes clear. Probably, he is already aware of his more public function as judge of Israel and does not want to be seen to be avenging a merely family matter, using his position to pursue personal ends. It would be natural to request his son to avenge the family's honor, rather than any of his servants or members of the three hundred. But in the end Gideon kills them himself. This would seem to mark the peak of his power, prestige, and influence for good, in Israel.

Perhaps the main lesson of these verses is that God's work very often calls for persistence. Gideon faced physical dangers and hardships and opposition from those whom he might reasonably have expected to support and encourage him. He pressed doggedly on until the victory was complete and the enemies of his people were no more. He had every incentive to give up. If anyone had legitimate cause for burnout, he did. He could easily have argued that if the other Israelites were no more concerned to get rid of the Midianites than the men of Succoth and Penuel, why should he go on bothering?

But then, where would we be if God were to treat us like that? Robert Murray McCheyne, the great Scottish missionary and preacher of the nineteenth century, was once asked what he considered to be the greatest wonder in the world. He considered the question for some time and then replied that it was not creation, or even redemption that moved him most, but, he said "that God goes on bothering with a man like me." Our God persists, and if that is a quality of his own perfect character we can be sure that he is delighted when he sees it mirrored in the lives of his imperfect servants.

The Test of Personal Popularity

22 Then the men of Israel said to Gideon, "Rule over us, both you and your son, and your grandson also; for you have delivered us from the hand of Midian."

23 But Gideon said to them, "I will not rule over you, nor shall my son rule over you; the Lord shall rule over you."

24 Then Gideon said to them, "I would like to make a request of you, that each of you would give me the earrings from his plunder." For they had golden earrings, because they were Ishmaelites.

25 So they answered, "We will gladly give them." And they spread out a garment, and each man threw into it the earrings from his plunder.
26 Now the weight of the gold earrings that he requested was one thousand seven hundred shekels of gold, besides the crescent ornaments, pendants, and purple robes which were on the kings of Midian, and besides the chains that were around their camels' necks.
27 Then Gideon made it into an ephod and set it up in his city, Ophrah. And all Israel played the harlot with it there. It became a snare to Gideon and to his house.

Judg. 8:22–27

It must have been a real test for Gideon to turn down the tempting offer the people made him. To be invited to become king was heady stuff for a man who had risen so comparatively recently from virtual obscurity. Of course, it made good sense, in human terms, and Gideon would not have been hard pushed to rationalize it in an acceptance speech. The nation needed a sense of solidarity and unity, which the judges were to some extent beginning to provide. But what of the succession? It all seemed so haphazard; surely it would be preferable to establish a royal house. Gideon represented the best option in terms of security from further invasions.

But their offer is fatally flawed and Gideon, to his great credit, seems to have had no real difficulty in rejecting their flattery. The Israelites' mistake is the classic one which occurs over and over again throughout this book. They attributed the deliverance which God had secured for them to a human leader: *"You have delivered us from the hand of Midian"* (v. 22).

Gideon, however, remembered how he came to be in that position. How could he forget? It was not he who had saved them, but God. They already had a king. "The Lord shall rule over you" (v. 23b). He knew that his own "appointment" was not by a committee of the elders, or even by the popular vote of the people, but by the Spirit of the Lord. How then could he usurp a role which God had not given him? Israel already had a king, and all of her problems stemmed from her stubborn refusal to give him his royal rights. To put a human being in God's place would only worsen matters irretrievably.

But as the story of the Book of Judges unfolds, we find that the desire for a human monarch develops in intensity until, in Samuel's day, God finally gives them what they clamored for (1 Sam. 8:4–9).

Although Gideon was able to resist the temptation of political power, he did not lose the opportunity of developing for himself a position of religious leadership to which he had no right. Seizing the momentum of his popularity, he asks for the gold earrings which were taken as spoil from the defeated Ishmaelites. With this large quantity of gold, Gideon made an ephod. This was not an idol, but a garment. Exodus 28:5–14 gives us a detailed description of this, an upper garment worn by the high priest. On the shoulder straps that held the ephod in place were two onyx stones on which were engraved the names of the twelve tribes of Israel. The linen breastplate contained the Urim and Thummim used for divine revelation. Leon Wood describes the ephod as "a sort of extravagant apron, covering both the front and back of the person."[1] Certainly it was extremely valuable, woven throughout with golden thread and containing various jewels.

The main point, however, is that God had prescribed that it should be worn only by the high priest. It was therefore confined to his service within the Tabernacle. This was one of the ways in which the Lord intended to preserve the one geographical focus of worship at the "tent of meeting," rather than allowing numerous shrines and, with them, local cults and deities.

All this Gideon seems now to have ignored. He wanted to have his own ephod, to receive his own direct guidance from God. It would not be hard to work out a justification of his actions. The high priesthood at Shiloh does not seem to have been very effective at this time and Gideon's plan could be argued to be a better and more accessible substitute. If Gideon was to judge Israel, he knew how much he needed divine wisdom. And we have already seen that his faith constantly required confirmation and support. He had a real weakness for the spectacular and for special revelation, which the ephod could provide on his very own doorstep.

"And all Israel played the harlot with it there" (v. 27). The deliberately shocking language forces us into realizing how wrong Gideon was. Effectively, he was consecrating himself as an alternative high priest to the one whom God had chosen. Worship and inquiry of God's will would now focus on both Shiloh and Ophrah, in the people's minds.

Gideon became the slave of his own inner desire to be rewarded, applauded, and revered—but at a great cost. *"It became a snare to Gideon and to his house"* (v. 27b). When we insist on having what God has not given us, we always are ensnared.

God does not always frustrate our sinful longings. Sometimes he allows us to have what we have been determined to get, but with bitterness and vexation.

If we determine to go our own way and set ourselves up in conscious opposition to his purposes, he may teach us to trust him through the sour experience of getting *what* we want, at the expense of *whom* we need. A man is determined to enter the ministry, in spite of negative advice from others and no true call from God. The life appeals to him. It seems to offer prestige, the exercise of authority, a respected public role, influence, a chance genuinely to help others. Sometimes it is the ephod itself, the vestments and trappings of office, that attracts. He persuades a church to sponsor him and a college to train him, and eventually he is ordained. But at what cost? The reality of the ministry's demands, with its constant draining of resources, soon begins to tell. Marriage and family life suffer. The glamour wears off and the daily round becomes a drudgery, or else the golf course calls and other interests take over. "The hungry sheep look up and are not fed." The man has all that he wanted, but often with a bitter spirit and a frustrated life, because it was not what God wanted.

Many a Christian has been carried on a tide of personal popularity far beyond what God was calling him or her to do. It is a desperate situation when a church imagines that the way to recognize and reward its most devoted young servants is to package them up and send them off to seminary. The old advice is still true. "Don't go into the ministry, if you can avoid it." For if you can avoid it, with a good conscience before God, you are not called.

THE TEST OF RETIREMENT

> 28 Thus Midian was subdued before the children of Israel, so that they lifted their heads no more. And the country was quiet for forty years in the days of Gideon.

29 Then Jerubbaal the son of Joash went and dwelt
in his own house.
30 Gideon had seventy sons who were his own
offspring, for he had many wives.
31 And his concubine who was in Shechem also
bore him a son, whose name he called Abimelech.
32 Now Gideon the son of Joash died at a good old
age, and was buried in the tomb of Joash his father, in
Ophrah of the Abiezrites.
33 And it was, as soon as Gideon was dead, that
the children of Israel again played the harlot with the
Baals, and made Baal-Berith their god.
34 Thus the children of Israel did not remember
the Lord their God, who had delivered them from the
hands of all their enemies on every side;
35 nor did they show kindness to the house of
Jerubbaal (Gideon) in accordance with the good he had
done for Israel.

Judg. 8:28–35

On the face of it, in verse 28, life looks pretty rosy. A quiet land for forty years must have been a great blessing to Gideon's generation, for which they were doubtless extremely grateful. The Midianites had been dealt with really decisively and everybody knew that Gideon was to be credited with that success. By calling him Jerubbaal in verse 29 the author reminds us of the lasting effect he had in destroying the Baal cult, even if he did assume a role God had not given him.

But look a little more closely. Gideon's many wives and seventy sons reflect the sort of expensive and ostentatious life-style of many an eastern monarch. The man who declined the title of king seems to have surrounded himself with the outward trappings of royal power. Even his son by a Shechemite concubine is ironically called *"Abimelech"* by him, a name which means "the father is king." The fact that his influence reached as far south as Shechem is eloquent testimony to the authority he exercised and the respect he commanded in Israel, as verse 32 implies. But it is significant that no mighty exploits are recorded of these forty years in which Gideon was judge. They seem to have been years of personal luxury, but their legacy was a sad one.

"As soon as Gideon was dead" (v. 33) the spiritual and moral condition of the people reverted back to its previous state. It almost seems as though they were waiting impatiently for the old hero to go. A new generation chose to forget what the true situation had been when God's angel met Gideon at the winepress. The judge failed to secure any deep or lasting reforms in the religious life of the nation, because he himself failed to preserve the purity of the worship of Yahweh, as He had commanded. His legacy was therefore bound to be flawed; and with the passing of the man it was blown away, like chaff. Syncretism again took hold of Israel, and now the Baal is given a new name—"Baal of the covenant," a direct substitution for their true covenant Lord who had brought them out of the land of Egypt and constituted them as a people. There was no respect for Gideon's family either (v. 35). Indeed, the family becomes the focus for the next chapter, which reveals how far covenant people can sink when Baal replaces Yahweh.

If the true test of successful leadership is what happens when the leader moves on, then Gideon was a failure. Perhaps the most potent lesson of these last verses is that Gideon was unable to change the heart of the nation because his own heart had not changed. When we first met him he was an idol worshiper; and although he did not apparently return to the cult of Baal, nevertheless the end of his life sees him barely holding on in a situation where the wheel has virtually turned full circle. It is the sad downward spiral of Judges, once again.

So, how are we to apply this? We need to ask ourselves whether we are really learning our own lessons. Am I really changing? Where is God making a difference in my life? We all know how easy it is to be spiritually hollow on the inside, however well we may appear outwardly.

Christians often fall into one of two extremes. Some are tempted to say, "I've done enough. I've changed sufficiently, and now I can settle down with a Christianity I feel comfortable about." That is the way to become cemented in to our own weaknesses and inadequacies and ultimately to lose all spiritual vitality completely.

Others sigh and say, "I can't change. I've tried so often and I'll never be any different." The net result is the same. But this is where we, as New Testament Christians, have so much more than Gideon enjoyed. We have the blood of Jesus to cleanse us, the Scriptures to guide us, and the Holy Spirit to empower us. That is the new initiative we so much need, the fresh start we are all looking for. It provides a new beginning that cuts the infinite loop in which we are otherwise caught. It locks our inherent human weakness into the divine power grid, so that we are no longer running on our own batteries. A life like that can weather even the tests of success.

NOTES

1. Leon Wood, *The Distressing Days of the Judges* (Grand Rapids: Zondervan, 1975), 227.

CHAPTER NINE

The Power That Corrupts

Judges 9:1–57

The Book of Judges is often perplexing, to our modern minds, in terms of the amount of space it gives to its constituent characters and their activities. Nowhere is that more the case than in this ninth chapter.

Why devote fifty-seven verses to a character such as Abimelech, when he isn't even a judge at all? He does not deliver his people from any outside oppressor. Rather, he plunges a part of the nation into civil conflict, which shakes it to the very core. The chapter is the story of a man of blood, beginning with his accession to power through the murder of seventy of his half-brothers and ending with his own violent death. It's a grisly story of conspiracy and mass murder to rival anything that the history of medieval Europe can provide.

In fact, the chapter has a special position and purpose. The story of Judges is almost halfway through, and the chronicler seems deliberately to focus on Abimelech to provide his readers with a microcosm of the rampant progress of evil in the life of the nation. Here we see in one man's life and in one specific geographical area the devastating effects of sin which are spreading on the macro-scale throughout the nation. When we come to the end of the book, we shall see that the last four chapters provide a summary, in a series of representative incidents, of the whole sorry process which the narratives have progressively unfolded. This present chapter performs the same function, as it enables us to draw breath and to learn just what is happening to Israel through her spiritual rebellion and decline.

Structurally, we need to remember that this chapter is an epilogue to the Gideon sequence. There is an irony in the mention of Abimelech's father by his other name, Jerubbaal, at the beginning of the story. That honorable nickname which Gideon had been awarded—"Baal-fighter" we might translate it—is about to be trampled in the mud by his son. Through Abimelech, Baal, or rather the prince of darkness who lies behind all forms of idolatry, is about to strike back.

Chapter 9 is a commentary on Gideon's legacy. Although he had refused the people's attempts to make him king, his illegitimate son has no such modesty. As we have seen, his name means "my father is king." The chapter is underlining the drift toward a human monarchy in Israel, which is the inevitable outcome of the dethronement of Yahweh. The idols have no power to rule because they cannot speak or act. Those are the prerogatives of the living God alone (see Psalm 115:2–8 and Isaiah 44:9–20).

But if God is not reigning, someone else must. So, as the spiritual life of the nation declines, the clamor for a king increases until it reaches its climax in 1 Samuel 8 and God grants them their request in the person of Saul.

> We will have a king over us, that we also may be like all the nations, and that our king may judge us and go out before us and fight our battles.
>
> *1 Sam. 8:19–20*

Is that not exactly what the Lord had done for them all down the years? That was why they had any foothold at all in the promised land. So God tells Samuel,

> they have not rejected you, but they have rejected Me, that I should not reign over them.
>
> *1 Sam. 8:7*

And at this much earlier stage we are being warned that the Abimelech story is representative of the outcome that will always follow the rejection of the Lord, as night follows day.

Though Gideon refused the title of king, he seems not to have vanquished the temptation. In retirement, his household exhibited all the indulgence of a developing dynasty, with his many wives and seventy sons. In addition, there is the one son of his concubine, Abimelech, who will prove, as history has done so often, that the illegitimate sons of princes make the best usurpers.

Parallel to this kingship theme runs that of Israel's growing idolatry. They are twin streams from the same source. Again, it is partly Gideon's responsibility, through his setting-up of the golden ephod in Ophrah (8:27–33). If their deliverer encourages the people to prostitute themselves in superstitious idolatry at an unauthorized shrine (8:27), then perhaps we should not be surprised to find a temple in existence in Shechem dedicated to a pagan deity, Baal-Berith—"lord of the covenant" (9:4).

The provocation to the Lord is as horrifying as it is tragic. The city of Shechem was only a few miles north of Shiloh where the ark of God was situated. At Shechem generations before, the living God had renewed his own covenant commitment to Joshua and the people of Israel, as the blessings had been recited from Mt. Gerizim and the cursings from Mt. Ebal (see Josh. 8:30–35). And it was here at the end of his life that the people answered Joshua's challenge, "We also will serve the Lord, for he is our God" (Josh. 24:18). To build a shrine to Baal, at Shechem of all places, was to be guilty of trampling the covenant grace of God under their feet and provoking the God of the covenant to rise up in judgment, to defend his holy name and honor.

The theological significance of chapter 9 is to teach the doctrine of divine retribution, which is in essence the reality of just punishment, a fair deal. If a people who have been as greatly privileged as Israel turn their back on the grace of their God who is a consuming fire (Heb. 12:29), then they will be burnt up by his righteousness. Twice in the chapter the point is made. In verses 23–24, *"God sent a spirit of ill will between Abimelech and the men of Shechem. . . . that the crime done to the seventy sons of Jerubbaal might be settled and their blood be laid on Abimelech. . . ."* The point is made again at the conclusion to the whole episode in verses 56–57: *"Thus God repaid the wickedness of Abimelech . . . and all the evil of the men of Shechem God returned on their own heads. . . ."* This interpretative key opens our understanding of the whole chapter. Israel may turn her back on the Lord, but that does not mean that he reciprocates. God is still intimately involved in the life of his covenant people, however little they may realize it. He loves them too much and too persistently to allow them to continue in their sin unchecked. But the way in which that love is demonstrated is by allowing the consequences of sin to work themselves out.

There is a recurring biblical logic about this. If people choose deliberately to live without reference to God, then God may well leave them to their own devices. It is the same chilling possibility to which Paul alludes in the opening chapter of Romans. Three times he tells us that when human beings chose to worship the created order rather than the Creator, "God gave them up" (Rom. 1:24, 26, 28). It is as though God says, "You can have what you want, but there will be consequences."

A generation that is obsessed with sexual gratification reaps a harvest of devastating abortion and divorce rates, incest and child abuse and an AIDS epidemic, on a world-wide scale. God is allowing sin to work itself out. Hell itself is the end of the road. If the whole of life is spent refusing and denying God, rebelling against his laws and distancing oneself from him as much as possible, why should we expect God to reverse that process, after death? Hell is what the ungodly have literally asked for—separation from God. The tragedy is that they have not realized what that means—separation from love and light and life itself. But God is not unjust. He respects man's choices. He insists on treating everyone of us as a responsible human being. That is what is being worked out in Judges 9 with an almost mathematical precision.

Powerful Arrogance

1 Then Abimelech the son of Jerubbaal went to Shechem, to his mother's brothers, and spoke with them and with all the family of the house of his mother's father, saying,

2 "Please speak in the hearing of all the men of Shechem: 'Which is better for you, that all seventy of the sons of Jerubbaal reign over you, or that one reign over you?' Remember that I am your own flesh and bone."

3 And his mother's brothers spoke all these words concerning him in the hearing of all the men of Shechem; and their heart was inclined to follow Abimelech, for they said, "He is our brother."

4 So they gave him seventy shekels of silver from the temple of Baal-Berith, with which Abimelech hired worthless and reckless men; and they followed him.

5 Then he went to his father's house at Ophrah and killed his brothers, the seventy sons of Jerubbaal, on one stone. But Jotham the youngest son of Jerubbaal was left, because he hid himself.

6 And all the men of Shechem gathered together, all of Beth Millo, and they went and made Abimelech king beside the terebinth tree at the pillar that was in Shechem.

Judg. 9:1–6

If Israel was acquiring a taste for kingship, then Abimelech wanted to ensure that he would be the front runner. While there is no indication in the text that the seventy sons of Gideon had any aspirations to assume and enlarge their father's role, Abimelech's insatiable appetite for power is made abundantly plain. He attributes a similar thirst to his half-brothers, in order to win over the men of Shechem. The fact that his mother came from among them surely gave them a tenuous foothold on the ladder of influence in Israel. Abimelech was a "son" of Shechem. Here was an opportunity for them to have a taste of power. His illegitimacy would only serve to underline his rights, in his own mind. Also, if Shechem was a center of idolatry, the sooner they acquired power in the vacuum caused by Gideon's death, the sooner the idolaters could confirm their pagan rites and resist any of the sons of Jerubbaal actually living up to their dead father's name.

There is little doubt, however, that for Abimelech the naked motivation of his actions was personal power. He shamelessly uses family loyalties and jealousies to feather his own nest. Having persuaded his uncles of his candidacy, he is able to use a large sum of money from the Baalite temple treasury to put together a task force of mercenaries to remove all the sons of Gideon who stand in his way. In the most ruthless and cold-blooded way he murders his seventy brothers at the family home and he is himself proclaimed king in Shechem. His jurisdiction is still limited. In effect, Abimelech is a local war lord; but it is a beginning, and no doubt his arrogance and ruthlessness combined to make plans for the extension of his power.

The power that corrupts, like any narcotic, eventually demands total control. Keil and Delitzsch describe this action as "a bloody omen of the kingdom of the ten tribes, which was afterwards founded at Shechem by the Ephraimite Jeroboam, in which one dynasty overthrew another, and generally sought to establish its power by exterminating the whole family of the dynasty that had been overthrown."[1] The whole story unfolds in 1 Kings 15:27ff. and 2 Kings 10:1ff.

We do not have to look far for contemporary illustrative material of the same sad mechanism. The stories coming out of Romania, for example, following the fall of Ceausescu, demonstrate the paranoia of the dictator who can never be 100 percent sure that he is in total control, or that he has quashed every opponent. The lust for power can and does lead to the most outrageous actions in the business world, in family struggles, and even in the church of Jesus Christ. People will do terrible things when they are consumed by the desire to come out on the top. Such arrogance destroys relationship, because it kills trust and silences dialogue.

Recent church history has provided us with examples of what can happen when anyone—even well-motivated and apparently godly men—moves beyond personal accountability to anyone else. None of us is immune from the corrupting influence of power and position. We can all too easily lose our perspective on ourselves, and with it our moral and spiritual balance. As pastors, we need faithful friends who will pastor us and bring us down to earth from some of our wilder flights of fancy. It is not for nothing that the pulpit is sometimes caricatured as "six feet above contradiction," or "cowards' castle." In a chapter full of irony, we must be careful to see that we do not succumb to the supreme idolatry of worshiping at the shrine of our own infallibility, or power, or pride. The more "successful" a ministry is perceived to be, the greater will be the danger that we start to believe our own press releases! Many a pastor has allowed himself to be "made king" in his little corner of God's world-wide field, by an enthusiastic band of supporters, and those people have lived to rue the day.

Prophetic Insight

> 7 Now when they told Jotham, he went and stood on top of Mount Gerizim, and lifted his voice and cried out. And he said to them:
>
> "Listen to me, you men of Shechem,
> That God may listen to you!

8 "The trees once went forth to anoint a king over them.
And they said to the olive tree,
'Reign over us!'
9 "But the olive tree said to them,
'Should I cease giving my oil,
With which they honor God and men,
And go to sway over trees?'
10 "Then the trees said to the fig tree,
'You come and reign over us!'
11 "But the fig tree said to them,
'Should I cease my sweetness and my good fruit,
And go to sway over trees?'
12 "Then the trees said to the vine,
'You come and reign over us!'
13 "But the vine said to them, 'Should I cease my new wine,
Which cheers both God and men,
And go to sway over trees?'
14 "Then all the trees said to the bramble,
'You come and reign over us!'
15 "And the bramble said to the trees,
'If in truth you anoint me as king over you,
Then come and take shelter in my shade;
But if not, let fire come out of the bramble
And devour the cedars of Lebanon!'
16 "Now therefore, if you have acted in truth and
sincerity in making Abimelech king, and if you have
dealt well with Jerubbaal and his house, and have done
to him as he deserves—
17 "for my father fought for you, risked his life,
and delivered you out of the hand of Midian;
18 "but you have risen up against my father's
house this day, and killed his seventy sons on one
stone, and made Abimelech, the son of his female servant, king over the men of Shechem, because he is your
brother—
19 "if then you have acted in truth and sincerity
with Jerubbaal and with his house this day, then rejoice in Abimelech, and let him also rejoice in you.
20 "But if not, let fire come from Abimelech and

> devour the men of Shechem and Beth Millo; and let fire come from the men of Shechem and from Beth Millo and devour Abimelech!"
>
> 21 And Jotham ran away and fled; and he went to Beer and dwelt there, for fear of Abimelech his brother.
>
> *Judg. 9:7–21*

A low outcrop of rock on Mt. Gerizim, that formed a natural platform about Shechem, is still called Jotham's pulpit today. The voice from Mt. Gerizim would have strong historical reminders of the voice of Joshua, who had spoken God's Word from the same location to the assembled tribes, years before. Now the one son of Gideon who has escaped the massacre assumes a prophetic role, as he tells a fable designed to awaken and spur the consciences of his hearers. It is as powerful as it is memorable. Indeed, Jotham himself claims that their hearing and reaction to his story will determine God's reaction to them (v. 7). This is in effect a claim to be the voice of God, akin to the later prophetic formula, "thus says the Lord." If the Shechemites are to know the grace of God in averting the tragedy they have precipitated by making Abimelech king, they must listen to the meaning of the fable. Only then will they repent of their sinful stupidity, so that God can hear and forgive them.

Like Israel, the trees are looking for a king, but no one wants the job. The olive, fig, and vine all decline for the same basic reason. They will not tear themselves from the soil, in which they have been planted and bear their fruit, in order *"to sway over trees."* The verb literally means to float about or soar above. Oil, figs, and wine are among the most valuable products of the land of Israel. The trees' argument, therefore, is that they are not willing to leave the useful tasks they are currently performing in order to take on the dubious privilege of an exalted, but uncertain, superiority, waving over the other trees. The concept behind it makes its own comment on the value, or otherwise, of the kingly office.

However, rather than reject the idea of having a king at all, the desperate trees approach the totally unsuitable bramble, or thornbush. But because all the trees are now involved (v. 14), it seems that no other candidate is forthcoming. The bramble is only too pleased to accept. After all, it has no useful task to perform, and nothing to offer but thorns. The shelter of its shade is insufficient to protect anyone from the burning sun. It has nothing positive to give, for the trees will soon discover that all it can do is to hurt and wound. But it can threaten (v. 15b). Having once given the invitation, if the trees do not proceed to recognize its exalted position, the bramble will become the source of a forest fire so fierce that even the cedars of Lebanon will be destroyed. Thus, "the most insignificant and most worthless man can be the cause of harm to the mightiest and most distinguished."[2]

At verse 16, the prophet turns preacher. The people of Israel had asked Gideon to be their king, but he had declined. How much he had done for them was a matter of indisputable history (v. 17). But now they have sided with the murderer of his dynasty, who is to Gideon as a bramble is to an olive tree. They will soon find that they will be set on fire and consumed by their "king" and the foolishness of their actions (v. 20) and in this course of events, the thornbush itself will also be destroyed.

The principle of retribution is enshrined in the prophetic curse with which Jotham ends his proclamation. As the men of Shechem have not acted *"in truth and sincerity with Jerubbaal,"* so they can have nothing to look forward to but reaping the reward of their actions, in the outworking of circumstances. "A friendship based on ambition, ingratitude, disloyalty and bloodshed could only have disastrous consequences for both sides."[3] Jotham's flight to watch the unfolding of events from a safe distance (v. 21) is hardly surprising!

Rampant Evil

22 After Abimelech had reigned over Israel three years,

23 God sent a spirit of ill will between Abimelech and the men of Shechem; and the men of Shechem dealt treacherously with Abimelech,

24 that the crime done to the seventy sons of Jerubbaal might be settled and their blood be laid on Abimelech their brother, who killed them, and on the men of Shechem, who aided him in the killing of his brothers.

25 And the men of Shechem set men in ambush against him on the tops of the mountains, and they robbed all who passed by them along that way; and it was told Abimelech.

26 Now Gaal the son of Ebed came with his brothers and went over to Shechem; and the men of Shechem put their confidence in him.

27 So they went out into the fields, and gathered grapes from their vineyards and trod them, and made merry. And they went into the house of their god, and ate and drank, and cursed Abimelech.

28 Then Gaal the son of Ebed said, "Who is Abimelech, and who is Shechem, that we should serve him? Is he not the son of Jerubbaal, and is not Zebul his officer? Serve the men of Hamor the father of Shechem; but why should we serve him?

29 "If only this people were under my authority! Then I would remove Abimelech." So he said to Abimelech, "Increase your army and come out!"

30 When Zebul, the ruler of the city, heard the words of Gaal the son of Ebed, his anger was aroused.

31 And he sent messengers to Abimelech secretly, saying, "Take note! Gaal the son of Ebed and his brothers have come to Shechem; and here they are, fortifying the city against you.

32 "Now therefore, get up by night, you and the people who are with you, and lie in wait in the field.

33 And it shall be, as soon as the sun is up in the morning, that you shall rise early and rush upon the city; and when he and the people who are with him come out against you, you may then do to them as you find opportunity."

34 So Abimelech and all the people who were with him rose by night, and lay in wait against Shechem in four companies.

35 When Gaal the son of Ebed went out and stood in the entrance to the city gate, Abimelech and the people who were with him rose from lying in wait.

36 And when Gaal saw the people, he said to Zebul, "Look, people are coming down from the tops of the mountains!" But Zebul said to him, "You see the shadows of the mountains as if they were men."

37 So Gaal spoke again and said, "See people are coming down from the center of the land, and another company is coming from the Diviners' Terebinth Tree."

38 Then Zebul said to him, "Where indeed is your mouth now, with which you said, 'Who is Abimelech, that we should serve him?' Are not these the people whom you despised? Go out, if you will, and fight with them now."

39 So Gaal went out, leading the men of Shechem, and fought with Abimelech.

40 And Abimelech chased him, and he fled from him; and many fell wounded, to the very entrance of the gate.

41 Then Abimelech dwelt at Arumah, and Zebul drove out Gaal and his brothers, so that they would not dwell in Shechem.

42 And it came about on the next day that the people went out into the field, and they told Abimelech.

43 So he took his people, divided them into three companies, and laid in wait in the field. And he looked, and there were the people, coming out of the city; and he rose against them and attacked them.

44 Then Abimelech and the company that was with him rushed forward and stood at the entrance of the gate of the city; and the other two companies rushed upon all who were in the fields and killed them.

45 So Abimelech fought against the city all that day; he took the city and killed the people who were in it; and he demolished the city and sowed it with salt.

46 Now when all the men of the tower of Shechem had heard that, they entered the stronghold of the temple of the god Berith.

47 And it was told Abimelech that all the men of the tower of Shechem were gathered together.

48 Then Abimelech went up to Mount Zalmon, he and all the people who were with him. And Abimelech took an axe in his hand and cut down a bough from the trees, and took it and laid it on his shoulder; then he said to the people who were with him, "What you

> have seen me do, make haste and do as I have done."
> 49 So each of the people likewise cut down his own bough and followed Abimelech, put them against the stronghold, and set the stronghold on fire above them, so that all the people of the tower of Shechem died, about a thousand men and women.
>
> *Judg. 9:22–49*

From the very beginning of this chilling episode, the note of irony is struck yet again. Abimelech's reign is despotic, but as yet limited. He would no doubt have referred to himself as reigning over Israel, but in fact it is highly unlikely that his actual authority extended any further than the tribe of Ephraim and half of Manasseh. However, the important point theologically is to note the divine initiative recorded in verse 23. Undoubtedly there were discernible political reasons for their actions, but the Bible very clearly shows us the real cause. No longer is the covenant name, *Yahweh*, used, but the more general term, *God*, because the people concerned had fallen so far short of their special relationship with him. He therefore treats them as the same as the pagan tribes, whose gods they have adopted to worship. The devil's power behind all idolatrous worship often results in the devotees becoming the victims of evil spirits, and it seems that this is what God permitted to happen in the relationship between Abimelech and the Shechemites. The text reminds us that this is the outworking of his justice (v. 24).

If Abimelech was already living at Arumah (v. 41), with his officer Zebul (v. 28) being left to control Shechem, we can understand the political reason why relations deteriorated and why Abimelech's agents became subject to ambushes. It was a strategy of destabilization. The government of Abimelech was not even able to guarantee safe travel in the immediate area of its control, so what sort of king was he?

Into this situation comes the opportunist, Gaal, son of Ebed (v. 26). Perhaps he was something of a Robin Hood figure, traveling the country and righting wrongs. He and his freebooters look something like an original Israelite "A-team." The Shechemites welcomed him as an ally in their cause and soon, in the context of a drunken, pagan, temple party, Gaal's words are flowing as lavishly as the wine. He despises Abimelech not because of his character or his record, but because he is the son of the man who destroyed the altar of Baal. The Shechemites should be true to their ancestry, the pagan prince

Hamor, the Hivite who had founded the city. Why tolerate any more the descendant of a man who had attempted to destroy their cultural and ethnic religious origins in favor of a foreign god, Yahweh?

In this context, Gaal is making his bid for power. Zebul, Abimelech's agent, however, is incensed. He masterminds the counterattacks, informing his master of the danger and suggesting a surprise, early morning, preemptive ambush. The strategy is devastatingly successful. Gaal is surprised by the four companies coming at him from different directions and routed with comparative ease (v. 40). Returning into the city for protection, he is eventually expelled by Zebul (v. 41). Everything seems to have returned to normal, but fire is to come forth from the bramble.

Next day, as the Shechemites are working the fields outside the fortified city, they too are ambushed and massacred by Abimelech. The "bramble king" turns his attention to the city, which he takes and destroys along with all its inhabitants. The mark of Abimelech's total victory is that he sprinkled the ruined city with salt (v. 45) as a symbol that it was to be forever an uninhabited, barren desert. Even those who had escaped to the tower, or stronghold, (no one is sure of the translation) cannot avoid Abimelech's wrath. At the place where they had crowned the bramble king, the fire literally shoots out from him and consumes them all (v. 49; cf. v. 15). It is a blood bath of senseless revenge and wanton destruction. Jotham's curse is fulfilled as a tidal wave of unstoppable evil, terrifying in its power and magnitude, engulfs and destroys Shechem.

In application, we must draw the unpalatable but salutary lesson of the "exceeding sinfulness of sin." Once the tide of evil builds, nothing can contain it in the end. This was the unlearned lesson of the 1930s as the evil Nazi power base in Germany grew stronger and stronger, almost unchallenged, until the whole world was caught up in its cataclysmic outcome. We think that sin can be contained; but it cannot. We talk of "little" sins and "white" lies, to persuade ourselves that we can stop whenever we wish, but it is not like that.

One of Dr. Paul White's famous "Jungle Doctor" stories tells of the African family who took pity on an orphaned leopard cub, took it into their home, nurtured and cared for it, and treated it as a pet. Frequently they were warned to return it to the wild before it became too powerful for them to handle. But the warnings were disregarded; they knew the animal so well—it was one of the family.

Then, one day, it showed its true nature and the "domesticated" beast of prey became a killer. The jungle doctor's message was clear and plain: "Little leopards become big leopards, and big leopards kill!" The characteristic nature of sin is contempt for anything of value (contrast Philippians 4:8). "The thief does not come except to steal, and to kill, and to destroy" (John 10:10a). That is why he is no friend of the shepherd or the sheep.

> Do not love the world or the things in the world. If anyone loves the world, the love of the Father is not in him. For all that is in the world—the lust of the flesh, the lust of the eyes, and the pride of life—is not of the Father but is of the world."
>
> *1 John 2:15–16*

In a culture like ours, where the very concept of sin is an endangered species, under threat of extinction, we need to hear this lesson over and over again. It is common to view individual sins as nothing more than a nuisance or an irritation, rather like minor traffic offenses. They will only cause us difficulties if we are foolish or unfortunate enough to accumulate too many, we tell ourselves. This chapter is a powerful corrective to that sort of self-indulgent weakness which all too often infects our thinking, even as Christians.

Cigarette advertising now carries a government health warning because the habit does have an effect. Alcohol abuse will lead to cirrhosis of the liver and damage to the brain cells, just as sexual promiscuity creates disease. The compulsive liar ends up isolated and friendless, having forfeited everyone's trust. If we flaunt God's rules, we must be prepared to face the consequences. We would accept it in the physical realm, but we imagine we can avoid it in the spiritual. No one in his or her right mind would organize a party to defy the law of gravity by jumping off the tallest building in the city. We all know that the law defied in that way would exact its own price.

It is part of our creatureliness, in the world, as God has made it, that our fragile lives are not free to play fast and loose with the structures of reality. Why should we expect it to be any different in the moral or spiritual realms? In these spheres, too, God has determined how his creatures should live, for he knows how he has made us to function at our best. His laws are designed not to enslave but to liberate, much as the laws of the road free us to travel, or the rules of a sport free us to enjoy the game. True freedom is living in conformity with the will of God. Every act of sin is an attack on that principle.

Covenant Discipline

> 50 Then Abimelech went to Thebez, and he encamped against Thebez and took it.
> 51 But there was a strong tower in the city, and all the men and women—all the people of the city—fled there and shut themselves in; then they went up to the top of the tower.
> 52 So Abimelech came as far as the tower and fought against it; and he drew near the door of the tower to burn it with fire.
> 53 But a certain woman dropped an upper millstone on Abimelech's head and crushed his skull.
> 54 Then he called quickly to the young man, his armor-bearer, and said to him, "Draw your sword and kill me, lest men say of me, 'A woman killed him.'" So his young man thrust him through, and he died.
> 55 And when the men of Israel saw that Abimelech was dead, they departed, every man to his own place.
> 56 Thus God repaid the wickedness of Abimelech, which he had done to his father by killing his seventy brothers.
> 57 And all the evil of the men of Shechem God returned on their own heads, and on them came the curse of Jotham the son of Jerubbaal.
>
> *Judg. 9:50–57*

Crazed by his obliteration of Shechem, Abimelech decides to add Thebez to his list. The town was situated a few miles north of Shechem and we are given no reason as to why he decided suddenly to set siege to it. Most probably the revolt that had been simmering in Shechem had its supporters in Thebez too. As at Shechem, Abimelech seems to have seized the city without too much difficulty and again many of its citizens took refuge in the strong tower. Once again, Abimelech reveals his total contempt for human life and his unimaginable cruelty by immediately seeking to set fire to the tower, in a repeat of the incident at Shechem. But this time he is thwarted—and by a woman. From her position directly above him on the top of the tower, she drops an *"upper millstone"* and crushes his skull (v. 53). "Hand mills were made from two circular stones (see Deut. 24:6, Job 41:24), between one and two feet in diameter and two to four inches thick, that were particularly hard and heavy" notes Goslinga.[4]

As Abimelech's armorbearer killed him, so the fire created by the "bramble king" was abruptly extinguished. The final verses of the chapter underline the ingredient of divine retribution to which our attention has already been drawn. "God caused the wickedness to return" is the literal rendering of the Hebrew text of verse 56, and again Goslinga has a pithy summary which illuminates the meaning for us.

> [It] not only means that God punished them, but also draws an inner connection between the crime and the punishment and shows that the partnership in evil was disastrous for both sides. The Shechemites' disloyalty to Gideon's family reduced them to servitude under Abimelech's tyranny, and the cruel king met his own cruel death in his subjects' revolt.[5]

What possible encouragements can we draw from such a uniformly depressing record of human sinfulness? Perhaps the emphasis we need to make is on the controlling hand of God through it all. Yes, he does permit the evil to thrive and develop, with disastrous consequences, but he also limits its extent. He cuts Abimelech short in the midst of his career. He extinguishes the flames when they seem certain to spread and overwhelm the whole land.

So, we are not looking at a forest fire that is out of God's control. Nothing ever is, in this world or the next. Our God reigns, and he uses the adverse circumstances of life to teach his people that fundamental truth over and over again. The whole perspective is changed when we begin to understand this sad chapter as a record of covenant discipline, expressing the loving faithfulness of our God. He cares what his people do with their lives and whom they worship. He will stop at nothing to win them back to that personal relationship of trust and love for which he redeemed them. As with any earthly father worth the name, part of his devotion to his children is his commitment to discipline them, for their good. We can be sure that even when the rod is in his hand there are tears in his eyes.

The proof of that conviction is quite simply in the Cross of our Lord Jesus Christ. That is where we see God's retributive justice, in all its intensity of wrath, launched against human sin. There, at Calvary, is the place where the covenant God exacts the full penalty and punishment that our sin deserves. And that is precisely the place where we also see the climax of his covenant faithfulness and redeeming love. For we are not bearing the holy wrath of a righteous God, but his beloved Son is. Not that we see a vengeful God punishing an innocent third party, Jesus; that is a travesty of the atonement. Rather "God was in Christ," carrying the full effect of our sin, as our representative and substitute, dying in our place, so that we might be forgiven and never be forsaken.

Moreover, in that conquering death, he overcame all the hostile forces that were ranged against us (Col. 2:14–15) as he demonstrated beyond refutation, by his glorious resurrection. If God was prepared to do *that*, then he will be committed to right every wrong and to bring in his everlasting kingdom of justice and peace. That is covenant faithfulness and God will stop at nothing to see that all is fulfilled.

In that New Testament perspective, we can learn the lessons of Judges 9 with joy and confidence. We can seek to cooperate with his loving discipline in our lives, confident that the God who gave his only Son for our salvation will bring every adopted son and daughter safely home to glory. In those splendid words of John Newton (1725–1807), the converted slave trader, who knew so well the covenant grace of God to sinners:

> Let us love, and sing, and wonder,
> Let us praise the Saviour's name!
> He has hushed the Law's loud thunder,
> He has quenched Mount Sinai's flame;
> He has washed us with His blood,
> He has brought us nigh to God.
> Let us wonder; grace and justice
>   join, and point to mercy's store;
> When through grace in Christ our trust is,
> Justice smiles, and asks no more:
> He who washed us with His blood,
> Has secured our way to God.[6]

NOTES

1. C. F. Keil and F. Delitzsch, *Joshua–Samuel*, Vol. 2 of *Commentary on the Old Testament* (Grand Rapids: Eerdmans, 1973), 362.

2. Ibid., 364.

3. Goslinga, *Judges*, 361.

4. Ibid., 374.

5. Ibid.

6. "Let Us Love, and Sing, and Wonder," in *Christian Praise*, published by Inter-Varsity Press, London, 1957.

CHAPTER TEN

Sin's Dead End

Judges 10:1–18

If chapter 9 solved nothing, chapter 10 is a drama in four acts demonstrating the unquenchable grace of God. It reveals how the covenant Lord Yahweh intervened yet again on behalf of his rebellious people to discipline, reform, and at last deliver them.

SIN RESTRAINED

> 1 After Abimelech there arose to save Israel Tola the son of Puah, the son of Dodo, a man of Issachar; and he dwelt in Shamir in the mountains of Ephraim.
> 2 He judged Israel twenty-three years; and he died and was buried in Shamir.
> 3 After him arose Jair, a Gileadite; and he judged Israel twenty-two years.
> 4 Now he had thirty sons who rode on thirty donkeys; they also had thirty towns, which are called "Havoth Jair" to this day, which are in the land of Gilead.
> 5 And Jair died and was buried in Camon.
>
> *Judg. 10:1–5*

In these few verses we have outlined for us the careers of Tola and Jair, which together spanned a period of forty-five years. They are among the so-called "minor" judges, not because they are personally unimportant, but because we have so little recorded about them. Tola is said to have *"judged,"* or "saved," Israel, although there is no mention of any external threat while he was in office. Probably the mention of Abimelech in verse 1 is sufficient background. To rescue Israel from the chaos which Abimelech left behind him was indeed a "salvation" of enormous proportions. During Tola's time there seems to have been a period of stable government that saved the nation from the accelerating disintegration into which it was relentlessly sliding. If we were to visualize the movement of this whole book, it seems to me that a downward spiral would be the most appropriate. But that process is restrained by these two men, whom God raised up.

Similarly, with Jair, about whom we know hardly anything, his twenty-two years as judge were clearly a period of relative peace and prosperity (v. 4). Jair seems to have enjoyed considerable prestige and popularity, so that during his lifetime the government of Gilead became something of a family business. But the good times can be even more testing than the hard ones, as we have already learned. The time of peace once again became a time of complacency. Nepotism rarely produces quality leadership in the second or third generations. The thirty pampered sons, who each had his own town or settlement to rule over, seem to have been completely ineffectual in the crisis described in verse 7, when Gilead was invaded and oppressed by the Ammonites for eighteen years. Jair seems to have followed and developed the kingly life-style, begun by Gideon and carried on by Abimelech. Undoubtedly he did much good, but once he was removed it seems that the old influences to sin began to reassert themselves.

We are reminded by this that godly men and women in positions of responsibility, within our communities, can have a real and positive influence for good and in restraining evil. It is right that Christians should take their full role as citizens in the spheres of national and local government. It is right that through the mechanisms of a democratic society we should seek to influence popular thinking and legislative decision making to bring our society more in line with the standards of God's revelation in Scripture. But we must recognize that these measures will always be limited, and even temporary, unless the hearts of the people are being changed by the gospel of God's grace. Otherwise, when the brake is removed, when the Christians of influence are voted out or die, the old downhill movement will soon take over again.

The judgeships of Tola and Jair provided a breathing period, a time of God's grace in which the people had the opportunity once again to mend their ways and turn back to God wholeheartedly. But they failed to do so. Surely, the application is abundantly plain. Nothing short of a work of God's Spirit in the hearts and lives of thousands of "ordinary people" can turn the juggernaut of our increasingly godless Western materialism back from the slippery slope of collapse and disintegration. While we are right to pray and work to restrain sin and to enact Christian legislation to prevent the corruption of our society and the upholding of God's moral absolutes, we shall never change the hearts of people that way. Law can restrain, for a while, but only the gospel can liberate.

Twenty years ago in London, England, Christians inaugurated a nationwide Festival of Light, under the slogan "moral pollution needs a solution." Over those two decades there have been many commendable initiatives and there is a growing sense of social responsibility among evangelicals throughout Britain today, as a result. But the solution is still needed, as the leaders of the movements to which the festival gave birth would be the first to recognize. A time of restraint should be a time of intercession for a new initiative by God, in power, to turn the hearts of men. It is noteworthy, for example, that the great social reforms of the nineteenth century, including the abolition of slavery, followed the spiritual revivals of the late eighteenth century, under George Whitefield and John Wesley. When the hearts of men and women are changed in large numbers, the laws of their society soon follow.

Sin Resurgent

> 6 Then the children of Israel again did evil in the sight of the Lord, and served the Baals and the Ashtoreths, the gods of Syria, the gods of Sidon, the gods of Moab, the gods of the people of Ammon, and the gods of the Philistines; and they forsook the Lord and did not serve Him.
>
> 7 So the anger of the Lord was hot against Israel; and He sold them into the hands of the Philistines and into the hands of the people of Ammon.
>
> 8 From that year they harassed and oppressed the children of Israel for eighteen years—all the children of Israel who were on the other side of the Jordan in the land of the Amorites, in Gilead.

> 9 Moreover the people of Ammon crossed over the Jordan to fight against Judah also, against Benjamin, and against the house of Ephraim, so that Israel was severely distressed.
>
> *Judg. 10:6–9*

Once the restraining hand of godly men had been removed, the downward spiral quickly accelerated. This does not mean that idolatry was entirely absent from Israel in the days of Tola and Jair, but that after their deaths it flourished more and more. The sad evidence for this is provided by the extensive catalogue in verse 6 of pagan deities served by Israel. They included not only the Baals and the Ashtoreths, the gods of the Canaanites which were already in the land, but also the importation of deities from every direction. The gods of Sidon (in the north), Ammon (east of the Jordan), and the Philistines (to the south) all came pouring into Israel. It is as though Israel's obsessive greed for idolatry could only be satisfied by idols flooding into the land from every point of the compass. This also demonstrates that the spiritual poison was beginning to penetrate and infect the bloodstream of the whole nation, and not just a few tribes on the borders. As gross evil multiplied, so *"the anger of the Lord was hot against Israel"* (v. 7).

Pagan religion was based on a system which can best be summarized by the term *sympathetic magic*. We have to go back a stage to understand the attraction of idolatry. It is the harnessing of supernatural power to achieve the ends which the "worshiper" requires. In spite of mankind's rebellion against God and rejection of his moral law, it remains stubbornly true that because we are made in the image of God, men and women always have been and always will be incurably religious. There will always be an appetite for the divine, which can ultimately only be satisfied in the deep personal relationship with God, through the Lord Jesus Christ, which is the essence of Christianity.

But man, in rebellion, is always looking for substitutes. The root of all sin is to want to be my own god. It is clear that idolatry will always be attractive to the sinful human heart. It removes the uncomfortable aspects of the living God, with his perfect knowledge, total power, and moral demands, summed up by C. S. Lewis in his memorable description as "the transcendental interferer," and replaces the god-need with an idol which I can create and control.

The only problem is that the idol has no power, because it is lifeless. Therefore, I have to persuade myself that like any human being (after all it is made in the image of man!) my "god" has to be cajoled, or encouraged, or bribed to give me what I desire. This need lies at the root of all pagan worship.

So, if the requirement is for fertile soil and rich harvests, as it was with the Canaanites, the temple worship logically involves ritual prostitution, in the hope that the demonstration and dedication of human potency and fertility will persuade the god to act similarly in the natural, physical realm—to increase the crops or the flocks of animals.

Canaanite religion was largely a fertility cult of the mother goddess. Other gods, such as Molech (god of Ammon), required human sacrifice, especially of children, in a fire pit, as did Chemosh (god of Moab). These horrifying and ultimately devilish delusions were expressly forbidden to Israel from the time of Moses onward. For example, Leviticus 20:1–5 clearly states that any worshiper of Molech, from among God's people, is to be stoned. But the many warnings which God had given his people were either ignored, or else deliberately disobeyed (v. 6).

Their sin was twofold. They forsook their living Lord, to whom they were bound by covenant oaths, and turned instead to gods of their own choosing. Centuries later, Jeremiah was to capture the essence of his own generation's similar rebellion in his famous oracle (Jer. 2:11–13).

> "Has a nation changed its gods,
> Which are not gods?
> But my people have changed their Glory
> For what does not profit.
> Be astonished, O heavens, at this,
> And be horribly afraid;
> Be very desolate," says the Lord.
> "For my people have committed two evils:
> They have forsaken Me, the fountain of living waters,
> And hewn themselves cisterns—
> Broken cisterns that can hold no water."

Disaster is inevitable. The idols we create and choose to worship can never satisfy because ultimately every man-made cistern is flawed. We can only hew out leaking containers, which are destined to run dry. We do not have the spiritual technology to create a fountain of living waters, however much we may fool ourselves. So, God's wrath is always kindled when anyone or anything is allowed to take over his place in our lives. It is not a vindictive, punitive anger, but a jealous yearning that those whom he has redeemed, at such great cost, should live in the enjoyment of that exclusive relationship with himself, for which he recreated them. "I will be your God and you shall be my people." Such anger is the other side of a love that will not let us go, a love that disciplines, in order to restore.

That's why the cycle begins again (cf. Judg. 2:11–15). In the bitter regret of his wounded love, God hands his covenant people over to the Philistines and Ammonites (10: 7) and from the very beginning the effect is devastating. They were *"harassed and oppressed,"* "shattered and crushed" (NIV), for eighteen years. Not only did the invaders subdue the land of Gilead, east of the Jordan, but they crossed the river into the land itself to devastate Judah, Benjamin, and Ephraim. The resulting distress was severe and widespread. But that is where sin always gets us. Its promises are never fulfilled. A little compromise with the surrounding tribes seemed such a sensible policy. Take on board a little of their culture and religion and peaceful coexistence would become a certainty.

Peace and prosperity were the goals, but instead it turned God's face against them. It was, and is, a bitter pill to swallow; but can there be a more important lesson for a human being to learn? When has the devil ever produced what was promised? He never produces the alluring fruit for which we have yielded to his temptation in the first place. He cannot, and has not the slightest interest in doing so. We are at our most foolish when we imagine that Satan has anyone's interests at heart, other than his own. All he wants to do is to trap and destroy his victims, to shatter and crush men and women made in God's image.

Jesus warned us all: ". . . your father the devil, . . . was a murderer from the beginning, and does not stand in the truth, because there is no truth in him. When he speaks a lie, he speaks from his own resources, for he is a liar and the father of it. But because I tell the truth, you do not believe Me" (John 8:44–45). Sin always produces great distress, even though sometimes, by God's grace, its effects are delayed. Nevertheless, a broken relationship with God will always result in broken relationships with others—an isolation and aloneness which are sin's dead end.

Sin Rebuked

10 And the children of Israel cried out to the Lord, saying, "We have sinned against You, because we have both forsaken our God and served the Baals!"
11 So the Lord said to the children of Israel, "Did I not deliver you from the Egyptians and from the Amorites and from the people of Ammon and from the Philistines?
12 "Also the Sidonians and Amalekites and Maonites oppressed you; and you cried out to Me, and I delivered you from their hand.
13 "Yet you have forsaken Me and served other gods. Therefore I will deliver you no more.
14 "Go and cry out to the gods which you have chosen; let them deliver you in your time of distress."

Judg. 10:10–14

It took eighteen years for Israel to understand the reality of her situation. Sin is like a drug that paralyzes the will, and it can take a very long time for the victim to realize it. That was the problem for the prodigal son in the story Jesus told. Before he could return to his father in true repentance, casting himself on the father's mercy, which was the prerequisite for his restoration, he had to come to himself. And that only happened when he faced the choice of eating pig-swill or starving. He was that desperate before he decided to make his way back home and confess "I have sinned" (Luke 15:16–19). So it was with Israel, and so it often is with us, too.

Eventually they recognized and confessed the two major ingredients of their sin—forsaking God and serving idols (v. 10). But if they had expected this to trigger an "open sesame" from their problems, they were disappointed. The downward spiral has an intensifying effect. As the sin pattern repeats throughout the book, so God deals with it more severely each time. As judges are raised up, so each one is more flawed and failing than the last. God may still deliver, but days of victory and prosperity can only be enjoyed by an obedient and faithful people. Discipline resisted has to be stepped up.

God's rebuke comes through a prophetic utterance (v. 11). As so often in Old Testament instruction, God counsels his people to look back and learn lessons in the present from their past. Their very existence as a nation, created through the Exodus from Egypt, was totally dependent on the divine initiative. It was he who had enabled them to overthrow Sihon, king of the Amorites, and settle his land (see Numbers 21:26–31). Their deliverance from the Ammonites through Ehud (3:12ff.), and from the Philistines through Shamgar and his ox goad (3:31), were mighty acts of God. While the present book gives no documentation of a Sidonian oppression, the Amalekites and Maonites (probably the Midianites, as in the Septuagint) referred to in verse 12 take us back to Gideon's story (chapters 6–8). *"I delivered you"* is the constant refrain in all these incidents. Again and again God had stepped in to rescue them when all seemed lost. How many times he had called them back to himself!

But verse 13 shows that there comes a point at which sin's dead end has to be faced for what it really is. God's logic is irrefutable. Since Israel has chosen to forsake her covenant responsibilities so consistently and so determinedly, why should he any longer regard his commitment to them as binding? Let them turn to the *"gods"* they have chosen, in preference to the living Lord, to ask for their deliverance (v. 14).

The simplicity of the language and the clarity of the indictment combine to bring home, in a sickening way, to the pit of the stomach, the awful emptiness and hopelessness of being under God's rebuke. Yet God is only being true to his word, for this is what he warned them he would do, back in Deuteronomy 32:37–38.

> "Where are their gods,
> The rock in which they sought refuge?
> Who ate the fat of their sacrifices,
> And drank the wine of their drink offering?
> Let them rise and help you,
> And be your refuge."

It is the classic Old Testament argument against idolatry which we have already noted. There are no other gods, for the idols made by men, however impressive or expensive, are artifacts without life.

Recently I was watching a TV profile of the yuppies of London, who are feeling the pinch of economic stringency in a changed climate from the heady days of the mid-1980s, before the stock market collapse. One young man had been earning £86,000, not far short of 140,000 U.S. dollars, per annum selling commodities, at the age of nineteen. His comment was that the eighteen to twenty-five-year-olds had made money their god and that became the only purpose of life. But the bubble burst; their debts were mountainous, their life-style untenable. Thank God that he still loves his lost world of rebellious human beings enough, sometimes, to rebuke us by leaving us to our own devices until we realize what a desperate dead end sin is. We need to expose our contemporary God-substitutes to the penetrating light of the Old Testament's exposure of idolatry, for what it really is and where it really leads.

SIN REJECTED

> 15 And the children of Israel said to the Lord, "We have sinned! Do to us whatever seems best to You; only deliver us this day, we pray."
> 16 So they put away the foreign gods from among them and served the Lord. And His soul could no longer endure the misery of Israel.
> 17 Then the people of Ammon gathered together and encamped in Gilead. And the children of Israel assembled together and encamped in Mizpah.
> 18 And the people, the leaders of Gilead, said to one another, "Who is the man who will begin the fight against the people of Ammon? He shall be head over all the inhabitants of Gilead."
>
> *Judg. 10:15–18*

The Greek word *metanoia,* which we translate "repentance," means a change of mind. It is in our thought processes that the transformation which issues in a change of action has to begin. Repentance is more than a mere admission of sin, though that confession *"we have sinned"* (v. 15) is the first step. What the people had once regarded as a legitimate expression of their own self-determination is now recognized for what it always was—an offense against God.

But admission, on its own, can mean little more than remorse. The small boy caught pulling his sister's hair may howl in apparent contrition at the punishment he receives, but he may simply be peeved that his misdeed has been discovered. Do the tears signify repentance, or merely remorse? Everything depends on what happens when the adult leaves the room. True repentance is being sorry enough to quit! Just as Israel had chosen to turn away from the Lord, so now they must choose to turn away from idols.

The reality of their repentance is demonstrated, in verse 15, in the request, *"Do to us whatever seems best to You."* That reveals a heart change. While recognizing the justice of what God has said, they would still rather cast themselves upon his mercy than be left in the misery of their sin, without him. They realize that they have no grounds on which to appeal for mercy, but they determine nevertheless to commit their cause to their gracious covenant Lord.

There are no extenuating circumstances. There can be no logical appeal-grounds for clemency. Still, it is better to fall into the hands of the Lord than to be left, isolated in one's sins, a prey to the nations around them. At the same time, they demonstrate the reality of their words by removing the foreign gods and restoring their right and proper worship of Yahweh (v. 16). They turn to him, not in words only, but in deeds and therefore in truth. There was a public break with sin which signified a true change of heart, and this was acceptable to God.

"And his soul could no longer endure the misery of Israel" (v. 16b). Literally, the Hebrew means, his soul became "short" or "impatient." God could bear it no longer. Interestingly, the same word is used in Numbers 21:4 to describe the people becoming very discouraged on their wilderness journey round the borders of Edom, just before they grumbled against God and against Moses and suffered the plague of fiery serpents. Here, in this much more positive context, the Lord can no longer look down at the miseries his people are suffering. As their covenant God he is obligated to help; but in that the covenant expresses his heart toward them, this is no grudging duty, but a deep-rooted response of love. The same love that withdrew his protection and help in order to bring his sinful people to recognize the true consequences of their sin and rebellion now demonstrates itself in pity and compassionate grace. It has achieved the goal of turning them back from their rebellion, to love and serve the Lord. "Punishments and benefits flow from the love of God, and have for their object the happiness and well-being of men."[1] As Israel turned to the Lord, so he also turned, from their sins to their suffering.

The last two verses of the chapter open up a new way through the dead-end sin, as hope is reborn. The scene is set for a dramatic confrontation between the forces of Ammon and of Israel, in Gilead.

The great need, however, is for a leader, a captain; but that lies in the gift of God alone. Strengthened by their renewed repentance and dependence on the Lord, the leaders of Gilead resolve to make a stand against their oppressors and this seems to have startled the Ammonites and delayed their attack. We wait, with bated breath, to see whether and how God will fill the leadership vacuum in Israel. Will he be gracious and raise up another judge?

Meanwhile, in applying this chapter, we need to stress the nature of true repentance, which casts itself upon the mercy of God. There were none of the excuses that so often dilute or even nullify our attempts to repent. Whenever we find ourselves excusing the sins of which God convicts us, we need to realize that our repentance is as yet incomplete. We need to come to the point where we can say with Augustus Toplady:

> Nothing in my hand I bring,
> Simply to Thy cross I cling;
> Naked, come to Thee for dress,
> Helpless, look to Thee for grace;
> Foul, I to the fountain fly,
> Wash me, Savior, or I die!

True repentance realizes that we can do nothing to save ourselves or make ourselves even a fraction more acceptable to God. But the mercy and grace of God are such that, "If we confess our sins, He is faithful and just to forgive us our sins and to cleanse us from all unrighteousness" (1 John 1:9). Repentance and faith are always the only way out of sin's dead end.

> Not the labor of my hands,
> Can fulfill Thy law's demands;
> Could my zeal no respite know,
> Could my tears for ever flow,
> All for sin could not atone;
> Thou must save, and Thou alone.[2]

The tragedy was that it took Israel (and still takes us) so long to learn the lesson.

NOTES

1. Keil and Delitzsch, *Joshua–Samuel*, 377.
2. "Rock of Ages," written by Toplady (1740–1778).

CHAPTER 11

Learning from God's Providence

Judges 11:1–28

Imagine your feelings if you had the misfortune of being one of the soldiers in the Israelite army encamped in Mizpah (10:17). Behind you, you have eighteen years without a single victory—defeat, after massacre, after rout. In front of you are the crack troops of Ammon who by now really believe themselves to be unconquerable. How would you rate your chances, given that there is no Israeli general present who is remotely willing to assume the role of commanding officer? A British poet might well opine, as the sun set on the Empire, "It matters not who won or lost, but how you played the game!" But war with the Ammonites is not a game, and if you lose, you're dead! Either way, life could not have looked very attractive to the soldiers of Israel that day.

However, as readers of the book, we know that another unseen factor is operative, of which they probably had not the remotest idea. The Lord could no longer endure the misery of Israel (10:16b). That is the key to chapter 11, which now unfolds as a demonstration of God's unseen providential love and care.

The lessons of providence still need to be learned in our contemporary congregations. Not long ago an older Christian lady came to see me pastorally about a number of problems that troubled her. None of them was much more than trivial in itself, but together they had become a debilitating burden. In the course of her conversation, I asked her whether she felt that God had begun to answer her prayer about any of her difficulties. She look at me, astonished. "Oh, no," she replied, "I haven't prayed about any of them. They are far too small and insignificant for me to bother the good Lord about them. He's got far more important things to do than be bothered with my little worries!" Gently, I pointed out that this was almost a blasphemy against the "good Lord," whom she had somewhat domesticated and reduced to pocket-size.

The splendor of the living God is not that he is too big to bother with the details of our lives, but that he is so great that he can, and does.

> "Are not two sparrows sold for a copper coin? And not one of them falls to the ground apart from your Father's will. But the very hairs of your head are all numbered. Do not fear therefore; you are of more value than many sparrows."
>
> *Matt. 10:29–31*

The words of Jesus affirm the doctrine of God's providence. Or, as Shakespeare expressed it, in the more secular context of "Hamlet," "There's a divinity that shapes our ends, rough-hew then how we will." The old myth of deism, that God's interest in his creation extended only to setting it all in motion, dies hard. The God of the Bible is not an idle, disinterested heavenly observer, however, but the governor of all that happens in his cosmos, the keeper of the keys. In this chapter, we can see his providential care at work.

The Early Circumstances of Jephthah's Life

> 1 Now Jephthah the Gileadite was a mighty man of valor, but he was the son of a harlot; and Gilead begot Jephthah.
>
> 2 Gilead's wife bore sons; and when his wife's sons grew up, they drove Jephthah out, and said to him, "You shall have no inheritance in our father's house, for you are the son of another woman."
>
> 3 Then Jephthah fled from his brothers and dwelt in the land of Tob; and worthless men banded together with Jephthah and went out raiding with him.
>
> *Judg. 11:1–3*

The power vacuum in Israel's army is about to be filled. The mighty warrior of Gilead exists all right, but he is not where you might expect to find him. Like Gideon, David, Jeremiah, and many of God's great men, Jephthah would not have gotten far in the interview stage for a leadership post. From the beginning, he had all the built-in disadvantages of the outsider. Like Abimelech, he lacked breeding, even legitimacy; he was the son of a prostitute. His half brothers soon got rid of him so that he could have no claim or part in the family inheritance (v. 2).

Jephthah fled to Syria where his natural leadership gifts seem to have attracted to him a band of adventurers who, like their leader, lived outside normal society. In the upheavals of this time when everyone did what was right in his own eyes it would be increasingly difficult to stop marauding bands of hoodlums who were out to make all they could for themselves from the prevailing insecurity. The history of the Wild West, both real and celluloid, doubtless provides plenty of examples of the Jephthah gang syndrome. They were "soldiers of fortune," who lived by their wits.

It would be difficult to imagine a less promising background, but in the providence of God this was how he had been training his deliverer, through the long years of the Ammonite oppression. With that sort of background, Jephthah's personality was not going to score high on the "compliance" or "introvert" scales. This man was used to fighting for everything he had. He had developed into a shrewd and effective leader who was not afraid of standing up for his rights, and who commanded loyalty and respect. He was clearly a man of considerable personal strength and resourcefulness. Most important of all, he was God's man who had been tailor-made through the rough, tough experiences of life to take on the job when the time came for it.

Jephthah's story is a powerful reminder to us Christians today, with our highly developed personality inventories and assessment packages, not to write anybody off from having a place to fulfill in the work of God's kingdom. Our danger is that we become too controlled by the perceptions of the secular world around us, so that we apply its criteria unchanged to the operations of God's work. Without in any way condoning the mediocre or losing sight of our quest for excellence in the work of God, we must nevertheless ensure that we make room for a biblical balance.

> Not many wise according to the flesh, not many mighty, not many noble, are called. But God has chosen the foolish things of

> the world to put to shame the wise, and God has chosen the weak things of the world to put to shame the things which are mighty; and the base things of the world and the things which are despised God has chosen, and the things which are not, to bring to nothing the things that are, that no flesh should glory in His presence.
>
> *1 Cor. 1:26–29*

If God is "able to raise up children to Abraham from these stones" (Matt. 3:9), then he does not need to advertise or headhunt the situations vacant for his work.

It is worth applying this principle a little more closely. There are churches around the world that would not think of appointing a senior pastor who did not have an earned doctorate. Some of these pastorates, in the Far East for instance, remain vacant for long periods for this reason. While I am second to none in arguing for a highly educated ministry, I cannot help asking whether such a criteria is the right one. Could this elevation of the academic over spiritual maturity and gift actually frustrate God's work? Gladys Aylward, whose ministry was so greatly used in China, was turned down by the societies as being unsuitable material. Were they right? Some of our criteria regarding evangelical background or pedigree may prove to be quite irrelevant, in the last analysis, to the spread of the kingdom. God has a way of sidetracking our official channels and raising up his Jephthahs, which we ignore or despise at our peril. Church history is liberally sprinkled with stories of the Lord's "irregulars," who have been used to turn the tide, often in spectacular ways.

In fact, the very band of disciples chosen by our Lord would not have impressed most management consultants. Jim Graham quoted the following "Memorandum" at the 1989 Keswick Convention in England:

> To: Jesus, Son of Joseph, Woodcrafter's Shop, Nazareth
> From: The Jordan Management Consultants, Jerusalem
> Subject: A Staff Aptitude Evaluation
> Thank you for submitting the résumés of the twelve men you have picked for management positions in your new organization. All of them have now taken our battery of tests and we've not only run the results through our computer, but also arranged personal interviews for each of them with our psychologist and

vocational aptitude consultant, bless him. It is the staff opinion that most of your nominees are lacking in background, education, and vocational aptitude for the type of enterprise you are undertaking. They do not have the team concept. We would recommend that you continue your search for persons of experience in managerial ability and proven capability. Simon Peter is emotionally unstable and given to fits of temper. Andrew has absolutely no qualities of leadership. The two brothers James and John, the sons of Zebedee, place personal interest above company loyalty. Thomas demonstrates a questioning attitude that would tend to undermine morale. We feel that it's our duty to tell you that Matthew has been blacklisted by the Greater Jerusalem Better Business Bureau. James, the son of Alphaeus, and Thaddaeus definitely have radical leanings and they both registered a high score on the manic depressive scale. One of the candidates, however, shows great potential. He is a man of ability and resourcefulness, meets people well, has a keen business mind, and has contact in high places. He is highly motivated, ambitious, and innovative. We recommend Judas Iscariot as your controller and right-hand man. All the other profiles are self-explanatory. We wish you every success in your new venture.

One further application is also worthy of our consideration. We need to encourage those in our churches, who feel they are nobodies, not to allow disadvantages in their backgrounds or setbacks in life to discourage or disqualify them from serving the Lord. Let us affirm that God has something for each of his dearly loved children to do, something that is precious to him and unique to us as individuals.

So many Christians waste their time and energy grieving over something they never had, and that is very counterproductive. This is all the more the case in a day like our own, when there is a great interest in the healing of memories. Of course it is often right and helpful to try to understand why we react wrongly to the problems and disappointments of life, and even to work through old bitternesses and grievances that have lain undealt with, festering in our souls, perhaps for years. I can think of a lady, over eighty now, who has found new peace in the last two years by being able to forgive her mother for the verbal and physical abuse she suffered at her hands seventy years ago. That is one thing; but to pine for a past, which in his providence God did not permit us to enjoy, can be a paralyzing exercise in self-indulgence and self-pity that sours the soul and alienates our friends. There is not a human being alive who has not suffered in some way from his or her parenting, since we all had fallible, sinful human beings to parent us, and are no different ourselves. As one has observed, "the trouble with parenting is that by the time you have the experience you are redundant."

To be always looking back over one's shoulder wishing that father had been more demonstrative, mother less demanding, and that the family circumstances had been different, is to be both ungrateful for God's providence and unrealistic about life in a fallen world. Some of us have had a raw deal out of life, but we need to recognize that God's providence means that he weaves the strands together to make each of us the unique individual we all are, and that is for his glory. There are no mistakes, no accidents with God; no pages to be torn up. It all counts. The story of Jephthah provides us with a key example to encourage our "no hopers" not to write themselves out of the script, but to make themselves freshly available to their totally ingenious Lord.

The Wise Negotiation of Gilead's Elders

4 It came to pass after a time that the people of Ammon made war against Israel.

5 And so it was, when the people of Ammon made war against Israel, that the elders of Gilead went to get Jephthah from the land of Tob.

6 Then they said to Jephthah, "Come and be our commander, that we may fight against the people of Ammon."

7 So Jephthah said to the elders of Gilead, "Did you not hate me, and expel me from my father's house? Why have you come to me now when you are in distress?"

8 And the elders of Gilead said to Jephthah, "That is why we have turned again to you now, that you may go with us and fight against the people of Ammon, and be our head over all the inhabitants of Gilead."

9 So Jephthah said to the elders of Gilead, "If you take me back home to fight against the people of

> Ammon, and the Lord delivers them to me, shall I be your head?"
>
> 10 And the elders of Gilead said to Jephthah, "The Lord will be a witness between us, if we do not do according to your words."
>
> 11 Then Jephthah went with the elders of Gilead, and the people made him head and commander over them; and Jephthah spoke all his words before the Lord in Mizpah.
>
> *Judg. 11:4–11*

After sketching in the background, verse 4 now brings us right up to date. We are back in the battle zone at Mizpah, with our understandably nervous Israeli soldiers. The ineffective military leaders, who seem to have been unable to make up their minds as to who should draw the short straw to take on the Ammonites for the next round, are now overruled by the civic elders of Gilead, whose decisive action is to recruit Jephthah. This cannot have been an easy decision since it involved them swallowing their pride to recall a man whose very banishment they had apparently sanctioned (v. 7). The dialogue between them, recorded in verses 6–10, is a fascinating piece of boardroom politics.

The elders' opening ploy is to offer Jephthah a limited role as military commander (v. 6). This is the immediate need and he has the experience to fill it. But the outlaw leader is more than a match for the smooth-talking politicians. He is going to extract the maximum personal benefit from this unexpected change of fortunes.

Jephthah's response in verse 7, *"Why have you come to me now when you are in distress?"* bears a very close resemblance to the response of God in 10:14. The Lord's unwillingness to be used by Israel, on their terms, is closely paralleled here by Jephthah's. In this reflective irony, with which Judges abounds, surely we are meant to get the point again. They cannot cope with the enemy unless they are helped by the very person whom they have rejected. And there is the same initial rebuttal, which eventually leads to a renewed awareness of dependence and a deeper commitment. In their relationship with God, this meant that Yahweh must have no rivals in their affections. In the case of Jephthah, they have to offer him a much more extended authority, as *"head over all the inhabitants of Gilead"* (v. 8), a role at once more prestigious and more permanent.

Jephthah, however, has still not finished his bargaining. The rags-to-riches story has to be hardened into a firm contract while the elders are hardly in a position to deny him (vv. 9–10). Both parties appeal to the Lord as their witness. For Jephthah, victory over the Ammonites will be divine endorsement of his right to rule. For the elders, the Lord is a silent witness to their new leader's commitment. Indeed, so relieved are the people at the success of the elders' diplomatic excursion in bringing Jephthah back that they confirm him as both their civil and military head in a formal ceremony before the Lord in Mizpah, even before the battle is joined.

In all of this, the writer means us to recognize the providence of God at work. But if there are parallels with Israel's approach to God in chapter 10, there is also a wide divergence in terms of the response. Their God can bear his people's misery no longer because his heart is moved with love and pity toward his covenant people, in spite of their stubborn rebellion. Their human leader, however, is interested only in his personal position and prestige. He has driven a hard bargain because he is more interested in being ruler than in those he is to rule.

Yet even in this we see the providential hand of God. He is giving the people the leadership they deserve. Although they are going to be delivered from their oppressors, there is still a price to pay. The downward spiral of sin pays its own wages. God never ceases to be gracious, but one aspect of his love may be to teach us the hard lesson that we cannot go on sinning with impunity. We cannot expect God to raise up quality leadership, at the drop of a hat, to airlift us out of the pits we have dug through our sinfulness. His providence is active in the chain of spiritual cause and effect which he has built into his government of the world. We are responsible human beings, so the moral and spiritual choices we make do have repercussions.

We may live in a society in which "it doesn't matter" has become a popular exit route from accepting our personal responsibilities; but it does matter to God. There can be no substitute for obedience. It is the height of spiritual folly to open the lion's mouth, insert one's head, and then pray fervently to the Lord that it will not be bitten off! God's providence does not remove human responsibility, but works through it. To change the image and culture, in the words of the old Chinese proverb: "You can't stop the birds from flying over your head, but you can stop them building their nests in your hair!"

His Sovereign Control of Israel's History

12 Now Jephthah sent messengers to the king of the
people of Ammon, saying, "What do you have against
me, that you have come to fight against me in my land?"
13 And the king of the people of Ammon answered the messengers of Jephthah, "Because Israel
took away my land when they came up out of Egypt,
from the Arnon as far as the Jabbok, and to the Jordan.
Now therefore, restore those lands peaceably."
14 So Jephthah again sent messengers to the king
of the people of Ammon,
15 and said to him, "Thus says Jephthah: 'Israel
did not take away the land of Moab, nor the land of the
people of Ammon;
16 "'for when Israel came up from Egypt, they
walked through the wilderness as far as the Red Sea
and came to Kadesh.
17 "'Then Israel sent messengers to the king of
Edom, saying, "Please let me pass through your land."
But the king of Edom would not heed. And in like
manner they sent to the king of Moab, but he would
not consent. So Israel remained in Kadesh.
18 "'And they went along through the wilderness
and bypassed the land of Edom and the land of Moab,
came to the east side of the land of Moab, and encamped on the other side of the Arnon. But they did
not enter the border of Moab, for the Arnon was the
border of Moab.
19 "'Then Israel sent messengers to Sihon king of
the Amorites, king of Heshbon; and Israel said to him,
"Please let us pass through your land into our place."
20 "'But Sihon did not trust Israel to pass through
his territory. So Sihon gathered all his people together,
encamped in Jahaz, and fought against Israel.
21 "'And the Lord God of Israel delivered Sihon
and all his people into the hand of Israel, and they
defeated them. Thus Israel gained possession of all the
land of the Amorites, who inhabited that country.
22 "'They took possession of all the territory of the
Amorites, from the Arnon to the Jabbok and from
the wilderness to the Jordan.

23 "'And now the Lord God of Israel has dispossessed the Amorites from before His people Israel; should you then possess it?
24 "'Will you not possess whatever Chemosh your god gives you to possess? So whatever the Lord our God takes possession of before us, we will possess.
25 "'And now, are you any better than Balak the son of Zippor, king of Moab? Did he ever strive against Israel? Did he ever fight against them?
26 "'While Israel dwelt in Heshbon and its villages, in Aroer and it villages, and in all the cities along the banks of the Arnon, for three hundred years, why did you not recover them within that time?
27 "'Therefore I have not sinned against you, but you wronged me by fighting against me. May the Lord, the Judge, render judgment this day between the children of Israel and the people of Ammon.'"
28 However, the king of the people of Ammon did not heed the words which Jephthah sent him.

Judg. 11:12–28

Although Jephthah was a mighty warrior, he seems also to have been a shrewd diplomat. He begins his campaign not by mobilizing the army, but in negotiation with the enemy. By seizing the initiative, he is able to occupy a position of moral strength. So the new ruler of Israel sends messengers to discover the cause of Ammon's antagonism, which is declared to be all about territory (v. 13). The simple request is that all the territory (*"my land"*) settled by Israel east of the Jordan should be returned to Ammonite sovereignty.

Jephthah's answer is a detailed one. In fact, what we are seeing here are two diametrically opposite views of history in collision with each other, and that not just about boundary disputes, but about who is in charge of this world. The fundamental issue is whether the Creator God has the freedom to allot territories and boundaries in the world he has made, or whether man is in charge of its living space.

Jephthah's tactics take both dimensions into account. He answers the human arguments at a political level, but is not content to allow the discussion to remain there. His first strategy is to establish the facts. This is plain common sense, but amazingly it is often ignored in all sorts of disputes. Jephthah denies the charge that Israel had taken the land of Moab or of the Ammonites when the nation came out of

Egypt (vv. 14–18). On the contrary, they had been careful to ask for permission even to travel through. They only fought King Sihon when he refused them such permission and massed his armies to oppose them. It was Yahweh who delivered him and his people into their hands (v. 21), enabling them to take possession of Amorite territory (see Numbers 21:21–31). Though the Ammonites bordered on this territory it had never belonged to them.

Having stated the facts, Jephthah next takes care to establish the ground rules. He reminds the enemy that Balak, king of Moab, had not questioned Israel's right to the land she had conquered, although he had resisted Israel's advance and tried to hire the prophet Balaam to curse the nation. Why then should the king of Ammon raise the matter three hundred years later when he could establish no right to the disputed territory anyway? Clearly, the reality was that Ammon was in an expansionist phase, had mopped up Moab, and was now ambitious to add Israel to her empire. Even on these political grounds, Israel was morally in the right, facing an unprovoked attack by a greedy colonializing power (v. 27).

However, Israel's judge is not content for the dialogue to remain at the level of human politics. In Jephthah's view there is a third clinching argument, which involves the recognition of God's sovereignty. Why had Israel originally taken the land? The answer is made abundantly plain. Yahweh, God of Israel, had given it to his people (v. 21). He drove out the Amorites (v. 23). So Jephthah does not hesitate to lift the struggle above the level of political dispute or military engagement to a conflict between the two nations' gods. Verse 24 states the issue beautifully. *"Will you not possess whatever Chemosh your god gives you to possess? So whatever Yahweh our God takes possession of before us, we will possess."*

Jephthah sees this conflict as an earthly battleground for a supernatural encounter between the living God and the false idols which had oppressed the people for so many years. Chemosh was the god of the Moabites, who were the original owners of the land. He had been worshiped by the idolatrous Israelites as part of their pantheon (10:6). If, however, he had any power at all, would he not have used it to keep his possession? Will he not use it now to retrieve it? The implication is that he is powerless. He can do nothing because he is nothing. The battle is therefore a direct challenge to the false religion represented by Ammon which has been the root cause of Israel's eighteen years of misery. As Jephthah commits his and the nation's cause to the living God, Israel is restored from her folly, to faith (v. 27). But this is a totally different way of looking at the world and we should not be surprised that the Ammonites dismiss it as totally irrelevant. The same will often happen today when pagan people are asked to introduce God into the equation. They have no need of that hypothesis!

We live in a world where the two systems are still in conflict. Recently, in Britain, we have been celebrating the fiftieth anniversary of the evacuation of the British army from the beaches of Normandy, and especially from Dunkirk. At a time when it seemed that Hitler's Germany was about to obliterate our forces, in the darkest days of 1940, the country witnessed an amazing deliverance. An armada of small boats crossed the English Channel to the French coast to rescue the troops. Many of the vessels were hardly seaworthy, but the channel was remarkably calm for several days and a miraculous evacuation was achieved. At the time, many attributed this to a direct intervention by God, in answer to a nation's prayers, as the thanksgiving services afterward testified.

Fifty years on, and much further away from any national belief in a living God, a leading national newspaper, the London *Times*, in recalling the event could only speak of being lucky with the weather. There are two fundamentally different ways of looking at the world, the movements of the nations, the rise and fall of leaders, as well as the detailed circumstances of our individual lives. Everything depends on whether God really exists.

Bible believers know that there is an unseen hand that guides and governs. "We know that all things work together for good to those who love God . . ." (Rom. 8:28). That can sometimes seem a rather glib statement, because the translation often puts the emphasis on the "things" rather than on "God" (as in the New King James Version). This could imply the sovereignty of circumstances, rather than of God. It might even indicate a sort of desperation as God tries to cope with unexpected, dangerous, or difficult situations, as though he had no control over their appearance. That is why I prefer what I believe to be the more accurate and helpful rendering of the New International Version, "We know that in all things God works for the good of those who love him. . . ."

Trust in a sovereign God is one characteristic mark of believers. We may not understand why things happen as they do. It would not necessarily help us to cope if we did. We come back often to the recognition of Deuteronomy 29:29 that "'the secret things belong to the Lord our God, but those things which are revealed belong to us and to our children for ever, that we may do all the words of this law.'" This is the faith that goes on obeying the revealed counsel of God, even when it cannot see where the road leads or why it has to be traveled. This is what being a believer is all about. We cannot call God to render an account to us, but in the words of John Calvin,

> We must reverence his secret judgments, since his will is the truly just cause of everything.

Such a faith does not relieve us of the proper human responsibility for our actions. It does not excuse us from a watchful care in the way that we make our decisions and conduct our lives. Nor does it ignore the problem of human sin or change the fact that we may often have to live with the consequences of our own wrong choices, perhaps for a very long time. All that would tend toward fatalism. Rather, this biblical faith in a God "whose love is as great as his power," who is constantly operating in sovereignty for the good of his loved ones, enriches our confidence in the divine promises (he *will* act) and increases our gratitude for all the blessings that we do already enjoy. It develops our perseverance when things are tough by releasing us from an energy-sapping anxiety about the future, because we know it could not be in safer hands. When we are unjustly attacked, it teaches us to commit our way to God (see 1 Peter 4:19). Rightly to grasp the great truth of God's providence means that we can fearlessly and unreservedly commit ourselves to him. "For He Himself has said, 'I will never leave you nor forsake you.' So we may boldly say: 'The Lord is my helper; I will not fear. What can man do to me?'" (Heb. 13:5–6).

CHAPTER 12

The Enemy Within

Judges 11:29–12:15

It was the Greeks who made an art form out of human tragedy. The heroes of their tragic dramas rose too high, grew too confident, flew too free until one fatal misjudgment or mistake unraveled all that they had so diligently achieved. Shakespeare developed the genre in his greatest plays. We think of Macbeth's ambition, Hamlet's indecision, Lear's incredulity—and we see our own weaknesses reflected in them as we watch them being precipitated from the heights of influence and power into a tragic nemesis over which they have no control. What the playwright creates for the stage is the stuff of human life, played out in a million obscure dramas of secret sorrow and tragedy.

In the words of Carl E. Armerding, the account before us in Judges 11 is a tragic story "tenderly told, with emphasis on the emotions of both parties taking the place of gruesome details of the sacrifice. It stands as one of the most beautiful expressions of tragedy in the entire Bible."[1] A wise preacher will be particularly sensitive to the hurting hearts and the personal tragedies of his congregation as he seeks to bring this ancient story alive today.

Overactive Doubt Brings Tragedy

> 29 Then the Spirit of the Lord came upon Jephthah, and he passed through Gilead and Manasseh, and passed through Mizpah of Gilead; and from Mizpah of Gilead he advanced toward the people of Ammon.

30 And Jephthah made a vow to the Lord, and said, "If You will indeed deliver the people of Ammon into my hands,

31 "then it will be that whatever comes out of the doors of my house to meet me, when I return in peace from the people of Ammon, shall surely be the Lord's, and I will offer it up as a burnt offering."

32 So Jephthah advanced toward the people of Ammon to fight against them, and the Lord delivered them into his hands.

33 And he defeated them from Aroer as far as Minnith—twenty cities—and to Abel Keramim, with a very great slaughter. Thus the people of Ammon were subdued before the children of Israel.

34 When Jephthah came to his house at Mizpah, there was his daughter, coming out to meet him with timbrels and dancing; and she was his only child. Besides her he had neither son nor daughter.

35 And it came to pass, when he saw her, that he tore his clothes, and said, "Alas, my daughter! You have brought me very low! You are among those who trouble me! For I have given my word to the Lord, and I cannot go back on it."

36 So she said to him, "My father, if you have given your word to the Lord, do to me according to what has gone out of your mouth, because the Lord has avenged you of your enemies, the people of Ammon."

37 Then she said to her father, "Let this thing be done for me: let me alone for two months, that I may go and wander on the mountains and bewail my virginity, my friends and I."

38 So he said, "Go." And he sent her away for two months; and she went with her friends, and bewailed her virginity on the mountains.

39 And it was so at the end of two months that she returned to her father, and he carried out his vow with her which he had vowed. She knew no man. And it became a custom in Israel

40 that the daughters of Israel went four days each year to lament the daughter of Jephthah the Gileadite.

Judg. 11:29–40

With the failure of diplomacy (v. 28), the time has come for action. It is significant that the Spirit of God takes the initiative in empowering Jephthah for the task of military leadership against the pagan oppressors. In spite of the natural gifts and experience Jephthah had, which led the elders of Israel to select him in the first place, the writer of Judges wants us to realize that divine enabling stands behind the great victory over Ammon recorded in verse 33. It is significant, too, that the sequence, which began back in 10:6 and comes to its fulfillment here, concludes with only the briefest of descriptions of the battle itself. The Bible's agenda, reflecting the concerns of its divine author, is always more concerned about God's work in the life of the man he chooses to take up and use, than with what he does through him. In our activist age we need to be reminded often that what we are before God is more important than what we accomplish for him. Relationship matters more than service. Indeed, the one is the precondition of the other.

In the light of this, Jephthah's error is truly tragic. The effect of verses 29 and 33 is of a man whose progress is irresistible because the wind of God is blowing in his sails. Gathering troops in Gilead and Manasseh, he devastates the Ammonite occupied towns, forcing the invaders back behind their own borders. But in between those verses, the tragic mistake has already occurred. What Jephthah promised God is in itself very strange. Modern translations tend to translate the word in verse 31 as neuter—"*whatever comes out of the doors of my house to meet me.*" It is as though he might be expecting a pet animal, or a sheep or an oxen to be the referent. But it would be very strange to speak of being met by one's animal; and also, the feminine form would generally be used to denote the neuter, whereas here the form is masculine. It seems then that Jephthah had in mind the extraordinary expedient of a human sacrifice with which to honor the Lord, if victory was granted to him.

This presents us with a number of problems. Surely, even in a time of spiritual decline such as this, Jephthah could not possibly have been ignorant of the Lord's abhorrence of human sacrifice. While it is true that the prohibitions in Leviticus 18:21 and 20:2–5 are particularly against sacrificing children to Molech, in Deuteronomy 12:29–31 and 18:9–10, the instructions are much wider ranging and could hardly be more specific. "You shall not worship the Lord your God in that way; for every abomination to the Lord which he hates they have done to their gods; for they burn even their sons and daughters in the fire to their gods" (Deut. 12:31). Jephthah must have known that such an offering would be abhorrent to God. So why did he make the vow?

In an attempt to solve this problem, commentators from the Middle Ages onward have claimed that Jephthah's daughter was not sacrificed. Taking the picture of Jephthah's exemplary devotion to the Lord from these two chapters and adding the other biblical commendations of him as a man of faith, sent by God (1 Sam. 12:11; Heb. 11:32), these commentators argue that he could not have actually sacrificed his daughter, but that he used the two months of verse 39 to reflect on his vow and concluded that to perform it literally would be a more serious sin than to break it. Accordingly, it is claimed, he kept the spiritual intent of his vow by dedicating his daughter to a life of perpetual virginity, banishing her from his home and normal human society, so that she was effectively dead to him, leaving him without hope of an heir. This would have been a very costly sacrifice for Jephthah if that is how the vow was fulfilled. While that interpretation is ingenious and would commend itself to our humanitarian feelings, I cannot personally find any cause to disagree with Luther's characteristically blunt assertion, quoted by Goslinga, "One would like to think that he did not sacrifice her, but the text clearly says that he did."[2]

So we are left with the question Why? Surely, we should explore what lies behind the action. A vow always starts with "if"; it is an attempt to strike a bargain. If God does his part in granting a particular request, then the person in need will do his part for God as an act of sacrificial thanksgiving. If God will prove in a tangible, undeniable way that he really is there and that he is active on behalf of the petitioner, then he or she will pay up what is due. It's a way of buying God off. How many men in battle have prayed, "God, if you get me out of this alive, I'll give my life to you!" And how many have forgotten him as soon as the emergency was over? How many prayers for healing, or for financial security, have had the same motivation and contents?

Jephthah's action is showing us something that is endemic in the human heart. We all tend to act this way. We Christians say we believe in God's unconditional love, but when we get into a tight scrape, our lives betray us. We begin to bargain with God, because we don't really trust him. We so desperately want to see his power at work on our behalf, to improve our circumstances, or grant us what we call success, that we offer him anything if he will only intervene. And that is really creating God in *our* image, in our human faithlessness, rather than believing his revelation, as, for example, it is declared in the ringing assurances of Romans 8:31–39.

The tragedy is that Jephthah had no need to make the vow. God was already with him. The Spirit of the Lord was already upon him. But Jephthah's experience of the Spirit, in common with all the great heroes of the Old Testament, lacked the personal dimension of indwelling, which is the birthright of the New Testament believer. John tells us that Jesus spoke concerning the Spirit:

> whom those believing in Him would receive; for the Holy Spirit was not yet given, because Jesus was not yet glorified.
>
> *John 7:39*

The Holy Spirit, as the divine, eternal Third Person of the holy trinity, was present and active from the very beginning (Gen. 1:2), but his ministry in the Old Testament was to "come upon" certain individuals, to equip them with power, in order to accomplish God's will. The fruit of the Cross and the Resurrection of our Lord Jesus Christ guarantees the indwelling of the Spirit in the lives of all who turn to him in repentance and faith. That is how the quality of holiness is increasingly produced in the life of the believer, and Jephthah did not enjoy that privilege.

Perhaps he feared that God's presence and power would be withdrawn, leaving him and his forces exposed to the enemy. His fatal mistakes were to fail to trust God, and to believe that he could drive a bargain with the Almighty. These were the products of overactive doubt, which always wants to ensure that we are in control. At its root, every failure of faith is a failure to leave things in God's hands and let him work them out according to his sovereign will. Every desire to manipulate God puts us in control rather than him. We become God, and he becomes our powerful servant. That was the unbelief which ultimately led to Jephthah's tragedy.

God was faithful. The victory was accomplished, but not because of Jephthah's vow. There is a grave danger in seeing faith as a means by which we persuade a reluctant God to give us what we want. We may not necessarily express it by a vow; sometimes we use fasting in the same way. If I deny myself food, that will prove to God how much I mean business. Then surely he will be more inclined to give me what I am asking for. We don't often put it as baldly as that, but we ought to, so as to understand the mechanisms of our own divided self-seeking hearts!

The sovereignty of God means that we cannot coerce him, and some of us mere mortals have a hard time accepting that. Our motivation in tithing can be similarly warped. If I give my tithes and offerings, then God is under obligation to pour in more, so that I shall be better off than had I not tithed. This reduces a relationship of loving, submissive faith to the plane of a manipulative, depersonalized mechanism. And of course it doesn't work! Nothing that we try in order to bring God to heel ever works, except to destroy faith in the true and living God and reduce our religious experience to a self-deluded trust in a pocket-sized, man-made idol.

But, like us, Jephthah was a casualty of the day in which he lived. As has already been pointed out, each of the succession of judges is progressively more flawed, spiritually, than his or her predecessor. Jephthah was clearly influenced by the syncretism of his culture, to the extent that he tried to conduct his own relationship with Yahweh, much as one of the pagans from the nations around Israel would have conducted his. Human religion is always a matter of driving bargains, taking up positions, controlling powers, all to the advantage of oneself. But you cannot interact with the living God in that self-centered way.

Faithlessness has its own consequences. God's faithfulness in providing the victory required the fulfillment of Jephthah's incautious, faithless vow. The story is poignantly told and heart-rending in its tragedy: "*There was his daughter* . . . she was his only child" (v. 34). ". . . 'Alas, my daughter!'" (v. 35). What is remarkable is that the girl submitted to the fulfillment of the vow, because of her father's word, given to the Lord. This at least illustrates the residual faith and respect in Israel, and is perhaps a recognition on her part that her life was the cost of the national victory (v. 36). The rest of the story is recounted sparingly. For two months the daughter and her friends bewail her fate. The emphasis on her virginity, rather than her death, is used by some to support the idea that she was not in fact sacrificed. But the denial of her opportunity to bear children would in itself be a cause of great sorrow. It was as though her life purpose had been denied. And Jephthah had an annual reminder of it, that must have been very difficult to bear (v. 40).

In applying the passage, we need to bear in mind two extremes which are likely to be exemplified in most congregations. There will be those who are careless in their relationship with the Lord, who have made reckless promises in the past which have never been fulfilled and who need to be made aware of the sin of faithless bargaining with God. Repentance and renewed submission to his sovereign control of their lives can be the only ways forward.

But there will also be those who, in their heightened sensitivity, are only too well aware of tragic mistakes in the past, mistakes for which they have never really been able to forgive themselves, in spite of confession and repentance. The fact that we have to live with the consequences of our foolishness is clearly a biblical lesson from Jephthah, but it can be applied in a demoralizing, paralyzing way. For such hearers, it may be helpful to take a New Testament illustration, such as Saul of Tarsus, before his conversion, persecuting the church. Paul never was able to forget what it meant to be the "chief" of sinners (1 Tim. 1:15). Doubtless he often looked back to the martyrdom of Stephen, or to the imprisonment of other disciples with deep sorrow and regret. There was a sense in which he had to live with the consequences throughout his life, but he knew that they were not held against him by God. He was forgiven! Nor did they disqualify him from being called and used in God's service. Nor did they lessen his confidence in God's plans and purposes for his life.

The purpose of the past is not to haunt the present, but to make us cleave the harder to Christ. If we learn something of the depravity of our own hearts, of the mistakes we are capable of making and the sins we are capable of plunging headlong into, we shall find ourselves readier to hold onto the grace of God in Jesus Christ, and to walk humbly with him (Mic. 6:8; Gal. 5:16).

Inactive Criticism Brings Tragedy

1 Then the men of Ephraim gathered together,
crossed over towards Zaphon, and said to Jephthah,
"Why did you cross over to fight against the people of

Ammon, and did not call us to go with you? We will burn your house down on you with fire!"

2 And Jephthah said to them, "My people and I were in a great struggle with the people of Ammon; and when I called you, you did not deliver me out of their hands.

3 "So when I saw that you would not deliver me, I took my life in my hands and crossed over against the people of Ammon; and the Lord delivered them into my hand. Why then have you come up to me this day to fight against me?"

4 Now Jephthah gathered together all the men of Gilead and fought against Ephraim. And the men of Gilead defeated Ephraim, because they said, "You Gileadites are fugitives of Ephraim among the Ephraimites and among the Manassites."

5 The Gileadites seized the fords of the Jordan before the Ephraimites arrived. And when any Ephraimite who escaped said, "Let me cross over," the men of Gilead would say to him, "Are you an Ephraimite?" If he said, "No,"

6 then they would say to him, "Then say, 'Shibboleth'!" And he would say, "Sibboleth," for he could not pronounce it right. Then they would take him and kill him at the fords of the Jordan. There fell at that time forty-two thousand Ephraimites.

7 And Jephthah judged Israel six years. Then Jephthah the Gileadite died and was buried among the cities of Gilead.

Judg. 12:1–7

The last episode of Jephthah's story takes another nose dive. We have already learned from the story of Gideon that victory can sometimes be harder for people to handle than defeat. And other people's victories can be even more difficult. Once again the enemy is within; not this time in Jephthah's own distorted spirituality but among his kinsmen, from the tribe of Ephraim. Jealousy is a terrible monster. Back in Gideon's day the Ephraimites had complained that they were left out of the battle with the Midianites, but Gideon's diplomacy had avoided conflict with them (8:1–3). Not so with Jephthah. A posse of Ephraimites crosses the Jordan near Zaphon to present an ultimatum to the judge in Gilead (v. 1). They will incinerate him inside his house because he did not call on their help to fight the Ammonites. But this time they are met, not by diplomacy, but by a forceful assertion that they are in the wrong, followed up by military force (v. 4).

Jephthah's case (vv. 2–3) is that he did call on the Ephraimites for help, though there is no record in the text of that happening. However, since they declined to be involved in the great struggle, they can hardly hope to have had any part in the celebrations and glory of the victory. The implication is that they lacked the courage to get involved, and that must clearly be traceable to a lack of faith in the Lord. He it was who secured the victory, but they were not prepared to trust him and fight. This reminds us that faith is not a comfortable address at which to live.

We like to think of faith growing and developing quietly, in a peaceful, favored situation, without the need for conflict or struggle. Actually, faith is like a muscle. It only grows strong when it is exercised, and that may well involve us in breaking through successive pain barriers if its full potential is going to be developed. Nobody ever won a gold medal for weightlifting painlessly! Faith usually has to be exercised in the middle of confusion and uncertainty, when the battle is at its toughest and its outcome undecided. For those who have been armchair spectators to come along and criticize after the event, when they were not prepared to accept the risk of participation, is indefensible. The faithlessness of the Ephraimites led them to the choice not to be involved in what God was doing.

Verse 4 seems to indicate that there was an additional taunt concerning the origin of the Gileadites, which may well reveal that the particular circumstances were merely being used as an excuse to ventilate a longstanding jealousy and breathe new life into an ancient feud. The settlers of Gilead were not a pure tribe like Ephraim, which could trace back its inheritance to the origins of Israel. Instead, they were a mixture of the tribes of Manasseh and Gad. What right, then, did these "half-castes" have to wage war for Israel? Ephraim's arrogance and derision were clearly deep-seated.

But they seem to have underestimated the military leader they had chosen to confront. Jephthah was not one to take their challenge lying down; so when it became clear that a battle was unavoidable, he was ready for them. Not only were they pushed back into their own territory, but when they came to cross the Jordan fords, they found them under the control of Jephthah's men who applied a pronunciation test to determine their identity. The word *"Shibboleth"* means "torrent." In its pure Hebrew form the first consonant is pronounced "sh," but it seems that the Ephraimite dialect pronounced it as a simple "s." The staggering number of those who were killed in the battle, or murdered on the basis of the speech test, reached forty-two thousand. It is that note which sounds in our ears as Jephthah's career comes to its end. His was a comparatively short tenure of office, and a very violent one (v. 7).

Sadly, the green-eyed monster—jealousy—is still alive and well, and living in God's church. A new congregation is planted in a developing housing area as a town overspills into new lots. The existing adjacent congregations demand to know why their permission was not asked before these intruders (who live there anyway) began the new work. They would then have had the opportunity to refuse them. A new pastor comes to a church and begins to develop different avenues of ministry which reach newcomers more effectively than ever before. But the "old guard" do not approve of doing things differently and resist his ideas, refusing to welcome the newcomers in their midst. I have seen both happen in the past five years. Division is the child of jealousy. Instead of seeing ourselves as one people of God, we are back with denominations and personalities, what we like and approve, or dislike and reject. All too often such critics are themselves merely passengers, like the Ephraimites. Wasn't it D. L. Moody who, on being criticized for his evangelistic methods by inactive "permission-withholders," responded by saying, "Well, on the whole, I think God prefers the way I do it, to the way you don't!" It is those who stay outside the battle and gripe from the sidelines who are always the losers, because of their lack of faith.

While we cannot justify Jephthah's extreme revenge against the men of Ephraim, it is at least clear that he did not regard them as being in the category of "weaker brethren." So often, inactive criticism is allowed to bleed away the life of a ministry, or a local church, on the grounds that we must bear with the weaker member who cannot tolerate change, or does not feel comfortable with what is happening. But as one of my colleagues, Trevor Waldock, has expressed it, "Isn't it amazing how the weaker brethren seem to have the loudest voices, and when you come back to a church, a year later, the weaker brethren are the same—still moaning, still blocking, still griping?" What passes for weakness can sometimes be sin, and that must not be allowed to hinder the forward movement of God's work. As New Testament Christians we shall want to deal with jealousy and envy graciously, but we also need to deal with them ruthlessly.

There is one other important strand we must note before we pass on from the Jephthah story. When the Ephraimites take issue with him, it is with the one man, as an individual, in his capacity as leader. They are going to kill him by burning his house down (v. 1). But, in his defense, Jephthah identifies himself with his own tribal group (*"My people and I,"* v. 2). Barry Webb comments, "This at once sets the particular point at issue in the broader context of Ephraimite-Gileadite relations and prepares the way for an escalation of the conflict into a full-scale inter-tribal war."[3] This in turn points us to the developing disintegration of the nation as the period of the judges proceeds. The process will reach its appalling climax in the civil war involving the whole nation of Israel at the end of the book (chapters 19–21). Meanwhile, Jephthah's distinction is that he judged the whole land for six years (v. 7) and perhaps the point is being made that only a leader as strong and uncompromising militarily, as he seems to have been, could possibly have held the increasingly warring groups together. Certainly the writer does not mean to cast Jephthah in either the role of hero or of villain. He is raised up by God, and used by him to achieve his purposes in delivering Israel, but he is not commended by God.

In his penetrating analysis of the Jephthah episode, which he uses as a sounding for the whole book, Barry Webb stresses the different levels on which the story is working. "It is about the tendency to accommodate religion to political norms. It shows this happening at both the national and the personal level. It shows us Yahweh's reaction to it, and how (in one particular case at least) it brought tragedy in its wake." He continues, "Yahweh saves Israel under protest. He is angry at Israel's apostasy and affronted by its "repentance." Yet he cannot tolerate its continued misery; he cannot simply leave it to its fate. He intervenes briefly to relieve Israel of the Ammonite yoke. But he does not intervene to relieve Jephthah's anguish, or to spare his daughter. He uses Jephthah to deliver Israel, but he never really approves of him. His silence is the other side of his anger." So the man he uses is capable, but also fatally limited; flawed in his insecurity and self-centeredness. Webb concludes, "He may judge Israel, but he can never care about it as Yahweh does."[4]

Before we close this chapter, we must balance what we have just read with the forward perspective of the remaining verses of chapter 12, in which three more "minor" judges are briefly chronicled.

Divinely Active Faithfulness Brings Stability

> 8 After him, Ibzan of Bethlehem judged Israel.
> 9 He had thirty sons. And he gave away thirty daughters in marriage, and brought in thirty daughters from elsewhere for his sons. He judged Israel seven years.
> 10 Then Ibzan died and was buried at Bethlehem.
> 11 After him, Elon the Zebulunite judged Israel. He judged Israel ten years.
> 12 And Elon the Zebulunite died and was buried at Aijalon in the country of Zebulun.
> 13 After him, Abdon the son of Hillel the Pirathonite judged Israel.
> 14 He had forty sons and thirty grandsons, who rode on seventy young donkeys. He judged Israel eight years.
> 15 Then Abdon the son of Hillel the Pirathonite died and was buried in Pirathon in the land of Ephraim, in the mountains of the Amalekites.
>
> *Judg. 12:8–15*

The story of Jephthah and his daughter almost seems to underline his disqualification from fatherhood because of the fatal flaws in his character. In a sense, his action in rendering to God a needless vow reflected the nation's wrong attitude and relationship toward Yahweh. They thought of him too much in terms of the pagan deities around them. They imagined that he too could be bribed or appeased. They forgot the uniqueness of his holiness, the majesty of his creatorial power, and the sheer "aloneness" of the one true and living God. Jephthah, like his contemporaries, erred in reducing God to pocket-size dimensions.

In contrast to Jephthah, the comments about Ibzan, his immediate successor, seem to be almost exclusively domestic. Where the one lost his only daughter, the other had thirty, as well as thirty sons (v. 8).

His main preoccupation (understandably!) seems to have been in seeing them all successfully married, and it seems as though his moving outside his clan to do this may well have been designed to strengthen his own position. However, if he had thoughts of founding a dynasty they do not seem to have materialized. Elon, who succeeded him, came from the same area of Zebulun, but we are told nothing more than the length of his time as judge and his burial place (vv. 11–12). With Abdon (v. 13) we are back on the domestic front, with his seventy descendants on their donkeys (v. 14) recalling Jair and his family (10:4). They were clearly a wealthy and influential family, and yet they seem to have achieved nothing worthy of note in the history of their nation.

But while there may have been an absence of the dramatic after Jephthah's death, this does seem to have been a period of considerable stability in the life of the nation. There were no major incursions from hostile neighbors and certainly in Abdon's time a fair degree of prosperity seems to have been restored to Israel. It is perhaps a breathing space before the high drama of the Samson saga, about to begin. Births, marriages, and deaths may rarely hit the headlines, but there will not be a day when a paper's columns do not carry notices of these life-changing situations. There is almost an air of normality about the second half of the chapter, described by one commentator as "a chronicle of trivialities." But if that is so, it is a lull before the storm. It reminds us, however, that there are periods in God's purposes when comparatively little seems to be happening—the day of small things. Nevertheless, the ordinary events of ordinary lives are just as meaningful to God as the headline stories. Indeed, the heroism of the judges was only really required in order to enable a return to the stability of normal family life, which is the hallmark of God's blessing and security. Faithfulness in little things is, after all, a very great thing.

NOTES

1. Carl E. Armerding, *Judges*, in *The International Bible Commentary*, ed. F. F. Bruce (Grand Rapids: Zondervan, 1979), 329.
2. Goslinga, *Judges*, 393.
3. Webb, "Judges—An Integrated Reading," 71.
4. Ibid., 74–75.

CHAPTER 13

Samson: God Intervenes

Judges 13:1–25

We now come to the last and most famous of all the judges—Samson. The saga of his life stretches over four chapters, so that we know more about him than about any of his predecessors. The irony is that Samson is the one judge who did not deliver Israel, in spite of his auspicious beginning. Ultimately he was ensnared by his own folly and weakness, though he was a man of such prodigious strength. So, the story of Samson is one of wasted opportunities and disappointed hopes, and in that it accurately reflects the conditions within the nation at that time.

Samson is representative of Israel. The lessons of his life are the lessons God's people, as a whole, should be learning. It is sometimes said that a nation gets the government it deserves. Perhaps it would be a truer comment to say that it often elects or accepts the government which most closely reflects its own mood and values. Certainly, that seems to have been the case in the Samson saga. As Israel's spiritual decline progressively deepens, so each deliverer is seen to be more flawed than the last. The cycle of sin does not merely repeat; it intensifies, and escape becomes increasingly difficult. Indeed, the situation of the nation is such, at the end of Samson's life, that it seems only direct intervention by the Lord will be able to save his people from disintegration politically and assimilation by the pagan religions spiritually.

If the basic problem of Judges is that "everyone did what was right in his own eyes" (21:25) then Samson is the supreme example of that attitude. But the book is always also about a God who does intervene, because he is committed by covenant mercy and promise to a disobedient and rebellious people. The parallels for the New Testament Christian and church are pertinent and exact.

While Jephthah was delivering the tribes east of Jordan from the Ammonite invasion, west of the Jordan right up to the seacoast, the Philistines were in control for forty years (13:1). This seems to have run roughly parallel with the lifespan of Samson. We are told in 15:20 that he led Israel for twenty years, the second half of this long period of oppression. During the first half, Samson was growing up. They were years of desperate spiritual decline in Israel, when the influences on the younger generation were almost universally unhelpful. Eli was high priest, and we know that far from being able to give the nation any effective spiritual leadership, he was even unable to discipline his own family. His sons treated God's offerings with contempt and practiced immorality with the women who served in the tabernacle (1 Sam. 2:12ff). Eventually the ark of God was captured in battle and returned only after a period of seven months when its captors had been smitten by boils and the idol of their god Dagon had been smashed to pieces in their temple by the hand of Yahweh (1 Sam. 5). It seems to have been at this time that Samson began his active service, to prove that the God of Israel still had the power and the commitment to come to the aid of his people and to defeat their enemies. It was a lesson the Philistines were to learn repeatedly over a period of twenty years.

But behind the straightforward outward story of the historical events, there lies a great enigma. What are we to make of Samson himself? Many sermons have doubtless been preached (and will be!) picking out aspects of Samson's character, good or bad, and using him as an example to follow or a warning of what to avoid. This may be legitimate, though we need to be sure that our criteria of judgment are contained within the text itself, or at least within the rest of Scripture, rather than imposed from the outside.

But there is more to Samson's story than a moralizing saga. Why did the glorious start of chapter 13 come to the desperate end of chapter 16? The events leading up to his birth are described in such a detailed way that they constitute a veritable fanfare of trumpets for a mighty hero. But then most of the rest of the story is such a letdown. The focus is on his love affairs and his amazing feats of physical strength. But above all it is on his moral weakness culminating in his eventual defeat at the hands of Delilah, and his blindness and slavery, from which he could only escape by bringing about his own violent death. And whenever we are given an insight into the man's character or motivation, it seems to be dominated by selfishness, lust, spite, vengeance, or brutish stupidity and foolhardiness. What *is* God doing? He is intervening for the blessing and good of his people. Let's see how.

On God's Terms

1 Again the children of Israel did evil in the sight of the Lord, and the Lord delivered them into the hand of the Philistines for forty years.

2 Now there was a certain man from Zorah, of the family of the Danites, whose name was Manoah; and his wife was barren and had no children.

3 And the Angel of the Lord appeared to the woman and said to her, "Indeed now, you are barren and have borne no children, but you shall conceive and bear a son.

4 "Now therefore, please be careful not to drink wine or similar drink, and not to eat anything unclean.

5 "For behold, you shall conceive and bear a son. And no razor shall come upon his head, for the child shall be a Nazirite to God from the womb; and he shall begin to deliver Israel out of the hand of the Philistines."

6 So the woman came and told her husband, saying, "A Man of God came to me, and His countenance was like the countenance of the Angel of God, very awesome; but I did not ask Him where he was from, and He did not tell me His name.

7 "And He said to me, 'Behold, you shall conceive and bear a son. Now drink no wine or similar drink, nor eat anything unclean, for the child shall be a Nazirite to God from the womb to the day of his death.'"

Judg. 13:1–7

For the last time, the depressingly familiar formula, which has introduced all the main episodes of the book, is reiterated (v. 1). The problem of Israel's apostasy remains and the work of God's chastisement therefore has to be repeated. The downward spiral of sin will always be followed by punishment.

What is different now is that there is no record of repentance, no desperate calling on God, such as we have seen in earlier chapters. Israel's heart has hardened that much. It is a peril that besets us all. We need often to be reminded that our relationship with God is not static. Every time we hear God's Word, we either make ourselves more open and responsive by receiving and obeying it, or we harden our hearts in unbelief and disobedience. The danger which the writer to the Hebrews warns about in Hebrews 3:12–13 is that of a hardened, or dried-out, heart. The unbelief which is endemic to our sinful human nature and the deceitfulness of sin combine to persuade us that we do not need to respond to God's voice today. And the result is that the heart starts to dry out, as surely as apricots or raisins left in the sun. Successive acts of resistance to God make it increasingly difficult to respond positively. We can illustrate this biblically from the story of Pharaoh who hardened his heart until God confirmed that decision and there was no way out. Or we can think of Dr. Faustus, in Christopher Marlowe's play of the same title, who is brought in the end to lament bitterly, "My heart's so hardened I cannot repent." "Will not" hardens into "cannot."

Yet these verses also show that God loves his sinful, rebellious people too much to let them stew in their sin. He refuses to write them out of the script. He insists on intervening in their lives, but he will do it in such a way as to drive home the lesson that he is God. No wonder C. S. Lewis refers to him as "the transcendental interferer." The covenant commitment of God to Israel, his first-born, is to be understood as a unilateral action by which God's will is carried out in the lives of his people, for his glory and their benefit. But that is what we all find ourselves resisting. We are prepared to let God intervene, provided it is on our terms, for our comfort, to boost our morale, to help us out of a fix. That we are very happy to permit, even eager to experience. What we have to realize, and this is part of our growth to spiritual maturity, is that the God of the Bible is never on a string. He is not in anybody's pocket. He is the sovereign controller of the entire universe. So when he does intervene, it is always on his terms.

The appearance of the angel of the Lord to Manoah's wife is by any standards an extraordinary event. Her barrenness was an accepted fact, rather like the spiritual emptiness and fruitlessness of Israel had come to be accepted as the normal situation. But God is going to change all that (v. 3b). He will see to it that she has *"a son."* Furthermore, that son is going to be a Nazirite throughout his life, and she is therefore to follow Nazirite practices in preparation for the child's birth (vv. 4–5). The background to this announcement is given in some detail in Numbers 6:1–8.

It was possible to make a special vow of separation to Yahweh which would be characterized by abstinence from all forms of fruit of the vine, by growing the hair, and by never allowing oneself to be made unclean by going near a dead body. This was usually for a restricted period of time, as a particular act of dedication. For Samson, however, it is to be lifelong (v. 7b). But most significant of all were the angel's words: *"he shall* begin *to deliver Israel"* (v. 5b). That process was only to be completed by King David's great victories later (2 Sam. 5:17–25). This child would make a start.

Clearly the Nazirite consecration and the deliverance of Israel are linked. The message of God's intervention for his people is that you only find deliverance from the oppression of your enemies by seeking after a life of consecration to the Lord. That is a matter of divine imposition. We are not told why Mr. and Mrs. Manoah were chosen. They lived in Zorah, right on the Philistine border, in a town that had no doubt capitulated totally in terms of compromise with Philistine culture and religion. But the only reason given to us that the wife's barren state is being miraculously changed by divine intervention, is to prove that this child has a special purpose to fulfill. This is a child given by God to his people, on his terms. And Manoah's wife underlines that in her excited report in verse 6.

There was so much she didn't know, as there always will be when God intervenes, but she accepted everything that the angel told her. Her husband, Manoah, however, is not so easily satisfied. It may well have been his natural incredulity at his wife's message about "a man of God" who looked *"like the countenance of the Angel of God"* (v. 6) which made him request further confirmation from the Lord, in prayer. God never scorns honest doubt or the desire to know more, and the reappearance of the angel in the next section takes his, and our, understanding of God's intervention a stage further.

In God's Time

8 Then Manoah prayed to the Lord, and said, "O
my Lord, please let the Man of God whom you sent

come to us again and teach us what we shall do for the child who will be born."

9 And God listened to the voice of Manoah, and the Angel of God came to the woman again as she was sitting in the field; but Manoah her husband was not with her.

10 Then the woman ran in haste and told her husband, and said to him, "Look, the Man who came to me the other day has just now appeared to me!"

11 So Manoah arose and followed his wife. When he came to the Man, he said to Him, "Are you the Man who spoke to this woman?" And he said, "I am."

12 And Manoah said, "Now let Your words come to pass! What will be the boy's rule of life, and his work?"

13 So the Angel of the Lord said to Manoah, "Of all that I said to the woman let her be careful.

14 She may not eat anything that comes from the vine, nor may she drink wine or similar drink, nor eat anything unclean. All that I commanded her let her observe."

15 Then Manoah said to the Angel of the Lord, "Please let us detain You, and we will prepare a young goat for You."

16 And the Angel of the Lord said to Manoah, "Though you detain Me, I will not eat your food. But if you offer a burnt offering you must offer it to the Lord." (For Manoah did not know He was the Angel of the Lord.)

Judg. 13:8–16

Manoah wants to know more about how it is all going to work out. His concern is about the boy's education, his "rule of life" and future work (v. 12). That's very natural, especially to a responsible father who has been told that his son will begin a great work of national deliverance, which his nation manifestly needs urgently. Supposing a man in Czechoslovakia, in 1968, had been told, just after the Russian tanks had invaded and extinguished the "Prague Spring" of Alexander Dubcek, that in twenty years' time his son would deliver the nation from its oppressors. Would not that father be keen to nurture his son, educate him, train and develop him to the very best of his ability? Surely that is the essence of good and responsible fatherhood, whatever the particular circumstances of life may be.

Significantly, the angel returns, in answer to Manoah's prayer, to his wife, who this time quickly runs to fetch her absent husband (vv. 9–10). Perhaps the emphasis on the mother is, as Webb suggests, "anticipating the significant role that women will play in his [Samson's] career."[1] Perhaps it is making the point in Samson's life of the formative role played by women in the life of any nation, whether it is Manoah's wife at one end of the spectrum seeking to be a responsible and committed mother, or Delilah at the other in the role of seducer and temptress. Manoah now has an interview to conduct. First, he establishes the angel's identity and then he asks for additional information (v. 12). But all that he receives by way of reply is a repeat of the instructions already given. Twice it is stressed that obedience is required without any more knowledge (vv. 13–14). That is the essence of faith, to accept what God has revealed, to believe it to the point of being determined to act upon it, irrespective of what the outcome might be, or of how the unknown factors will pan out in the future.

Centuries later, a New Testament writer would teach us that "faith is the substance of things hoped for, the evidence of things not seen" (Heb. 11:1). By way of illustration this writer goes on to remind us that it is "by faith we understand that the worlds were framed by the word of God, so that the things which are seen were not made of things which are visible" (Heb. 11:3). This is a very important concept which we need to grasp, especially in our modern world of scientific materialism. How did the world come about? Was there a "big bang" at the beginning; and, if so, how did that occur?

Science, properly, only concerns itself with the question "how?" not the question "why?" That is where we need God's self-revelation in the Scriptures. But the atheist position is that the world just happened, by chance. The world made the world. The visible evolved from the material. The Christian view is that the Word made the world. It sprang into being by the creative power of God, who expressed his divine will in a divine word. "Then God said, 'Let there be light'; and there was light" (Gen. 1:3). That is the essence of faith. It believes the word of God even where it cannot see, not only in its acceptance of the origins of the world, but also in its sure and certain hope about the future realities that are promised by the same sure word, but are as yet neither seen nor experienced. This was the lesson Manoah was being taught, and it needs to be underlined firmly in our generation too. If God says it, then I believe it—and that settles it! Manoah had to learn that he didn't need to have the answers at that point. He and his wife had been told all they needed to obey God. Other things would become clear in his time, not theirs. Ultimately faith must recognize that there is a divine inscrutability which our inquisitive minds can never penetrate.

The same is true about Manoah's hospitable suggestion in verse 15. He has not yet come to the point where he sees the visitor as anything more than a man of God. But the angel of the Lord is only willing to wait for one thing—a *"burnt offering"* by which Manoah can show his gratitude to God (v. 16).

Thankfulness is perhaps the way in which we express our faith most clearly. In the busy round of modern life, it is all too easy to occupy our time with what we fondly imagine are more productive, or at least more necessary, activities. We are concerned about time to eat, time to talk—these are part of our humanity and must not be denied. But as with any other part of life, we can overemphasize the trivial and spend too much time on a self-centered activism, which subtly pushes life out of its true perspective. Heaven is concerned about time to thank, time to worship, time to reflect on the nature of God, to rejoice in his goodness and enjoy his friendship. Perhaps a good check-up question to ask oneself is—"If I were God, how satisfied would I be with the way I have been treating him lately?" If husbands and wives need time just to be together (and they do!), is that not equally true of the Lord and his people?

WITH GOD'S TRUTH

> 17 Then Manoah said to the Angel of the Lord, "What is Your name, that when Your words come to pass we may honor you?"
>
> 18 And the Angel of the Lord said to him, "Why do you ask My name, seeing it is wonderful?"
>
> 19 So Manoah took the young goat with the grain offering, and offered it upon the rock to the Lord. And He did a wondrous thing while Manoah and his wife looked on—

20 it happened as the flame went up toward
heaven from the altar—the Angel of the Lord ascended
in the flame of the altar! When Manoah and his wife
saw this, they fell on their faces to the ground.
21 When the Angel of the Lord appeared no more
to Manoah and his wife, then Manoah knew that he
was the Angel of the Lord.
22 And Manoah said to his wife, "We shall surely
die, because we have seen God!"
23 But his wife said to him, "If the Lord had de-
sired to kill us, He would not have accepted a burnt
offering and a grain offering from our hands, nor
would He have shown us all these things, nor would
He have told us such things as these at this time."
24 So the woman bore a son and called his name
Samson; and the child grew, and the Lord blessed him.
25 And the Spirit of the Lord began to move upon
him at Mahaneh Dan between Zorah and Eshtaol.

Judg. 13:17–25

Manoah is still conducting his interview, but now he is getting to the heart of the matter, which is to recognize that God is God. The announcement of Samson's birth is accompanied by this totally unusual theophany in which God discloses himself, in the person of the angel of the Lord, because what is about to happen is miraculous—the birth of a son to a barren woman. It is not surprising then that as the story reaches its climax with the request for the revelation of the visitor's name, Manoah is told *"it is wonderful"* (v. 18).

We need to remember that in Hebrew thought the name reveals the nature. It is true also to some extent in our own culture, but only in a very limited way. In the city of Southampton, where I live, on the south coast of England, the main road north from the city is at one point called "London Road." That describes its nature, because it does eventually lead to London. But mostly we use names as meaningless labels, unlike the Bible. The name "wonderful" here reminds us of the inscrutability of God, that his ways are past our finding out. Those magnificent chapters, Job 38–40, are a marvelously healthy corrective to an arrogant obsession with man and all his works. We can only know anything of God at all because, in his sovereign wisdom, he has chosen to reveal himself to us. So it is here that as God touches the lives of this very ordinary couple, by his word of promise and his presence with them, the one whose name is "wonderful" chooses to do *"a wondrous thing"* (same root, v. 19).

Manoah offers the young goat and the grain offering to the Lord who works wonders, and as the sacrifice kindles, the angelic visitor ascends to heaven in the flames. Now there can be no doubt as to his supernatural identity, as the Lord himself appearing to his people (vv. 21–22).

Many believe that the appearances of the angel of the Lord in the Old Testament are in fact preincarnation appearances of our Lord Jesus Christ, since the identity of the angel seems to be that of Yahweh himself. Alternatively, it may be that the angel's visit is considered to be as if Yahweh were himself present, because he conveys Yahweh's words directly. This would be rather like the presence of an ambassador who so represents his head of state, or government, that he or she is, as it were, that authority speaking. The outcome, however, is to bring Manoah and his wife face down on the ground (v. 20), prostrate and terror-struck, recognizing that they have been in the presence of God and all that they deserve is destruction (v. 22). Every real meeting with God must surely bring us all to that same point.

But the touch of God is a touch of grace. As they recover from the shock they begin to gather themselves. Manoah's wife had survived the previous encounter. Had not the offering been accepted? And was not the whole visit with a future purpose of grace? So she applied her enlightened mind to the situation (v. 23) and in due time the child was born. The name *"Samson"* means the strong, the daring one. And the same Lord began to touch the boy's life as he grew, stirring him by his Spirit toward the tasks for which he had been born (v. 25).

As we end this chapter, let us return to the question we were asking at the start. What *is* God doing in this strange and unexpected encounter, which heralds the Samson story?

The answer, as so often, exists on a broader canvas than the personal lives of the main characters in the drama. God was intervening in the affairs of his covenant people, as he always does. He was shaping a man who would tower over his generation in terms of strength, because God had separated Samson for himself, as a Nazirite. This man would be a living demonstration of what that strength, which only God can give, is able to accomplish in a life that is dedicated to him. It was to be a living demonstration to Israel (and to the church) that God's strength can transcend human weakness, when that weakness is consecrated to him. Paul was to teach the New Testament believers the same lesson from the crucible of his own experience when he wrote in 2 Corinthians 12:9 of God's more than adequate promise to him.

> "My grace is sufficient for you, for My strength is made perfect in weakness."

Our problem is that we do not really believe that to be true. We imagine that we have to find resources of strength or capability within ourselves and, consequently, we tend to spend inordinate amounts of energy and effort on trying to generate within ourselves that which God has already promised to give us. We are amazed that Paul can go on to affirm,

> Therefore most gladly I will rather boast in my infirmities, that the power of Christ may rest upon me. Therefore I take pleasure in infirmities, in reproaches, in needs, in persecutions, in distresses, for Christ's sake. For when I am weak, then I am strong.
> *2 Cor. 12:9b–10*

It so cuts across all that we have been brought up to believe. But we are wrong and God is right!

Samson was to be a continual reminder of spiritual potential; but sadly, he is also a reminder of actual failure. The strong man sank into weakness and uselessness through his unfaithfulness to his covenant vows and through his liaisons with heathen women. In that, he was an exact replica of the nation of Israel. He was more flawed in character than any of the previous judges. It seems as though the downward spiral intensifies hopelessly. But in fact, as the picture gets darker, the glory of Yahweh grows more brilliant. When his Holy Spirit came upon as flawed an agent as Samson, even he could do such mighty deeds as made the Philistines feel the power of God. Everything depended upon his commitment to that consecration vow which God had imposed on him. It was not until he finally betrayed that, when it lay shattered and broken, that his strength evaporated. So the period of the judges ends in failure. Their weakness culminates in Samson, as well as their strength. No man could, or can, win the battle against God's enemies, for the flesh will always lust against the Spirit. That is why we Christians cannot live a day without the God who intervenes—but on his terms, not ours, and that means consecration.

NOTES

1. Webb, "Judges—An Integrated Reading," 164.

CHAPTER 14

Samson: God Overrules

Judges 14:1–20

This chapter and the next are the story of Samson's marriage with a Philistine woman in Timnah, and the contrasting strife which emanated from that decision. As the story of Samson's life begins to unfold, we certainly begin to appreciate the background we have already been given in chapter 13, which helps to explain actions and attitudes which would otherwise seem almost meaningless. One view of the story is expressed by Goslinga in his introduction to the section. He writes:

> Judges 14 and 15 present a thrilling account of Samson's unusual relationship to the Philistines. To confront them he even went so far as to marry a Philistine woman. This became a source of constant quarrelling and strife in which the Philistines displayed their savagery and depravity, while Samson had the opportunity to demonstrate his obvious superiority.[1]

That analysis seems to beg a number of important moral questions, but it is a coherent way of explaining what happened. On this reading Samson's actions were carefully calculated to generate strife between himself and the Philistines so that he could eventually overcome them.

A variant reading is to see God's providence as overruling Samson's intemperate demands and working through his very weaknesses to demonstrate the strength of the Lord in using such an agent. Either way, it was through this unusual set of circumstances that the Lord opened the way for Samson to become Israel's judge, as the angel had foretold. My own inclination is that we should read the chapter as an exposition of God's providence at work in overruling human sin and weakness, to accomplish his glorious and gracious purposes.

Through Apparently Bizarre Behavior

> 1 Now Samson went down to Timnah, and saw a woman in Timnah of the daughters of the Philistines.
> 2 So he went up and told his father and mother, saying, "I have seen a woman in Timnah of the daughters of the Philistines; now therefore, get her for me as a wife."
> 3 Then his father and mother said to him, "Is there no woman among the daughters of your brethren, or among all my people, that you must go and get a wife from the uncircumcised Philistines?" And Samson said to his father, "Get her for me, for she pleases me well."
> 4 But his father and mother did not know that it was of the Lord—that He was seeking an occasion to move against the Philistines. For at that time the Philistines had dominion over Israel.
>
> *Judg. 14:1–4*

The editorial comment of verse 4 is clearly the key to understanding this strange and difficult situation. We know the Spirit of the Lord was already moving on Samson (13:25), which must mean that as a man he already had a sense of destiny that he must enter into conflict with the Philistines. Obviously, his parents would have explained the special circumstances surrounding his birth and the reasons for his Nazirite vow. Perhaps Samson suffered something of the pressure of parental expectations in his teens. He must certainly have grown up knowing that much would be expected of him "one of these days," and that is not always easy to handle. We can imagine, then, something of his parents' horror at his blunt demand in verse 2. This cannot be the plan working out properly. They would be quite happy with him visiting a Philistine outpost like Timnah, to weigh up the possibilities of attacking it, to work out some sort of military strategy, but not to look for a wife. Timnah was only a few miles west of Zorah. Although it was allotted to the tribe of Dan

(Josh. 19:43), they had failed even to occupy it, having been forced into the mountains by the Amorites (Judg. 1:34). It is currently a Philistine town and is typical of their incursion and dominance throughout the border region. So while his parents probably looked forward to the day when their son would lead an Israeli army to liberate the area, the idea of marrying one of the enemy would be an anathema to them.

Intermarriage with foreigners was forbidden by the Mosaic Law (Exod. 34:16), and few were regarded as less suitable than the *"uncircumcised Philistines."* Not surprisingly, therefore, from every point of view, Samson's parents are determined to resist his demands, but without any success whatever. The request is simply repeated (v. 3b). You can imagine the late night conversations between Mr. and Mrs. Manoah in their bewilderment. Why is God allowing this to happen? What will it mean about his future usefulness, if Samson persists in this crazy headstrong way? Didn't God promise us a deliverer, not a delinquent?

That is why we need verse 4, which they did not know, at that point in time. As William Cowper puts it, "God moves in a mysterious way, his wonders to perform." In his total sovereignty he does not need to manipulate man or mechanize him like a puppet. He gives the individual free play, but through our human choices, right and wrong, wise and foolish, "he treasures up his bright designs and works his sovereign will."

God is going to break the dominion of the Philistines over his people, and he alone decides how that is going to be done. It is a recurrent Old Testament theme. When Isaiah informs the generation of Israelites in exile in Babylon that their deliverance will come through a pagan emperor, "Cyrus . . . My Shepherd" (Isa. 44:28), the very next chapter finds the people who are about to be delivered complaining about the method God has chosen to effect their salvation. To their question as to how God could possibly use a Gentile to carry out his purposes, the only answer they receive is the rebuke, "'Shall the clay say to him who forms it "What are you making?"'" (Isa. 45:9). Was this not the same sort of problem the Pharisees had with Jesus? How could he be the Messiah if he did not meticulously keep the traditions of the elders? As George Bernard Shaw once pithily expressed it, "God made man in his own image, and man has returned the compliment." We make "God" after our likeness and imagine that we can dictate to the sovereign Creator what he can or cannot do. This chapter shows us that his ways are not ours.

There is an important application here in our preaching. One of the most prevalent mistakes of our generation is to imagine that we have God in a box, that we have tied him down to working only in ways which we approve. In short, God belongs to our denomination! He could not possibly use a man who does not agree with us 100 percent. He could not possibly work through channels that are doctrinally unsound or lives that are immature and undisciplined.

The implication of such thinking is that you have to be good enough for God to use you, to have reached a certain standard (set by us!) of moral maturity or theological accuracy. Do you see what we have done? We have perverted the doctrines of grace with a religion of works.

The Book of Judges shoots holes through all of that. It is above all a book about grace, undeserved mercy, as is the whole Bible. Some of the most exciting and far-reaching spiritual advances in the world have been accomplished by God using people whom we might not be willing to accept into our church memberships, or who (worse!) might not even apply! Can we not have an expanded view of the mercy of God? That is not to play down theological accuracy or doctrinal soundness, or to pretend that it does not matter what we believe or how we behave because God will still use us. Far from it! Nothing excuses Samson from contracting this forbidden marriage. God's opinions do not change and waver. He always stands by his word. But we can rejoice that he is also in the business of righting our mistakes and using our failures as the foundations for his success. Let us never imagine that we have God taped, or that we know how he will work, or when. As soon as we start to say "God cannot or will not . . . until . . ." we are wrong-footed.

I like the story of the British general of two hundred years ago, who was surveying the enemy's battle lines drawn up and ready to engage. His equerry warned him that he was too near the enemy to dawdle and that his life was in danger. To which the distinguished soldier replied, in what must be among the most cautionary famous last words ever uttered, "Don't be silly, man! At that distance they couldn't hit a. . . ." God has his ways of putting us in our place when we think we know better than he. What he calls for is that element of trust which allows him to know best, and rests in his sovereignty even when we have no idea what the eventual outcome will be. If we really love him, we shall not need to know what God is planning in order to move forward with him. We know that we can leave him to work out all the details. He can even include our mistakes in his overruling plans and turn our most bizarre behavior to his purposes. Take heart!

By Empowering with His Spirit

> 5 So Samson went down to Timnah with his father and mother, and came to the vineyards of Timnah. Now to his surprise, a young lion came roaring against him.
>
> 6 And the Spirit of the Lord came mightily upon him, and he tore the lion apart as one would have torn apart a young goat, though he had nothing in his hand. But he did not tell his father or his mother what he had done.
>
> 7 Then he went down and talked with the woman; and she pleased Samson well.
>
> 8 After some time, when he returned to get her, he turned aside to see the carcass of the lion. And behold, a swarm of bees and honey were in the carcass of the lion.
>
> 9 He took some of it in his hands and went along, eating. When he came to his father and mother, he gave some to them, and they also ate. But he did not tell them that he had taken the honey out of the carcass of the lion.
>
> *Judg. 14:5–9*

We are not told how Samson managed to persuade his parents to agree to his scheme, but they eventually capitulated. Perhaps this too was the Spirit's pressure through the persistence of their son. Clearly they went down to Timnah separately, since the parents knew nothing of the incident with the lion (v. 6). Presumably they went down first to make the negotiations, and Samson followed to celebrate the wedding. But instead of the young woman we meet a young lion!

There follows the first demonstration of Samson's supernatural strength and we are intended to be as surprised about it, as Samson was by the beast. We find this difficult because we have been reared on centuries of Christian art which has usually delighted to represent Samson as our Old Testament Rambo or Mr. Universe. In fact, the text would seem to indicate the opposite. Up to this point there has been no indication of Samson's proverbial strength. Indeed, had he spent hours "pumping iron" to build a magnificent physique, Delilah would hardly have needed to ask him, "Please tell me where your great strength lies . . ." (16:6). It was a mystery to everybody. But the text explains it to us. *"The Spirit of the Lord came mightily upon him"* (v. 6).

Samson did not ask for it; he was overcome by it, and he seems to have been as surprised as the lion was! The Hebrew verb in verse 6a means "rushed into" or "penetrated powerfully." It is used again in verse 19, in 15:14, in 1 Samuel 10:10 of Saul prophesying, and in 1 Samuel 16:13 of David at his anointing by Samuel. This supernatural endowment enabled Samson to deal with a young lion as easily as he would a kid goat "probably in the manner Near-Easterners rend a young goat, pulling it in half by the hind legs."[2] You have only to stop and imagine it to see how remarkable the incident was.

Significantly, too, we are told twice (vv. 6b, 9b) that Samson did not inform his parents about the exploit or the honey in the carcass. What was he learning? He was learning above all that he, of whom so much was expected, was totally dependent on God for power and strength, but that God could be relied upon in the hour of need. And that was a very personal and private revelation. It was an explosion of spiritual power for one man at one particular time to accomplish one particular task.

The visit to his prospective wife (v. 7) is almost incidental, as the interest focuses for the rest of the story on the honey and the ensuing conflict. There are puzzles as to why he revisited the spot (reliving the triumph?) and especially as to whether the Nazirite vow strictly precluded contact with a dead animal body as well as that of a human being. But as the animal was killed by divine power working through Samson, there seems little point in being overconcerned about such niceties.

In detailed narratives like this we must be careful not to force unnatural spiritual applications, as though the story were some kind of allegory and every ingredient had a hidden meaning. However, it does seem legitimate to connect Samson's Nazirite consecration with the accessibility of the divine power, when it was needed. The fact that he is eventually overcome (because the Lord's strength no longer comes upon him) when that vow is finally revealed and then broken further establishes the connection (16:16–20). Our ability to serve God is equally dependent upon the power of the Holy Spirit, and he is never more easily grieved (Eph. 4:30) or quenched (1 Thess. 5:19) than when our consecration to Christ is compromised by sin. If the church in our generation seems strangely bereft of the equipping power of God to push back the enemies of the Cross, it must merely be in large measure because of the deficiencies of our consecration. Too often we are found like Augustine before his conversion, praying, "Lord, make me holy; but not yet!" It is the passion for God himself, for the honor and glory of his name and cause, that leads to a full-hearted consecration, which is the prerequisite for the unhindered flow of the power of the Holy Spirit in and through our lives.

In Transcending Human Weakness

10 So his father went down to the woman. And Samson gave a feast there, for young men used to do so.

11 And it happened, when they saw him, that they brought thirty companions to be with him.

12 Then Samson said to them, "Let me pose a riddle to you. If you can correctly solve and explain it to me within the seven days of the feast, then I will give you thirty linen garments and thirty changes of clothing.

13 "But if you cannot explain it to me, then you shall give me thirty linen garments and thirty changes of clothing." And they said to him, "Pose your riddle, that we may hear it."

14 So he said to them:

"Out of the eater came something to eat,
And out of the strong came something sweet."

Now for three days they could not explain the riddle.

15 But it came to pass on the seventh day that they said to Samson's wife, "Entice your husband, that he

may explain the riddle to us, or else we will burn you and your father's house with fire. Have you invited us in order to take what is ours? Is that not so?"

16 Then Samson's wife wept on him, and said, "You only hate me! You do not love me! You have posed a riddle to the sons of my people, but you have not explained it to me." And he said to her, "Look, I have not explained it to my father or my mother; so should I explain it to you?"

17 Now she had wept on him the seven days while their feast lasted. And it happened on the seventh day that he told her, because she pressed him so much. Then she explained the riddle to the sons of her people.

18 So the men of the city said to him on the seventh day before the sun went down:

"What is sweeter than honey?
And what is stronger than a lion?"
And he said to them:
"If you had not plowed with my heifer,
You would not have solved my riddle!"

19 Then the Spirit of the Lord came upon him mightily, and he went down to Ashkelon and killed thirty of their men, took their apparel, and gave the changes of clothing to those who had explained the riddle. So his anger was aroused, and he went back up to his father's house.

20 And Samson's wife was given to his companion, who had been his best man.

Judg. 14:10–20

Verse 10 sends another warning note. The *"feast"* is to be translated more literally a "drinking party." If his scooping of honey from the lion's carcass violated his consecration vow, this wedding party may well have broken the Nazirite commitment to abstain from fermented liquor. Against this, however, it can be argued that although these were two of the usual requirements of the vow for a Nazirite, they were not specifically mentioned by the angel in chapter 13. The only stated requirement then was "no razor shall come upon his head" (13:5); and, as mentioned above, it is only when that requirement was finally infringed that the Lord left him. We should therefore probably not place too much significance on these other infringements, though they certainly do indicate the general carelessness and indiscipline of Samson's life-style. I am reminded of the minister who, when asked by one of his young people what was wrong with smoking, replied, "Well, there may not be anything wrong with it, but it certainly shows which way the wind is blowing!" That was presumably in the days before our present knowledge of the injurious effect of tobacco on the body's health.

The stag party proceeds with his thirty groomsmen, apparently provided by the bride's family, and the riddle is introduced. Whether or not the drink loosened Samson's tongue, the purpose of the riddle seems to have been twofold. Its very obscurity meant that the Philistines would almost certainly be unable to solve it, thus establishing Samson's superiority over them. Firstly, he would take from them thirty suits of clothes, both undergarments and outer clothing. The word is often used to mean "Sunday best," festive garments, probably with embroidery. Secondly, in order to explain the riddle he would tell them of his exploit with the lion, secret until now, which would further establish his superiority in terms of his supernatural strength. The purpose of the whole exercise is about to be fulfilled; God is *"seeking an occasion to move against the Philistines"* (v. 4).

Although cross-cultural weddings of this sort were probably quite common in the syncretistic climate then prevailing in Israel, there was naturally a good deal of residual suspicion and distrust between the two nations. When the party was in its third day, it became clear to the Philistines that they were not going to solve the riddle and they began to suspect that they had been duped. They even accused Samson's wife and father-in-law of being in on the plot (v. 15). In fact, the only way to solve the puzzle, they reasoned, was by threatening Samson's wife, for she represented the only chink in his armor. They put pressure on her, and she put pressure on Samson (v. 16). Not for the last time he succumbed to the combination of a woman's tears and reproaches, and the secret was revealed. Not even his father or mother knew of the event; but once his wife knew, it was immediately passed on by her to the Philistines.

This may have been in self-defense, but the interaction of the young bride and her husband reveal that there was very little real love or loyalty between them. The situation can hardly have been improved by Samson's speedy recognition of the source of the answer when the men of Timnah presented it to him. It was hardly complimentary to describe his wife as *"my heifer"* (v. 18). The animal was known proverbially for its untamed stubbornness.

Samson acknowledged that the riddle had been solved and that the wager had to be paid, but the way he did it was to demonstrate who was really superior. The Philistines were paid back for their trickery. Again, the emphasis in verse 19 is on the Spirit of the Lord taking the initiative. We are not to see this as a personal revenge, but as an act of God through his chosen deliverer. Goslinga expresses it well when he writes:

> The author explicitly states that the Spirit of the Lord drove him to do all this. The Spirit seized him and filled him with power so that he could punish the Philistines. . . . He was acting as a judge called by God who wanted to demonstrate to the Philistines that he was their most formidable foe. It was really the Lord, Israel's covenant God, who was fighting through Samson against the oppressor of his people.[3]

They may have won the riddle, but they lost thirty of their own men from Ashkelon, and the clothes they received were those of their own dead countrymen. And as Samson stormed off to his parents' home, the woman he had wanted to be his wife was being married instead to the best man (v. 20). There never was any real future for the marriage and the unfortunate Philistine family has yet to pay the price for it (15:6).

What is being demonstrated throughout the incident is the impossibility of mixed marriages or, indeed, of any compromise or political union between the people of God and a pagan nation. The truth of separation is deeply embedded in the law code of the Old Testament, reflecting as it does the character of Israel's God. When he instructs his people, "You shall be holy, for I am holy" (Lev. 11:44), Yahweh is calling them to a distinctive moral purity based on his own righteous character. But there is more to it than that. The holiness of God is not so much one attribute among others as a description of his essential being. He is utterly "other," transcendent, separate from his creation. He calls his people into an exclusive relationship with himself, in which they are increasingly to reflect his character and manifest his glory. He is a "jealous" god, who will not share his glory with another and who will never allow his people to worship at other altars.

The whole basis of Israel's easygoing religious and cultural syncretism in the days of the judges was an offense toward the Lord. In the Samson story, he is demonstrating again the impossibility of any sort of alliance between those who belong to him and those who worship idols. It will never work, because they operate from fundamentally different presuppositions. That remains the basis of the prohibition of mixed marriages between Christian believers and unbelievers in 2 Corinthians 6:14–18. It remains the reason why all pluralism in worship and interfaith services or celebrations (so-called) are unacceptable to God. The existence of Truth means also the existence of falsehood, and if the one is to be received the other must, by that very action, be rejected. That is not prejudice or bigotry; it is logic and common sense. The Israelites of Samson's day needed to learn it, and so do we.

In application, we need to draw attention to how much the contemporary climate is against what it sees as divisive dogmatism, which is really the statement of absolute Christian truth. At a recent evangelistic supper party I was speaking to about forty professional middle-class couples, mostly non-Christians, about the message of Christ. All was well with the first half of John 14:6, Christ's incomparable words, "I am the way, the truth, and the life." No one blinked an eyelid at that. Doubtless they mostly accepted the conventional picture of Jesus as a fine moral teacher and a wonderful ethical example, encouraging us all to do our best in the confidence that, in the end, all will be well. If you want to follow Christ, believe his teaching, practice his precepts, that's fine! Religion is a privatized area of our culture. It's OK between consenting adults, preferably behind closed doors, but don't bring it out into the open and don't, above all, expect other people to believe it. That's the way the argument usually goes.

But even I was unprepared for the tirade of abuse and sheer resistance that came when I expounded the second part of John 14:6—"No one comes to the Father except through Me." That is intolerable because it is intolerant! It is bigotry of that sort that causes all the problems in the world . . . and so on.

You are allowed to have your own private religious truth, but nothing that claims to be absolute or exclusive. We are going to run into that sort of opposition more and more as the "global village" expands its population and uses up its resources in the next decades.

Anything that divides will be increasingly rejected. Isn't that why the Hindu syncretism that underlies the New Age mysticism is already so popular in the West? We shall need to have Samson's lesson very firmly engraved in our minds and on our hearts if we are to be faithful to the God of Truth in our generation.

NOTES

1. Goslinga, *Judges*, 419–20.
2. F. Duane Lindsey, *Judges, The Bible Knowledge Commentary*, eds. John F. Walvoord and Roy B. Zuck (Wheaton, Ill.: Victor Books, 1988), 405.
3. Ibid., 428.

CHAPTER 15

Samson: God Empowers

Judges 15:1–20

This is not a very flattering chapter, either for Samson or for Israel. Yet it is the only one of the four chapters on Samson's life which describes in any detail the sort of activities he was involved in during his twenty years as judge of Israel (v. 20). During that time he made a few dents in the Philistines, but, by and large, their oppression of Israel continued and, as this chapter shows us, Israel was only too happy to accept that state of affairs. Samson is both the most powerful of the judges physically and the weakest morally. He does more singlehandedly than the others, but less for the nation as a whole. He is an individualist, but hardly a leader.

Revenge on God's Enemies

1 And after a while, in the time of wheat harvest, it happened that Samson visited his wife with a young goat. And he said, "Let me go in to my wife, into her room." But her father would not permit him to go in.

2 Her father said, "I really thought that you thoroughly hated her; therefore I gave her to your companion. Is not her younger sister better than she? Please, take her instead."

3 And Samson said to them, "This time I shall be blameless regarding the Philistines if I harm them!"

4 Then Samson went and caught three hundred foxes; and he took torches, turned the foxes tail to tail, and put a torch between each pair of tails.

5 When he had set the torches on fire, he let the foxes go into the standing grain of the Philistines, and burned up both the shocks and the standing grain, as well as the vineyards and olive groves.

6 Then the Philistines said, "Who has done this?" And they answered, "Samson, the son-in-law of the Timnite, because he has taken his wife and given her to his companion." So the Philistines came up and burned her and her father with fire.

7 And Samson said to them, "Since you would do a thing like this, I will surely take revenge on you, and after that I will cease."

8 So he attacked them hip and thigh with a great slaughter; then he went down and dwelt in the cleft of the rock of Etam.

Judg. 15:1–8

The first episode of the chapter centers around two key statements from Samson. After discovering that his intended wife has been given in marriage by her father to the best man, Samson's reaction is *"This time I shall be blameless . . . if I harm them"* (v. 3). The New International Version translates this, "I have a right to get even." The wording may show that he had some initial remorse for the deaths of the men of Ashkelon, or, at least, a sense that he might have overstepped the mark. But no such restraints operate to quell his anger at the insult of being offered the younger sister (v. 2).

The other statement is in verse 7, *"I will surely take revenge on you, and after that I will cease,"* which is perhaps better translated, "I won't stop till I get my revenge on you." Together they express Samson's determination to settle the score and so free himself from the obligation of continuing revenge, which is how the New English Bible translates verse 3. In fact, the retaliation against the Philistines for being deprived of the wife he had intended to marry is out of all proportion to the offense. The episode with the three hundred foxes, recorded in verses 4–5, was clearly designed to cause as much damage and mayhem as possible.

Presumably, the revenge took some time to accomplish since catching three hundred foxes would not be an easily accomplished task, even if we do accept the view of many commentators that the Hebrew term can also mean "jackals," which run in packs and are therefore more easily caught! I wonder how many learned exegetes have tried it! The point is surely that a great deal of effort and application was needed to prosecute this revenge, which reveals a side of stubborn determination that was a potential strength in Samson's character.

The devastation was very great. Grain that had already been harvested, together with the standing grain waiting to be cut, as well as vineyards and olive groves, were all casualties of the fire-borne destruction, so that the three main crops of the land were wiped out for that year, in the one action. That triggers a chain reaction from the Philistines, who appear to be too frightened of Samson to tackle him, but who wreak their own vengeance on his prospective wife and father-in-law, whom they consider responsible for introducing the cause of all this chaos into their midst. Their threat first made in 14:15 to burn them and their house is now carried out, in a further act of senseless anger and revenge. So sin multiplies. This, in turn, provokes a further revenge on Samson's part in the vicious slaughter referred to in verse 8.

The whole story is a classic example of conflict escalation, fueled by anger, pride, jealousy and fear. We are all too familiar with this pattern as human relationships disintegrate, whether in marriage and the family, or in the board room, on the factory floor, between social groupings and races, and even sometimes in the church of Jesus Christ. It is recorded here, step by step, to remind us of the furious power of developing evil, of where sin leads and how totally destructive it always is.

Yet there can be little doubt that God was at work in the process, as 14:4 persistently reminds us. This can hardly be called a deliverance of Israel from foreign oppressors, but it is an act of judgment on her enemies. Though we may question Samson's motivation and extreme reactions there is little doubt that he could not have accomplished either episode, with the foxes or the massacre, apart from supernatural help. They are not the work of unaided man. This is stressed by the descriptions of verse 8, where *"hip and thigh"* is a term taken from wrestling, indicating a ferocious attack, as the rest of the verse reiterates. We have to recognize God's empowering in this—and more is to come.

Rejection by God's People

9 Now the Philistines went up, encamped in Judah, and deployed themselves against Lehi.

10 And the men of Judah said, "Why have you come up against us?" So they answered, "We have come up to arrest Samson, to do to him as he has done to us."

11 Then three thousand men of Judah went down to the cleft of the rock of Etam, and said to Samson, "Do you not know that the Philistines rule over us? What is this you have done to us?" And he said to them, "As they did to me, so I have done to them."

12 But they said to him, "We have come down to arrest you, that we may deliver you into the hand of the Philistines." Then Samson said to them, "Swear to me that you will not kill me yourselves."

13 So they spoke to him, saying, "No, but we will tie you securely and deliver you into their hand; but we will surely not kill you." And they bound him with two new ropes and brought him up from the rock.

14 When he came to Lehi, the Philistines came shouting against him. Then the Spirit of the Lord came mightily upon him; and the ropes that were on his arms became like flax that is burned with fire, and his bonds broke loose from his hands.

15 He found a fresh jawbone of a donkey, reached out his hand and took it, and killed a thousand men with it.

16 Then Samson said:
"With the jawbone of a donkey,
Heaps upon heaps,
With the jawbone of a donkey
I have slain a thousand men!"

17 And so it was, when he had finished speaking, that he threw the jawbone from his hand, and called that place Ramath Lehi.

Judg. 15:9–17

Samson is camping out in a cave at Etam because he knows a Philistine reprisal will come and he does not want the people of Zorah to suffer. An invading army deploys itself without resistance in Judah and the people whose deliverance Samson is beginning to achieve prove not to be in the least bit interested. In fact, verse 10a is an expression of their fear and their great desire to be on the best possible terms with their oppressors. The two sides agree that Samson is the real troublemaker and so his own people agree to hand over their hero to the enemy. In much the same way the Philistines had turned on Samson's wife and father-in-law and treacherously murdered them, so now the men of Judah are prepared to play traitor to their own defender. Apparently they do not feel the slightest embarrassment that their land is occupied by the enemies of the Lord. All they want is a quiet life. They are only too happy to go to Samson and arrange to trade him in, for terms of peace; only they very sensibly take three thousand men (v. 11) in case he thinks of trying on them the treatment which was meted out to the Philistines.

We should not let the horror of their complacent question in verse 11 escape us. This is the depth to which Israel has been prepared to sink. Their consuming desire for peace and quiet means that the nation which affirms that their god is the king of the whole earth is quite content to live in the land God has given them as insecure tenants of a foreign power, devoted to the worship of pagan idols. Can you believe it? But of course we can when we think of many of the mixed denominations of the church in Western Christendom today.

How is it that pulpits and presbyteries, bishoprics and synods can be occupied by those who deny by word and behavior some of the most fundamental doctrines of the faith and basic moral tenets of the Christian revelation, and all in the name of Christ, without so much as a protest by large sections of the believing orthodox church? It's the same motivation. Don't rock the boat! Don't challenge the status quo! We are ruled over by these people. They may deny the deity of our Lord Jesus Christ, his substitutionary atoning death, his bodily resurrection, ascension into glory, and his coming again. They may bless adulterous and homosexual "marriages," sanction abortion and euthanasia, and support radical subversive elements in society. But we are ruled over by them. They occupy university chairs of theology or the places around our denominational and seminary committee tables. We give them titles of honor and esteem them as great men. Why? Is it because the alternative would be too uncomfortable for us? We might find our own secure positions under threat. So there is an uneasy alliance in many church associations, an unwritten agreement not to challenge error or expose heresy. Where that is the case, we are not in a position to lift a finger in condemnation of the men of Judah.

Samson agrees to be bound and delivered up to the Philistines, having secured the promise of his fellow countrymen that they will not murder him themselves. What an irony it all is! He is bound with new strong ropes and brought up through the narrow defile which led to the rock Etam and taken to Lehi (which means "jawbone"). There the Philistines fall upon him with shouts of triumph (v. 14a), only to find the tables suddenly turned. For the fourth and last time we are told that *"the Spirit of the Lord came mightily upon him"* (v. 14). God empowers. Filled with superhuman strength, Samson snaps the ropes that bind him and, seizing a donkey's jawbone, wields it to such devastating effect that a thousand Philistines are slaughtered by it. Their corpses are left piled up in heaps (v. 16).

So this man who in verse 11 states, *"As they did to me, so I have done to them,"* ends up in verse 16 declaring, "I have made donkeys of them." And not only of his enemies, but of his own cowardly, compromising people as well. This was indeed a great deliverance, achieved by one man with God against a thousand. It is one of the most spectacular victories in the whole of the Old Testament record in that it was achieved singlehandedly without the mobilization of any army. "But the lack of follow-up indicates both Samson's failure as a leader and the depth of Judean acceptance of its plight."[1] Jawbone Heights may be the triumphant name Samson assigns to the location of his great victory (v. 17), but the nation, morally and spiritually, is still in the depths.

This is perhaps the peak of Samson's achievements, and yet so much still remains undone. "One swallow doesn't make a summer," we say, and one battle doesn't win a war. All too often in the history of the church God's people have experienced a great deliverance or forward movement only to discover the enemy regrouping with intensified ferocity, or that their own shallow optimism has led them to be unaware of the long and arduous campaign needed to see any really lasting change.

At this point it may be helpful to review where the whole narrative complex from Othniel to Samson has brought us with regard to our understanding of the function of the judges in Israel. Barry Webb's comments are illuminating.

> After the example of Othniel in 3:7–11 we think we know what a judge is. But almost at once that initial understanding is challenged: Ehud is a devious assassin rather than a warrior, Shamgar is probably not an Israelite, Deborah is a woman, and so

> on until finally we are presented with Samson, who is the polar opposite of Othniel. Othniel's marriage is exemplary, Samson's liaisons with foreign women are the reverse; Othniel leads Israel in holy war, Samson is a loner who doesn't even *want* to fight the Philistines; Othniel saves Israel and ushers in an era of peace, Samson leaves the Israelites under the Philistine yoke. And yet the narrator insists that Samson was a judge, and the point is made with particular emphasis. . . . Samson's judgeship began effectively at Ramath-Lehi and concluded with his death at Gaza. To be a judge then, is to be the person in whom Yahweh's administration of Israel is realized at a particular time. Retrospectively we see that what we initially thought were the defining characteristics of the institution were its outer husks: the Samson episode discloses the "vital essence."

Recognition through God's Provision

> 18 Then he became very thirsty; so he cried out to the Lord and said, "You have given this great deliverance by the hand of Your servant; and now shall I die of thirst and fall into the hand of the uncircumcised?"
> 19 So God split the hollow place that is in Lehi, and water came out, and he drank; and his spirit returned, and he revived. Therefore he called its name En Hakkore, which is in Lehi to this day.
> 20 And he judged Israel twenty years in the days of the Philistines.
>
> *Judg. 15:18–20*

This was June or July, and it requires no great stretch of the imagination to appreciate the expenditure of energy required to achieve this great victory. The power of the Spirit does not make us immune from the ordinary needs and weakness of our humanity. With the task complete, Samson is ready to collapse. But here we see another perspective. The man who until now has appeared to be motivated only by revenge and spite recognizes that this great victory is not his but God's, and that he is as dependent on God after it as he was during it. This is surely why Samson appears among the great heroes of faith recorded in Hebrews 11. He casts himself on God's mercy, recognizing himself as Yahweh's servant and calling on God to defend him against dying of thirst and his body being mutilated by his enemies. That would be no way for God to celebrate his victory.

And God answers his faith with a miracle in the provision of a spring. The need is met. Samson is restored and revived; but above all, he is recognized to be God's chosen agent by a divine action of which everyone soon became aware (v. 19b). It was presumably on that basis that he was able to lead Israel for twenty years (v. 20), as the man whom God had sovereignly raised up, equipped, and preserved.

On one level, all this is a graphic and exciting story which lends itself to the Hollywood epic treatment. But at a deeper level it restates the serious moral problems we have already noted, which can best be expressed in the question: Can God really be at work in all this? If we shrug that off with an easy yes or no, we shall miss much of what God wants to say to us. That is why some of our Bible study is so predictable and unexciting. We think we know the answers and are not prepared to dig deeper and to worry at the difficult questions. Samson is a real challenge! Empowered by the Holy Spirit, he nevertheless appears sensual and sometimes completely irresponsible. Although a Nazirite, he seems to sit loose to the implications of his position, and even his patriotism is motivated by selfish envy and bitterness. How can this be a man of faith? Perhaps the best way to answer these problems is to draw out two lessons about ourselves and two about God, from the tangled web of Samson's saga.

Lesson One is that we are all products of our time. That is always a conditioning factor, at least in the early stages of our personal adventures in pilgrimage with God. When the amateur player goes to his first session of coaching with the professional, all sorts of natural bad habits have to be unraveled and unlearned. It takes time, patience and perseverance. But it is a hundred times worse if the natural talent has been misled or wrongly shaped by bad or inept coaching. Then you have to undo the work of the memory and try to unscramble all sorts of consciously assimilated errors. That's how it is with us when God takes us on to begin to lick us into shape. We have acquired so much cultural baggage from our own generation and we have assumed so much to be unquestionably right, that is actually totally wrong from God's perspective, that we all start hopelessly conditioned by our contemporary cultural limitations.

By now, we know that Samson's cultural climate was one of spiritual decline and apostasy from the living God. We have often drawn attention to the downward spiral movement of this book, in which the pattern of idolatry and punishment intensifies with each repetition of the cycle. Samson stands at the end of that long, destructive process.

Furthermore, he is an Old Testament man, by which I mean that although he was stirred, empowered and used by the Holy Spirit, he did not know the permanent indwelling of the Spirit which is the birthright of the New Testament believer, and one of the distinctive qualitative differences between the two covenants.

Indeed, Samson follows what we might call the Old Testament norm in that the Holy Spirit comes upon him to equip him to do a particular job of work, but can then depart. Is this not why David prays in his penitential confession psalm, "Do not take your Holy Spirit from me" (Ps. 51:11)? The point is made transparently clear by John when dealing with our Lord's great claim on the final day of the Feast of Tabernacles. "On the last day, that great day of the feast, Jesus stood and cried out, saying, 'If anyone thirsts, let him come to Me and drink. He who believes in Me, as the Scripture has said, out of his heart will flow rivers of living water.' But this He spoke concerning the Spirit, whom those believing in him would receive; for the Holy Spirit was not yet given, because Jesus was not yet glorified" (John 7:37–39). It is that last comment of the evangelist which is so illuminating. Only when the Lord Jesus had carried the sins of a lost world in his own body on the cross, only when God had vindicated the person and work of his Son through his glorious resurrection and ascension—only then could the Spirit be given ("poured out," Acts 2:33) to indwell every one of God's believing people as the gift of the ascended, conquering Christ. Paul makes the same point in Ephesians 4:7–12, where he identifies the gift of Christ's grace as the spiritual gifts bestowed on the church for her service and growth. These gifts of the Spirit are in themselves the fruit of Christ's passion and victory. Quoting Psalm 68:18, Paul links Christ leading captivity captive with his gifts to men.

But Samson did not have these benefits. He was empowered, anointed even, but not indwelt. So the greater conditioning factor for him was not the life of the Spirit of God within, but the views of the people around him, the culture of which he was a part. We need to be aware of that process at work also in our own discipleship.

For example, living in a generation where we are constantly told that "seeing is believing," we shall be only too likely to make our estimates of what God can do by what we have already seen or experienced. We limit God by our blindness to his potential. We take on the color of our Christian environment, chameleon-like, following the latest fads and fashions, copying one another, hunting for the newest and most impressive success model, instead of being totally radical, which is another way of saying *thoroughly biblical*. In our day, obsessed with personal comfort and pleasurable self-indulgence, it is not popular to call congregations to hard work in evangelism, self-denying prayer, and sacrificial service. We would rather have the cheapest, quickest route to numerical growth, with the least bother or disturbance. We too are the products of our time. Jesus was killed by his contemporaries because he refused to toe the line to their religious and cultural norms.

Lesson Two is that we are the prisoners of our feelings. This was clearly the case with Samson, as the passage remorselessly points out. Verses 3, 7, 11, and 16 of chapter 16 all expose his bitter pride and envy which fueled his unrelenting, cold-blooded revenge. The great danger for Christian congregations is that we fail to see ourselves in a man like Samson. Every Sunday school child knows that the Pharisees are the "baddies" in the Gospels, so that when we grow up it never occurs to us for one moment that they are a frightening mirror-image of the hypocritical legalistic pietism that passes for evangelical Christianity in so many places in the Western church. "Lord, is it I?" And the answer must be yes to the extent that the Pharisaical heart is still unchecked in us, for we are all natural "play actors" when it comes to religion (as well as many other areas of life).

Similarly, we are all one with Samson in our natural attitudes; but we don't have to remain at that address. One of the gracious ministries of the Holy Spirit within our lives as believers is to empower us to move, to live somewhere different, emotionally. He can free us up from simply reacting to the circumstances of life on the basis of what we happen to be feeling. We need his help to enable us to start looking beyond ourselves and the limited horizons of our own emotions. Self-pity is perhaps the commonest sin of many of us Christians in this generation. We need toughening up, which is one of the most neglected ministries of the Spirit. We need to look beyond what we feel to what we know by renewing our focus on the truth of God, in his Word. On that basis, we can ask the Holy Spirit, who indwells us, to give us his enabling power so that we can live according to his truth.

Then we shall begin to make right choices and carry out right actions because we are right with God and because his life is flowing into our minds and hearts without hindrance or restriction.

The last two lessons are convictions about God, which the sad story of Samson should surely burn into our understanding and spiritual consciousness.

Lesson Three is that God always remains committed to his covenant promises. He never goes back on his Word; he cannot deny himself (2 Tim. 2:13). This explains what God was doing, even with a tool as flawed and weak as Samson. Through these amazing incidents of personal victory, God was holding up a mirror to his rebellious people, Israel, of what they could yet be, if only they would turn to him. He had not deserted them. It was they who were ignoring him.

Unusual power was considered to be evidence of the presence of God, even by these unspiritual people. It is a sort of bottom-rung spirituality to be impressed by physical power, so God accommodates himself to their weakness. He raises up a man whom he endows with superhuman strength, to demonstrate what *God* can do. He makes him a Nazirite, to show them that it is only by separation to God—letting him do what he wants with us—that this divine power can be experienced with any degree of consistency in our lives. Yet all the time God is holding it out to his people as a possibility. He still does!

The tragedy of Samson is that nothing was really solved by his life. God's power was demonstrated, but not appropriated, by his rebellious people. The amazing thing is that in spite of this he never lets them down and never lets them go. Even when they want to settle down and merge with the Philistines, the Holy Spirit is always seeking a showdown, a confrontation. That is why he raises up a Samson. He will do the same in our lives whenever we compromise. The unbreakable nature of his covenant-love is that he will never leave us to our own sinful devices, however much we may rebel against him. The love of God is literally the strongest force, the greatest power, in all the world.

Lesson Four is that this God remains constantly accessible and available to all who pray, whatever their background or situation, according to their need. He is always ready and willing to demonstrate his sovereign power for the renewal and refreshment of all those who call out to him in faith. That is the meaning of the miraculous provision of the spring at En Hakkore.

As we apply the passage, we need to encourage God's people to call on the Lord in any and every circumstance. All too often Christian people allow their past failures to stand between them and the enjoyment of God's present provision. Certainly, unresolved conflicts with God have first to be confessed and repented of, where there is sin, so that there may be true forgiveness and reconciliation. But when the matter has been properly dealt with, it is no mark of spiritual maturity to keep resurrecting it. We are not compelled to keep reliving the lessons of history if we truly learn from them.

We should learn from Samson never to think that we predict what God can, will, or should do. Though we may question how God could use a man like Samson, that does not alter the very clear fact that he did! In fact, we find him constantly using what many Christians would describe as "the most unlikely people" not only in the pages of Scripture, but also in the contemporary church. Your church has many of them. You are probably one yourself! There will always be an inscrutability to God's ways which we shall never be able fully to understand. The great thing is that we don't need to have it all worked out in order to ask.

When Samson was in need, he cried out to God. That is faith! And in response he did not receive an ethical lecture; he got the drink of water he desperately needed. There is superhuman power available to those who trust in God. He exactly matches the colors of his grace to the spectrum of our human need. In that confidence, we can afford to leave the insoluble mysteries we shall never be able to resolve with God, and instead concentrate our spiritual energies on the things we do know and can be absolutely sure about—the commitment of the covenant Lord to his people, in unfailing love, and the indwelling of the Holy Spirit to empower us in his service.

> But we have this treasure in earthen vessels, that the excellence of the power may be of God and not of us.
>
> *2 Cor. 4:7*

CHAPTER 16

Samson: God Judges

Judges 16:1–31

Throughout the Bible there runs a fundamental and, to our human way of thinking, an extraordinarily ironic strand of thinking. It is expressed most succinctly by Paul on two occasions during his correspondence with the Corinthian church. In 1 Corinthians 1:25 he writes that "the foolishness of God is wiser than men, and the weakness of God is stronger than men," in the context of his reflections as the centrality of the Cross in the message of the gospel. Toward the end of the second letter, reflecting on his experience of living that gospel of cross-bearing, he concludes with the message of God's grace as the answer to his repeated prayer for the removal of his "thorn in the flesh." "And He said to me, 'My grace is sufficient for you, for my strength is made perfect in weakness.' Therefore most gladly I will rather boast in my infirmities, that the power of Christ may rest upon me. Therefore I take pleasure in infirmities, in reproaches, in needs, in persecutions, in distresses, for Christ's sake. For when I am weak, then I am strong" (2 Cor. 12:9–10). That is such an amazing juxtaposition that we might well ask how it can possibly be true. Yet it is the substance of this final chapter of Samson's life story too, and the lessons it teaches are very penetrating. It begins with a strong man who is revealed to be weak, but ends with a weak man who is stronger than ever he was before.

Strength and Moral Weakness

1 Now Samson went to Gaza and saw a harlot there, and went in to her.

2 When the Gazites were told, "Samson has come here!" they surrounded the place and lay in wait for him all night at the gate of the city. They were quiet all night, saying, "In the morning, when it is daylight, we will kill him."

3 And Samson lay low till midnight; then he arose at midnight, took hold of the doors of the gate of the city and the two gateposts, pulled them up, bar and all, put them on his shoulders, and carried them to the top of the hill that faces Hebron.

Judg. 16:1–3

These three verses form a sort of bridge, from the summary statement of Samson's twenty years as a judge (15:20) to the account of his ultimate downfall at the hands of Delilah, culminating in his death. This begins in verse 4, with the introductory words *"afterward it happened . . ."* clearly marking it off as a fresh unit.

So, here we have Samson's story and tragedy, encapsulated in a representative incident, with an admirable economy of words. The strong man is a moral weakling. It would be easy to say that women were his downfall, and that is certainly true at the level of his personal morality. But it is also true that God was working through this weakness, overruling Samson's volitional sinful behavior to accomplish his purposes for his covenant people. The Lord "was seeking an occasion to move against the Philistines" (14:4). As this chapter proceeds, we shall see that the moment of Samson's eventual eclipse is also the moment of his greatest victory. *"So the dead that he killed at his death were more than he had killed in his life"* (16:30b).

Perhaps the greatest danger is to equate outward physical strength with inner moral and spiritual fiber; to imagine that because God's blessing seems to rest on the external circumstances of life, he must be pleased with, or at least condone, the inward, hidden moral and spiritual condition of what the Bible calls *the heart*. That seems to have been at the root of Samson's tragedy.

In view of his later blindness, it is significant that verse 1 stresses the role of the eyes in leading Samson into sin. The same mechanism of chapter 14 is triggered again. There he said to his father, "I have seen a woman in Timnah . . . get her for me . . ." (14:2). Now he sees a prostitute in Gaza and gets her for himself. What was Samson looking for? Not apparently a caring relationship of mutual love and trust so much as self-gratification. He wanted to feel good.

In our society, where sex is deified, we should not be surprised when it becomes the measure of life. People are hungry and thirsty for value, esteem, personal worth, and most of all, for real, unconditional love. They have to be because we are all made in the image of God, created for interpersonal relationships of love. But in a generation where belief in God is either nonexistent or distorted to belief in a cosmic Santa Claus whose only function is to keep the creatures he has created unendingly happy, we should not be surprised if the other great compulsions of humanity—sex, money, and power—usurp God's place.

Gaza, the most southerly city on the coast, had at one time been conquered by Judah (1:18) but was now firmly back under Philistine control. It must have been a threat to Samson's life for him even to enter Gaza. For him to spend the night there was suicidal. The gate, being the only way in and out of that walled city, was guarded all night so that no one could go out (v. 2). But that was no problem to a Samson in the full awareness of his immense strength which gave him such superiority over his enemies. Although his liaison with the prostitute demonstrated his moral weakness through his uncontrolled lust, yet the strength which God gave him was once again used to perform a heroic act of defiance against the Lord's enemies, albeit to save his own skin. This is the paradox. The brave man who could strangle a lion cannot control himself. He can break the fetters with which his enemies bind him, but he ends up the prisoner of his own appetites.

There is some dispute about where exactly Samson carried the gates of Gaza (v. 3). The feat of removing them at all is in itself Herculean. Keil and Delitzsch suggest that Samson carried them out to the range of hills that are about half an hour's walk to the southeast of Gaza. From the top of those hills the mountains of Hebron are visible, and it is there that tradition affirms Samson deposited the city gate.[1] However, Goslinga asserts, "I believe that Samson indeed brought the gates back to Israelite soil, and that the author included the name Hebron to show that he deposited them in the centre of Judah so that Israel would have tangible proof of his victory."[2] Admitting that this would involve a journey of forty miles, he nevertheless argues that the lifting of the gates at all was a miracle, and that such a great distance presents no additional problem for supernatural power. Certainly it would seem to give more purpose, both to the event itself and to its being recorded here, if the people of Israel saw this visible reminder of Yahweh's power over their enemies, within their own land.

Strength and Personal Vulnerability

4 Afterward it happened that he loved a woman in the Valley of Sorek, whose name was Delilah.

5 And the lords of the Philistines came up to her and said to her, "Entice him, and find out where his great strength lies, and by what means we may overpower him, that we may bind him to afflict him; and every one of us will give you eleven hundred pieces of silver."

6 So Delilah said to Samson, "Please tell me where your great strength lies, and with what you may be bound to afflict you."

7 And Samson said to her, "If they bind me with seven fresh bowstrings, not yet dried, then I shall become weak, and be like any other man."

8 So the lords of the Philistines brought up to her seven fresh bowstrings, not yet dried, and she bound him with them.

9 Now men were lying in wait, staying with her in the room. And she said to him, "The Philistines are upon you, Samson!" But he broke the bowstrings as a strand of yarn breaks when it touches fire. So the secret of his strength was not known.

10 Then Delilah said to Samson, "Look, you have mocked me and told me lies. Now, please tell me what you may be bound with."

11 So he said to her, "If they bind me securely with new ropes that have never been used, then I shall become weak, and be like any other man."

12 Therefore Delilah took new ropes and bound him with them, and said to him, "The Philistines are upon you, Samson!" And men were lying in wait, staying in the room. But he broke them off his arms like a thread.

13 Delilah said to Samson, "Until now you have mocked me and told me lies. Tell me what you may be bound with." And he said to her, "If you weave the seven locks of my head into the web of the loom"—

14 So she wove it tightly with the batten of the loom, and said to him, "The Philistines are upon you, Samson!" But he awoke from his sleep, and pulled out the batten and the web from the loom.

15 Then she said to him, "How can you say, 'I love you,' when your heart is not with me? You have mocked me these three times, and have not told me where your great strength lies."

16 And it came to pass, when she pestered him daily with her words and pressed him, so that his soul was vexed to death,

17 that he told her all his heart, and said to her, "No razor has ever come upon my head, for I have been a Nazirite to God from my mother's womb. If I am shaven, then my strength will leave me, and I shall become weak, and be like any other man."

Judg. 16:4-17

We now begin the last episode of Samson's life, the tragic fall of the man who had promised so much, but who produced so little. Once again, it begins with his weakness for women. His love affair with Delilah has become one of the world's classic stories of betrayal. It is suggested by Armerding that her name has been identified as meaning both "flirtatious" and "devotee," the latter suggesting that she may have been a religious prostitute.[3] Other derivations of her name point to a meaning such as "the weak or pining one," which would certainly fit with the irony of the drama where the naive strong man is brought down by the weak, but cunning, woman.

The Philistine leaders, doubtless well aware of Samson's weakness, must have been delighted to hear of his developing love affair with Delilah, which they saw as yet another opportunity to destroy their perplexing enemy. The fact that they could not account for his strength seems to indicate again that Samson's physique was not what we would expect of the strongest man in the world. They knew it was supernatural. From the background of their pagan superstition, they may have imagined that Samson had some lucky charm or amulet which gave him superhuman powers, but which could be rendered ineffective by a stronger charm. This at least seems to lie at the root of the false answers which Samson gave Delilah.

Of course, there was an element of truth in this. The Nazirite vow not to cut the hair was not a magic talisman, but it represented a physical pledge of obedient dedication to the Lord, to which his physical strength, subsequently granted by the Lord, was inextricably bound up. When the hair was removed by Delilah, the strength was removed by God. For the moment, however, the Philistine leaders are prepared to pay Delilah a huge sum of money if she can but discover the secret. The apparently excessive reward offered indicates the level of their frustration and anger.

What follows is a drama in four acts, each of which is a miniature of deception and falsehood. The relationship, within which the drama is played out, is supposed to be one of love. Actually it is one of self-satisfaction. Delilah is prepared to use Samson, in the context of a false "love" for him, in order to earn enough money to set her up comfortably for the rest of her life. We are not without contemporary examples of women whose affairs with some prominent public figures not only bring the downfall of the men they have professed to "love," but also set them up financially through the money offered by the press or publishers for their inside story or memoirs. On the other hand, Samson is perfectly prepared to play along with Delilah, telling her strings of lies in order to gratify his sexual appetite. Because they are both prisoners of themselves, they exploit each other in the name of a "love," which is no more than self-indulgent lust.

As the drama unfolds, we see Samson slipping by stages to his doom, apparently unaware of what is happening. It probably started as a game. His lover, Delilah, could ask Samson what nobody else had been able to discover. How hilarious it would be to see the strongman bound and unable to defend himself—but all at the hands of the woman who "loved" him, of course!

Samson's first reply is both cautious and foolish (v. 7). On the one hand, he suggests something totally irrelevant—*"seven fresh bowstrings"*—which the superstitious Philistines are gullible enough to believe. At the same time, he is foolish to begin the dialogue, much as Eve did with the serpent in the Garden, which eventually leads to his defeat. Each act of the drama increases the pressure and each time Samson yields a little more and slips a little nearer to revealing the secret of his Nazirite vow. The irony is that he seems blind to what is happening. Confident in his strength, Samson is well aware that fresh bowstrings and new ropes, though they could be tied the tightest and would be the hardest to break, hold no problem for him. What he does not see is how Delilah's persistent pressure on him is gradually wearing him down. It all seems a game that the strong man can easily control, but actually he is being morally tied up and thereby weakened and softened up, made ready for the kill.

Many of the applications are very obvious. We have already referred to Paul White's story about the little pet leopard which grew up to be a killer. Christians need to realize that sin which is regarded as harmless self-indulgence is doubly lethal, just because its killing power is unrecognized. A thought becomes an action; an action becomes a habit; a habit shapes a character; and a character reaps a destiny. Samson's defeat did not happen overnight. There was a hidden movement of the heart, by stages, long before the public denouement. We all need the warning because, while we tend to be very observant and critical of the sins of others, we are all inclined to be indulgent of our own "little weaknesses," with often frightening results.

The third act moves Samson nearer to his downfall, when he begins to talk about his hair as the source of his strength (v. 13). This is tempting providence, but still he seems to have felt secure—and indeed it was no great problem to him to pull out *"the batten and the web (fabric) from the loom"* (v. 14). His physical strength was still intact, but his power to resist the emotional pressure Delilah was exercising had all but eroded. The old hymn, "Yield not to temptation," is right when it states, "Each victory will help you some other to win." But the corollary is equally true. Every capitulation makes the next time easier.

So, when Delilah turns on her feminine wiles and charm, Samson is an easy target. The "pining one" pretends to be hurt and wounded that the man who professes to love her will not share his whole heart with her (v. 15). His lies mock her and mislead her. How can that be evidence of love? The question is hardly unreasonable.

Sadly, as we have seen, what Samson and Delilah have is not the love that gives itself, but the lust that grabs for itself. However, Samson is clearly wounded by this attack and very vulnerable to it. Verse 16 vividly describes the constant pressure, like water dripping on a stone, that eventually wore him down. Sensing that he was weakening, Delilah pressed, prodded, and plagued him relentlessly with her accusations and taunts until, as Armerding comments, "the continued emotional barrage exhausted his powers of resistance." He was literally sick to death with the whole business and determined to end it once and for all, by revealing the true source of his strength. *"He told her all his heart . . ."* (v. 17a).

But did Samson really understand it himself? In explaining his "secret" to Delilah he concentrates merely on the externals of the Nazirite vow; but they were never designed to be an end in themselves. The whole point was that the external signs represented the internal reality of a life devoted to God, in obedience to his will and commandments. If that reality had been there within Samson he would never have betrayed the secret of his strength. Indeed, he would never have had any relationship with a pagan woman like Delilah at all. It seems that Samson did not really understand the secret of his strength. His attitude was very similar to the superstitious practices of the pagan Philistines among whom he spent so much time. The outward, visible sign took over from the inward, hidden reality to such an extent that the spiritual reality ceased to exist. Samson began to imagine that outward conformity was all that was needed until, ultimately, even that disappeared, too.

It is dangerous when God begins to work in and through our lives. There is the danger that we shall imagine that somehow we are in such a favored relationship with the Lord that the usual disciplines of the Christian life can be abandoned because the demands for obedience have been waived. There is the danger of thinking that if we keep up outward appearances God will have to go on blessing us, even though our hearts may be hardening and our lives beginning to drift far from our spiritual moorings. Isn't that why the writer to the Hebrews identifies the great peril besetting his readers as "neglecting" so great a salvation. "Therefore we must give the more earnest heed to the things we have heard, lest we drift away" (Heb. 2:1). All we have to do to drift away is nothing. Just tie a loose knot around the bollard on the harbor quay and the tide will do the rest. No virtue is safe if it is not enthusiastic. No devotion is guaranteed if it is not passionate.

The greatest deceit is that we can have all the outward conformity to the behavioral norms of our particular Christian subculture, even to the point of exercising spiritual gifts in our apparently "successful" ministry, and yet in our hearts have no living love relationship with Jesus Christ. Samson points us to the peril of professionalism, in

Christian terms. His fulfillment of the office of judge seemed successful, even heroic. He regularly put the Philistines in their place. Surely it was clear that God was using this man, and did he not have all the outward signs of a man set apart for God? But we deceive ourselves, on the grand scale, when we begin to imagine that any of that guarantees a reality of inner relationship with the Lord.

Perhaps the key question is where we are actively putting our faith. For Samson, it was in the gifts God had given and in the external signs, but there seems to have been no heart-relationship with God. The strength that he did have was therefore only physical and external, rather than spiritual and inward. That was why he had to look to a succession of women, like Delilah, to try to give meaning and significance to life. Because he did not have a deep faith-relationship with God, he looked for a substitute in human relationships, as every pagan made in the image of God does, and must. It was this personal vulnerability, which never found its answer in God, that ultimately brought him crashing down.

Strength and Fatal Presumption

> 18 When Delilah saw that he had told her all his heart, she sent and called for the lords of the Philistines, saying, "Come up once more, for he has told me all his heart." So the lords of the Philistines came up to her and brought the money in their hand.
>
> 19 Then she lulled him to sleep on her knees, and called for a man and had him shave off the seven locks of his head. Then she began to torment him, and his strength left him.
>
> 20 And she said, "The Philistines are upon you, Samson!" So he awoke from his sleep, and said, "I will go out as before, at other times, and shake myself free!" But he did not know that the Lord had departed from him.
>
> 21 Then the Philistines took him and put out his eyes, and brought him down to Gaza. They bound him with bronze fetters, and he became a grinder in the prison.
>
> *Judg. 16:18–21*

Instinctively, Delilah knew that at last she had been told the truth. It all made sense, in a way that none of the earlier lies had. Presumably, Samson still regarded it as a game, and thought that his secret would be safe with a lover so committed to him. But Delilah lost no time in summoning the lords of the Philistines, who responded equally quickly, complete with payment of the money in advance, sharing her confidence that this time they had the true story. One cannot help feeling sorry for Samson as the drama works out to its inexorable conclusion. The personal moral blindness, which will all too soon be illustrated by the horror of his new physical blindness, leads him like a lamb to the slaughter. That is the essence of the tragedy. We can see what he cannot. But we also need to approach the story with the moral and spiritual realism that is reflected in Goslinga's comment. "In a sense the Lord had already abandoned him at this point; since he refused to take warning, he would have to suffer the consequences of his sinful folly."

The verbs of verse 19 bring home the full shock of Delilah's treachery. *"She lulled him to sleep"* as a mother might her child, with his head on her knees. She shaved off *"the seven locks of his head."* The Hebrew text makes Delilah the subject of the verb, because she is responsible for the treacherous act, though the New King James Version is probably right to attribute the actual shaving to the man who was lying in wait, as others had been in verses 9 and 12. *"Then she began to torment him."* It was the stated purpose of the Philistine rulers to subdue or *"afflict"* him (v. 5), and the same verb is used here. The writer of Judges is a superb dramatist, and the juxtaposition of the endings of verses 19 and 20 make his theological point with great irony and penetration. As soon as the Nazirite vow was broken and the locks of his hair lay on the floor of Delilah's room, Samson became, as he had himself prophesied in verse 17, *"like any other man."* Verse 19 describes it as *"his strength left him,"* but verse 20 states, *"the Lord had departed from him."* While Samson talks about his strength, the inspired author talks about the Lord. Awaking from sleep, he has no awareness of what has happened; but his resolve, *"I will go out as before,"* is absolutely powerless for, without God, Samson is nothing.

That seems to be the major lesson God wanted Israel to learn, as their judge learned it personally that day. In a sense, Samson, the last in the line of the twelve judges, stands in solidarity with his people—not above them as morally superior, but equally flawed and equally doomed. What happened to him, as representative of the nation, would happen to them all, so long as the downward spiral of sin continued. Samson was strong, not because his hair had never been cut, but because his life had been dedicated to God. As long as that vow was intact, God was with him. But long before his head was shaved, his heart had drifted, and what is going on in the hidden control center of the human personality will eventually show in the words and actions that inevitably issue from it.

Once he had dishonored the Lord by revealing his secret to a pagan woman (and that to satisfy his own appetite), God departed from him, and when God went, Samson's strength went. He had to learn in the hard school of experience that he was utterly powerless without God. His fatal mistake seems to have been to imagine that somehow the strength was his, almost as a natural attribute, rather than a totally supernatural endowment. Surely, that is something with which we can all identify.

When God begins to bless us we readily succumb to the temptation to think that there must after all be something particularly meritorious or worthy in us that has attracted God's attention and favor. We sinners find it very hard to admit that we are totally dependent upon grace. But we are! Surely that is why the Lord Jesus, after declaring himself to be the "true vine," the real Israel, which the nation had manifestly failed to be (Isa. 5:1–7; Ps. 80:8–10), warns his disciples not to fall into the Old Testament trap of imagining that they have any residual supplies of spiritual strength in and of themselves.

> I am the vine, you are the branches. He who abides in Me, and I in him, bears much fruit; for without Me you can do nothing.
>
> *John 15:5*

That is what Samson had to learn, blinded, tormented, and fettered in the prison at Gaza, grinding the grain like a donkey or an ox. Any of us may have enjoyed the highest privileges of God's grace, but any of us can equally be reduced to those depths if we begin to imagine that we have any spiritual strength whatsoever apart from a constant total dependence upon the grace of God in Jesus Christ our Lord.

The best designed and most efficient electrical appliance is totally useless until the flow of electricity is established. Sometimes the plug is not fully in contact with the socket, or maybe the switch has not been turned on. Either way, the flow of power is hindered and nothing will happen until contact is reestablished. If only we could see things that clearly in the spiritual realm. For example, to continue expending huge amounts of money and energy on all the spiritual technology so widely available today, while lacking that vital moment-by-moment contact with Christ, is tragic. Such a false presumption must eventually come under the judgment of a holy God, for it is an implicit denial of our creatureliness. Without God—nothing.

Strength and Divine Judgment

22 However, the hair of his head began to grow again after it had been shaven.
23 Now the Lords of the Philistines gathered together to offer a great sacrifice to Dagon their god, and to rejoice. And they said:

"Our god has delivered into our hands
Samson our enemy!"

24 When the people saw him, they praised their god; for they said:

"Our god has delivered into our hands
our enemy,
The destroyer of our land,
And the one who multiplied our dead."

25 So it happened, when their hearts were merry, that they said, "Call for Samson, that he may perform for us." So they called for Samson from the prison, and he performed for them. And they stationed him between the pillars.
26 Then Samson said to the lad who held him by the hand, "Let me feel the pillars which support the temple, so that I can lean on them."
27 Now the temple was full of men and women; all the Lords of the Philistines were there—about three thousand men and women on the roof watching while Samson performed.
28 Then Samson called to the Lord, saying, "O Lord God, remember me, I pray! Strengthen me, I pray, just this once, O God, that I may with one blow take vengeance on the Philistines for my two eyes!"

29 And Samson took hold of the two middle pillars which supported the temple, and he braced himself against them, one on his right and the other on his left.

30 Then Samson said, "Let me die with the Philistines!" And he pushed with all his might, and the temple fell on the lords and all the people who were in it. So the dead that he killed at his death were more than he had killed in his life.

31 And his brothers and all his father's household came down and took him, and brought him up and buried him between Zorah and Eshtaol in the tomb of his father Manoah. He had judged Israel twenty years.

Judg. 16:22–31

The word *"however,"* with which verse 22 begins, signifies another turning point in this amazing drama. Although Samson was down, he was not finally out. Naturally, his hair began to grow straight away, so that we are not to imagine that the following events happened very long after his humiliation. It is in keeping with Scripture to recognize that God does not punish his erring children longer than is needed, and the regrowth of Samson's hair is a sign that God has neither entirely deserted him, nor completed all his purposes in and through him. The Philistines may have imagined they had won a great victory over the Lord's agent, Samson, which indeed they had, but they had reckoned without the Lord himself. God may put one of his servants aside for a while, even in the discipline of correction through suffering, but that does not mean he has abandoned his purposes. A star player in the "sin bin" does not stop the team pressing all out for victory!

The Philistine feast of verse 23 is therefore at best ill-advised, but their attribution of this victory to their god Dagon is an affront to the glory of the Lord, which will not be tolerated. Here we are back on the main line of Judges with the clash between false gods and Yahweh, the resolution of which is the central agenda of the book. Dagon was an idol with the bodily shape of a fish but the head and hands of a man, one of the principal gods of the Philistines. The temple seems to have been in Gaza, the scene of Samson's earlier heroism, to which he now returns, utterly humiliated. That process continues and intensifies, as the crowd, intoxicated by their victory and probably also with wine (*"their hearts were merry"* v. 25), call

Samson out of his prison to amuse them. Like a bear being baited, Samson is mocked and provoked, and doubtless the name of Yahweh is dragged into the mud, along with the disgrace of his hero. The world is never slow to denigrate God, whenever any of his servants stumbles into public shame. But God is not to be mocked (Gal. 6:7).

So, the final scene of the drama is set. The temple is packed with all the socialites of Gaza and probably Philistia, while thousands of others gather on the roof to get a good look at their defeated enemy. The noise of praise to Dagon mixes with the guffaws and contemptuous laughter at Samson's expense, as he is forced to act the role of clown for the onlookers' delight. In a break in the proceedings, Samson puts himself in a strategic position, between the pillars that support the whole structure, and prays. It is perhaps the moment of Samson's greatest spiritual strength in the whole saga because it is the moment of his clearest dependence on God. Brought totally to the end of his own resources, he now knows that only God can meet him in all his need. So he calls upon the God who is faithful to his covenant promises to remember him by granting one last inflow of supernatural strength in order to avenge Samson's blindness. In so doing he will also vindicate his name as against that of the idol Dagon.

In faith, Samson grasps the central pillars on which the whole structure depended and, sensing for the last time the inflow of the divine strength, pulls the structure in on itself. In what could have been a harrowing description, the writer chooses simply to state a matter of sober fact. *"So the dead that he killed at his death were more than he had killed in his life"* (v. 30b). It was therefore entirely appropriate that his body should be recovered by his family, perhaps at no small risk to themselves, and given a hero's burial back home. He had restored his status as judge (v. 31b) in this climactic act of vengeance in which Yahweh had vindicated both his servant and himself.

The last heroic act shows how Samson ultimately put the honor and glory of God, whom he represented as judge of Israel, before his own life. This is why he is given his place in Hebrews 11:32 along with the other Old Testament men and women of faith. The most appropriate description of Samson from that chapter is surely that in verse 34, "out of weakness were made strong." We are inclined to see the chapter as a record of those who lived well, but it is perhaps more accurate to see it as a record of those who died well.

So many of the commendations center on the way in which they held on to the promises which they did not receive because of their conviction about what lay beyond this world. "Faith is the substance of things hoped for, the evidence of things not seen" (Heb. 11:1). Certainly, Samson fits very well into that scenario. Here was a man of faith who, in the end, sacrificed his own life for the glory of his sovereign Lord, and who saw that this was the only way to deliver his people from the tyranny of sin and false religion. To quote Keil and Delitzsch:

> Such a triumph as this the God of Israel could not permit his enemies and their idols to gain. The Lord must prove to them, even through Samson's death, that the shame of his sin was taken from him, and that the Philistines had no cause to triumph over him. Thus Samson gained the greatest victory over his foes in the moment of his own death. The terror of the Philistines when living, he became a destroyer of the temple of their idol when he died.[4]

The strong became weak, but not useless. Samson's defeat at the hands of the Philistines, permitted by God, was the first time in his life that he hit a brick wall he could not break his way through. He lost his sight and he lost his strength. He realized the unchanging reality of his own weakness. Peter had to sink to the depth of denying his Lord three times, with oaths and curses. Paul had to be blinded and humbled in the dust of the Damascus road.

While things are going our way, we can go on deceiving ourselves that all is well. Surely it is no coincidence that the Sinatra hit "My Way" has been recorded by more artists than any other popular song in the last twenty years. It is so true to our human nature. Only when our foolishness fails do we begin to see what our hearts are really like. It took his failure and abject humiliation to show Samson that he was not a strong man after all—only a weak man in whom God had demonstrated his mighty power. When we learn that, weak people like us become usable. Like Samson, we learn to depend upon God in a new, even desperate, way, which is the essence of true faith.

It was when Samson stood among the Philistines in Dagon's temple, exposed in all his folly and weakness but in total dependence on Yahweh, that he was actually at his strongest and won his greatest victory. That is the paradox with which we began this chapter, exemplified most fully in the Cross of Christ. "God has chosen the foolish things of the world to put to shame the wise, and God has chosen the weak things of the world to put to shame the things which are mighty . . . that no flesh should glory in His presence" (1 Cor. 1:27–29). That sort of weakness, resting in God's strength and grace, God uses to judge a world which prides itself on its self-sufficiency and its strength without God.

NOTES

1. Keil and Delitzsch, *Judges*.
2. Goslinga, *Judges*, 440.
3. Armerding, *Judges*, 333.
4. Keil and Delitzsch, *Judges*, 426.

CHAPTER 17

Beware of False Gods

Judges 17:1–18:31

We have now arrived at the closing section of the Book of Judges. The death of Samson concludes the accounts of the twelve judges and the history of the people of Israel under their leadership, which first began with Othniel back in chapter 3. The last five chapters of the book are given over to two representative incidents, recounted in very considerable detail, which provide typical examples of what life was like in Israel at this traumatic time of the nation's history. In this way they balance the introductory material of 1:1 to 3:6, where the inadequate conquest and settlement of the land and the carelessness of spiritual devotion were identified as the seedbed from which the events we have followed, from 3:7 to 16:31, sprang. The lives of the judges are the detailed sandwich filling between the bread of the introductory analysis and that of these representative incidents.

In these concluding chapters we find a refrain which appears, with some variation, on four separate occasions (17:6; 18:1; 19:1, and 21:25). *"In those days there was no king in Israel; everyone did what was right in his own eyes."* The end of the book relentlessly presses home the message that at its very best the period of the judges was a holding operation. With each judge more flawed and failing than the one before, it is clear that the national life and identity of Israel is under the threat of extermination. All that was accomplished under Moses and Joshua is in jeopardy. Even the covenant promises look set to fail, unthinkable though such a suggestion is theologically, unless some new initiative is taken to turn the people's hearts back to God.

These closing chapters are actually very dark indeed. They show the depths to which even God's covenant people can sink when once they begin to disobey his instructions and trample his grace and mercy under their feet. They prove beyond all doubt the truth that God has not chosen us because we are costly, or impressive, or morally any better than anyone else, for we are not. The grace of God is that he chooses to have mercy on totally undeserving sinners, such as Israel and today's church. In the end, we cannot get further than that magnificent statement to Israel about God's covenant love and mercy, recorded in Deuteronomy 7:7–8. "The Lord did not set His love on you nor choose you because you were more in number than any other people, for you were the least of all peoples; but because the Lord loves you. . . ." He loves us because he loves us!

Not surprisingly, the twin themes which are woven together throughout the book occur again in these closing chapters, in clear and challenging detail. Chapters 17 and 18 deal with the religious and spiritual chaos in Israel, as they explore the problem of idolatry. Chapters 19 to 21 focus on the moral chaos, with their treatment of the concomitant problem of immorality. Because spiritual belief (or lack of it) has an inevitable effect upon moral behavior, the two themes run so closely in parallel. Failure to love God will always lead to, and be expressed in, failure to love one's neighbor. Denial of God's revealed truth will always issue in a denigration of God's love. But, although these two accounts form an epilogue or summary of the book as a whole, we must remember that they did not take place chronologically at the end of the period of the judges. In fact, the migration of the tribe of Dan (chapter 18) happened very early in the period (see Joshua 19:47), soon after the death of Joshua. The inclination of the people toward idolatrous worship occurred very early on and was mixed with sinful behavior from the start. Micah's shrine, an example of the apostasy of a household, led to the apostasy of a whole tribe and stands as a terrible example of the rapidity with which spiritual decline can take hold. All the evidences of that decline which have been so vividly described for us in the rest of the book are already here in seed form.

What chapters 17 and 18 describe is not yet the situation at its worst, but all the ingredients of the downward spiral are already present. There is no king. The root problem is the breakdown of authority in Israel. Once the people have rejected God as their rightful ruler, they are no longer a theocracy. The unifying principle has been removed and, as a consequence, the threat of national disintegration becomes more and more prevalent. If God is not at the center, the tribes will increasingly splinter into warring factions. What the writer is especially concerned to point out, as always, is that such political and social consequences have spiritual roots.

Chapter 17 presents us with the story of a silver idol made for a man named Micah and installed in his private domestic shrine in the region of Mount Ephraim. Chapter 18 records how the tribe of Dan, having been unable to expel the Canaanite tribes from the territory allotted to them under Joshua, sends out a five-man search party to look for alternative quarters. En route, they encounter Micah's priest who confesses God's blessing on them, after which they discover a city called Laish, which is undefended and vulnerable. Six hundred Danites move to take over Laish, but to ensure their success they first collect Micah's idols and then appropriate his priest, in spite of all his protests. They overwhelm and destroy Laish, resettling it and the area and setting up their own idol shrine and alternative priesthood. The overall message is clear. We are to see how the sins of one man are multiplied on a tribal scale, which will in turn become the sins of the whole nation.

The Marks of False Religion

1 Now there was a man from the mountains of Ephraim, whose name was Micah.

2 And he said to his mother, "The eleven hundred shekels of silver that were taken from you, and on which you put a curse, even saying it in my ears—here is the silver with me: I took it." And his mother said, "May you be blessed by the Lord, my son!"

3 So when he had returned the eleven hundred shekels of silver to his mother, his mother said, "I had wholly dedicated the silver from my hand to the Lord for my son, to make a carved image and a molded image; now therefore, I will return it to you."

4 Thus he returned the silver to his mother. Then his mother took two hundred shekels of silver and gave them to the silversmith, and he made it into a carved image and a molded image; and they were in the house of Micah.

Judg. 17:1–4

Make Your Own Idol

These verses graphically portray the irony of an almost farcical situation. Virtually everything about the situation bristles with highly irregular and questionable religious practices. To start with, the man who blithely thinks he can set up his own "do-it-yourself" domestic shrine to Yahweh is a thief—and from his own mother. His name, *"Micah,"* in its shortened form carries the ironic meaning in its original "who is like Yahweh?" or "Yahweh, the incomparable." But there is certainly no reflection of the content of the name in the character of its bearer. That in itself is significant. It is making the point that simply to acknowledge the Lord in a superficial way, without reflecting his character in our behavior is an affront to his deity and holiness, which brings its own inevitable consequences.

Micah steals eleven hundred shekels of silver from his mother. Terrified by the curse which she calls down on the thief, in his hearing, he makes a clean breast of the crime and returns the money to his mother, only to be blessed by her, in the Lord's name, surely taken in vain. She then reveals that she had already decided to dedicate the entire amount to the Lord to make a carved and molded image. But in fact, only two hundred shekels are handed over to the silversmith to produce this object. Truth and honesty are clearly nonstarters in this family.

However, the focal sin is their direct contravention of the Second Commandment:

> "You shall not make for yourself a carved image—any likeness of anything that is in heaven above, or that is in the earth beneath, or that is in the water under the earth; you shall not bow down to them nor serve them."
>
> *Exod. 20:4–5*

Micah and his mother chose to ignore this clear instruction of the Lord so as to respond to the customs of the pagan tribes all around them. Many images have been excavated by archaeologists working on this period in that area of Palestine. Doubtless, Micah and his mother convinced themselves that they were worshiping the true God in this socially acceptable way; but it was an abomination to the Lord. In fact, they were making God in their image, reducing him to man-size and thereby trying to tame and control him. That is always both the attraction and peril of idols.

We must not be so naive as to imagine this to be a problem confined to ancient Israel or to primitive tribal communities. The essence of idolatry is *to want to bring God within our pockets, so as to control him.* Foolishly, we imagine that we can deal with the source of life on the same level as ourselves, so that we can bribe him, or drive a bargain, or compel him to do what we want, to give us what we want out of life. Above all, and at all costs, what natural human beings want is a god that will not make demands on our lives—one that will give us what we need, but require nothing in return. It may be an attractive shape or a quality product; it can be a status symbol much admired and envied. But we worship idols for their imagined power, which is given into our hands as their devotees. In that sense, all forms of idolatry are an extension of works-oriented religion, a man-made invention by which I hope to save myself by the works of my own hands.

In applying this passage, it is helpful not just to point out the more obvious materialistic idols of our culture, but to explore their Christian equivalents, which we so often justify and sanctify. Religious idols are the most dangerous of all. We may be liberated from idolatry to the toys of our society—the cars and boats, the airplanes and swimming pools, the exotic travel trips and even larger houses—but at the same time, in Christian circles, we can often substitute our own much more respectable and accepted idol shrines. After all, if lots of other people worship there too, that gives the idol greater credibility. An idol is anything that usurps the place of God, because I am looking to it to give me real life, to protect or to enrich me. It is anything that squeezes God into the margin of my life because that thing has now become worth more to me than he is. It could be our marriage or family life, the achievements of our kids, the success of our church, our position as a valued Christian leader or a growing disciple, our service for the Lord, our financial generosity, our biblical or doctrinal knowledge, our spiritual gifts. Once we fall in love with any of these good and potentially godly ingredients of life rather than with the Lord as the undisputed Number One in our experience, we are casting our idol, as surely as Micah did.

For behind each of these good things when it usurps the central position of our affections and worship lies ourselves. I am really worshiping acceptable extensions of little me, while all the time fooling myself and my fellow Christians that it's all for the Lord. Only God can read our hearts, and we each have enough to do coping with our own depravity without trying to sit in judgment on one another, but we do need to take the closing injunction of John's first letter with deadly seriousness. "Little children, keep yourselves from idols" (1 John 5:21). The Bible places the responsibility fairly and squarely with us.

> 5 The man Micah had a shrine, and made an ephod and household idols; and he consecrated one of his sons, who became his priest.
> 6 In those days there was no king in Israel; everyone did what was right in his own eyes.
> *Judg. 17:5–6*

Set Up Your Own Shrine

The setting up of his own shrine was a further necessary step if idolatry was going to thrive in Israel. But in the Mosaic Law code, God expressly prohibited it. A classic passage which demonstrates such prohibition is Deuteronomy 12:2–8, where the Israelites are specifically instructed to break down the idol shrines "on the high mountains . . . and under every green tree." Altars, pillars, and images are all to be destroyed. "You shall not worship the Lord your God with such things," Yahweh commanded. Instead, Israel is to seek out the one place chosen by the Lord "to put His name for His dwelling place" and to worship him there with the offerings he has prescribed. In fact, the passage ends by describing the idolatrous worship practices among the Canaanite tribes in exactly the same terminology as that used by the author of Judges—"every man doing whatever is right in his own eyes." That is clearly the essence of idolatry.

There was to be one sanctuary for all the people, which was the Tent of Meeting, now situated at Shiloh (18:31). This had been the only focus for acceptable worship of Yahweh since Israel had come out of Egypt. Here alone was the Ark of the Covenant, with its tablets of the Law, symbolic of the presence of God among his people, and so the principal focus of the nation's unity. Here alone could the proper worship of Yahweh be carried out, as he had dictated, by the priests whom he had appointed.

But it was so much more convenient to stay at home. It was so much easier not to have to cope with long journeys to Shiloh for the festivals, not to have to bother with the expensive business of providing animal sacrifices without blemish. It was so much handier to have a residential priest to pray for you. So Micah made his own shrine and set up one of his own sons in the business. He introduced small household gods, as well as his splendid status-symbol image. He even had his own ephod, as Gideon had done (8:27). Usually this refers to a part of the priest's garments, to which the Urim and Thummim were attached, means by which the will of God could be discovered. However, it may be that in Judges the term is being used to describe a metal idol. Whatever it means, clearly it is an indication that Micah was determined to worship God in the way he wanted to. But that is the one thing you cannot do if your god is greater than the worshiper. *He* dictates the terms. And so, because Micah's heart was not right with God, his so-called worship was an empty fake. Doubtless, he was very pleased with it all, as it was all on his terms; it is the mark of the idolater to presume that if he is pleased with it then his "god" must be also. But actually what Micah was doing was an abomination in God's eyes. All that he had succeeded in doing was to mirror the pagan culture all around him, of which he was increasingly a part, by bringing the Creator God who made him, the covenant Lord to whom he owed his very existence, down to his own human level.

At a time when subjective "worship experiences" are all the rage, these sobering reflections should provide a much-needed assessment of some of our current practices. Of course, we are liberated in the New Testament from geographical restrictions on corporate worship, as we are from the whole Old Testament cultus. But we are not free to worship God in any way we choose. There is still the qualification that he seeks those who will worship him "in spirit and in truth" (John 4:24). Do we actually worship God in the way he wants? Recently, a young lady came to our Sunday morning service, for the first time, and told me afterward that she felt God had constrained her to come, against her will. When I asked her to explain, she said, "Well, I wanted to go to (naming another local fellowship) to sing and dance and shout, but I felt God wanted me to come here to learn from the Bible." Now I am not suggesting for one moment that God is not present in that other fellowship, but what interested me was her approach to worship. It had been very much on her terms, on what she wanted to do. Whatever its form, we can easily leave a worship service saying, "We had a great time today"; but is that God's verdict? Because there was no truth content in Micah's false worship, satisfying to him and expensive though it was, it was the cotton candy of his own delusion.

> 7 Now there was a young man from Bethlehem in Judah, of the family of Judah; he was a Levite, and was staying there.
>
> 8 The man departed from the city of Bethlehem in Judah to stay wherever he could find a place. Then he came to the mountains of Ephraim, to the house of Micah, as he journeyed.
>
> 9 And Micah said to him, "Where do you come from?" So he said to him, "I am a Levite from Bethlehem in Judah, and I am on my way to find a place to stay."
>
> 10 Micah said to him, "Dwell with me, and be a father and a priest to me, and I will give you ten shekels of silver per year, a suit of clothes, and your sustenance." So the Levite went in.
>
> 11 Then the Levite was content to dwell with the man; and the young man became like one of his sons to him.
>
> 12 So Micah consecrated the Levite, and the young man became his priest, and lived in the house of Micah.
>
> *Judg. 17:7–12*

Employ Your Own Priest

Clearly Micah was not too happy about his unqualified son serving as priest, so when the wandering, young Levite came along, he seized the opportunity. But the Levite was not qualified, on God's terms, to serve in that capacity either. He had no right to be wandering from the one central sanctuary, no mandate to be a priest, and no authority to serve an individual or a family (see Numbers 3:6–10). But of course, false religion believes it can buy the services of important cult figures. Moreover, false ministers can usually be relied on to comply with such requests, if the career prospects are right.

This young man was not content with the job and place of work God had assigned to him. He was out to make his own way, on his own terms.

We can understand that this seemed too good an offer to decline—ten shekels a year, as well as food and clothing! Surely God has got to be in an offer as attractive and profitable as that! It must be a mark of his special blessing. Such is a trap we are all prone to fall into, but, of course, it is often a barrier to any sort of effective ministry at all. When the minister is in the pocket of a ruling elder, or a dominant personality in the local congregation, he has lost his independence of judgment and action. Many a young minister, scandalously poorly paid, has found the apparent generosity of a wealthy layman, in offering financial support to himself and his growing family, to have certain strings attached. He has to dance to a certain tune, and if he does not comply with the particular foibles of his patron, he can find himself not only without that extra financial help, but even ejected from his pastorate. It is a terrible thing for a local church when its ministers are at the beck and call of such wealthy supporters, though it has to be said that were the church to pay a proper salary instead of the pittance that is offered in some countries, the problem would never exist.

Listen to a church council or a congregational meeting discussing the sort of minister the church wants to call. So often, what God wants is assumed to be the same as what *we* want, because in practice God has become a pocket-sized idol. What churches always need is ministry that presents the true Word of God, without fear or favor, and a minister who serves for the glory of God, not the rewards of the church. We need to be alert to the danger of the church imagining that it employs rather than God calls, and of the minister pleasing men rather than God. We need to ask whether we are really open for God to work among us as he wants to.

> 13 Then Micah said, "Now I know that the Lord will be good to me, since I have a Levite as priest!"
>
> *Judg. 17:13*

Ensure Your Own Future

This last verse encapsulates the essence of both the appeal and the folly of idolatry. Whenever we human beings imagine that we have

God in our pocket, we are desperately misguided. Sometimes, on the road to faith, intellectual barriers have to be overcome. Intelligent but arrogant people refuse to believe God because they cannot understand his self-revelation in terms of their own logical arguments. They forget that when we have a "God" who can be encompassed within the limited intellect of the next brilliant human being, we have emptied the word *God* of all its essential meaning. He is infinite and we are not. That is why faith—not intellectual argument—is always the door to spiritual reality. Of course, the task of apologetics is vital, especially today when for many the door of faith is encrusted and overgrown by the intellectual skepticism and biblical ignorance of our culture. Those habits of mind die hard; many Christians seem to want a "God" who can be manipulated, who will dance when we pull the strings and who will produce the blessings when we put in the demands. By setting up an alternative cult in direct disobedience to God's clear commands (Exod. 28:1), Micah might have imagined that he was securing divine blessing on his life. But in fact he was acting stupidly. But that is the story of the Book of Judges, and we find the echo still in our sinful human hearts.

The true and living God does not have favorites. He loves the world. The attraction of the idol is that it belongs to me, so that I can control it and enjoy a special relationship of favor with it. When my church, or my work for the Lord, or my financial capacity, or my status in the community begin to whisper to me that now God's blessing is certain or inevitable, I can be sure that these things have become idols, by means of which I am actually worshiping myself. They provide only a thin veneer of godliness over the unmistakable features of a worldly idol (see 2 Timothy 3:1–5).

Such idols drain the church of the power of the Holy Spirit which could otherwise be experienced in all his fullness. They paralyze us (see 18:24). Their worshipers become as inert and ineffective as they are, so that far from the future providing certain blessings from God, it is condemned to be a predictable, boring round of self-worship. Then the devil has won. Spiritually, he has destroyed us because we were not prepared to venture out on the bare word of God's promises in faith. Instead, every time we chose to operate on the basis of sight and of what our own hands and minds could achieve for ourselves, we were playing the devil's game and becoming enmeshed in a web of idolatrous self-reliance. "Little children, keep yourselves from idols" (1 John 5:21).

Chapter 18 shows not only the spread of Micah's evil, as the Danites take over both his idols and his priest and appropriate them for their own ends. It also uncovers the deeper motivations we have begun to hint at, which are important to grasp if our preaching is to bring this passage alive—out of the pages of history right into our contemporary context.

THE MOTIVATION OF FALSE RELIGION

1 In those days there was no king in Israel. And in those days the tribe of the Danites was seeking an inheritance for itself to dwell in; for until that day their inheritance among the tribes of Israel had not fallen to them.

2 So the children of Dan sent five men of their family from their territory, men of valor from Zorah and Eshtaol, to spy out the land and search it. They said to them, "Go, search the land." So they went to the mountains of Ephraim, to the house of Micah, and lodged there.

3 While they were at the house of Micah, they recognized the voice of the young Levite. They turned aside and said to him, "Who brought you here? What are you doing in this place? What do you have here?"

4 He said to them, "Thus and so Micah did for me. He has hired me, and I have become his priest."

5 So they said to him, "Please inquire of God, that we may know whether the journey on which we go will be prosperous."

6 And the priest said to them, "Go in peace. The presence of the Lord be with you on your way."

7 So the five men departed and went to Laish. They saw the people who were there, how they dwelt safely, in the manner of the Sidonians, quiet and secure. There were no rulers in the land who might put them to shame for anything. They were far from the Sidonians, and they had no ties with anyone.

8 Then the spies came back to their brethren at Zorah and Eshtaol, and their brethren said to them, "What is your report?"

9 So they said, "Arise, let us go up against them.
For we have seen the land, and indeed it is very good.
Would you do nothing? Do not hesitate to go, and
enter to possess the land.
10 "When you go, you will come to a secure people
and a large land. For God has given it into your hands,
a place where there is no lack of anything that is on the
earth."
11 And six hundred men of the family of the
Danites went from there, from Zorah and Eshtaol,
armed with weapons of war.
12 Then they went up and encamped in Kirjath
Jearim in Judah. (Therefore they call that place Mahaneh
Dan to this day. There it is, west of Kirjath Jearim.)
13 And they passed from there to the mountains of
Ephraim, and came to the house of Micah.
14 Then the five men who had gone to spy out the
country of Laish answered and said to their brethren,
"Do you know that there are in these houses an ephod,
household idols, a carved image, and a molded image?
Now therefore, consider what you should do."
15 So they turned aside there, and came to the
house of the young Levite man—to the house of
Micah—and greeted him.
16 The six hundred men armed with their weapons of war, who were of the children of Dan, stood by
the entrance of the gate.
17 Then the five men who had gone to spy out the
land went up. Entering there, they took the carved
image, the ephod, the household idols, and the molded image. The priest stood at the entrance of the gate
with the six hundred men who were armed with
weapons of war.
18 When these went into Micah's house and took
the carved image, the ephod, the household idols,
and the molded image, the priest said to them, "What
are you doing?"
19 And they said to him, "Be quiet, put your hand
over your mouth, and come with us; be a father and a
priest to us. Is it better for you to be a priest to the
household of one man, or that you be a priest to a tribe
and a family in Israel?"

20 So the priest's heart was glad; and he took the
ephod, the household idols, and the carved image, and
took his place among the people.
21 Then they turned and departed, and put the little
ones, the livestock, and the goods in front of them.
22 When they were a good way from the house of
Micah, the men who were in the houses near Micah's
house gathered together and overtook the children of
Dan.
23 And they called out to the children of Dan. So
they turned around and said to Micah, "What ails you,
that you have gathered such a company?"
24 So he said, "You have taken away my gods
which I made, and the priest, and you have gone away.
Now what more do I have? How can you say to me,
'What ails you?'"
25 And the children of Dan said to him, "Do not let
your voice be heard among us, lest angry men fall
upon you, and your lose your life, with the lives of
your household!"
26 Then the children of Dan went their way. And
when Micah saw that they were too strong for him, he
turned and went back to his house.
27 So they took the things Micah had made, and
the priest who had belonged to him, and went to Laish,
to a people quiet and secure; and they struck them with
the edge of the sword and burned the city with fire.
28 There was no deliverer, because it was far from
Sidon, and they had no ties with anyone. It was in the
valley that belongs to Beth Rehob. So they rebuilt
the city and dwelt there.
29 And they called the name of the city Dan, after
the name of Dan their father, who was born to Israel.
However, the name of the city formerly was Laish.
30 Then the children of Dan set up for themselves the
carved image; and Jonathan the son of Gershom, the son
of Manasseh, and his sons were priests to the tribe of Dan
until the day of the captivity of the land.
31 So they set up for themselves Micah's carved
image which he made, all the time that the house of
God was in Shiloh.

Judg. 18:1–31

We need to treat chapter 18 as a unit, so as to catch the sweep of the whole narrative and understand the events of the story in sequence. From these the Holy Spirit enables us to see the spiritual significance of the history that is recorded, since the character of God and the heart of man are unchangingly independent of time and place. The best way of presenting this sad story to a contemporary congregation may well be to draw out the major strands of motivation behind the Danites' apostasy so that we may search our own hearts, in the light of God's Word.

Disobedience is identified as the root of the problem in verses 1–2. The irony of the opening sentence is that the King was always in Israel, among his people, as he had always promised to be, but his word was rejected and his availability ignored. That was why things went so badly wrong throughout this period. The people may "solve" the problem by appealing to God for "a king to judge us like all the nations" (1 Sam. 8:5), but as the Lord pointed out to Samuel, this symbolized their rejection of God (1 Sam. 8:7). They were right in recognizing the root of their problems lay in the absence of authority, but wrong in their solution. Only when their true King rode into Jerusalem on a donkey, centuries later, was the need for divine authority mediated through an earthly king really. And he was rejected.

The historical fact is that the Danites had chosen not to obey God's clear instructions to them to take over the territory which had been allotted to them. They were driven back by the Amorites into the hill country (Judg. 1:34). As their numbers increased and they needed more space, being unprepared for the hard work of obedience, which meant conflict, they chose their own apparently easier alternative, and it seemed to work. In fact, they won an easy victory, but it had devastating long-term effects. Their very remoteness from the other tribes led them further into idolatry, but that did not show up at first. In the short term, they undoubtedly congratulated themselves that they were on to a good thing; they felt comfortable, settled, at peace. Actually, they were totally disobedient.

Their actions show how bad a guide subjective feelings can be. We forget that the long-term results of disobedience are always devastating when everything seems to be going so well. Conversely, when we run into problems and difficulties, we begin to imagine that something *must* be wrong. The New Testament apostles, however, seem to have gone out of their way to alert the second generation of

Christians left behind that suffering would always be part of the package for a godly life (1 Pet. 4:12–13; 2 Tim. 2:3–4; 3:12).

The young couple who decide to live together before marriage, because they do not have any inner witness that it could possibly be wrong, since they love one another so much—and after all, God is love—are making the same fundamental error. Ignoring God's clear command (1 Cor. 6:18), they choose to disobey instructions on the ground that it feels OK and everything seems to be going well. No thunderbolts of judgment fall from heaven. But the long-term damage done to their relationship by the "trial" nature of the arrangement and their unwillingness to commit themselves lastingly to one another, by a public statement, is unseen and incalculable. The Danites' error is being repeated throughout the church whenever we move the goal posts or bend the rules to accommodate human desires that are actually contradictory to God's word.

It is not that the Bible is unclear, but that we don't like to do what God says. That is the problem, and it is as old as the Garden of Eden. Even while writing this chapter I have had a phone call from a fellow minister, asking my advice on whether to conduct a marriage ceremony between a Christian and an unbeliever, who is nevertheless very sympathetic to Christian things. The issue seems to me to be very clear-cut, in terms of 2 Corinthians 6:14–16. The danger is that because it is easier, in terms of pastoral relationships, not to enforce the biblical teaching, we gradually drift into disobedience. Surely this chapter provides an arresting enough example of where that can lead to make us stop in our tracks and question what we are doing when we countenance setting aside God's instructions.

Superstition is a second motivation, which is brought out very clearly in verses 5–6 and 14–20. Of course, the Danites wanted God to be with them—anybody who believes in God would be a fool not to want that—but it was all on their terms. This is what is often called "folk religion," which owes far more to pagan superstition than to divine revelation. It is especially prevalent in a country like Great Britain, where committed church attendance is running at less than 5 percent, but where the cultural traditions are embedded in a remembered, vibrant Christian faith.

The Danites were not too worried about the priest's credentials or spirituality. So long as they had a blessing from a religious leader, that was fine. Later they stole not only the priest, but Micah's idols and ephod as well. Religious symbols were important for them to possess if they were to be successful in conquering Laish. They were good luck charms; it was pure superstition. The emptiness of these false gods and their disobedience to the true and living God do not seem to have bothered them for a moment. They felt safe, without needing to have any dealings with a transcendent deity. That's always the attraction of false religions.

Back in contemporary Britain, this means that thousands of families will want their babies to be christened, thousands of couples will expect a church wedding, in white with all the trimmings, and almost everyone except the most convinced atheist will expect a minister to conduct the funeral. Such people have no living faith in God, rarely if ever attend public worship, and live their lives often in flagrant disobedience of God's commandments. But some holy water or religious words, administered by a properly qualified "holy man," in a properly sanctified place, give them feelings of security that ultimately all will be well spiritually in this world and the next. It is truly tragic. Such conformity to rites and ceremonies without a heart that is humbly submitted to God, in obedience to his Word, is just superstition. The aim is to have all of the benefits without any of the equivalent cost. It is welfare state religion, which uses Christianity rather than paganism as its foundational superstition. We need to realize that none of our evangelical citadels are immune from its penetrating attacks.

Selfish ambition takes us a step deeper into the analysis of our own hearts to see why false religion has such a strong hold over us. Here, verses 8–10 are particularly helpful and searching. It is remarkable how similar the report of the spies is to that of Joshua and Caleb at the time when God really had called the people to enter the land and trust him to give them success (Num. 13:25–14:9). False religion can very easily wear the same clothing as the real thing. When the wolf enters the flock, he does not carry a placard around his neck proclaiming his identity; he comes dressed in sheep's clothing.

It was the Danites' greed and their desire for ease that led them to massacre a peaceful and unsuspecting people (v. 27). It was their desire to be safe that led them to steal Micah's idols, just as that same desire had led him to have them made in the first place. It was the priest's ambition that led him to serve Micah and then to be drawn away to a more attractive and lucrative task (vv. 19–20). The living

God who always insists on interfering with our lives, by producing his plans, is rejected in favor of "godlets" that do not answer back because they cannot. Yet every time we make decisions without really seeking God, or insist on enforcing our will onto the situation, or choose what will be most easy and comfortable for us—are we not doing the same?

Personal power is the ultimate root of false religion, which this chapter exposes, especially in verses 25–31. The issue could not be more fundamental. It concerns who is going to be in charge in our lives, God or us. There are really only two candidates, however we may dress up ourselves in the trappings of human religions and philosophies. This was the issue put to Eve and Adam by the serpent in the Garden. "Are you going to let God be God, by doing what he says, or are you going to set up an alternative authority by which you put yourself in control?"

The age-old method is to question God's authority ("has God indeed said . . . ?" Gen. 3:1), deny its validity ("you will not surely die," Gen. 3:4), and present a more attractive alternative ("you will be like God . . ." Gen. 3:5). This was the issue that God articulated through Joshua to the people at the beginning of the period of the judges: "Fear the Lord, serve him in sincerity and in truth and put away the (foreign) gods . . ." (Josh. 24:14).

After this period, Elijah would issue the same challenge on Mt. Carmel, with memorable clarity. "'How long will you falter between two opinions? If the Lord is God, follow Him; but if Baal, follow him'" (1 Kings 18:21). The Lord Jesus addressed the same issue in the conclusion of his Sermon on the Mount, "'Enter by the narrow gate; for wide is the gate and broad is the way that leads to destruction, and there are many who go in by it. Because narrow is the gate and difficult is the way which leads to life, and there are few who find it'" (Matt. 7:13–14). Augustine grappled with the same issue when he affirmed that if Jesus Christ is not Lord of all, then he is not really Lord at all. It is the same battle in all our hearts.

Both Micah and the Danites acted as they did because, at root, they wanted to be in control. The Danites used their personal power first to intimidate Micah and steal his idols (v. 25), and then to attack and conquer Laish (vv. 27–28). They had it all their own way and God left them to it, just as he had left Samson. For God's way is not power or coercion, but the authority of love. That is the mark of true religion, or, in biblical terms, of real faith.

When the love of God, revealed in Christ crucified, captures our hearts and conquers our will the most amazing miracle takes place still. Instead of wanting to be in charge of our lives and do our own will, we acknowledge that Jesus is Lord (1 Cor. 12:3) and pray, "Your will [not mine] be done" (Matt. 6:10). Instead of wanting to secure and exercise our power, we look to Christ for his strength, made perfect only in our weakness (2 Cor. 12:9, 4:7). That is real Christianity, and it is a matter of the heart. Since there was none born of women greater than John the Baptist (Matt. 11:11), perhaps we should let his words summarize the lesson these two chapters teach about true devotion, as opposed to false religion, "He must increase, but I must decrease" (John 3:30). That is spiritual reality. Beware of false gods!

CHAPTER 18

The Infection of Godlessness

Judges 19:1–20:11

Chapters 19–21 form the last unit of the Book of Judges. That the three chapters have to be taken together is proved, not only by the unilinear development of the story as one event inexorably leads to another, but also by the editorial comment, with which it begins and ends. In this chapter, we take the first two sections of the unit, which describe the outrage at Gibeah (19:1–28) that leads to the preparations for civil war, of which it is the *casus belli* (19:29–20:11).

We need to remember that this refrain about there being no king so that everyone was doing what was right in his own eyes is not just a political comment, but a theological diagnosis. God was to be Israel's king. It was he who chose Abram and who entered into covenant with him and his descendants. There would have been no nation of Israel had God not seen their suffering in Egypt, identified them as "My people," "My firstborn" (Exod. 4:22), and come down to rescue them. He had set them apart to be his own people by giving them his law at Sinai. There was, therefore, no conceivable way in which anyone or anything could substitute for God as the ultimate authority in the lives of these people.

In the previous chapter, we explored the tragic story of a representative act of idolatry, beginning with one man, but ultimately affecting a whole tribe, and through them the nation. In turning from the living God to dumb idols, Micah and the Danites illustrated the false worship that lay at the heart of the nation's problems. It was in fact a thinly disguised substitution of self-worship for the worship of the true and loving God. In this final section our author demonstrates the social consequences of that shift as he documents the nation's slide into moral anarchy and civil war. The rejection of the Lord's authority led to such a breakdown of law and order that Israelite society stood on the verge of moral collapse and annihilation. The downward spiral, ending in national extinction, appears to be almost complete.

We are not without prophets in our own day, both within the popular media and the Christian church, who are more than ready to intone the funeral rites over the corpse of what was once called Western civilization. We may feel that we can agree with Mark Twain, who cabled London in 1897: "the reports of my death have been greatly exaggerated!" But with the international, political, and ecological challenges the world faces, it is not so difficult now to imagine the "worst scenario" of the extinction of planet earth. When we look at the insoluble problems faced by the developed, as well as the developing, nations, we can understand the mesmeric effects of doom watching at this point of time.

Part of our Christian discipleship consists in using our minds, carefully and prayerfully, to understand the times in which we live without becoming unduly influenced by the contemporary analyses or mood-shifts. Mature believers are not tossed around by every wind that blows (Eph 4:14). This is especially important when we come to present biblical material which is historically rooted, as these chapters are, to a very different contemporary culture. There will be both points of similarity and of discontinuity, about which the expositor needs to be very clear.

For example, Bible history is always written from a theological standpoint. Paul tells us that Old Testament history was specifically written down to help God's people in every age to persevere, to take heart, and to increase in hope (Rom. 15:4). That is why the Bible is strong on spiritual analysis rather than factual, biographical detail, which is anyway a Western preoccupation. Our civilization is not a parallel with Old Testament Israel, enabling us to transfer any and everything lock, stock, and barrel from the pages of Scripture to today's political or social debates. We do not live in a theocracy in rebellion against its God who has brought it into special covenant relationship with himself. We live in a secular democracy, which is multicultural in its life and religious beliefs. Personally, I am persuaded that the New Testament parallel to Israel is the church, within the secular state. And within that visible entity, there is also a parallel spiritual "remnant." In teaching a book like Judges, therefore, our first applications must always be to the people of God, and so to our own hearts. Unarguably, there is plenty that the church is needing to do, throughout the Western democracies, to put her own house in order.

But it is also true that God's moral law was given with the highest good in mind for the whole of mankind. It contains the Maker's Instructions for the right functioning of everything he has created, so that if we human beings ignore or deliberately flout it, we must not be surprised when individual lives disintegrate and society begins to crumble. A hundred years ago, seminal German thinkers like Nietzsche and Weber painted the picture of a world without values and without absolutes because it was a world without God. But they trembled on the brink of that abyss. The tragedy of our time is that we seem to have waltzed into it or perhaps "rock 'n' rolled" into it with total abandon. The history of our century shows just how contagious godlessness can be because, as in so many areas of life, fashions can influence, grip, and ultimately control whole societies. There is such a thing as a spiritual and moral climate which affects everyone living in that society more than they usually realize. Both godly and godless attitudes spread, sometimes very rapidly. This is the explanation of the great revivals in history, as well as the moral collapse of empires. The church is always facing the pressures of the world, which is trying to squeeze it into the culture's mold (Rom. 12:2). It is when we most mirror that culture, often obliviously unaware of what we are doing, that we are at our most worldly. This is much more subtle than the "shibboleths" of former generations, when worldliness was defined in terms of social "no go" areas like drinking, dancing, or the cinema. It is in the heart attitudes and the hidden thought-life that the world exercises its deepest influence upon us, merely to conform. That is all that's required of us. Don't be different!

In an age when we are perhaps tempted to place too much importance on the role of the opinion-formers—the journalists, the program makers, and popular media personalities—it is easy for us to imagine that our ordinary lives have no influence and so count for nothing. But that is not so. Each of us has a unique circle of relationships in which we have influence for good or ill. We need to remember that what we believe and how we behave does influence others all the time. How we conduct our family life, our attitudes toward our spouses and children, how we behave at work, among our friends, in the neighborhood, in our leisure pursuits—how we use our resources of time, money, skills, and energy—they all make an impact on others without our even recognizing it. We all make a contribution every day.

Writing in the British press recently, the bishop of Worcester characterized the moral climate of the last two decades in one pithy sentence. He said we live in a society where "it doesn't matter what you believe, so long as you believe that it doesn't matter." That was precisely the situation in Israel, throughout this Book of Judges, so the bridges of contemporary relevance should not be too hard to find. We, too, need to be on our guard against being subtly influenced by the thinking of our contemporary culture, particularly toward the area of accepting and making compromises with what God's Word clearly proclaims. Let's look at the text.

> 1 And it came to pass in those days, when there was no king in Israel, that there was a certain Levite staying in the remote mountains of Ephraim. He took for himself a concubine from Bethlehem in Judah.
>
> 2 But his concubine played the harlot against him, and went away from him to her father's house at Bethlehem in Judah, and was there four whole months.
>
> 3 Then her husband arose and went after her, to speak kindly to her and bring her back, having his servant and a couple of donkeys with him. So she brought him into her father's house; and when the father of the young woman saw him, he was glad to meet him.
>
> 4 Now his father-in-law, the young woman's father, detained him; and he stayed with him three days. So they ate and drank and lodged there.
>
> 5 Then it came to pass on the fourth day that they arose early in the morning, and he stood to depart; but the young woman's father said to his son-in-law, "Refresh your heart with a morsel of bread, and afterward go your way."
>
> 6 So they sat down, and the two of them ate and drank together. Then the young woman's father said to the man, "Please be content to stay all night, and let your heart be merry."

7 And when the man stood to depart, his father-in-law urged him; so he lodged there again.

8 Then he arose early in the morning on the fifth day to depart, but the young woman's father said, "Please refresh your heart." So they delayed until afternoon; and both of them ate.

9 And when the man stood to depart—he and his concubine and his servant—his father-in-law, the young woman's father, said to him, "Look, the day is now drawing toward evening: please spend the night. See, the day is coming to an end; lodge here, that your heart may be merry. Tomorrow go your way early, so that you may get home."

10 However, the man was not willing to spend that night; so he rose and departed, and came opposite Jebus (that is, Jerusalem). With him were the two saddled donkeys; his concubine was also with him.

11 They were near Jebus, and the day was far spent; and the servant said to his master, "Come, please, and let us turn aside into this city of the Jebusites and lodge in it."

12 But his master said to him, "We will not turn aside here into a city of foreigners, who are not of the children of Israel; we will go on to Gibeah."

13 So he said to his servant, "Come, let us draw near to one of these places, and spend the night in Gibeah or in Ramah."

14 And they passed by and went their way; and the sun went down on them near Gibeah, which belongs to Benjamin.

15 They turned aside there to go in to lodge in Gibeah. And when he went in, he sat down in the open square of the city, for no one would take them into his house to spend the night.

16 Just then an old man came in from his work in the field at evening, who also was from the mountains of Ephraim; he was staying in Gibeah, whereas the men of the place were Benjamites.

17 And when he raised his eyes, he saw the traveler in the open square of the city; and the old man said, "Where are you going, and where do you come from?"

18 So he said to him, "We are passing from Bethlehem in Judah toward the remote mountains of Ephraim; I am from there. I went to Bethlehem in Judah; now I am going to the house of the Lord. But there is no one who will take me into his house,

19 "although we have both straw and fodder for our donkeys, and bread and wine for myself, for your female servant, and for the young man who is with your servant; there is no lack of anything."

20 And the old man said, "Peace be with you! However, let all your needs be my responsibility; only do not spend the night in the open square."

21 So he brought him into his house, and gave fodder to the donkeys. And they washed their feet, and ate and drank.

22 As they were enjoying themselves, suddenly certain men of the city, perverted men, surrounded the house and beat on the door. They spoke to the master of the house, the old man, saying, "Bring out the man who came to your house, that we may know him carnally!"

23 But the man, the master of the house, went out to them and said to them, "No, my brethren! I beg you, do not act so wickedly! Seeing this man has come into my house, do not commit this outrage.

24 "Look, here is my virgin daughter and the man's concubine; let me bring them out now. Humble them, and do with them as you please; but to this man do not do such a vile thing!"

25 But the men would not heed him. So the man took his concubine and brought her out to them. And they knew her and abused her all night until morning; and when the day began to break, they let her go.

26 Then the woman came as the day was dawning, and fell down at the door of the man's house where her master was, till it was light.

27 When her master arose in the morning, and opened the doors of the house and went out to go his way, there was his concubine, fallen at the door of the house with her hands on the threshold.

28 And he said to her, "Get up and let us be going." But there was no answer. So the man lifted her onto the donkey; and the man got up and went to his place.

29 When he entered his house he took a knife, laid hold of his concubine, and divided her into twelve pieces, limb by limb, and sent her through out all the territory of Israel.

30 And so it was that all who saw it said, "No such deed has been done or seen from the day that the children of Israel came up from the land of Egypt until this day. Consider it, confer, and speak up!"

20:1 So all the children of Israel came out, from Dan to Beersheba, as well as from the land of Gilead, and the congregation gathered together as one man before the Lord at Mizpah.

2 And the leaders of all the people, all the tribes of Israel, presented themselves in the assembly of the people of God, four hundred thousand foot soldiers who drew the sword.

3 (Now the children of Benjamin heard that the children of Israel had gone up to Mizpah.) Then the children of Israel said, "Tell us, how did this wicked deed happen?"

4 So the Levite, the husband of the woman who was murdered, answered and said, "My concubine and I went into Gibeah, which belongs to Benjamin, to spend the night.

5 "And the men of Gibeah rose against me, and surrounded the house at night because of me. They intended to kill me, but instead they ravished my concubine so that she died.

6 "So I took hold of my concubine, cut her in pieces, and sent her throughout all the territory of the inheritance of Israel, because they committed lewdness and outrage in Israel.

7 "Look! All of you are children of Israel; give your advice and counsel here and now!"

8 So all the people arose as one man, saying, "None of us will go to his tent, nor will any of us turn back to his house;

9 "but now this is the thing which we will do to Gibeah: We will go up against it by lot.

10 "We will take ten men out of every hundred throughout all the tribes of Israel, a hundred out of every thousand, and a thousand out of every ten thousand,

> to make provisions for the people, that when they come to Gibeah in Benjamin, they may repay all the vileness that they have done in Israel."
>
> 11 So all the men of Israel were gathered against the city, united together as one man.
>
> *Judg. 19:1–20:11*

This is a grisly and horrific passage, which we might well prefer to avoid; but it is part of the "all Scripture" of 2 Timothy 3:16 which is "useful for teaching, rebuking, correcting and training in righteousness . . ." (NIV). The Bible never squeamishly closes its eyes to the awfulness of human depravity. Three strands of godlessness run throughout the incident.

Sexual Immorality

One of the themes of chapter 19 is the moral depravity which runs all the way through it. The Levite, who should have been faithful to one wife, decides to take a girl friend whom he lives with (v. 1). In turn, she is unfaithful to him (v. 2). The implication is that, as a result, the Levite sends her packing, and she decides to go back home to daddy. After four months the Levite decides he wants her back and so he goes off to find her.

The scene at the father's house is one of undisciplined self-indulgence (v. 4). A three-day "binge" extends to a fourth day (v. 6) and a fifth (v. 8). "Refresh yourself, enjoy yourself" are the keynote ideas. This is an atmosphere of total moral laxity. Eventually the girl and the Levite leave the home, but too late to complete their journey before nightfall. So, rejecting the alien city of the Jebusites (vv. 11–12), they go on to the Israelite town of Gibeah (v. 15), where they are eventually offered hospitality by an old man from Ephraim (v. 20). The house is besieged by a homosexual gang who eventually satisfy their lust on the Levite's girl friend. She is left like discarded rubbish, on the doorstep, unconscious, if not dead (vv. 26, 28). All of this behavior was clearly contrary to the Law of God and an abomination to him. But what we need to understand and explain is that once we do away with the worship of God and with the moral absolutes that are grounded in his character, there is then no barrier against sexual license of the most violent kind.

The Levite and his girl friend had already dismissed God's commandment against adultery, which reflects God's commitment in loving faithfulness to his people. That is not an arbitrary restriction, but an expression of the nature of true love, which is grounded in God's own character. Because human beings are made in God's image, we can only function properly and find true fulfillment and security when we obey his ground rules. Once these are set aside we become depersonalized and less than truly human. All our sin is a self-inflicted attack on our true humanness.

It is, therefore, no surprise to find that in a society where God's moral law of love is rejected, the gift of sex—designed by him to enrich and deepen the exclusive relationship of one man and one woman as an expression of their total self-giving to one another—is reduced to becoming an end in itself. Love then becomes equated with sex. The physical dominates everything, and human beings are reduced to pleasure machines. No wonder it is easy to walk away from one "machine" when its attractions begin to pall, and go on to the next.

But human beings are not infinitely plastic. God has not made us that way. No one can walk away from the deepest act of physical union between two people totally unchanged by it. That is why we see so many people, who drift in and out of relationships, who are ultimately unable to give themselves to any lasting relationship of trust and commitment at all. There is a price to pay for jettisoning God's laws—emotionally, psychologically, and physically.

In the same way, homosexual activity is a rejection and reversal of God's purpose for human sexuality. That is why its characteristic is frustration, which, in the story, explodes into violence. And yet, in spite of all this, we live in a society that exalts sex to the place of God. That is what people are encouraged to live for. Popular entertainment shouts it all the time. "This is what life is for. If it feels good, it is!" Of course, powerful commercial influences are exploiting the appetites of vulnerable young people. But we need to remind people that wherever you find unrestrained sexual appetite, there you have the seeds of moral collapse. People will then deny themselves nothing that they want. We need to teach Christian sex ethics without compromise or apology, to explain the moral responsibility to say no, and to teach our people *why* God's commandments are good.

Personal Violence

Another chilling theme runs throughout chapter 19—personal violence. The sexual morals of these people indicate the total lack of respect they have for one another and for human life in general. Sexual ethics and violence are closely interrelated. When marriage is held in disrepute and family breakup becomes the expected norm, the two are symptoms of a profound malaise in which human life itself will be progressively devalued.

The Levite seems totally unconcerned for the welfare of his girl friend. He kicks her out, and then goes to get her back, entirely on his whim. She is expendable. When the house is attacked, the old man is prepared to offer his own virgin daughter to the mob (v. 24) and eventually the Levite takes his girl friend out to them (v. 25) to save himself. He is *"her master"* (v. 27) and as such he is quite happy to sleep while she endures the most fearful treatment. His callous treatment of her, as though she were a sack of potatoes (v. 28), is almost unbelievable. Finally, the dismemberment of her body (v. 29) shows he had no respect for her at all.

A society that reduces love to lust will not long have any residual respect for human life. Other people become mere objects. Human life is expendable and cheap, so a baby in the womb becomes "the fetus"; "it," not he or she. And a woman has a right to choose to do away with *it* if *it* is inconvenient. If old people increase in number and become a drain on the state, then let the state's medically approved agents "put them out of their misery." Abortions and euthanasia "on demand" are symptoms of the same disease that surfaces in rape, crimes of violence, and the mental cruelty, petty tyrannies, and personal violence that characterize so many homes. We must not be surprised to find child abuse, incest, robbery with violence, and murders increasing. "If God is dead," said Nietzsche, "then everything is permitted." It's all perfectly logical.

So the Christian response which simply wrings its hands in despair, or washes them in resignation, is unworthy of followers of Christ. We have grown far too sentimental about evil in our cozy Christian ghettoes. Cushioned from its effects through the Christian heritage and capital on which the church in the West has lived for decades, we have somehow imagined ourselves and our churches to be immune from sin's ravages. We have believed the liberal humanists, who tell us that man is getting better and kinder, without reminding us that all such advances have had Christian foundations and impetus. We often seem surprised, if not overwhelmed, when we encounter evil head-on, because we do not really believe the Bible's teaching about human depravity and about our own hearts.

Last Christmas I heard that several Christian girls in a large evangelical church known to me had received pornographic Christmas cards, which could only have been sent by someone on the inside of the church who had access to their private addresses through the church's mailing list. It was an extremely unpleasant and disturbing experience for the young ladies concerned, but their predominant reaction was one of horror that it should have come from someone inside the church. I understand that, of course—they felt betrayed. But should they have been so surprised? The human heart, even the Christian heart, is a past master in self-deception and deceit. The appalling list of sins in 2 Timothy 3:2–4, which Paul says will characterize times of stress in the days between Christ's ascension and his second coming ("the last days"), make all too familiar reading, until we are suddenly stabbed awake by his prediction that they will be *within the church*, going along with "a form of godliness," but without the power of spiritual reality. Interestingly, Paul confirms the Judges diagnosis by attributing these manifestations of evil to misplaced love. "People will be lovers of themselves, lovers of money . . . lovers of pleasure rather than lovers of God . . ." (NIV). These are sober calls to Christian realism and to Christian action. Again, we need clear thinking and wise counsel, to which the rest of the unit directs us.

Moral Paralysis

Verse 30 of chapter 19 is one of those brilliant, vivid summaries of attitude which the writer of Judges so often catches in dialogue form. The words are a picture of outrage mixed with confusion, impotence, and inability to know what to do. If everybody is used to doing what is right in his or her own eyes, how can anyone get a grip on the situation? The dismembered body of the Levite's concubine circulated among the twelve tribes brought home in an unmistakably violent and horrific way the appalling moral degradation into which the nation had sunk. But so often in the contemporary scene, as we see the bastions of our Christian society being dismantled, one by one, all we do is react with the "tut tut" of the Israelites (v. 30). We are genuinely outraged, as are other responsible members of our society, who share the Judeo-Christian ethical basis of our civilization, if not our spiritual faith. But there's a sense of overwhelming moral paralysis because the ultimate answers are neither social nor political, but spiritual. We may hold our protest rallies and marches and proclaim on our banners that "moral pollution needs a solution," but where is that solution to come from, and how is it to be activated?

Chapter 20 provides the record of how the people of God tried to deal with the problem. They began by calling a solemn assembly (v. 2), in order to gather the facts about this *"wicked deed"* (v. 3). They heard the witnesses and received the report of the working party. They were so outraged that they knew they had to do something, so they decided to punish Gibeah. Without trying to deal with the root causes of the problem, they determined to pay back the men of Gibeah and give them what they deserved. That was a very natural human reaction, and an extremely destructive one. As Shakespeare puts it in *The Tempest*, "the rarer action is in virtue than in vengeance"; rarer in the double sense of less frequent, but also more valuable. Revenge is sweet, the proverb says, but Sir Walter Scott called it "the daintiest morsel ever cooked in hell." The moral collapse exemplified by this incident was in all their hearts, as it is, at least potentially, in all our ours, too. Because their hearts were equally culpable in being turned away from the living God, they escaped from their paralysis into greater confusion and, eventually, civil war.

What does this say to our congregations today? It reminds us of the emptiness of human solutions. Neither the right wing law-and-order brigade, nor the left wing redistribution-of-wealth advocates can change the hearts of people. There always will be a moral paralysis in society until those hearts are transformed by men and women being set free from their sin and themselves to live as God's children. The passage reminds us that we shall not bring in God's kingdom by programs of legislation, by marches and lobbying, by committees, or by law and politics.

That is not to despise or downgrade Christian action in any or all of these areas. Undoubtedly, it is part of our Christian duty, as salt and light in a secular society, to work in every way available to us to see that the laws of our country are in the greatest possible conformity to the will of God, as revealed in Scripture. We need Christians in national and local government, in action groups, in the media, on school and community boards, who will present biblical arguments coherently and confidently, with love and compassion. They need the prayerful support and understanding of the whole church. In a democracy, laws cannot be imposed by force; they have to be accepted through the ballot box, and I imagine we would not want it any other way. So we have to be ready and willing to argue our case, to the limits of our lawful rights; but also to be outvoted. To impose laws which do not command the respect of the majority is simply to devalue the currency of the legal system and to make it unworkable, as some of the Reformers and their heirs discovered generations ago.

We are not looking to bring in the kingdom of heaven on earth by political means. The only way that hearts will be changed lastingly in a way that will transform society is by the gospel of the Lord Jesus Christ. That is what Judges looks forward to.

We should remember that this story occurred early on in the chronology of the book. Having studied Judges, we might be tempted to say that Israel was already ripe for judgment, but God did not. Instead, he raised up the judges. Romans 1:18 tells us that God's wrath is *being revealed* from heaven against all ungodliness. That verb is in the present (continuous) tense, indicating a norm throughout human history, which suggests the downward spiral effect that we have noted so often in this book. Sin contains its own judgment, as it separates the sinner progressively from the only solution to his needs and problems. But Romans 5:20 reminds us that "where sin increased, grace increased all the more" (NIV).

If the effects of judgment are always being worked out, thank God that grace is always superabounding. And that inexhaustible grace will lead us to take three practical steps to stem the tide of godlessness. Firstly, we shall live very close to Christ, our Savior, so that in his strength we may gain the victory over sin in our own lives. Nothing harms the cause of Christ more than half-hearted disciples, who want to have one foot in the world and one foot in the kingdom. We need constantly to look to ourselves as well as to our doctrine (1 Tim. 4:16) so that we do not allow any secret compromise with sin in the recesses of our own hearts. Next, we must dedicate ourselves to prayer, conscious that the battle is the Lord's, and that we must use the spiritual weapons he has provided for us (2 Cor. 10:3–4; Eph. 6:10–18). Lastly, we must get the good news of Christ out to as many people, in as many places, by as many avenues, as we possibly can. Only the proclamation of the saving authority of the King of kings can bring those who do what is right in their own eyes to submit their minds to his truth, their hearts to his love, and their wills to his lordship.

CHAPTER 19

The Purging of Evil

Judges 20:12–21:25

It would be hard to find a darker or more depressing episode in the whole Old Testament story of God's people than this account of civil war in Israel, with which the Book of Judges concludes. Certainly there were many black moments to come later when the armies of Assyria and Babylon swept the nation into exile; but this appalling, self-inflicted genocide with 40,000 Israelites cut down in the first two days of the battle, and 25,100 Benjamites on the final decisive day, is a massacre of gruesome proportions. No wonder the survivors of the catastrophe are to be found weeping before God at Bethel, "Why has this come to pass in Israel?" (21:3). The answer is the story of the Book of Judges. The sins of idolatry and immorality always lead, in the end, to self-destruction. The spreading infection of godlessness eventually surfaced in sexual immorality, personal violence, and moral paralysis (19:30). Now the whole process comes to its inevitable and depressing climax in the determination of the eleven tribes to punish their erring brother Benjamin. But far from the evil being purged, it is multiplied to the thousandth power.

The outcome is a civil war, which almost totally wipes out one of the twelve tribes of Israel. The aim stated in 20:13 is the sentence of death passed on the perverted men of Gibeah to *"remove the evil from Israel,"* but the result echoes with an even more somber bleakness in the refrain of 21:25, with which the chronicler ends his book, "In those days there was no king in Israel; everyone did what was right in his own eyes." We leave Israel at the end of Judges greatly weakened, tottering on the edge of anarchy and dissolution.

Today, the preacher's problem is clearly that this is not going to be anybody's favorite Old Testament passage. It makes profoundly disturbing and depressing reading. People are not going to rush home to Sunday lunch full of joy and optimism if this material is preached in morning worship. This is where we shall need to muster our conviction that

> *whatever* things were written before were written for our learning, that we through the patience and comfort of the Scriptures might have hope
>
> *Rom. 15:4, emphasis added*

For "all Scripture is given by inspiration of God, and is profitable . . ." (2 Tim. 3:16).

It seems to me that there are two practical dangers to guard against. One is the spirit of the age, which says that we only want to hear the positive and encouraging things that Scripture has to say, and that the preacher must always be "merry and bright." To do that is not only to opt for the devastatingly superficial, but also to ignore a considerable amount of the Bible's instruction.

However, the other danger is to preach so depressingly that our congregation leaves church in a worse state than when they arrived, and with the mistaken idea that the Old Testament is negative, discouraging, and ultimately better left alone. The answer is to realize that biblical history always has a spiritual purpose, that, depressing as the historical details may be, they uncover much about our human depravity that we need both to know and to learn from. If we learn the lessons, we need never experience the devastation. This gives the sermon a positive thrust, which can actually stimulate the congregation to a biblical fear of the Lord and a renewed appetite for holiness.

We need to put ourselves in Israel's shoes and face the question as to why God's people failed so spectacularly to purge themselves of this evil. The division of the material which follows underlines the three external symptoms of their moral weakness. We shall give attention to those before homing in on the underlying disease. If we can see the parallel areas of weakness in our own lives, however incipient, so as to take action while we have the opportunity, this Scripture will certainly have done its work.

No Recognition of Guilt

12 Then the tribes of Israel sent men through all the tribe of Benjamin, saying, "What is this wickedness that has occurred among you?
13 "Now therefore, deliver up the men, the perverted men who are in Gibeah, that we may put them to death and remove the evil from Israel!" But the children of Benjamin would not listen to the voice of their brethren, the children of Israel.
14 Instead, the children of Benjamin gathered together from their cities to Gibeah, to go to battle against the children of Israel.
15 And from their cities at that time the children of Benjamin numbered twenty-six thousand men who drew the sword, besides the inhabitants of Gibeah, who numbered seven hundred select men.
16 Among all this people there were seven hundred select men who were left-handed; every one could sling a stone at a hair's breadth and not miss.

Judg. 20:12–16

There is not the slightest doubt as to the action the leaders of the tribe of Benjamin should have taken when they were confronted with the moral responsibility of the crime they allowed the citizens of Gibeah to perpetrate. Either they should have punished the offenders themselves or handed them over to the nation's representatives, as demanded in verse 13. But they refused to do this, although the guilt of the men of Gibeah was proved beyond question. Instead, they chose to regard the accusation as a personal attack on the tribe and began to mobilize an army of twenty-six thousand men to defend the guilty.

By way of application, we need to remember that there is no clearer indication of moral sickness than when wrongdoing is condoned or even defended on the grounds of family or national solidarity and loyalty. All school teachers are familiar with the child who can do no wrong in its parents' eyes, but who does little right in anyone else's. Adept at manipulating circumstances in its favor, the child will appeal to the parental defense instinct by representing any punishment for its misdemeanors as victimization. The parents, who have always made concessions to keep little Johnny happy, are ultimately deceived by a spoiled and self-indulgent offspring who has them dancing, like puppets on a string, to his every whim. In a situation like that, there is no longer any true sense of right and wrong, since there has been no real exercise of discipline.

In our society, among adults, it is often a matter of vocabulary. Sins are laundered verbally to make them acceptable, or at least tolerated, to an increasingly undisciplined populace. Adultery is redefined as "wife swapping" or "having an affair." Homosexuality becomes "a gay life-style." Theft at work is acceptable if it is "the perks of the job." Lies are always "white," the truth always "selective." Greed is sanitized as "upward social mobility." The examples are endless. The purpose is always the same—to remove my sense of moral guilt, and so to pretend that if something sounds OK and people feel comfortable with it, that's all that matters. Whether it is in the TV ads or in the newspapers, the circumstances are glamorized and visual images of social acceptability, fun, wealth, and vitality are all used to anaesthetize the conscience, to pretend that "anything goes."

This was the situation in Israel; but the lesson, then and now, is that a society that refuses to accept guilt, in the sense of distinguishing right from wrong and punishing the offender, will soon prove impossible to govern. Everyone will do what is right in his or her own eyes, and there will be no ultimate restraints. Might becomes right, and civilization ceases. The principle is clear and can be seen to have application to self-discipline, to family life, to a community, state or nation, as well as internationally. It is also relevant to the church of Jesus Christ, whether locally or universally. The tragedy of Israel was that these symptoms were not dealt with when they first appeared, because there was no king. Those of us who are entrusted with authority within the biblical structures of home, church, or nation, have a heavy responsibility before God to use it responsibly in love to him and to our neighbor (Rom. 13:1–14).

No Restriction on Revenge

17 Now besides Benjamin, the men of Israel numbered four hundred thousand men who drew the sword; all of these were men of war.

18 Then the children of Israel arose and went up to the house of God to inquire of God. They said, "Which of us shall go up first to battle against the children of Benjamin?" The Lord said, "Judah first!"

19 So the children of Israel rose in the morning and encamped against Gibeah.

20 And the men of Israel went out to battle against Benjamin, and the men of Israel put themselves in battle array to fight against them at Gibeah.

21 Then the children of Benjamin came out of Gibeah, and on that day cut down to the ground twenty-two thousand men of the Israelites.

22 And the people, that is, the men of Israel, encouraged themselves and again formed the battle line at the place where they had put themselves in array on the first day.

23 Then the children of Israel went up and wept before the Lord until evening, and asked counsel of the Lord, saying, "Shall I again draw near for battle against the children of my brother Benjamin?" And the Lord said, "Go up against him."

24 So the children of Israel approached the children of Benjamin on the second day.

25 And Benjamin went out against them from Gibeah on the second day, and cut down to the ground eighteen thousand more of the children of Israel; all these drew the sword.

26 Then all the children of Israel, that is, all the people, went up and came to the house of God and wept. They sat there before the Lord and fasted that day until evening; and they offered burnt offerings and peace offerings before the Lord.

27 So the children of Israel inquired of the Lord (the ark of the covenant of God was there in those days,

28 and Phinehas the son of Eleazar, the son of Aaron, stood before it in those days), saying, "Shall I yet again go out to battle against the children of my brother Benjamin, or shall I cease?" And the Lord said, "Go up, for tomorrow I will deliver them into your hand."

29 Then Israel set men in ambush all around Gibeah.

30 And the children of Israel went up against the children of Benjamin on the third day, and put themselves in battle array against Gibeah as at the other times.

31 So the children of Benjamin went out against the people, and were drawn away from the city. They began to strike down and kill some of the people, as at the other times, in the highways (one of which goes up to Bethel and the other to Gibeah) and in the field, about thirty men of Israel.

32 And the children of Benjamin said, "They are defeated before us, as at first." But the children of Israel said, "Let us flee and draw them away from the city to the highways."

33 So all the men of Israel rose from their place and put themselves in battle array at Baal Tamar. Then Israel's men in ambush burst forth from their position in the plain of Geba.

34 And ten thousand select men from all Israel came against Gibeah, and the battle was fierce. But the Benjamites did not know that disaster was upon them.

35 The Lord defeated Benjamin before Israel. And the children of Israel destroyed that day twenty-five thousand one hundred Benjamites; all these drew the sword.

36 So the children of Benjamin saw that they were defeated. The men of Israel had given ground to the Benjamites, because they relied on the men in ambush whom they had set against Gibeah.

37 And the men in ambush quickly rushed upon Gibeah; the men in ambush spread out and struck the whole city with the edge of the sword.

38 Now the appointed signal between the men of Israel and the men in ambush was that they would make a great cloud of smoke rise up from the city,

39 whereupon the men of Israel would turn in battle. Now Benjamin had begun to strike and kill about thirty of the men of Israel. For they said, "Surely they are defeated before us, as in the first battle."

40 But when the cloud began to rise from the city in a column of smoke, the Benjamites looked behind them, and there was the whole city going up in smoke to heaven.

41 And when the men of Israel turned back, the men of Benjamin panicked, for they saw that disaster had come upon them.

42 Therefore they turned their backs before the men of Israel in the direction of the wilderness; but the battle overtook them, and whoever had come out of the cities they destroyed in their midst.

43 They surrounded the Benjamites, chased them, and easily trampled them down as far as the front of Gibeah toward the east.

44 And eighteen thousand men of Benjamin fell; all these were men of valor.

45 Then they turned and fled toward the wilderness to the rock of Rimmon; and they cut down five thousand of them on the highways. Then they pursued them relentlessly up to Gidom, and killed two thousand of them.

46 So all who fell of Benjamin that day were twenty-five thousand men who drew the sword; all these were men of valor.

47 But six hundred men turned and fled toward the wilderness to the rock of Rimmon, and they stayed at the rock of Rimmon for four months.

48 And the men of Israel turned back against the children of Benjamin, and struck them down with the edge of the sword—from every city, men and beasts, all who were found. They also set fire to all the cities they came to.

Judg. 20:17–48

The numbers involved in the conflict may seem out of all proportion to the issue of contention. Four hundred thousand is a huge army, similar in size to the land forces deployed by Iraq in the Gulf War in 1990–91. For Benjamin to mobilize its twenty-six thousand fighting men was a comparatively straightforward task, but how could the colossal national army be best organized? Such large numbers provided no solution to the problem in themselves.

The memory of God's past guidance in the days of Joshua sends them to the shrine at Bethel, not to ask God *what* they should do, or seek his help, but to go through the religious motions of receiving the divine guidance and blessing. We already know that their motivation is revenge (v. 10b) so they could not possibly expect God's approval. Several commentators have pointed out the similarity between verse 18 and 1:1–2, but the differences are even more striking. Here there is no promise of victory because the operation has not been initiated by the Lord. Indeed, the Lord's brief reply proved to be a death sentence on the men of Judah, of whom twenty-two thousand fell that day in battle.

The result is typical of superstitious, external religiosity. They *"encouraged themselves"* and resumed their plans (v. 22), determined to do better on the next assault. At the same time they went through the religious ritual, presumably with Phinehas inquiring of God before the ark of the covenant (vv. 27–28). But the tears which accompanied the ceremony were more of remorse than repentance since they had no intention of changing their purposes. Again, God's answer is a judgment on the people, of whom eighteen thousand are killed the next day (v. 25).

The preparations for the third day indicate a definite change of heart. Goslinga notes:

> The Israelites had lost all confidence in themselves. Finally, they had come to understand that victory could be won, not by their own power, but only by the grace of Yahweh. They realized that they should go no further till they were absolutely sure of the Lord's help, which obviously had left them.[1]

This time the weeping is accompanied by fasting, but it is the sacrificial offerings which remove the barriers between them and God and open the way not only for the guidance of God to be given but also for the promise of success. The consumption of the burnt offering was a symbol of their complete dependence on God, in self-surrender, totally at his disposal. No attention is drawn to the reality of their repentance, but their third offensive proves successful in the capture of Gibeah.

The fact that they were far more interested in winning the battle than in returning to God is illustrated by the massacre that followed. The slaughter of the 25,100 Benjamites was their revenge, not only, or perhaps even mainly, for the original outrage, but for the 40,000 victims of the previous reversals. In this way they became the agents of God's judgment on Benjamin, just as Israel had been judged on the first two days.

Surely this is an Old Testament illustration of the principle expounded by Paul in Romans 1:18ff. that "the wrath of God is [being] revealed from heaven against all ungodliness and unrighteousness of men." It is by allowing evil to feed on itself and to grow to such proportions as this that God gives us up to the outcome of our own sinful choices. We live in a world that is always under judgment in the present, as well as in the ultimate future.

The course of the battle is first described in verses 29–35, and then elaborated in more detail in verses 36–44. The tactical withdrawal of the Israelite army produced a display of overconfidence by the Benjamites, who assumed they were winning another round. This opened the way for the ambush to enter Gibeah and massacre its inhabitants, which in turn panicked the Benjamite forces as they realized they were trapped on both sides. This led to their rout. Only six hundred managed to escape to the rock of Rimmon (v. 47). However, the most shocking verse of the whole episode is the last (v. 48), which describes an orgy of destruction. The problem about revenge is that it is uncontrollable. This was one of the main reasons the Old Testament punishment code, "an eye for an eye, and a tooth for a tooth," was first given. It was to restrict the escalation of revenge before things got out of control. But the Israelites chose to jettison that principle. If every man does what is right in his own eyes, then force becomes the arbiter while truth and justice are the first casualties.

The truth of 1 Peter 2:21-23 is perhaps the best positive application of the negative example taught us by Israel's actions: "For to this you were called, because Christ also suffered for us, leaving us an example, that you should follow His steps: 'Who committed no sin, nor was deceit found in His mouth'; who, when He was reviled, did not revile in return; when He suffered, He did not threaten, but committed Himself to Him who judges righteously." The true vine (John 15:1), the real Israel, showed his disciples a more excellent way, the way of love. We follow a Savior who prayed, "Father, forgive them, for they know not what they do." That is the only power in the world which is totally indestructible. Any root of bitterness or morsel of revenge is a denial of the Cross and the character of Christ.

No Respect for Human Life

1 Now the men of Israel had sworn an oath at Mizpah, saying, "None of us shall give his daughter to Benjamin as a wife."

2 Then the people came to the house of God, and remained there before God till evening. They lifted up their voices and wept bitterly,

3 and said, "O Lord God of Israel, why has this come to pass in Israel, that today there should be one tribe missing in Israel?"

4 So it was, on the next morning, that the people rose early and built an altar there, and offered burnt offerings and peace offerings.

5 The children of Israel said, "Who is there among all the tribes of Israel who did not come up with the assembly to the Lord?" For they had made a great oath concerning anyone who had not come up to the Lord at Mizpah, saying, "He shall surely be put to death."

6 And the children of Israel grieved for Benjamin their brother, and said, "One tribe is cut off from Israel today.

7 "What shall we do for wives for those who remain, seeing we have sworn by the Lord that we will not give them our daughters as wives?"

8 And they said, "What one is there from the tribes of Israel who did not come up to Mizpah to the Lord?" And, in fact, no one had come to the camp from Jabesh Gilead to the assembly.

9 For when the people were counted, indeed, not one of the inhabitants of Jabesh Gilead was there.

10 So the congregation sent out there twelve thousand of their most valiant men, and commanded them, saying, "Go and strike the inhabitants of Jabesh Gilead with the edge of the sword, including the women and children.

11 "And this is the thing that you shall do: You shall utterly destroy every male, and every woman who has known a man intimately."

12 So they found among the inhabitants of Jabesh Gilead four hundred young virgins who had not known a man intimately; and they brought them to the camp at Shiloh, which is in the land of Canaan.

13 Then the whole congregation sent word to the children of Benjamin who were at the rock of Rimmon, and announced peace to them.

14 So Benjamin came back at that time, and they gave them the woman whom they had saved alive of the women of Jabesh Gilead; and yet they had not found enough for them.

15 And the people grieved for Benjamin, because the Lord had made a void in the tribes of Israel.

16 Then the elders of the congregation said, "What shall we do for wives for those who remain, since the women of Benjamin have been destroyed?"

17 And they said, "There must be an inheritance for the survivors of Benjamin, that a tribe may not be destroyed from Israel.

18 "However, we cannot give them wives from our daughters, for the children of Israel have sworn an oath, saying 'Cursed be the one who gives a wife to Benjamin.'"

19 Then they said, "In fact, there is a yearly feast of the Lord in Shiloh, which is north of Bethel, on the east side of the highway that goes up from Bethel to Shechem, and south of Lebonah."

20 Therefore they instructed the children of Benjamin, saying, "Go, lie in wait in the vineyards,

21 "and watch; and just when the daughters of Shiloh come out to perform their dances, then come out from the vineyards, and every man catch a wife for himself from the daughters of Shiloh; then go to the land of Benjamin.

22 "Then it shall be, when their fathers or their brothers come to us to complain, that we will say to them, 'Be kind to them for our sakes, because we did not take a wife for any of them in the war; for it is not as though you have given the women to them at this time, making yourselves guilty of your oath.'"

23 And the children of Benjamin did so; they took themselves enough wives for their number from those who danced, whom they caught. Then they went and returned to their inheritance, and they rebuilt the cities and dwelt in them.

24 So the children of Israel departed from there at that time, every man to his tribe and family; they went out from there, every man to his inheritance.

> 25 In those days there was no king in Israel; everyone did what was right in his own eyes.
>
> *Judg. 21:1–25*

There are two regular reactions of the human conscience when it is convicted of guilt. The first is to shift the blame, as Adam did to Eve and Eve to the serpent. The second is to make every effort to avoid the consequences of the wrong action, no matter what hypocrisy this may require. It is the second strand that chapter 21 particularly illustrates.

It begins with the senseless oath of verse 1 which effectively excommunicated the tribe of Benjamin and placed its survivors on the same level as the Canaanite peoples all around them. Presumably the point of the oath was either to exterminate Benjamin totally, or to ensure that the survivors were subsumed into other people-groups, but had no continuing part in Israel. The senseless slaughter of women, children, and animals, as well as the wanton destruction of the towns was suicidal enough; but this further oath had future ramifications, which fundamentally altered the state of Israel.

As the cold light of day dawned on the people, we find them once again weeping before the Lord at Bethel,[2] but again more from remorse than repentance (vv. 2–3). They demand an answer from God as to why he has allowed their own actions to produce such devastating results; but there is no reference to any acceptance of blame or confession of sin, unless verse 4 is meant to signify this. It seems more likely that the offerings speak of a glib assumption that their relations with God are intact, and that if they do what is ritually required, he will get them out of their predicament. How often we think the same way! And how we need to learn, as much as they did, that "to obey is better than sacrifice, and to heed than the fat of rams" (1 Sam. 15:22). Significantly, there is no answer from God at all. His judgment has fallen; but the absence of any true repentance ensures the absence of any divine guidance. He has given his people up to the consequences of their sin.

We are not to be surprised that the solution to the problem which remains involves further multiplication of evil, because the heart of man is "deceitful above all things, and desperately wicked . . ." (Jer. 17:9).

When left to its own devices, sin will always multiply. Paul's indictment of the whole human race in Romans 3:15–18 is especially appropriate to Israel at this point:

> "Their feet are swift to shed blood;
> Destruction and misery are in their ways;
> And the way of peace they have not known."
> "There is no fear of God before their eyes."

Realizing just how foolish the oath of verse 1 was (cf. Jephthah), the leaders might have repented of it before the Lord and sought his overruling. But their hearts were too spiritually hardened to think of that. Instead, they look for a way of keeping the oath, by using a scapegoat. Jabesh Gilead had refused to come up to Mizpah at the time of the national council and was therefore deemed guilty, by association with Gibeah (vv. 8,9). Another episode of senseless violence follows (vv. 10–12) in which the whole city is exterminated apart from four hundred young virgins who are to become the wives of the six hundred Benjamite survivors at Rimmon. It seems almost incredible that they could try to remedy the effects of one massacre of their own people by another, but that is where sin always leads.

When the devil is on the rampage there is a blind fury at work which leaves rational thought and behavior far behind. You have only to examine the history of our century to see how its cataclysmic upheavals have been generated by megalomaniac dictators, with whom it has been impossible to deal on any rational basis of normal civility. That is the great mistake of the appeaser, because sin is not rational. Indeed, from the standpoint of Scripture it is the most irrational behavior imaginable in God's universe.

However, the cull at Jabesh Gilead still does not yield enough wives for Benjamin, and the question is posed again (vv. 16–18). There is no question of breaking the oath of verse 1, not because of any true devotion to the God of Truth or even loyalty to the national covenant, but because of the loss of face involved. Sin always sees to it that its victims act entirely out of self-interest and thus eventually consume themselves. The "solution" is the plan devised in verses 19–22 for the annual festival at Shiloh. The casuistry of the argument in verse 22 is truly appalling. When the people of Shiloh complained of the abduction of their daughters, they were to be informed that this kept their oath intact. Nothing could have been further from the truth. In fact, it was a backdoor way of giving their daughters to the Benjamites, by setting up the whole charade and assuring the men of Benjamin that no action would be taken against them. This was to answer injustice with injustice.

The point being made, that must be applied to our contemporary situation, is that once God, whose righteous character is the only source and guarantee of truth and justice, is neglected, then such fine-sounding moral concepts are inevitably reduced to hollow verbiage. In the words of Jean Paul Sartre, "Finite man is meaningless without an infinite reference point." The existentialist philosophy and the history of nations in the twentieth century surely confirms this age-old message of the Book of Judges. Even the most advanced technological societies are covered with only the thinnest veneer of civilization when once the Christian foundations are eroded away. As the Duke of Wellington once remarked, the problem is that if you educate devils all you get is clever devils.

Given the scenario of Judges, it is wholly logical that the four hundred young women of Jabesh Gilead should lose their parents and relatives, and be forced into a mass marriage with the men of Benjamin. Where there is no respect for human life, there will certainly be no protection of individual rights. The dancing girls of Shiloh similarly have no choice, no rights (v. 23). But that is the sort of society that is produced when verse 25 holds true. People exist simply to be used by others who are more powerful, favored, or wealthy. Their labor can be exploited until the worn-out "machine" is thrown out on the scrap heap of redundancy, a sacrifice to the great god Mammon. Others become sex objects, pleasure-machines to satisfy the passing whims of a moment's desire, easily discarded when something new takes the fancy.

The society of the end of Judges is uncomfortably akin to that of this twilight era of our Western world. The advertising media tempt us to even greater and easier credit facilities until couples end up hopelessly in debt and under strain. The interest rates suddenly rise and whole family units break up under the pressure. The successful young professional is assumed to belong to the company, body and soul, to ditch his private morality in the interests of corporate success, to work all hours to the neglect of his wife and children, with the result that the marriage breaks up, the family disintegrates, and he burns out. Illustrations abound throughout our increasingly godless society, and we do our young people no service if we do not expose the roots of the problem and nerve them to live lives that are distinctively different in an increasingly alien society. Pietistic withdrawal and superspiritual platitudes will not do!

If ever things are going to change it will be through those who know that there is a King, the Lord Jesus Christ. Like salt and light, they need to penetrate the godless, hopeless world, as they get stuck into its problems, at every level of society. We can see it in the classic issues such as abortion and euthanasia; but we are often like Israel, failing to see how compromised we are in the ordinary, everyday issues. And that is where it matters most! Perhaps more than any others we Western Christians need to learn the meaning of Christ's warning: "'No servant can serve two masters . . . You *cannot* serve God and mammon'" (Luke 16:13, emphasis added). This leads us, finally, to identify the basic inner reason for Israel's dreadful condition, the root cause of her decline.

No Reverence for God

This is the key not only to this whole sad episode, but also to the Book of Judges as an entity. Israel had rejected Yahweh, her only true king, and every other monarch would be a completely inadequate substitute for him. Even David, the Old Testament king par excellence, would be but a pale foreshadowing of the coming King of kings, who alone would be able to rule in righteousness and equity. Only when God returned as king, in the person of Christ, could the new Israel be gathered out of all the peoples of the earth, and the true theocracy begin of all those who confess that Jesus is Lord. In a parallel way, only with the return of the King at his second coming will the kingdom come in all its fullness. So, Judges chronicles the downward spiral of a society that rejects God as king. We shall see that worked out in the secular context, but we need to be especially vigilant about its replication in the church and in our own personal lives, since the pressure of the world will always want to squeeze us into its mold (Rom. 12:2).

The trick is as old as mankind itself (Gen. 3:1–6). It looks so attractive to cast off the creaturely role of obedience to God and to make up our own ground rules. But what offers to be freedom ends up as slavery, to our own passions and ultimately to our own selves. Malcolm Muggeridge, the British media figure who became a Christian late in life, spoke of our need to "break out of the citadel of our own inflated ego" in order to live for something bigger and better. We know that the "something" is Someone. The tragedy of contemporary atheistic thought is its impeccable logic. Once God is denied, then we really are on the road to the abyss of despair, where life is ultimately only a sick joke, a hollow delusion, and where human beings are nothing but a few cents worth of chemicals. If anything goes, then in the end everything goes.

What is so dangerous, however, is that the Israelites did not set out to deny God in that way; they simply tried to domesticate him. That is much more likely to be the problem for the church, too. The evidence can be found there in the solemn assembly (20:1). It was *"before Yahweh,"* but he was not consulted. They had already assumed and decided that God would be with them, especially if they adopted the correct procedures and appropriate rituals (20:18). What they did not think of doing was submitting their plans to God.

We have already noted the comparison between this and the opening verses of Judges. The heavy irony implicit in this is that at the beginning of the book the struggle is against their common enemy, the Canaanites; but by the end of the book Israel is turned in on herself in civil war. This is due in large measure to the sin of presumption that, irrespective of Israel's actual behavior, Yahweh was committed, on covenant oath, to be with them.

It is the most frightening of all situations to imagine that we have God in our pockets, only to wake up and discover that our sins have alienated us from him. Whenever we imagine that we have only to meet the formal, ritual requirements to ensure that God is "on our side," we are in for a shock. The successive humiliations they suffered, which Judges chronicles, should have driven them to their knees in abject repentance, but they seem only to have hardened Israel's heart.

Before there could be real restoration there had to be the loss of all their false self-confidence, demonstrated in their blasphemous attitude which assumed they could actually manipulate God. It was because their hearts were so far from God that they were so much more motivated by revenge than by righteousness. If the evil was to be purged it would be only by the power of God, and if victory was to be theirs, it would be only by his grace.

The book closes on an enigmatic, almost inconclusive, note. Verse 24 shows a nation outwardly living in God's plan, in the land he has given them, apportioned by God according to their inheritance. That was why he brought them out of Egypt. That was why the land was conquered under Joshua. God's promises had not failed, but the people's loyalty had.

So the last verse of the book reveals the true situation, the invisible declension of their hearts away from God the king. This has been the real dilemma recorded in this book, and it ends unresolved. In this last conflict, both sides had profound lessons to learn from their appalling losses. Certainly, it was Yahweh who *"defeated Benjamin"* (20:35), but that carried with it a sense of terrible loss and disintegration; for in that "victory" God was judging the whole nation. *He* had made the gap in the tribes of Israel (21:15) which was to be a lasting reminder to the whole nation of their apostasy. He was teaching Israel that sin always pays its wage (destruction) and that although his love for his people is unchanging and constant, he does not always intervene to shield them from the consequences of their own persistent rebellion.

Real love is tough; it disciplines (Heb. 12:7–11). He is teaching us that if we refuse to submit to the ultimate reference point beyond ourselves, the authority of God as king, we put ourselves under his chastening discipline and judgment, whatever outward professions of faith and loyalty we may continue to make. If evil is to be purged, it must begin in our own personal lives, in our families and in God's family, the church, as we submit daily to our Lord and King, in repentance and faith, in love and obedience.

Judges ends with a great longing for a better order, which depends upon a fundamental change of heart. It looks for a king who will reign to bring about justice and peace. Thank God the longing was finally met when Jesus came into Galilee proclaiming the gospel of God and saying, "'The time has come. . . . the kingdom of God is near. Repent and believe the good news!'" (Mark 1:14–15 NIV). There is a king in Israel, whose government and peace will increase for ever, and who reigns on David's throne and over his kingdom, establishing and upholding it with justice and righteousness eternally (Isa. 9:6).

Thank God that there is a day still to come when it will finally be revealed that "'the kingdoms of this world have become the kingdoms of our Lord and of His Christ, and He shall reign forever and ever" (Rev. 11:15). That is the only ultimate answer to the problems of the Book of Judges, which are the problems of our sinful human hearts. Once we have read ourselves into the book, as Israel, we shall never be able to forget its poignant and powerful lessons.

NOTES

1. Goslinga, *Judges*, 493.

2. On the question whether Israel was at Bethel or Shiloh, Keil and Delitzsch comment: "They went to Bethel, not to Shiloh, where the tabernacle was standing, because that place was too far from the seat of war. The ark of the covenant was therefore brought to Bethel, and Phinehas the high priest inquired of the Lord before it through the Urim and Thummim (vs. 27–28). Bethel was on the northern boundary of the tribe of Benjamin, and was consecrated to this purpose before any other place by the revelations of God which had been made to the patriarch Jacob there (Gen. 28 & 35)." Keil and Delitzsch, *Joshua-Samuel*, 451.

SECTION TWO

The Book of Ruth

Ruth 1:1–4:21

Introduction to the Book of Ruth

Although in our English Bibles the Book of Ruth follows Judges and precedes Samuel, that seems to have been the result of decisions by the translators of the Septuagint, the Greek version of the Old Testament. It is not difficult to see why, since the very first verse establishes its historical context as *"the days when the judges ruled."* However, in the original Hebrew canon, Ruth was always placed in its third division—the Writings—while Judges was found among the former prophets. Within the Writings, Ruth was usually second among the five Festival Scrolls (i.e., Song of Solomon, Ruth, Lamentations, Ecclesiastes, and Esther) which were each used at the annual festivals or commemorations in Israel. Ruth was traditonally read at the Feast of Pentecost, or Weeks. The importance of this information lies in the reminder that this little gem of a book stands in its own right, as an independent work, and not simply as an addition to Judges. In fact, it provides a commentary and a reflection on the whole period covered by Judges, in a much more narrow and personalized focus.

The book is telling us that while the broad sweep of Israel's history was moving them further and further away from God and increasingly under the divine judgment, this was not the whole story. There were still men like Boaz who were faithful to the Lord and obedient to his word. There were still people like Ruth who were brought into the family of God's people, through faith in Yahweh, although she was born a foreigner and a stranger. Above all, God was still faithful in keeping his covenant promises and demonstrating his covenant love (*hesed*) to those who were faithful to him. The story of Ruth is a microcosm of what life in Israel might have been, and would have been, if only the people had sought the Lord and followed him. Set in the context of the Judges, it contains several reminders of the pressures within the culture to turn away from the living God, but yet it shows clearly how God honors those who honor him, and encourages its readers to trust and obey him.

On the larger scale, concerning the book's place in the whole revelation of Scripture, the concluding genealogy of David (4:17b–22) is the key. The message of Ruth is not only about God's moving behind the scenes to reverse a family situation of collapse and despair by a series of remarkable providences. The genealogy makes the point that God is at work in these ways on the macroscale of his governorship of Israel and the nations, throughout history. He is actively at work, unseen and unperceived, in the darkness of the judges' days, to bring about the sequence of events which will lead to the emergence of King David and the establishment of his dynasty. That, in turn, points us forward to the New Testament fulfillment of all that the old foreshadowed, in the appearance of "great David's greater Son," who will rule the whole world, in truth and love.

Not surprisingly, then, Ruth has her own honored place, as a foreigner brought into the royal line, in the genealogy of our Lord Jesus Christ (see Matthew 1:5). As he is the ultimate answer to the unresolved dilemma of Judges, so he is the final fulfillment of all that the Book of Ruth points toward.

Most conservative scholars date the book in the early monarchy, probably during Solomon's reign, characterized as Israel's golden age. Some have suggested royal interest and patronage for the research into the king's ancestry. The events of the book would therefore have occurred nearly two centuries earlier.

This is a great book for the preacher. Its size makes it very suitable for a short series, so when I was preaching through Judges I tucked Ruth into the middle, both as a change of focus and as a window of light on the unrelieved darkness which the accounts of Judges sometimes produce. All the world loves a love story, and the unexpected twists of the drama of Ruth and Boaz, told as they are in a highly effective and tension-filled style, carry the congregation along from episode to episode in a way that far outshines any contemporary TV soap opera!

The success of the exposition, however, will not depend so much on a lively retelling of the story as on the preacher's ability to identify the central theological and spiritual principles of the narrative and apply them to today's listeners. It is worth taking time to build the bridges from the text into the life of our hearers, so that God's message can travel across it with authority and conviction.

An Outline of Ruth

I. When You're at the End of Your Tether: 1:1–22
   A. Elimelech—A Questionable Decision: 1:1–5
   B. Naomi—A Bitter Experience: 1:6–13; 19–22
   C. Ruth—A Growing Faith: 1:14–18
II. The Mechanics of Grace: 2:1–23
   A. Experiencing God's Providence: 2:1–10
   B. Holding on to God's Faithfulness: 2:11–12
   C. Enjoying God's Provision: 2:13–23
III. Acts of Faith and Love: 3:1–18
   A. Naomi—Following God's Signposts: 3:1–6
   B. Ruth—Trusting God's Protection: 3:7–9
   C. Boaz—Reflecting God's Character: 3:10–18
IV. There Is a Redeemer: 4:1–22
   A. The Heart of the Matter: 4:1–10
   B. The Answer to the Problem: 4:11–17
   C. The Hope for the Future: 4:18–22

CHAPTER ONE

"When You're at the End of Your Tether . . ."

Ruth 1:1–22

Notice boards outside churches can be a fascinating indicator as to what goes on inside. I remember seeing one years ago, on a grimy, downtown, ancient building in Manchester, which looked as though no one had cared for it, or even entered it, in years. Its message read, "Most people's minds are like concrete—thoroughly mixed and permanently set." I wondered what sort of despair had led that remnant of a congregation to express themselves to the world at large by what amounted to (as we say in Britain) blowing a verbal raspberry (called in America, I understand, a "Bronx cheer")! Last year, in Melbourne, I saw a much more upbeat slogan. "Trust a great God," it read, "to help you fulfill your potential." After all, that's what God is there for, wouldn't you agree? I somehow think God would not!

But the title of this chapter is one of the best messages I have ever seen outside a church anywhere: "When You're at the End of the Tether," the notice said, "Remember That God Is at the Other End." That is certainly what Ruth chapter 1 is all about, as it introduces us to three crisis situations, only to reveal the controlling hand of the sovereign God who constantly watches over every one of his people and really does order the circumstances of life for our greatest good. This whole book is an exposition of that great assertion of faith, made by the apostle Paul in Romans 8:28: "And we know that in all things God works for the good of those who love him, who have been called according to his purpose" (NIV).

ELIMELECH: A QUESTIONABLE DECISION

1 Now it came to pass, in the days when the
judges ruled, and there was a famine in the land. And a

> certain man of Bethlehem, Judah, went to dwell in the country of Moab, he and his wife and his two sons.
>
> 2 The name of the man was Elimelech, the name of his wife was Naomi, and the names of his two sons were Mahlon and Chilion—Ephrathites of Bethlehem, Judah. And they went to the country of Moab and remained there.
>
> 3 Then Elimelech, Naomi's husband, died; and she was left, and her two sons.
>
> 4 Now they took wives of the women of Moab: the name of the one was Orpah, and the name of the other Ruth. And they dwelt there about ten years.
>
> 5 Then both Mahlon and Chilion also died; so the woman survived her two sons and her husband.
>
> *Ruth 1:1–5*

It is an undeniable fact that many of the life problems we grapple with in the present are the result of what has happened to us in the past, whether as a result of our own deliberate choices or because of circumstances which were quite beyond our control. So these verses of background to the story form an important introduction, which we need to understand. This is an elementary principle of good pastoral counseling. The person before me today is the product of all their yesterdays, just as I am myself. There is a tendency for us to see that truism today in a somewhat fatalistic way, as though we are the inevitable product of our genetic inheritance and our early environment. It makes it easier for us to shift the blame for our problems on to others, but that is not the whole story. More important than the circumstance of the past are the ways in which we have decided to react to them. Such behavior often crystalizes into patterns, which harden into settled convictions, which in turn condition and dictate our present feelings.

Naomi faced a complex set of problems because of her husband's decision well over ten years before. Yet that decision was brought about by his measured response to circumstances which were quite outside his control. The famine of verse 1 may have been an act of God's judgment through drought, or because of marauding invaders like the Midianites, in Gideon's day, as recorded in Judges 6. Whatever the cause, the fact remains that at Bethlehem (which means "the house of bread") the supply had stopped and a man whose name means "my God is King" made the difficult decision to take his wife and two sons off to live as resident aliens in the land of Moab.

Was he right or wrong? The biblical text does not encourage us to be dogmatic, but certainly the decision was questionable. Why go off to a country and people whose god Chemosh demanded human sacrifice? Why join a nation whose king Eglon had pressed Israel into servitude for eighteen years (Judg. 3:14)? At the time Elimelech chose to go to Moab, it seems that Israel and Moab must have been on friendly terms, and clearly Elimelech had no intention of staying there forever. It was just "for a while," during the famine.

Although they would not be Moabite citizens, they would be able to make a living, food would be more plentiful, and no one would stop them practicing their religion, in what was a syncretistic society. It seemed like a good deal. Certainly decisions like this can have life-changing effects for generations. A Christian friend has recently visited her grandmother and cousins in the Soviet Union for the first time. In the 1920s, her father and mother, newly wed, decided to flee the Leninist state and make a perilous escape through China, eventually reaching Australia. Her father's brother decided to remain. The differences in life-style of his children, her cousins, from her own have been enormous. So much for the future hung on that one decision.

Was Elimelech turning his back on the Lord? There is certainly no record in the text that he consulted God about it. Was it lack of faith on his part? The fact that he was an Ephrathite (v. 2) probably means that he belonged to a well-established, even wealthy family, and certainly Naomi's remark in verse 21 would seem to support this. She not only contrasts the conditions in which she left and returned ("full" and "empty") but also the different reasons behind her experiences. *"I went out full,"* but *"the Lord has brought me home again empty."* Were material comforts and prosperity too high on Elimelech's agenda? Certainly the purpose of the move, to escape discomfort and death, was not fulfilled (vv. 3, 5). First the father and then Mahlon ("sickly") and Chilion ("failing") died. It is clear that the names were intended to be significant. They were Canaanite names, frequently in use, which may again imply a detachment from the worship of Yahweh.

Whatever the reasons for Elimelech's decision, Naomi is left, widowed and childless, without sons or grandsons to continue the family line, which is a situation of great deprivation and despair. All this has happened in a foreign land, far away from the support of those who speak her language or worship her God. Yet, equally clearly, Naomi is a believer in the Lord. Ruth's subsequent confession of faith in Yahweh (v. 16) confirms that. Nevertheless, the woman whose name means "pleasant" is brought to the place where she renames herself "bitterness." Can the God she believed in really be at the other end of that tether?

In any congregation today, many people will identify only too readily with Naomi's experience. Some will have gone through similar traumatic times of bereavement. Others will have made life decisions they now feel very bitter about—the job move that led to being laid off, the marriage that broke up almost from the beginning, the disappointment of children who have overthrown their parents' faith and are sowing wild oats. "Where did I go wrong?" is very often followed by "why did God let this happen to me?" There is no problem about relevance in these opening verses. What the preacher needs is love and sensitivity, gently to identify and articulate the problems, in terms that are up-to-date and nonjudgmental.

NAOMI: A BITTER EXPERIENCE

6 Then she arose with her daughters-in-law that she might return from the country of Moab, for she had heard in the country of Moab that the Lord had visited His people in giving them bread.

7 Therefore she went out from the place where she was, and her two daughters-in-law with her; and they went on the way to return to the land of Judah.

8 And Naomi said to her two daughters-in-law, "Go, return each to her mother's house. The Lord deal kindly with you, as you have dealt with the dead and with me.

9 "The Lord grant that you may find rest, each in the house of her husband." Then she kissed them, and they lifted up their voices and wept.

10 And they said to her, "Surely we will return with you to your people."

11 But Naomi said, "Turn back, my daughters; why will you go with me? Are there still sons in my womb, that they may be your husbands?

12 "Turn back, my daughters, go—for I am too old to have a husband. If I should say I have hope, if I should have a husband tonight and should also bear sons,

13 "would you wait for them till they were grown? Would you restrain yourselves from having husbands? No, my daughters; for it grieves me very much for your sakes that the hand of the Lord has gone out against me!"

Ruth 1:6–13

The turning point in Naomi's experience comes with a direct intervention by the Lord in the larger circumstances which have indirectly led to her problems. God comes to the aid of his people by providing food (v. 6); and that situation having changed, the widowed Naomi decides to go back empty to the House of Bread where she really belongs. Hers is a common-sense response to outward circumstances; but spiritually, it is a move toward the Lord, not away from him.

God is putting the pieces together for Naomi although at this stage she has no conscious awareness of that at all. She merely does what seems right. This is an interesting feature of the theology of this book. *There is not the faintest hint that the total control being exercised by the Lord in any way limits the freedom of activity of the people involved.* But as the book proceeds, we see the detailed and delicate way in which God in fact works all their actions together into his plan. The more the story seems to hide the hand of God, the more it actually affirms, even more firmly, his total sovereignty. For the great theological insight revealed here is that God does not act intermittently, but continuously. Though he may appear to step into the scene at given key moments, he is actually and actively there *every* moment, albeit hidden. Now it is *that* consciousness that keeps Naomi sweet in the midst of life's bitterness, and trusting the Lord even where she cannot see where he is leading her.

The point is well made by Professor Ronald M. Hals in his helpful monograph, *The Theology of the Book of Ruth*. He writes:

> While in the Book of Judges the Lord is described as periodically stepping in to punish or deliver his people, here he remains on

> the scene every moment, but hidden. While in the Book of Judges he acts through charismatic agents and in holy wars, here he acts in the needs and hopes of ordinary people. . . . So deeply has the author hidden God's directing of history that the thread of God's plan disappears completely into the tapestry of everyday events. And here precisely lay a tremendous problem for the Israel of the author's time, for apart from the skillful subtleties of this narrator, how would God's acting ever have been seen here?[1]

But that is the point of Scripture. It is written precisely to reveal the divine prospective on the uncertainties of what the old Prayer Book calls "this uncertain and transitory life." It is when, like Naomi, we learn to see God's hand in every scene that we truly begin to understand his sovereignty and omnipotence. Yet only because God has chosen to reveal it can we know that (Deut. 29:29). To recognize that is to realize why Paul asserts that "faith comes by hearing . . . the word of God" (Rom. 10:17). Let us look at the evidence of Naomi's faith, in spite of all she was enduring.

It is seen, first, in her prayer and care. There is no doubt that Naomi not only kept in touch with people at home, but also with the Lord. If he has visited his people by ending their time of famine, then Naomi knows that to be with God is going to be the best both for her and her daughters-in-law. But in verse 8 her concern for them also surfaces. To accompany her would be to separate them from their cultural and family background. Naomi also knows that her Lord is as much able to bless them in Moab as in Bethlehem, if that is his will, and so she prays for them (vv. 8–9). She asks for Yahweh's covenant-love, which Alec Motyer has described as "combining the warmth of God's fellowship with the security of God's faithfulness." In spite of all her suffering, she knows that God is love, and so she commits them to him, praying also that they will each find the security and comfort of a new husband and home. And when, in verse 10, they affirm through their fears that they want to go with her, she reminds them of the consequences. She is no longer able to produce sons to be their husbands (vv. 11–13). So she fulfills her duty in seeking to persuade them to return to their own people, as she will to hers.

At this point in the text we have the first example of a technique which the writer uses on other occasions as well. We are used to the "flashback" method in a film, to fill in details about a character's past. Here there is a verbal "fast-forward wind," since the basis of Naomi's argument is not hyperbole about her age, but a reference to the practice of levirate marriage, which is actually to feature in a very central role later in the book. If a man died without children, his brother had to marry the widow to continue the family line. The first-born son of such a marriage would then be considered the dead brother's child and heir. Naomi dismisses this as totally out of the question both because of her age and the time Ruth and Orpah would have to wait for such hypothetical sons to reach marriageable age (vv. 12–13). Yet it is this very provision which provides the means of rescue for herself and Ruth, in a different set of circumstances, later on.

Perhaps the key statement to note in verses 6–13 is Naomi's open recognition of God's hand in her circumstances, as she expresses it in verse 13b. It demonstrates how she met her bitter experience with acceptance and trust. There is pain and anger in this verse, but there is also honesty and faith, for Naomi knows that her life is in God's hands. These things have not happened by chance. God rules. How else can we comfort one another when we are facing life's tragedies? If we deny God's sovereignty, we have to say, in effect, that God's back was turned, which means that either he didn't know, or didn't care. What sort of a God is that? No, we have to admit that we cannot know why a particular tragedy has happened, but then that is not what would help us most, anyway. We want to come to the point, with Job, where we can say amid all the tears and pain and anger, "though He slay me, yet will I trust Him" (Job 13:15). That is not submitting lamely to a vengeful or capricious deity, but actively cooperating with the God of all power, all wisdom, and all love, who is working all things together for the good of those whom he loves, as the book will go on to prove.

One of the hardest tasks I had to fulfill in my first year in the ministry, as a young pastor, was to visit a man in his late sixties whose wife had just died suddenly of a heart attack. He had served with distinction in the Royal Air Force during the Second World War, from which he had suffered permanent invalidity. He was a strong man who had been through his fair share of danger and suffering, but when I arrived at his home he was howling disconsolately. He and his wife had been married only six weeks, neither having been married before. The joy they had found so late in life in one another had now been shattered. Through his sobs and bellows he repeated again and again to me, "why . . . why has God made this happen?"

Nothing at college had prepared me for a situation quite like this. I knew that whatever theological answer I might stumble toward articulating would be bound to have a hollow ring in the midst of his suffering. On the other hand, I knew that I could not sit silent and unresponsive. I believe it was the Holy Spirit himself who prompted me with the thought, "read the Word." Murmuring something about there not being any easy answers, but affirming my faith in God's wisdom, love, and power, I began to read some of the psalms, as calmly and deliberately as I could, declaring the character of God.

At first I thought he would never hear me for his weeping, but within ten or fifteen minutes a total change came over this broken, wretched man. The heaving and howling stopped. He began to sit still, to look up, and to take hold of what was being read. The picture of the man called Legion, in Luke 8:35, came to my mind: He was found "sitting at the feet of Jesus, clothed and in his right mind." It was a powerful lesson to me, early in my ministry, of the power that resides in the Word of God. We do not need clever philosophical arguments; they do not mend broken hearts. We need the revelation of God in his holy word, for that is the substance of all truly Christian ministry.

Before we move on from Naomi, we need to take in the final paragraph of this first chapter.

> 19 Now the two of them went until they came to Bethlehem. And it happened, when they had come to Bethlehem, that all the city was excited because of them; and the women said, "Is this Naomi?"
>
> 20 But she said to them, "Do not call me Naomi; call me Mara, for the Almighty has dealt very bitterly with me.
>
> 21 "I went out full, and the Lord has brought me home again empty. Why do you call me Naomi, since the Lord has testified against me, and the Almighty has afflicted me?"
>
> 22 So Naomi returned, and Ruth the Moabitess her daughter-in-law with her, who returned from the country of Moab. Now they came to Bethlehem at the beginning of barley harvest.
>
> *Ruth 1:19–22*

We shall look at Ruth's decision next, but here we see even more clearly Naomi's almost relentless trust in God (vv. 20–21). The contrast observed by her friends must have been startling to them (v. 19). But the fact that she calls herself "Mara" does not mean that she was bitter against God in her own heart, but rather that her experience had been bitter, and, for some reason which she could not understand, God had dealt harshly with her. There is a pun implicit in the sound of the original which could be translated "Call me Mara, for the Almighty has cruelly marred me" (v. 20).

In our easygoing materialism we need to be reminded that the Lord does sometimes empty us, but only in order to fill us with his goodness. The name by which Naomi refers to *"the Almighty"* is El Shaddai, a title used mainly in the Pentateuch. No one is exactly sure of its derivation, though it is common to relate it to the idea of mountain-like stability and so to God's attribute of unchanging faithfulness and dependability. Its use in the life of Joseph, for example, indicates that this is the God who comes, when the situation is at its worst, to do his best. El Shaddai breaks through all the barriers and roadblocks with fresh supplies of his inexhaustible grace just at the point when all the human resources are totally spent. Certainly, this is Naomi's faith.

She consciously places all her pain, bitter experiences and hopelessness within the structure of God's sovereignty, and she leaves the explanation and responsibility with him. Whether that is escapism or realism entirely depends on the character of God. This book is designed to vindicate that character of steadfast love and dependability and to generate a similar faith in the Lord. He provides in his person the only context in which faith can learn to cope with the uncertainties, pain and bitterness of life. For he is also *Yahweh*—the God of covenant-love and faithfulness.

Isn't that what the Cross is saying? God takes upon himself our aching load, our griefs and sorrows, as well as our sins and guilt, and he cries out in agony as we do, "My God, why . . . ?" All the pain and anger and pent-up bitterness of sinful human beings is experienced and expressed by the holy Son of God. The Lamb has been provided to carry it all away. The essence of sin is not letting him do it, not trusting him to take it and to bury it in the depths of the sea. El Shaddai is the Lamb, and he is always there for those who will accept and trust him.

In the little town of Olney in Buckinghamshire, England, famous these days for its pancake race every Shrove Tuesday, lived the English poet and hymn writer William Cowper (1731–1800). For nineteen years (1767–86) his home was a modest and rather gloomy red-brick house, which adjoined the vicarage garden of the parish church. The vicar of Olney at that time was John Newton (1725–1807), the converted slave-ship captain who became a minister and who with Cowper wrote many hymns for their congregation to sing. These were published as a collection called "Olney Hymns" in 1779. Newton wrote, "How Sweet the Name of Jesus Sounds" and "Glorious Things of Thee Are Spoken," while Cowper contributed "Oh! for a Closer Walk with God," "There Is a Fountain Filled with Blood," and what we now know by its first line, "God Moves in a Mysterious Way." This was originally entitled, "Light Shining Out of Darkness."

Between Cowper's house and the vicarage garden a little doorway was made for the friends to visit each other. Cowper was prone to periods of deep depression which later in his life tended toward suicide, but Newton was a faithful pastor to him; and the two men would always be found together at the prayer meeting on a Wednesday evening. The *Oxford Dictionary of Quotations* contains twelve columns of well-known lines by Cowper, including almost the whole of his best-known hymn.[2] Naomi could certainly have sung its words with conviction.

> God moves in a mysterious way His wonders to perform;
> He plants His footsteps in the sea and rides upon the storm.
>
> Deep in unfathomable mines of never-failing skill
> He treasures up His bright designs and works His sovereign will.
>
> Ye fearful saints, fresh courage take; the clouds you so much dread
> Are big with mercy and shall break in blessings on your head.
>
> Judge not the Lord by feeble sense, but trust Him for His grace;
> Behind a frowning providence He hides a smiling face.
>
> His purposes will ripen fast, unfolding every hour;
> The bud may have a bitter taste, but sweet will be the flower.
>
> Blind unbelief is sure to err and scan His work in vain;
> God is His own interpreter, and He will make it plain.

RUTH: A GROWING FAITH

14 Then they lifted up their voices and wept again; and Orpah kissed her mother-in-law, but Ruth clung to her.

15 And she said, "Look, your sister-in-law has gone back to her people and to her gods; return after your sister-in-law."

16 But Ruth said:
"Entreat me not to leave you,
Or to turn back from following after you;
For wherever you go, I will go;
And wherever you lodge, I will lodge;
Your people shall be my people,
And your God, my God.
17 "Where you die, I will die,
And there will I be buried.
The Lord do so to me, and more also,
If anything but death parts you and me."

18 When she saw that she was determined to go with her, she stopped speaking to her.

Ruth 1:14–18

The title figure of the book now becomes the focus. The first thing to notice about Ruth is that she is a foreigner, outside the covenant community. Yet she is going to be brought into the royal line of the King of kings because of God's grace and her faith in his covenant-love. That faith began its life as borrowed. Indeed, faith often starts that way. It started by being Naomi's faith in which Orpah and Ruth shared, but a borrowed faith won't get you far. However, it can become your own!

Undoubtedly Ruth would have been moved by the quality of Naomi's faith in the face of all her trials, and she wanted to share it. She knew that Naomi's God could be relied on. Even a little faith may be called on to face great testing as Ruth was through her bereavement, her poverty as a widow, and her leaving behind the prospect of marriage in Moab if she decided to go with Naomi. Doubtless she was further tested by the return of Orpah, but through it all she "*clung*" to Naomi (v. 14), and by clinging to Naomi she came to believe in Naomi's God. Verse 16 expresses Ruth's decision in memorable terms. The choice is very stark and it's put in a very interesting way by Naomi (v. 15). The choice Ruth faces is between the familiar and the unknown. The opportunity is wide open for Ruth to go back to her people, her old customs and culture, and above all her old gods. The challenge to a borrowed faith always culminates in its becoming personal or its being rejected. Faith that is tested will either wither and die or, as in Ruth's case, be openly declared and rewarded. It cannot be kept secret for long.

In verse 16, Ruth's loyalty to Naomi is shown to have its roots in her loyalty to Naomi's God (*"your God, my God"*). What began as a borrowed faith is now declared to be her own, and her further statement in verse 17 reveals her commitment to the powerful, sovereign hand of Yahweh over her life.

This is undoubtedly the turning point in Ruth's life, but she is brought to it along a path of suffering, disappointment, and grief. In her way, she too meets God when she is at the end of her tether, and is prepared to venture everything for her future onto him. Whatever our past or present experience, the moment of change always comes at the point where we are prepared to stop fighting God and to start trusting him, to stop going it alone and start giving it to God, to determine never to go back to Moab with its pseudosatisfaction, but to bring our emptiness to God and move forward into the unknown, with all its problems, with him. That is when the clouds begin to lift.

The chapter ends by reminding us that barley harvest was beginning, as Naomi and Ruth arrived at Bethlehem (v. 22). There will be food for them both, and who knows what other possibilities may lie ahead of them in the providence of God? The chapter ends on an upbeat because the future is always as bright as the promises of God, for those who trust him.

> For no matter how many promises God has made, they are "Yes" in Christ. And so through him the "Amen" is spoken by us to the glory of God.
>
> *2 Cor. 1:20* NIV

NOTES

1. Ronald M. Hals, *The Theology of the Book of Ruth* (Philadelphia: Fortress Press, 1969), 19.

2. Arthur Temple, *Hymns We Love* (London: Lutterworth Press, 1954), 81–82.

CHAPTER TWO

The Mechanics of Grace

Ruth 2:1–23

The second chapter of Ruth operates on a formally stylized pattern of interrelated dialogues, of which there are five: Ruth and Naomi (vv. 2–3), Boaz and the reapers (vv. 4–7), Boaz and Ruth (vv. 8–15a), Boaz and the reapers (vv. 15b–16), and Ruth and Naomi (vv. 19–22).[1] This follows the well-established pattern (a,b,c,b,a) of Hebrew narratives, usually called *chiasm*. The emphasis in such a pattern is always on the central unit, which is the exchange between Ruth and Boaz; and at the heart of that lies what many take to be the key verse of the whole book, the words of Boaz in verse 12b, *"a full reward be given you by the Lord God of Israel, under whose wings you have come for refuge."* Now that we have seen the structure, it may be more helpful to the preacher and congregation to analyze the material more according to the subject matter, in three sections.

Experiencing God's Providence

1 There was a relative of Naomi's husband, a man of great wealth, of the family of Elimelech. His name was Boaz.

2 So Ruth the Moabitess said to Naomi, "Please let me go to the field, and glean heads of grain after him in whose sight I may find favour." And she said to her, "Go, my daughter."

3 Then she left, and went and gleaned in the field after the reapers. And she happened to come to the part of the field belonging to Boaz, who was of the family of Elimelech.

4 Now behold, Boaz came from Bethlehem, and said to the reapers, "The Lord be with you!" And they answered him, "The Lord bless you!"

5 Then Boaz said to his servant who was in charge of the reapers, "Whose young woman is this?"

6 So the servant who was in charge of the reapers answered and said, "It is the young Moabite woman who came back with Naomi from the country of Moab.

7 "And she said, 'Please let me glean and gather after the reapers among the sheaves.' So she came and has continued from morning until now, though she rested a little in the house."

8 Then Boaz said to Ruth, "You will listen, my daughter, will you not? Do not go to glean in another field, nor go from here, but stay close by my young women.

9 "Let your eyes be on the field which they reap, and go after them. Have I not commanded the young men not to touch you? And when you are thirsty, go to the vessels and drink from what the young men have drawn."

10 Then she fell on her face, bowed down to the ground, and said to him, "Why have I found favor in your eyes, that you should take notice of me, since I am a foreigner?"

Ruth 2:1–10

Immediately as the chapter begins, Boaz is introduced. In one of the author's foreword "flashes," we are left in no doubt as to whom the future hope of Naomi and Ruth rests on. Here is the first step in the fulfillment of all that the symbol of barley harvest stands for. Boaz, whose name means "in him is strength," is introduced as a man of standing, through his great wealth; but much more important, he is a kinsman of Elimelech. This is the first indication to the reader that God is already working his purposes out.

The providence that will soon introduce Boaz has already provided for the needs of the poverty-stricken, widowed, foreigner Ruth, in the general rights laid down in the Levitical law code. "When you reap the harvest of your land, you shall not wholly reap the corners of your field, nor shall you gather the gleanings of your harvest . . . you shall leave them for the poor and the stranger: I am the Lord your God" (Lev. 19:9–10). On both counts, Ruth was qualified. She was poor and an alien. But within that general providence there comes a special providence to which Ruth 2:3 refers, in the words *"and she happened to come to the part of the field belonging to Boaz. . . ."* This establishes that Ruth was not only acting deliberately in choosing the field of Boaz, but was doubtless guided by God.

The same point is made by the start of the next verse, *"Now behold, Boaz came. . . ."* The timing was perfect, because it was God's. He is the chief actor in the unfolding drama, but his actions are concealed. This is not a story of direct revelations, angelic visitors, or visible miracles as in the story of Gideon, for example, in Judges. No judge, or prophet, or priest is involved in these events, but the hand of God is just as discernible to the eye of faith as if it had been literally visible. And yet the wonder of his providence is that each of the protagonists is able to make his or her choices without there being even the slightest sense of them being mechanized or programed.

In these small details we see a pale reflection of the greatest of all biblical miracles—the miracle of God's grace. There will always be mystery here. The work of salvation is all of God's grace, even the faith by which we believe in his gift (Eph 2:8); and yet we are called upon to exercise our wills to repent and believe the gospel. When we enter the narrow gate of Christ's kingdom, we are conscious of a decision of the will by which we turn from sin and trust Christ, as an expression of our free choice. Yet no sooner have we entered the door than we look back, as it were, and see inscribed over the entrance, "You did not choose Me, but I chose you . . ." (John 15:16). Peter struck the balance beautifully in his Pentecost sermon, when, preaching Christ, he affirmed, "'Him, being delivered by the carefully planned intention and foreknowledge of God, you have taken by lawless hands, have crucified, and put to death" (Acts 2:23).

The blend of divine sovereignty and human responsibility runs throughout all the comparatively insignificant details of our lives, as it did through the lives of Boaz and Ruth. It is a conviction we need to see restored running through our contemporary Christianity. Abraham Kuyper, who founded the Free University of Amsterdam in 1880 and was later prime minister of Holland, affirmed in his inaugural lecture, "There is not an inch in the whole area of human existence of which Christ, the sovereign of all, does not cry, 'It is mine!'"[2]

As we get to know Boaz better through his dialogue with the reapers' manager, we see that he is the model Israelite, even in the dark days of the judges. His greeting to his employees and their relationship with him are grounded in the centrality of Yahweh to the whole of life (v. 4). He inquires about the stranger and confirms that it is the young woman from Moab about whom, verse 11 reveals, he has already heard a good deal. Her character, in the foreman's report, is equally impeccable, as he stresses her modesty and devotion to hard work (v. 7). So the scene is set for their first encounter.

Verses 8–10 provide a most attractive picture of the mechanics of grace at work. Motivated not by duty but by compassion, Boaz goes out of his way to meet Ruth at the point of her need. In this he is a foreshadowing of the Lord Jesus in whose genealogical line he and Ruth will stand, who was and is himself "full of grace and truth" (John 1:14).

In calling Ruth *"my daughter"*—she had referred to herself as *"a foreigner"*—Boaz sweeps away at a stroke any doubt she might have had as to whether he would ever recognize her as a kinsperson. Next, he grants her permission to continue gleaning in his field and actually asks her not to go elsewhere (v. 8). Permission is followed by the promise of personal protection (v. 9a) and the provision of water whenever she needs it (v. 9b). These are such tokens of grace and favor that Ruth abases herself before her benefactor and marvels that he should be so compassionate as to notice a foreigner (v. 10). Goslinga comments that there is a play on words in the Hebrew terms translated "notice me" and "foreigner," and suggests as a rough English equivalent "respect a reject."[3]

We are not wrong to see in this generous provision a picture of the gracious dealings of Christ, the true Israelite, with his people the church who once were aliens and strangers. The answer to her question "why me?" lies ultimately not even in Boaz's compassion, but in the grace of God which has planned to bring an alien widow into the royal line of David.

Holding onto God's Faithfulness

11 And Boaz answered and said to her, "It has been fully reported to me, all that you have done for

> your mother-in-law since the death of your husband, and how you have left your father and your mother and the land of your birth, and have come to a people whom you did not know before.
>
> 12 "The Lord repay your work, and a full reward be given you by the Lord God of Israel, under whose wings you have come for refuge."
>
> *Ruth 2:11–12*

If Ruth describes herself as a "foreigner," in terms of the Sinai covenant by which the nation was constituted as God's people following the Exodus, Boaz goes back further to the Abrahamic covenant and identifies her with the father of the faithful. Like Abraham, Ruth had left her home and family to come to an unknown land, out of loyalty to Naomi and through faith in Naomi's God. Recognizing both these aspects of her loyalty, Boaz prays that she will experience the full blessing of Abraham's faithful God, who provides refuge for all who come to him. Her faith will be met by God's faithfulness.

The figure of the eagle is used in the Pentateuch as an image of God's power being utilized for the protection and nurturing care of his people. Speaking of Jacob (Israel), Moses declares, "As an eagle stirs up its next, hovers over its young, spreading out its wings, taking them up, carrying them on its wings, so the Lord alone led him" (Deut. 32:11–12). Moreover, God himself compares the Exodus deliverance to an eagle's activity. "'You have seen what I did to the Egyptians, and how I bore you on eagles' wings and brought you to Myself'" (Exod. 19:4). The *"wings,"* of which Boaz speaks (v. 12), symbolize the power of the grace that Ruth is experiencing, in protection and provision.

People today have the most extraordinary ideas about the nature of faith, but it is hard to better the definition that it is "holding on to a God who is faithful." This removes the emphasis away from the subjective experience of believing and on to the object of our trust, the God who is faithful. It is a very important point to make to a feelings-centered generation, who tend to measure reality by the rating on the internal, emotional Geiger counter. But biblical faith is not something that we work up by exciting music or corporate worship experiences, which soon fade. Such emotional dependency always has to have its next "fix" and can never live in the real world effectively. Biblical faith, by contrast, is responding to the divine initiative, as expressed in the words of Scripture, believing what God says to be true and acting consistently upon it. It is far more a matter of activity than feeling, just as love is. It means that if God says it, I believe it and that settles it.

Hudson Taylor, pioneer missionary to China and founder of the China Inland Mission (now Overseas Missionary Fellowship), told how he learned this lesson when translating the New Testament. He came upon Mark 11:22, "Have faith in God," at a time in his own personal life when he felt that was the hardest thing to do because of adverse outward circumstances and inward doubts and fears. But as he probed the text, he saw that "to have" is to hold on to something, and that godly faith is grounded in the God whose very nature is dependable faithfulness. Holding to this faithful God is all that we are called upon to do. Even though we may sometimes feel it is only by our fingernails, yet faith is still holding on, knowing that underneath are the everlasting arms of the Lord who will never let us down and never let us go. Under his wings there is refuge for all who trust him, however hostile the climate or violent the opposition. Can there be any sadder words than those spoken by the king when eventually he came to rescue his people and was rejected by them?

> "O Jerusalem, Jerusalem, the one who kills the prophets and stones those who are sent to her! How often I wanted to gather your children together, as a hen gathers her chicks under her wings, but you were not willing!"
>
> *Matt. 23:37*

ENJOYING GOD'S PROVISION

> 13 Then she said, "Let me find favor in your sight, my Lord; for you have comforted me, and have spoken kindly to your maidservant, though I am not like one of your maidservants."
>
> 14 Now Boaz said to her at mealtime, "Come here, and eat of the bread, and dip your piece of bread in the vinegar." So she sat beside the reapers, and he passed parched grain to her; and she ate and was satisfied, and kept some back.

15 And when she rose up to glean, Boaz commanded his young men, saying, "Let her glean even among the sheaves, and do not reproach her.
16 "Also let some grain from the bundles fall purposely for her; leave it that she may glean, and do not rebuke her."
17 So she gleaned in the field until evening, and beat out what she had gleaned, and it was about an ephah of barley.
18 Then she took it up and went into the city, and her mother-in-law saw what she had gleaned. So she brought out and gave to her what she had kept back after she had been satisfied.
19 And her mother-in-law said to her, "Where have you gleaned today? And where did you work? Blessed be the one who took notice of you." So she told her mother-in-law with whom she had worked, and said, "The man's name with whom I worked today is Boaz."
20 Then Naomi said to her daughter-in-law, "Blessed be he of the Lord, who has not forsaken his kindness to the living and the dead!" And Naomi said to her, "This man is a relation of ours, and of our close relatives."
21 Ruth the Moabitess said, "He also said to me, 'You shall stay close by my young men until they have finished all my harvest.'"
22 And Naomi said to Ruth her daughter-in-law, "It is good, my daughter, that you go out with his young women, and that people do not meet you in any other field."
23 So she stayed close by the young women of Boaz, to glean until the end of barley harvest and wheat harvest; and she dwelt with her mother-in-law.

Ruth 2:13–23

Ruth's response to the generosity of Boaz is an important step forward in their relationship. Having noted her loyalty to Naomi, Boaz cannot fail to have been impressed by her humility toward him. Her petition in verse 13 reflects her willingness to express her total dependence on his grace, which has already been indicated by her posture in verse 10. She is happy to accept the relationship of a *"maidservant"* to her lord, although she considers herself not worthy to be compared with the least of Boaz's actual servants, since she is still aware that she is a foreigner. Yet because of the great man's kind words and practical help, she is bold enough to petition him for continued grace and favor, to meet her great need (v. 13).

In interpreting Old Testament passages like this, commentators have sometimes used an allegorical approach. Boaz represents Christ and Ruth the sinner, brought in from outside God's family. Her response then becomes a model for us as we receive the riches of God's grace in Christ. There is a danger with this in that to press every detail of the story for an allegorical significance can force some fanciful interpretations which come more from reading into the text, than out from it. Impository preaching is alive and well in some church circles still, but our concern is to be expository.

The important factor to bear in mind is that the text is operating on different levels. We only interpret it properly when we begin by asking what it means to the original readers, and taking the text at its original face value. If we do not get right what it meant to them, we are unlikely to get right what it means to us. Hard work at the exegesis of the text is indispensable to good expository preaching. Otherwise, it will lack real biblical authority, and congregations notice when that is not present.

But, as Christian preachers, we are not to give Jewish sermons. So, we must also always read the Old Testament Scriptures through our New Testament spectacles, so that we interpret the particular in the light of the whole revelation of God, in all the Scriptures, finding their focus and fulfillment in our Lord Jesus Christ. The clue in Ruth lies in the genealogy at the end of the book, where her place with Boaz in the line of David points forward to the greater fulfillment of grace and truth in the Savior.[4]

The response of Boaz in verses 14–16 underlines the New Testament affirmation that there is always more grace. When the mealtime comes, Ruth is personally welcomed as one of the reapers by Boaz, to his table. She is invited to share fully in the servants' meal of bread dipped in wine vinegar, though she is working only for herself and Naomi, not for Boaz. But there is more to it than that. Boaz personally shares his own side dish of roasted kernels of grain with her, in such quantity that she is able to eat her fill and still have some left over, presumably for Naomi. Grace provides a welcome at the table and more than adequate supplies to satisfy. When Jesus fed the five thousand, were there not twelve basketsful left over?

But there is still more. Having granted her permission to reap, protection, and a generous provision of food and water, Boaz now goes a stage further in arranging for Ruth to have privileged reaping facilities (vv. 15–16). This is far beyond the letter of the law, and we are becoming aware that the actions of the wealthy farmer must stem from more than mere duty. The law regarding the welfare of the poor was always intended to reflect love for God, as well as for those in need, which is why love is the fulfilling of the law (Gal. 5:14). In his overflowing generosity Boaz demonstrates something of the character of God, who gave the law, "made known more fully to us in Christ, who, so the apostle teaches, is 'able to do far more abundantly than all that we ask or think' (Eph. 3:20)."[5] The unexpected bonus meant that Ruth was able to glean a very large amount of barley, which, after it had been beaten out to separate the grain from the husk, yielded an ephah, "twenty to twenty-two litres by the latest reckoning," according to Goslinga.[6]

The chapter's final dialogue finds us back with Ruth and Naomi after the day's work. Gratefully, Ruth produces the day's gleanings plus the roast grain she *"kept back"* at lunchtime (v. 18). Amazed at the quantity, Naomi realizes that someone has been extra generous to herself and her daughter-in-law. On hearing that it was Boaz, Naomi recognizes Yahweh's hand in this marvelous provision (v. 20). For Naomi, this is confirmation that the Lord has not deserted her, but is fulfilling his promises to provide for the widow and the stranger. It must have been a tremendous encouragement to her, confirming that she had done the right thing in returning to Bethlehem, and that God's favor rested on the Moabitess she had brought with her, too.

But we can also imagine her mind racing ahead with all sorts of ideas, as the author provides another "fast forward wind" with her mention of Boaz as *"one of our close relatives"* (v. 20b). Indeed, the Hebrew word *goʾel* carries with it more than the simple meaning of "relative." It implies "kinsman-redeemer," a concept which will be developed in the next chapter. Already, Ruth has found a place among all that Boaz owned, which is entirely the product of his grace; and the promise that this will continue until the end of the season (v. 21) is their guarantee of their adequate supply of good, not only for the three months of harvest (v. 23) but for the year beyond. Such generous compassion must, of course, be met by loyalty (v. 22).

In our Western civilization, we have come a long way from the sentiments sung by the children of Victorian Britain, in Mrs. C. F. Alexander's hymn "All Things Bright and Beautiful." Indeed, you will not find this verse from that favorite hymn in any contemporary hymn book.

> The rich man in his castle,
> The poor man at his gate,
> God made them, high or lowly,
> And ordered their estate.

That may belong to feudal Europe, but it does not sit easily with our contemporary democracy. One of the casualties of that old view's passing, however, has been the embarrassment many people feel about receiving grace, or charity, as we would probably call it. In Britain, we react strongly against the traditional picture of the aristocratic landowners doling out largesse at Christmas to their exploited workers, whose underrewarded labor has been the foundation of their wealth. We have perhaps swung too far the other way in producing a society where the weak or underprivileged, the sick or unemployed, go to the wall. Many are too ashamed to ask for help, and many are too unconcerned to offer it.

Our problem is that human definitions of grace are never as pure as God's grace. Here in Britain we have certain stately residences which are in the gift of the sovereign. These homes are known as "grace and favor" residences. They cannot be bought or rented; they can only be received, as a gift from the Queen. But of course, they are usually given to distinguished people, who have rendered considerable service to the state. You may find retired public servants or officers of the armed forces living in them, but you will not find down-and-outs from the streets of London. Human grace always conveys with it the idea of reward, or worthiness, or it is with a view to future business. God's grace is totally disinterested, in that sense. It is utterly undeserved, and the only strings attached are the obedient reception of all that he offers, in order to keep the channels of grace open to receive still more.

To be self-sufficient is a biblical goal, but only so that others will be able to be helped. The New Testament has no time for scroungers. "If any one will not work, neither shall he eat" (2 Thess. 3:10; see also 1 Thess. 4:11–12). However, Paul also ordered the converted thief to work hard, not simply to support himself, but "that he may have something to give to him who has need" (Eph. 4:28). There will always be a need for grace and generosity, because whatever the welfare schemes, "the poor you have with you always" (John 12:8). We must not become more hard-nosed than God simply because our culture pushes us in that direction. Many Christians need to take a leaf from Boaz's book and begin to reflect the grace of Christ as daily, compassionate grace. As John Wesley wrote,

> Let me do all the good I can, to all the people I can, by all the means I can, as often as I can, for I shall not pass this way again.

By demonstrating the character of the God whom Ruth had come to worship, Boaz won her heart and brought upon himself a happiness and an honor greater than either of them could ever have imagined.

NOTES

1. See *The Faith of Israel*, by William J. Dumbrell (Leicester, England: Inter-Varsity Press, 1989), 231–32.
2. Quoted by David Atkinson in *The Wings of Refuge* (Leicester, England: Inter-Varsity Press, 1983), 61.
3. Goslinga, *Ruth*, 531–32.
4. For help on this vital strand of Old Testament interpretation, see *The Unfolding Mystery: Discovering Christ in the Old Testament*, by Edmund P. Clowney (Colorado Springs: NavPress, 1988).
5. Atkinson, *The Wings of Refuge*, 79.
6. Goslinga, *Ruth*, 533.

CHAPTER THREE

Acts of Faith and Love

Ruth 3:1-18

For the three months of barley harvest there seems to have been no development in the Ruth-Boaz story. Life goes on. Day by day Ruth continues to glean with the servants of Boaz, and presumably, her daily needs are met, as chapter 2 describes. As readers of the story, we wonder what is going to happen. Will the relationship blossom or fade? Is this the answer to Naomi's prayers, or will there be a great disappointment?

If we are asking these questions, we do not need much imagination to realize what the two women were going through. Waiting is difficult at the best of times, but it depends largely on how we look at the world. We come back to the central theological message of the book which is that of the hidden, but active, God, who is at work continuously in the lives of his people, even when they think nothing is happening. There is not the slightest hint that this overruling sovereignty for one moment limits the freedom of our human actions or the dignity of our choices. Sometimes, God disappears completely into the tapestry of everyday life and we assume that he has forgotten us in our daily routine with its pressures, hassles, and uncertainties.

I believe it was Aldous Huxley who compared God to the Cheshire Cat in *Alice in Wonderland* by Lewis Carroll. This amazing animal was able to appear or disappear at will, and all that was left, at the end, was its grin. To an atheist, such as Huxley, that is all that is left of the outdated concept of God, presiding over a meaningless cosmos. But Christian experience is not in agreement. History is not a blind process, the product of chance, whether on the universal or personal scale. It has an Author, who will also conclude the drama. And when the Author steps onto the stage, he will bring down the curtain, finally. So behind the scenes, there is not an empty void, but the God "who works all things according to the counsel of His will" (Eph. 1:11).

In chapter 3 we can trace the actions of each of the major characters as they move forward, sometimes gropingly, in relationship with the God they trust, and so ultimately with one another.

Naomi: Following God's Signposts

> 1 Then Naomi her mother-in-law said to her, "My daughter, shall I not seek security for you, that it may be well with you?
>
> 2 "Now Boaz, whose young women you were with, is he not our relative? In fact, he is winnowing barley tonight at the threshing floor.
>
> 3 "Therefore wash yourself and anoint yourself, put on your best garment and go down to the threshing floor; but do not make yourself known to the man until he has finished eating and drinking.
>
> 4 "Then it shall be, when he lies down, that you shall notice the place where he lies; and you shall go in, uncover his feet, and lie down; and he will tell you what you should do."
>
> 5 And she said to her, "All that you say to me I will do."
>
> 6 So she went down to the threshing floor and did according to all that her mother-in-law instructed her.
>
> *Ruth 3:1–6*

Without some careful explanation, this third chapter of the story of Ruth is easily the strangest and most difficult to understand, from our contemporary, Western perspective. At first sight, Naomi might seem to be the archetypal scheming mother-in-law, pushing Ruth forward, determined that her plans will succeed. And couldn't Ruth's behavior be interpreted as somewhat forward, not to say immodest, literally throwing herself at Boaz? Are we meant to learn about how to arrange marriages from this chapter? Clearly, we need some vital background information if we are going to make sense of it all, because there are basic cultural practices written into the Law of Israel, which govern the story at this point.

The first concerns the "kinsman-redeemer." Israel was created, by God's call, to be a unique people. When we describe the nation-state as a theocracy we mean literally that Yahweh was its King, its covenant Lord. Indeed, several of the statements describing the covenant relationship in the Pentateuch reflect the treaties made in the ancient Near East by conquering monarchs with their subject peoples. From the origins of the people of Israel, in God's call to Abram (Gen. 12:1), the land of promise played a key role. This new land, "that I will show you," would be the location where God's blessing would be enjoyed by Abram and his descendants.

The Book of Exodus is the story of their deliverance from slavery in Egypt and their journey to the promised land, which they are on the verge of entering in the Book of Deuteronomy. This book introduces the new home of God's covenant people as the land for which God personally cares (Deut. 11:12), a "good land" (3:25; 4:21) "flowing with milk and honey" (6:3; 11:9).

Its description in Deuteronomy 8:7–10 reminds us of Eden, Paradise lost. But the emphasis is not on its natural fertility so much as on God's promise to give it to his people, as part of his blessing (7:13–15), a free gift (6:10–11), their "inheritance" (4:21; 21:23; 26:1). This is God's part of the covenant and the response he requires from those who are his beneficiaries is their love and loyalty, demonstrated by their obedience (4:1; 11:22–25). It is not that Israel's obedience is the means by which they earn God's grace and favor. Rather, obedience is seen as the expression of gratitude for the mercy already given. They were created to serve him, and obedience is an aspect of his comprehensive blessing. The alternative is a terrible possibility, however. Disobedience, or turning away from God, leads to his anger (6:14–15), the land's unfruitfulness (11:16–17), a curse (28:15–35), and ultimately, loss of the land (4:27).

We must remember in all this that Ruth is set "in the days when the judges ruled." If the Book of Joshua illustrates through the conquest of this land what happened when Israel responded positively to Yahweh's covenant-demands, Judges illustrates the downward spiral of apostasy and rebellion. The faithful obedience of Joshua's generation was completely overturned by their children, who did precisely what their fathers had sworn not to do (Josh. 24:16; Judg. 2:10). The Deuteronomic background is important if ever we are to understand the importance of the kinsman-redeemer concept. Indeed, the ownership of the land of Israel is still the most explosive issue in the precarious balance of contemporary world politics, and the Bible tells us why.

After the conquest under Joshua, the land was allotted by tribes, clans, and families as their inheritance from the Lord, so that they were leaseholders rather than freeholders. They had no absolute rights to the land. They could not part with the family portion or sell it whenever they wished, because it was not theirs. It belonged to Yahweh, but he had given it forever to that family as a mark of his blessing. But supposing poverty were to strike? Could the value of land be realized in order to alleviate suffering? The principles are clearly set out in Leviticus 25:23–28:

> "The land shall not be sold permanently, for the land is Mine; for You are strangers and sojourners with Me. And in all the land of your possession you shall grant redemption of the land. If one of your brethren becomes poor, and has sold some of his possession, and if his redeeming relative comes to redeem it, then he may redeem what his brother sold. Or if the man has no one to redeem it, but he himself becomes able to redeem it, then let him count the years since its sale, and restore the balance to the man to whom he sold it, that he may return to his possession. But if he is not able to have it restored to himself, then what was sold shall remain in the hand of him who bought it until the Year of Jubilee; and in the Jubilee it shall be released, and he shall return to his possession."

It was the duty of the nearest relation or kinsman to redeem the land, to buy it back for the family. That right also belonged to the original possessor, if his fortunes prospered and he could afford to compensate the buyer. However, if there was no redemption, at the next Year of Jubilee (every fiftieth year), the land reverted to the original owner or his heirs, without compensation. It is this provision which Naomi wants to invoke, but in order to do so she has to discover a kinsman-redeemer. We learn from 4:9 that Elimelech had owned property, which Naomi has had to sell because of her poverty. She, therefore, plans to call on Boaz, as a kinsman, to become the redeemer and thus to ransom the family property. But there is a further complication.

To the provision of the kinsman-redeemer she links a further levitical provision of what is called "levirate marriage" (from the Latin word *levir,* meaning brother-in-law). This refers to the provision in Jewish law for a man to marry the widow of his deceased brother if no heir has been born. The widow was not to remarry outside the family, but the brother of the deceased husband was to raise up an heir for his dead brother so that his name might be perpetuated and his family inheritance continue to be possessed.

It is this practice which is the basis of the Sadducees' hypothetical question to Jesus in Mark 12:18-27 about seven brothers, who each married the same wife and all died, without children. Whose wife would she be at the resurrection? The original provision is explained in Deuteronomy 25:5–10, where the force of the passage is that while such a marriage is the right of the nearest kinsman, it is not a duty to be enforced upon him. It is a right that he feels free to lay aside, though not without the possibility of some public denunciation and shame. However, the important point, of which Naomi was doubtless perfectly aware, concerns the fact that the kinsman-redeemer acts out of compassion and commitment rather than compulsion or mere duty. Naomi wants Boaz not only to ransom Elimelech's property, but also to marry the widow of her husband's rightful heir, and so to establish the name of her husband and son, and to return the family to its proper status in Bethlehem. How and whether all that is to happen is the drama unfolding in this chapter, as we follow God's providential control of the circumstances of all three characters.

We have seen how the message of the whole book is about God's providential overruling in the lives of his people, the classic New Testament statement of which is Romans 8:28, "We know that all things work together for good to those who love God. . . ." But the question remains, "What is our good?" If we were able to ask Naomi that, she would have had no doubt about the answer—she wanted to see her daughter-in-law married (1:9). But Ruth had stayed alongside her mother-in-law because she had come to accept Naomi's God as her own (1:16). This was a deeper love and loyalty than to Naomi alone. She had put herself into the hands of the God of Israel (2:12).

For us, there may be a variety of "goods" which we would like God to work in our lives, but in its fullest sense our greatest good is to become members of God's family, to grow in our likeness to the Lord Jesus, and to enter into the destiny for which we were created—to know God, to love him, and to enjoy him. That is what he is working out through all the changing scenes of our lives. And this book shows how he can use even the sinfulness of others for our good. Mahlon should never have married a Moabitess. Jews were not to marry Gentiles. Yet that action brought Ruth to the place where she trusted the true God for herself, and through Boaz entered into the line of descent of the Messiah (Matt. 1:5).

Now we would be wrong to deduce from that that sin does not matter. It does not, for example, give a Christian the liberty of marrying a non-Christian on the grounds that the marriage may be the means of bringing the partner to Christ. That would be wrong on two counts. First, it flies in the face of the clear teaching of the New Testament, such as 2 Cor. 6:14. In addition, we are not to use marriage as a method of evangelism! To break God's commandments always leads to suffering, and the predicament that Naomi and Ruth find themselves in is directly attributable to Mahlon's sin and Elimelech's wrong choice. Paul warns us not to argue that we can go on sinning so that grace can increase (Rom. 6:1). It is never right to do evil. But it is also true that this wonderful story prevents us from despairing of the future just because of past mistakes, whether for willful rebellion or evil that has come unbidden into our lives through the faults of others. What we have to do is to move forward with God.

Noami's reasoning is not difficult to follow as we see her trying to discern God's signposts. She has come home "empty," but she recognizes in her present condition the hand of El Shaddai, the Almighty, who is able to change situations. She does the sensible thing, the one thing she could do to provide for herself and her daughter-in-law, by sending Ruth to glean "amid the alien corn." On the very first day, Ruth is noticed by Boaz, and not only noticed, but singled out by him for special marks of compassion and favor. Is that not an answer to prayer? Naomi, at any rate, sees it as Yahweh's provision (2:20) and begins to follow the signposts. Perhaps Boaz is to be the answer to her dilemma. He is a kinsman, though not the nearest, but might he perhaps be persuaded to exercise his redemptive rights? The circumstances which Naomi had not engineered and the provisions in Scripture both for the kinsman-redeemer and the levirate marriage become the signposts on the basis of which she begins to plan her journey of faith.

But in all of this Naomi also demonstrates a down-to-earth, common-sense approach (vv. 3–4). The fact that God seems to be pointing in a certain direction does not ever mean that it is a foregone conclusion. Boaz may decline, and they are entirely dependent on his generosity. Will he resent Naomi's plan? Will it be counterproductive? Naomi's response is to test it out and see—to try this door that seems to be opening, but cautiously. Ruth will appeal to him to be their redeemer, privately. There is a blend of faith and activity here.

Naomi was not passive. She did not sit back, become a fatalist, and say "whatever will be will be," and call that faith. There is a false piety which is an excuse for laziness and lethargy. Naomi took the initiative, but she followed the direction which she believed God was already pointing out. It is still an important ingredient of guidance to discern God's direction and then follow where he is leading and moving, whether in our personal lives or in the life of God's church. U-turns are very rare with God after the first turnaround of our conversion. There is a sequence to his guidance by which all our yesterdays feed in what he is doing in our lives today. Our response is to act, in faith, as Ruth determined to do (vv. 5–6).

Ruth: Trusting God's Protection

> 7 And after Boaz had eaten and drunk, and his heart was cheerful, he went to lie down at the end of the heap of grain; and she came softly, uncovered his feet, and lay down.
>
> 8 Now it happened at midnight that the man was startled, and turned himself; and there, a woman was lying at his feet.
>
> 9 And he said, "Who are you?" So she answered, "I am Ruth, your maidservant. Take your maidservant under your wing, for you are a close relative."
>
> *Ruth 3:7–9*

Ruth, also, is a woman of active faith. In these verses we see her literally taking refuge under Yahweh's wings as she ventures forward in faith, to put Naomi's plan into action. To enter the barn, approach Boaz undetected, and lie down at his feet involved her in all sorts of danger. A single woman in a barn full of men in good spirits at the end of harvest celebration (v. 7) was vulnerable not only as to her own safety, but also as to her motives. Yet, behind these highly unusual actions lay a sincere trust in Yahweh's care and protection. Faith always grows when it acts on the basis of what the Lord has already accomplished and provided.

This is the burden of Ruth's request in verse 9, where she uses the word *"wing,"* as Boaz had done (2:12). Most modern translations take this to mean the corner of the garment or blanket which covered Boaz. If that is so, then Ruth's request is for more than protection. It is an appeal to him to marry her so that they will share the same covering. In the context of the chapter this seems to be the more likely meaning, especially in view of the response of Boaz in verses 11-13.

Knowing that Boaz is a man of God, Ruth asks from him the characteristics which she had already identified in, and experienced from, Yahweh. In this she provides a pattern for our faith. In all forward spiritual movement there are moments when we have to trust the bare word of God's promise and venture out in faith. There are many times when we cannot see how it is going to work out, but that is no reason not to trust God, commit our way to him, and act. Some Christians seem to be sitting down and waiting, throughout their entire lives, because they are always requiring God to show them more before they launch out and trust him. It is possible to be so afraid of making mistakes that we do nothing. But, provided our lives are in a right relationship with God and we honestly want to go his way and not our own, he gives us permission to launch out in faith, to risk for his sake, even to get it wrong and to fail, because "he who never made a mistake never made anything."

The balance between an adventurous faith and foolhardiness is not always easy to strike, especially when we are young. But Wesley spoke of preferring to have one firebrand working with him, whom he might have to cool down, to ten unenthusiastic men who had to be warmed up; and all of us involved in ministry can identify with that. Reckless faith may sometimes do things which in the cold light of rationality seem unwise, but God honors the heart that is set on attempting great things for him because it expects great things from him.

On that faith of William Carey, the modern missionary movement was largely built. Born near Northampton, England, in 1761, Carey worked as a shoemaker from the age of sixteen to twenty-eight, but after his conversion at eighteen he became a Baptist lay preacher. In 1792 he preached his now-famous missionary sermon, "Expect great things from God; attempt great things for God," and four months later founded the Baptist Society for Propagating the Gospel amongst the Heathen. This he did in spite of opposition from senior pastors. Their view was that if God wanted to effect the conversion of the heathen he could and would do so without resort to human means.

In 1793, Carey sailed for Bengal, India, where he translated the Bible into Bengali and by 1798 had also learned Sanskrit. His faith led to untiring activity, translating and printing the Bible, evangelism, church planting, education, and medical relief work. He supervised the translation of the Bible into thirty-six languages, produced a massive Bengali-English dictionary, and pioneered many social reforms. He was a man who took God at his word and opened many other areas of Asia, as well as the Indian subcontinent to the gospel.[1]

Boaz: Reflecting God's Character

> 10 Then he said, "Blessed are you of the Lord, my daughter! For you have shown more kindness at the end than at the beginning, in that you did not go after young men, whether poor or rich.
>
> 11 "And now, my daughter, do not fear. I will do for you all that you request, for all the people of my town know that you are a virtuous woman.
>
> 12 "Now it is true that I am a close relative; however, there is a relative closer than I.
>
> 13 "Stay this night, and in the morning it shall be that if he will perform the duty of a close relative for you—good; let him do it. But if he does not want to perform the duty for you, then I will perform the duty for you, as the Lord lives! Lie down until morning."
>
> 14 She lay at his feet until morning, and she arose before one could recognize another. Then he said, "Do not let it be known that the woman came to the threshing floor."
>
> 15 Also he said, "Bring the shawl that is on you and hold it." And when she held it, he measured six

> ephahs of barley, and laid it on her. Then she went into the city.
>
> 16 When she came to her mother-in-law, she said, "Is that you, my daughter?" Then she told her all that the man had done for her.
>
> 17 "And she said, 'These six ephahs of barley he gave me; for he said to me, "Do not go empty-handed to your mother-in- law."'
>
> 18 Then she said, "Sit still, my daughter, until you know how the matter will turn out; for the man will not rest until he has concluded the matter this day."
>
> *Ruth 3:10–18*

The situation begins to turn out better than Naomi or Ruth could ever have anticipated. Boaz not only understood Ruth's meaning, but blessed her for her readiness to marry him as the kinsman-redeemer, although he was clearly considerably older than she. He did not take offense at Ruth's open and guileless statement of her need, because he knew her heart and her motivation. When he commended her for her *"kindness,"* the word used is *ḥesed,* the term which so often designated the covenant-love and faithfulness of Yahweh for his people (1:8, 2:20) and which has already been shown to be a quality Boaz possessed in full measure. He sees that same quality in Ruth who is clearly growing in likeness to the God she has come to trust and worship. His reference to her kindness *"at the beginning"* may well have been to the fact that she was prepared to return to Bethlehem with Naomi at all (2:11), or possibly to her acceptance of his request not to reap in anyone else's fields throughout the harvest period (2:8).

Next, Boaz further demonstrates his compassion and sensitivity by calming her fears and promising his help (v. 11), a further reflection of the character of Yahweh. Clearly, that same God who had been prompting Naomi had been preparing Boaz. Indeed, it seems that Boaz would have taken the initiative as redeemer himself already, were it not for the fact that there was a nearer kinsman than he (v. 12). Boaz wanted to follow out the letter of God's instructions. In that, he reminds us that we never work for our good when we set aside Scripture. We need to be governed by God's own Word, because it is the expression of his character, which is the greatest and ultimate reality.

Lastly, Boaz shows again the character of Yahweh by literally loading Ruth down with a large amount of barley next morning. Clearly, their meeting had to be secret, so that no dishonor should be attributed to Ruth's behavior, which might disincline the nearer kinsman from fulfilling his role (v. 14b). But as a token and pledge of his commitment to her, and as an expression of his generous love, Boaz loads her shawl with *"six* [measures] *of barley"* (probably less than an ephah, but still a considerable amount; "measures" is the preferred reading rather than "ephahs") to carry back to Naomi. The picture is drawn of Ruth, in the first light of dawn, making her way back to Naomi's home, staggering under the weight of the generosity of her kinsman. No longer was Naomi to be "empty," but that gracious provision of Boaz surely strengthened her faith in Yahweh's overruling providence far more than it every nurtured her body. The waiting time is nearly over (v. 18).

Boaz is thus clearly a picture of our kinsman-redeemer, Jesus Christ. He became one with us, in all but our sinfulness, so that we might become adopted sons and daughters of God, through faith. "But when the fullness of the time had come, God sent forth His Son, born of a woman, born under the law, to redeem those who were under the law, that we might receive the adoption as sons" (Gal. 4:4–5). Having lived a life of moral righteousness in perfect obedience to the Father's will, the life that we have failed to live, he died the death that we deserve to die, and so he redeemed us by his precious blood (1 Pet. 1:18–19). As Boaz dealt with Ruth, so Christ deals with every one of his repentant, believing people. When we cast ourselves at his feet, dependent on his mercy, and claim the covering of his blood for all our sins, he welcomes us with a steadfast love and kindness that are limitless. He calms our fears and promises his help. He works out his purposes of grace in and through the circumstances of our lives. He daily loads us with his benefits. Isn't that just like the Lord? What we need to ask ourselves is how like him we really are. In all our dealings with one another here in God's world we need to remember that we never go wrong when we exhibit a gracious, generous spirit of love. Whenever we act selfishly we automatically wrong-foot ourselves. But whenever we act in faith and love we reflect the character of our God and open the way to unlimited progress, with him.

Perhaps the words of a woman can best express Ruth's confidence. Written nearly one hundred and fifty years ago by Anna L. Waring, a

Welsh woman from Glamorgan, before she was thirty, her words are still a powerful expression of the calm assurance of any disciple who knows the love of the Good Shepherd, who lays down his life for his sheep.

> Wherever He may guide me,
> No want shall turn me back;
> My Shepherd is beside me,
> And nothing can I lack.
> His wisdom ever waketh;
> His sight is never dim.
> He knows the way He taketh,
> And I will walk with Him."[2]

NOTES

1. See article on William Carey, by A. M. Derham, in *The New International Dictionary of the Christian Church*, ed. J. D. Douglas (Exeter: Paternoster Press, 1974).
2. From "In Heavenly Love Abiding," by Anna L. Waring.

CHAPTER FOUR

"There Is a Redeemer"

Ruth 4:1–22

From one point of view, Naomi's story is like anybody else's in Israel in the days of the judges, when there was no king in Israel. Elimelech made his decisions on the basis of what he thought would be best for himself and his family. He did what was right in his own eyes. It brought his wife to the brink of ruin, eventually, but he could not have foreseen that. Her only way out was through her foreign daughter-in-law, whose loyalty to her because of her loyalty to Yahweh, paved the way for the kinsman-redeemer to rescue them both. At one level, this might seem to be a rather ordinary, somewhat limited, story of family crisis. Yet it merits a whole book of the Bible, indicating that the revelation it contains is clearly strategic to our understanding of the mind and purpose of God. The necessity and provision of redemption is at the very heart of God's plan and the plan of his heart.

One cannot study this final chapter without seeing the centrality of Boaz, the redeemer, as the only resolution of the problems faced by Ruth and Naomi. He takes the initiative in bringing about the act of redemption (v. 1). He pays the price (vv. 8–9). He publicly claims his own (vv. 9–10). He provides a name and an inheritance where before there was only ruin (v. 14). He restores and sustains Naomi, even in old age, through the birth of Obed (v. 15). Ruth and Naomi could have done none of these things themselves. They were entirely dependent on the covenant-faithfulness and personal compassion of Boaz, their kinsman-redeemer. And in this way grace meets and answers the otherwise insoluble problems posed by the failure of the days of the judges.

Through New Testament eyes we can therefore see that what God did for Ruth and Naomi through Boaz, he has accomplished for all who cast themselves upon his mercy, in Christ. We, too, have suffered from the absence of a king in our lives, or rather by the usurpation by ourselves of the throne, which rightly belongs to God alone. We, too, need a redeemer as we suffer the deprivation of our inheritance as the just consequences of our sin and rebellion. We are equally unable to save ourselves, and no other kinsman could possibly meet our need. "But when the fullness of the time had come, God sent forth His Son, born of a woman, born under the law, to redeem those who were under the law . . ." (Gal. 4:4–5). By his incarnation, the Son of God became our kinsman so that by his sacrificial, atoning death he might also become our redeemer. All our fundamental human needs and problems find their solution at the Cross of Christ, and in his glorious resurrection.

> There is a Redeemer, Jesus, God's own Son;
> Precious Lamb of God, Messiah, Holy One.
> Thank You, oh, my Father, for giving us Your Son,
> And leaving Your Spirit 'til the work on earth is done.[1]

THE HEART OF THE MATTER

1 Now Boaz went up to the gate and sat down there; and behold, the close relative of whom Boaz had spoken came by. So Boaz said, "Come aside, friend, sit down here."

2 So he came aside and sat down. And he took ten men of the elders of the city, and said, "Sit down here." So they sat down.

3 Then he said to the close relative, "Naomi, who has come back from the country of Moab, sold the piece of land which belonged to our brother Elimelech.

4 "And I thought to inform you, saying, 'Buy it back in the presence of the inhabitants and the elders of my people. If you will redeem it, redeem it; but if you will not redeem it, then tell me, that I may know; for there is no one but you to redeem it, and I am next after you.'" And he said, "I will redeem it."

5 Then Boaz said, "On the day you buy the field from the hand of Naomi, you must also buy it from Ruth the Moabitess, the wife of the dead, to perpetuate the name of the dead through his inheritance."

6 And the close relative said, "I cannot redeem it for myself, lest I ruin my own inheritance. You redeem my right of redemption for yourself, for I cannot redeem it."

7 Now this was the custom in former times in Israel concerning redeeming and exchanging, to confirm anything: one man took of his sandal and gave it to the other, and this was an a confirmation in Israel.

8 Therefore the close relative said to Boaz, "Buy it for yourself." So he took off his sandal.

9 And Boaz said to the elders and all the people, "You are witnesses this day that I have bought all that was Elimelech's, and all that was Chilion's and Mahlon's, from the hand of Naomi.

10 "Moreover, Ruth the Moabitess, the widow of Mahlon, I have acquired as my wife, to perpetuate the name of the dead through his inheritance, that the name of the dead may not be cut off from among his brethren and from his position at the gate. You are witnesses this day."

Ruth 4:1–10

Naomi's prediction (3:18) that Boaz is a man of immediate action is fulfilled, as he makes for the town gate. Indeed, the tense indicates that he did this as soon as he got back to Bethlehem from the threshing floor. *"The gate"* was really the center of the community's life; there cases were heard and contracts were made. The *"elders"* dispensed justice, the poor waited for help, and the ordinary people met one another to exchange news. It had much the same function as the village square in medieval Europe. Everyone had to pass through the gate, so it was the obvious place to make for if you wanted to be sure of meeting someone, in a relatively small community.

Boaz has a plan to put into operation which involves him in meeting the nearer kinsman (3:12) as soon as possible. However, once he has met the man and persuaded him to sit down along with ten elders of the city who are presumably invited to be witnesses or arbiters (vv. 1–2), the story takes a sudden and unexpected twist.

Boaz begins to talk about the sale of land (v. 3) in which Naomi has been involved. This is, of course, the first time that we are told anything about this land *"which belonged to our brother Elimelech."* Much depends on the translation of the verb, which in turn depends on the pointing of the Hebrew text. The Masoretic text is vocalized to give a tense of completed action—Naomi *"sold"* (NKJV) or "has sold." However, if the vocalization is changed from the perfect tense to the active participle, which is equally possible, then the translation becomes "is selling" (RSV and NIV). There is considerable discussion among commentators as to which is to be preferred. Naomi might already have sold the land because of her poverty, though if this had happened it seems strange that Boaz could purchase it without the buyer being involved at all in the discussions. And why should he twice describe the action he is proposing as buying *"from the hand of Naomi"* (vv. 5, 9)? Moreover, Boaz would not need to redeem the land, since Naomi would already have been paid the market price. For these reasons, Goslinga and others suggest that "is selling" is a better translation, indicating that with harvest over, the land now has to be sold to keep Naomi and Ruth alive, but that Naomi's desire was to keep it within the family. Another suggestion, by Gunkel, is that the land was confiscated when Elimelech took his family off to Moab, but that if a kinsman would claim the land back, on her behalf, she might then be able to sell it for revenue. Whichever "solution" is preferred, the major significance is that the kinsman is invited to redeem because Naomi is at the end of her own resources. For Boaz, this was only the first stage of his plan.

His words in verse 4 indicate how important he regards the matter to be. The literal translation, "I thought I should uncover your ear," indicates something of almost revelatory significance about to be communicated. Working strictly to the letter of the law, Boaz presents the challenge to the nearer kinsman, recognizing his prior claim but also asserting his own readiness to act if the nearer kinsman declines.

We hold our breath, only to be amazed by the man's reply, "I will redeem it." What has gone wrong? All that we have been led to expect since chapter 2 seems about to be blown to smithereens! But verse 5 reveals Boaz's master stroke. The responsibility of the *goʾel* (the redeemer) is also at the same time the responsibility of the "levir." Probably the kinsman has dismissed the second idea, recognizing that Naomi's age made it impossible for her to raise up another heir for Elimelech were he to marry her. The property would therefore have reverted to him alone, there being no heir, and this may well explain his eagerness to buy it. But Boaz now introduces the fact that Elimelech's property, having technically passed to Mahlon and Chilion with his death, is somewhat entangled. The redeemer's duty involves not only the mother of the two sons but their widows, of whom only one, Ruth, is present in Bethlehem. So, it is not just a straight case of buying the land, but of contracting the levirate marriage with Ruth to raise up a grandson to Elimelech. The one cannot be divorced from the other. The privilege entails the responsibility (v. 5).

The kinsman's previous enthusiasm is stopped in its tracks (v. 6) and the reason he gives is that he would incur heavy financial obligations. David Atkinson comments, "Had he just been required to redeem the land, he would have been financially poorer, but at least the land would be his. The only way he could lose it would be if . . . a levirate son was born to Naomi, to whom the property would revert as legal heir of Elimelech. . . . But if he were to marry *Ruth* and give her a levirate son, the property would revert to the son, and the kinsman would lose both his money and eventually the land."[2]

We get the distinct impression that it is with not a little relief that he hands the responsibility back to Boaz. It underlines the personal cost of acting as kinsman-redeemer and magnifies the compassion of Boaz in doing all this for a "foreigner." This is a reflection of the covenant-love (*ḥesed*) of Yahweh for his people, and at the same time a very practical illustration of how the quality could be worked out in interpersonal human relationships. It provides a cameo of the sort of life-style God envisaged when he commanded, "Be holy, as I am holy."

The remaining verses detail the moves by which the nearer kinsman abrogates his right to redeem, in favor of Boaz. Verse 7 explains the giving of the sandal as the equivalent to our signature on a legal document, here witnessed by ten elders. The sandal probably assumed this significance as a symbol of ownership. If you owned land, then you were free to walk over it, wherever and whenever you wished to. The sandal transfer symbolized a change of ownership and came to be used as a sign of any agreement made and publicly witnessed between two parties.

Once the nearer kinsman has waived his rights in this way, Boaz immediately assumes them (vv. 9–10). Here is the resolution of the plot of the whole book. In exact, precise, legal language, but also with great compassion and kindness, Boaz makes two solemn affirmations before the witnesses. He accepts the role of kinsman-redeemer with regard to Elimelech's property, which had technically passed to his sons Mahlon and Chilion. Second, he marries Ruth, Mahlon's widow, so that the family name may not die out or disappear from the town's records. According to custom, Obed, the first-born son of Boaz and Ruth, would be known as Mahlon's son, and so the line would continue.

The spiritual application of these verses must be to underline again that at the heart of the law of God lies the character of the God of love. Where the nearer kinsman failed because, ultimately, he was governed by his own interests in providing for himself and preserving what he had, Boaz triumphed. What caused the other kinsman to step down was the ingredient which gave Boaz the greatest joy—marriage to Ruth. The provision of the kinsman-redeemer needed the motivation of compassionate love for it to be activated, and that Boaz, foreshadowing Christ, wonderfully demonstrates. We need constantly to be reminded that 1 Corinthians 13 comes between chapters 12 and 14. That is to say, the most spectacular gifts, the most skillful qualities, the most dutiful service are all as empty as "nothingness," if they are not motivated by love. So much that passes as service of the Lord is little more than religious duty. He is looking for the love of our hearts and he has given an example—in Christ and in those who, like Boaz, emulate him—that we should follow in his footsteps.

THE ANSWER TO THE PROBLEM

> 11 And all the people who were at the gate, and the elders, said, "We are witnesses. The Lord make the woman who is coming to your house like Rachel and Leah, the two who built the house of Israel; and may you prosper in Ephrathah and be famous in Bethlehem.
>
> 12 "May your house be like the house of Perez, whom Tamar bore to Judah, because of the offspring which the Lord will give you from this young woman."

13 So Boaz took Ruth and she became his wife; and
when he went in to her, the Lord gave her conception,
and she bore a son.
14 Then the women said to Naomi, "Blessed be the
Lord, who has not left you this day without a close
relative; and may his name be famous in Israel!
15 "And may he be to you a restorer of life and a
nourisher of your old age; for your daughter-in-law,
who loves you, who is better to you than seven sons,
has borne him."
16 Then Naomi took the child and laid him on her
bosom, and became a nurse to him.
17 Also the neighbor women gave him a name,
saying, "There is a son born to Naomi." And they
called his name Obed. He is the father of Jesse, the
father of David.

Ruth 4:11–17

By this time, we are surely to imagine that most of the inhabitants of Bethlehem have found their way to the town gate to witness these extraordinary events. Clearly, Boaz was a wealthy and powerful figure in the little town. The marriage of a man of substance was always an occasion of public interest and speculation. How much more when it is accompanied by dramatic pronouncements of this sort, and when it involves a Moabitess! So the elders and the people at the gate perform a dual function. Not only are they the legal witnesses to the transaction, but they convey a spiritual blessing through their prayers, much as we would today at the wedding ceremony in church of a couple from our own community.

In passing, it is worth pointing out that the public nature of the wedding ceremony, in the Bible and in Christian tradition, has its own special value and importance. Today, when there can be so much expense and so much social kudos invested in such an event, couples sometimes are tempted to wonder whether they need to bother. "What difference do a set form of vows or the signing of a piece of paper make if two people really love one another?" I am sometimes asked. My answer is, "All the difference." It is no accident that some form of public marriage ceremony exists in almost every culture of the world. It is important socially that others know publicly that two people are committing themselves to one another in marriage. But it is also very important for each individual within the partnership. If the love commitment which a man and woman have for each other is not prepared to go public, so that everyone knows they are man and wife, then I would question whether it is real love or a real commitment at all. Until it is affirmed in the presence of a witness, either partner has a right to question how deep the other's love truly is, however passionately it may be expressed.

The blessing of the townspeople in verse 11 illustrates that they have no prejudice against Ruth being brought within the community of God's covenant people. The Old Testament reveals that the nation of Israel corporately failed to fulfill its divinely given task of being a light to the Gentiles (Isa. 49:6) and became increasingly narrow in its religious nationalism and deluded in its false sense of privilege. The prophet Jonah's reaction to God's command to go to Nineveh by heading off in the opposite direction is the classic example of a widespread attitude, which came to its peak in the time of Christ when Gentiles were characterized as dogs. However, throughout the same period, there was a great willingness to accept proselytes within the community of Israel and a spirit of open welcome to those who recognized the supremacy of Yahweh, as is evidenced by this verse.

The parallels to the Christian church are often uncomfortably close here; both in our unwillingness to fulfill the great commission and in our reluctance to accept those whom God has brought into his family, until they accept some of the favorite "shibboleths" of our particular Christian subculture. But Ruth does not have to face that problem. Instead she is welcomed with what might seem to be extravagant prayers for blessing.

Prayer is a constantly recurring theme throughout this short book, which reminds us again of its major theological thrust regarding the constant presence and involvement of the sovereign Lord. It is worth recalling the specific occasions on which Yahweh is invoked in prayer as part of the normal everyday life-style of his people—see 1:8; 2:4, 12, 20; 3:10. To live in the grace of God means to realize consciously that he is always present and always active in love in the lives of all his people.

So, the people pray for a famous family line to spring from the union of Boaz and Ruth, just as the twelve tribes of Israel were built from the marriages of Jacob to Rachel and Leah. As the last verses of this chapter and, more importantly still, the first chapter of the New

Testament indicate, their prayer was to be answered in ways "exceedingly abundantly above" all that they had asked or even imagined (Eph. 3:20).

The same is true also of their second request regarding their prosperity and fame *"in Bethlehem."* For it was to Bethlehem that Samuel, the prophet, came (1 Sam. 16:4) to anoint the great grandson of Boaz and Ruth to be king over Israel. It was about Bethlehem that the prophet Micah later proclaimed,

> "Though you are little among the thousands of Judah,
> Yet out of you shall come forth to Me
> The One to be Ruler in Israel,
> Whose goings forth are from of old,
> From everlasting."
>
> *Micah 5:2*

And so it was to Bethlehem that Joseph from Nazareth came with Mary, under the decree of Caesar Augustus, to be registered, and in Bethlehem that the Savior of the world was born (Luke 2:1–11).

"Perez" (v. 12) was the more important of the two sons of the levirate marriage between Judah and Tamar, and also one of the ancestors of the Bethlehemites, who were of the tribe of Judah (see 1 Chronicles 2:5, 18, 51.) Some of the people praying this blessing on Boaz and Ruth were themselves descendants of Perez, as indeed Boaz himself was (v. 18). Not only do they long to see a son raised up for Elimelech, but a famous line of descendants from Boaz himself, as a reward for his faithful, compassionate love and kindness. They ask for God's blessing to be poured on the man who has acted faithfully for the preservation of the family line, by granting him a famous dynasty—a prayer which, again, was abundantly answered, reminding us that God is no man's debtor, and we can never outgive God.

The simple dignified description of verse 13 conveys within it a wealth of biblical doctrine on the theme of Christian marriage. The public commitment of Boaz and Ruth in the marriage ceremony before their sexual union reminds us of the context of sexual relations being always within married love. The "one flesh" of which Genesis 2:24 speaks is not referring exclusively to the physical union, but to the partnership of husband and wife within a lifelong commitment which produces a unitary experience at every level—physical, mental, emotional, and spiritual. Within that contract of friendship, the sexual relationship has an important symbolic and deepening function. Outside of that commitment it becomes a devaluation of our humanity by being reduced to the level of a sensory mechanism or a means of personal gratification.

The verse also stresses the gift of life as being from God from the moment of conception. This surely indicates that as human beings we have no right to interfere with God's gift from that moment on, much less to terminate it at our whim. It was Yahweh who watched over the child in Ruth's womb from conception to birth, and throughout his life. And why should what was true of Obed be any less true of you or me or any human being, for are we not all made in the image of God?

With the birth of Obed, it is interesting that congratulations go first to Naomi (v. 14) because she has always been the primary focus of the kinsman-redeemer motif. But the surprising ingredient of verses 14–15, is that the child Obed is being referred to throughout, and he is clearly regarded as the redeemer. The point seems to be that although Boaz married Ruth, if there had been no child there would have been no ultimate heir to Elimelech's property. Goslinga's comment is illuminating:

> The child was the real kinsman-redeemer, a word that here has the broad sense of "deliverer" and "helper" (a hint of this meaning is already present in 3:9). Only through the child was the yoke of affliction that the Lord had laid on Naomi completely removed.[3]

Similarly, only through the child of promise has our yoke been removed—see Isaiah 9:6. It would be a great comfort to Naomi's old age to see Obed grow up and perhaps even to see his infant son, Jesse. Every time she saw her grandson she would be reminded of her own redemption. Her future was assured, so that her Moabite daughter-in-law was indeed better to her than *"seven sons,"* an example of hyperbole, which is designed to convey the highest praise.

Verse 16 is a beautiful family picture to set beside the snapshot of "Mara," the empty widow returning from her bitter experiences in Moab. What a change grace has brought about in her life! Naturally, she regarded her grandson as a precious treasure and treated him as though he were her very own, as indeed he was. Obed means "servant," perhaps the idea being that the child was born for the sake of Naomi. As we look back we can therefore see God's answers to prayer in the birth of the child, and then suddenly, as we look forward to David (v. 17b), we see it even more dramatically. That is what God has been working toward behind the scenes all the time.

The stage is set for the final scene to trace the genealogical line from Perez to David, but before that, we need to reflect on the application of these verses. If we could imagine ourselves reading the Book of Ruth for the first time, we should be struck by the uncertainties and even vagaries of the plot. It is hardly ever straightforward or predictable from the reader's perspective. We are kept guessing, breathless even, until the final resolution. But God was never in doubt as to what he was doing. He was silently planning in love for Naomi, Ruth, and Boaz, and for the development of his purposes in the godly line of David, which would one day come to its complete fulfillment in the Lord Jesus Christ. There was never a shadow of a doubt that those purposes would one day be realized, although for the main characters, caught up in the problems and uncertainties of their lives, there was no way in which they could see that perspective.

This is a reminder to us all that "we walk by faith, not by sight" (2 Cor. 5:7). And yet, which of us does not often make the mistake of judging God's concern and involvement with us only in terms of what we can actually see in the present? We imagine that because things are not working out just as we would have chosen that God is no longer interested in us, that we have offended him irretrievably, or that he has gone off duty and is no longer working all things together for our good. In the light of the Book of Ruth and so many other Scriptures it is almost blasphemous to think in these terms, and yet how often we find ourselves doing just that.

This book encourages us to rely on the character of God, as revealed in his Word, and not to depend on our feelings or subjective assessments of how we "see" things. Listen to Isaiah: "Who among you fears the Lord? Who obeys the voice of His Servant? Who walks in darkness and has no light?" (Isa. 50:10a). Many Christians today have come to expect that if we fulfill the conditions of the first two questions, fearing the Lord and obeying Christ's words, the third could not possibly apply to us. Can a reverent, obedient Christian find him or herself walking in pitch-black darkness, trapped in a tunnel so long that there does not even appear to be a pinprick of light at the end of it? The answer of Isaiah would be, "Yes, certainly."

There is no guarantee built into our Christian discipleship that all will be easy and bright, or that our obedience to the Lord will automatically shield us from dangers or difficulties. Sometimes God's people do feel their name has become "Mara," just as Naomi did. But the second part of Isaiah 50:10 provides the answer in the form of a text of which this book of Ruth is really an exposition. How are we to live in the long, dark tunnel?

> "Let him trust in the name of the Lord and rely upon his God."

The *name* signifies the nature, as always in Hebrew thought. We are therefore to judge, not by what we see of our circumstances, but by what we know of the unchanging character of our God. That can only happen when our minds are soaked in Scripture and our thinking is informed by the certainty of God's sovereignty being exercised in love and grace, now, in the circumstances of our personal lives. It is usually only when we look back that we see this with clarity. The following anonymous lines put it well:

> I may not always trace the onward course
> my ship must take,
> But looking backward, I behold afar
> its shining wake,
> Illumined with God's light of love, and so
> onward I go
> In perfect trust that He who holds the helm
> the course must know.

THE HOPE FOR THE FUTURE

> 18 Now this is the genealogy of Perez: Perez begot Hezron;
> 19 Hezron begot Ram, and Ram begot Amminadab;
> 20 Amminadab begot Nahshon, and Nahshon begot Salmon;

21 Salmon begot Boaz, and Boaz begot Obed;
22 Obed begot Jesse, and Jesse begot David.
Ruth 4:18–22

The genealogy begins with Perez, son of Judah, the patriarch of the royal line (Gen. 49:10), because he held the scepter. It ends with the ideal king, who was the special recipient of God's grace and who exemplified in his character, with all its imperfections, a heart for God—King David. The position of Boaz and Obed in the line is the vital link to the rest of the book. The other names clearly do not constitute an exhaustive list of every generation. The Old Testament references can be traced through any concordance.

One other item of significance is that in Matthew 1:5 Salmon is said to have been married to Rahab, the citizen of Jericho who gave the spies lodging and who represents another foreigner in the line of David and ultimately of Christ. If Salmon to David (vv. 21–22) represented only four generations, it would be very difficult to square with the estimate of over three centuries between the fall of Jericho and David's birth. It seems, therefore, that the genealogy is not intended to be complete, but highlights the main names, as indeed Matthew 1 does.

Its major significance remains to remind us that in the days of the judges, when the national life of Israel was under such constant threat and when at times it seemed as though the very covenant itself might be dismantled, Yahweh was preserving his people and developing his purposes, taking fresh initiatives and demonstrating covenant-love in his continuing work of redemption. The story of Ruth and Naomi provides a microcosm of the whole. Surrounded by the Lord's covenant-love, they experienced his redemptive grace, not only in establishing and developing their personal relationships, but in those relationships reflecting what he was doing on the macroscale, in preparing his people for their coming king. "The Book of Ruth thus operates as a counter-point to the Book of Judges, indicating the type of kingship which was to operate as a result of convenantal fidelity, and the tranquillity that a true faith communicates," notes the commentator Dumbrell.[4] That is a message which is as relevant today as it was to those who first heard its captivating story.

NOTES

1. "There Is a Redeemer" is quoted by permission of The Sparrow Corporation.
2. Atkinson, *The Wings of Refuge*, 114.
3. Goslinga, *Ruth*, 552.
4. Dumbrell, *The Faith of Israel*, 233.

Bibliography

Armerding, Carl E. *Judges* in *The International Bible Commentary*, edited by F. F. Bruce. Grand Rapids: Zondervan, 1979.

Atkinson, David. *The Wings of Refuge*. Leicester: Inter-Varsity Press, 1983.

Auld, A. G. *Joshua, Judges and Ruth*, The Daily Study Bible. Philadelphia: The Westminster Press, 1984.

Bruce, F. F. "Judges," in *The New Bible Commentary: Revised*. London: Inter-Varsity Press, 1970.

Clowney, Edmund P. *The Unfolding Mystery—Discovering Christ in the Old Testament*. Colorado Springs: NavPress, 1988.

Cundall, Arthur E. and Morris, Leon. *Judges and Ruth, The Tyndale Old Testament Commentaries*. London: Inter-Varsity Press, 1968.

Davis, John J. *Conquest and Crisis*. Grand Rapids: Baker Books, 1969.

Dumbrell, William J. *The Faith of Israel*. Leicester: Inter-Varsity Press, 1989.

Goslinga, C. J. *Joshua, Judges and Ruth, Bible Students' Commentary*. Grand Rapids: Zondervan, 1986. Translated by Ray Togtman.

Hals, Ronald M. *The Theology of the Book of Ruth*. Philadelphia: Fortress Press, 1969.

Harrison R. K. *Introduction to the Old Testament*. London: Tyndale Press, 1970.

Keddie, Gordon J. *Even in Darkness*. Welwyn: Evangelical Press, 1985.

Keil C. F. and Delitzsch F. *Commentary on the Old Testament*. Vol. 2. Grand Rapids: Eerdmans, 1973.

Lindsey, F. Duane. *Judges, The Bible Knowledge Commentary*, edited by J. F. Walvoord and R. B. Zuck. Wheaton: Victor Books, 1988.

Mayes, A. D. H. *Judges* (Old Testament Guides). Sheffield: Journal for the Study of the Old Testament Press, 1985.

Webb, Barry G. "The Book of Judges—An Integrated Reading." *Journal for the Study of the Old Testament*, Supplement Series 46, 1987.

Wood, Leon. *The Distressing Days of the Judges*. Grand Rapids: Zondervan, 1975.